Ensemblance

A happy phrase is sometimes coined, so humanly expressive that barriers of language are swept aside and like music it becomes a universal sentiment. To the French we are indebted for such an expression, 'esprit de corps', which our English tongue has adopted and naturalized because it visualizes, as no idiom of our own does, the essence of co-operation [. . .] In proportion as 'esprit de corps' becomes a motivating force in men's lives do they transcend the narrow bounds of selfishness and become social beings, for it brings into action forces potent to lift men's thoughts from their own petty affairs to the contemplation of wider horizons.

John Scofield Rowe, 'Practical Philosophies: Esprit de Corps',
The Monroe Monitor, 9 August 1929

I do not care what methods a philosopher (or anybody else) may use so long as he has an interesting problem, and so long as he is sincerely trying to solve it. Among the many methods which he may use – always depending, of course, on the problem in hand – one method seems to me worth mentioning. It is a variant of the (at present unfashionable) historical method. It consists, simply, in trying to find out what other people have thought and said about the problem in hand: why they had to face it: how they formulated it: how they tried to solve it. This seems to me important because it is part of the general method of rational discussion.

Karl Popper, *The Logic of Scientific Discovery*,
Preface to the First English Edition, 1959

Ensemblance

The Transnational Genealogy of Esprit de Corps

Luis de Miranda

EDINBURGH
University Press

Edinburgh University Press is one of the leading university presses in the UK. We publish academic books and journals in our selected subject areas across the humanities and social sciences, combining cutting-edge scholarship with high editorial and production values to produce academic works of lasting importance. For more information visit our website: edinburghuniversitypress.com

© Luis de Miranda, 2020

Edinburgh University Press Ltd
The Tun – Holyrood Road
12(2f) Jackson's Entry
Edinburgh EH8 8PJ

Typeset in 10/12 Goudy Old Style by
Servis Filmsetting Ltd, Stockport, Cheshire
and printed and bound in Great Britain.

A CIP record for this book is available from the British Library

ISBN 978 1 4744 5419 3 (hardback)
ISBN 978 1 4744 5422 3 (webready PDF)
ISBN 978 1 4744 5421 6 (epub)

The right of Luis de Miranda to be identified as the author of this work has been asserted in accordance with the Copyright, Designs and Patents Act 1988, and the Copyright and Related Rights Regulations 2003 (SI No. 2498).

Contents

Acknowledgements

I wish, first, to thank the French language for its suggestive beauty. For as long as I can remember, the word *esprit* has always fascinated me because of its numerous nuances, *mind* being only one possible translation. The body, *corps* in French, is all too often considered as the antonym of mind. To see *esprit* and *corps* united in a globally recognised phrase was intriguing enough for me to spend several years wondering why and how.

My research was facilitated by institutional and human goodwill. My gratitude goes first and foremost to two academic institutions. I was able to conduct this extensive research mostly thanks to generous funding from the University of Edinburgh. I then moved from Scotland to Sweden, where a postdoctoral position at Örebro University offered me the time I needed to finalise the typescript. Thanks to Örebro's funding, the introduction of the present book is accessible as an open resource in partnership with Edinburgh University Press.

Institutions are represented by human beings; at the University of Edinburgh, I felt inspired by the encouraging welcome of Professor Marion Schmid and by regular and piquant Socratic dialogue with Professor Peter Dayan. More recently and at a distance, Professor Robin Howells (University of London) was an attentive reader of these pages, frowning upon a few Gallicisms, though sparing the most obvious one. Professor James Livesey (University of Dundee) cast an encouraging critical eye on the final version of the manuscript. Parts of the introduction and the third chapter have inspired two articles I authored for the journal *Global Intellectual History*: I warmly thank its editor-in-chief Professor Richard Whatmore (University of St Andrews) for accepting these echoes, as well as for his comments on an earlier version of the work.

My research on esprit de corps was also, incidentally, a personal reflection on the merits and pitfalls of academic institutionalisation. A typical product of rebellious French individualism, I believed for a long time that institutions could lead to uncreative groupthink: if I was to become an original author – I thought in my twenties and thirties – I had to avoid any kind of affiliation, and so I did for many years of precarious, reckless, consuming but exhilarating independence. I changed my mind in my early forties partly because I felt robust enough to find a good balance between freedom and incorporation. I had written a few unacademic essays and novels in French and I felt attracted by a new life and new thoughts expressed in a new language – this is the first book I have written directly in English. Because many universities around the world are threatened by the spirit of capitalist managerialism, it is never too late to join the transnational academic body in order to try and defend as far as possible the idealistic ethos of *knowledge for the sake of knowledge*.

I am grateful to Linda Ayres, supportive in many ways in the crucial early stages of this project, and to my young daughter Svea who was kind enough to remind me of how five little monkeys jumping on the bed can dangerously indulge in group entrainment. Learning to be a father during the first years of research that led to this book distracted me from the follies of excessive theoretical speculation.

Finally, my extended warm thanks go to commissioning editor Carol Macdonald at Edinburgh University Press, with whom I had a few inspiring chats around George Square when this book was but a possibility, and to Gerald Moore, Sam Coombes, Jean-Sébastien Hongre, Kirsty Woods, James Dale, Andrew Kirk and the numerous people – including the defunct authors quoted in the following pages – who have led to the slow and patient production of this monograph.

In what follows, the translations from French primary sources are almost always mine, and when not, the translators are gratefully cited – I also wish to thank Edinburgh University Press for allowing me to keep the original French quotations in the endnotes of each chapter for the benefit of francophone readers. Like the writing process leading to it, the genealogy of the notion of esprit de corps is a process of correspondences, variations, counter-interpretations, alliances, slippery metamorphoses, fears and dreams – a reflection, via one of the most influential Gallicisms in modern history, of our contemporary worries about identity, dependence and liberation.

Last but not least, and by anticipation, I thank the readers – *mes semblables, mes frères!* – for their patient engagement with the text.

Esprit de Corps: A Timeline

All quotations and citations below will be referenced, developed and contextualised in the following chapters.

1656–58   Pascal writes *Différence entre l'esprit de géometrie et l'esprit de finesse*.

1662   Louis XIV's historiographer René Bary publishes *L'esprit de cour*.

1721   Publication of Montesquieu's *Lettres persanes*, in which the author mocks the *esprit du corps* of the Académie française.

1732   *Lettres de Nedim Coggia*, by Germain de Saint-Foix, praises the esprit de corps of the French musketeers.

1752   D'Alembert, in the *Encyclopédie*, criticises the anti-national *esprit du corps* of the Jesuits.

1755   Voltaire, in the *Encyclopédie*, distinguishes esprit de corps from its supposedly worse version, *esprit de parti*. In the same volume, Diderot, more critical, suggests that the Encyclopaedists must avoid catching the esprit de corps by remaining objective.

1755   Lord Chesterfield, a friend of Voltaire, introduces 'esprit de corps' into the English language to describe the natural 'biased conduct' and 'inflamed zeal' in closed societies, a fatal aspect of 'human nature'.

1762   Rousseau explains in *L'Emile*: 'It is not only in the military that one acquires the esprit de corps, and its effects are not always good.'

1762   The formerly autonomous management of the French military corps, previously known for their respective esprit du corps, is centralised by the royal administration.

1764   The Jesuits are banned from France, after a long public campaign in which their esprit de corps was often attacked.

1765   The Parlement of Metz addresses a remonstrance to the King of France calling for a grand national esprit de corps, also called *l'esprit de patriotisme*.

1776   In the *Wealth of Nations*, the Scottish philosopher and economist Adam Smith criticises the 'corporation spirit', leading 'every man to consent that his neighbour may neglect his duty, provided he himself is allowed to neglect his own'.

1776   The French minister Turgot attempts to eradicate the *corporations* and their esprit de corps in the name of economic laissez-faire.

1779   In Calcutta, a local petition is signed by British inhabitants against the 'esprit de corps of the Professors of Law'.

1782   The Parisian author Louis-Sébastien Mercier predicts that the individualistic dissolution of esprit de corps in labour guilds might lead to a revolution.

1787   Mirabeau criticises 'the esprit de corps of the orders of the state that support despotism'.

1787   In America, the convention led by George Washington and the Founding Fathers debates the pros and cons of esprit de corps.

1789   Several French revolutionaries, one of whom is the Abbé Sieyès, call for a national esprit de corps to achieve the 'adunation' of France, against particular and local forms of esprit de corps.

1789   In the UK, Jeremy Bentham defines esprit de corps as 'professional zeal'.

1791   In Revolutionary France, the Le Chapelier law criminalises professional esprit de corps and proclaims that free trade and free working are the new economic standard: 'There are no longer *corporations* in the state, there is only the particular interest of each individual and then the general interest.'

1793   The French minister of war Jean-Baptiste Bouchotte strives to 'annihilate the esprit de corps' in military regiments and replace it with a unified army of citizens.

1793   In his Königsberg Lectures, Immanuel Kant violently criticises 'separatists and sectarians of every kind' and their immoral esprit de corps.

1793   A democratic reform to reduce the esprit de corps in British politics, inspired by the French Revolution, is officially discussed in the House of Commons.

1800   Napoleon and his minister of foreign affairs Talleyrand work on the organisation of a national programme of administrative esprit de corps, founded on several *grands corps d'État*.

1803   In France, the idea of esprit de corps is popular anew among the elites. Reversing the claims of the Enlightenment, Chateaubriand writes: 'Esprit de corps, which can be bad in the whole, is always good in the part.'

1803   US President Thomas Jefferson calls for less esprit de corps in the leadership of banks, via a frequent rotation of directors.

1805   Napoleon calls *corps enseignant* the national corporation of teachers and declares that the former esprit de corps of the Jesuits is a model to be revived in education: 'If we do not learn from childhood whether to be republican or monarchical, Catholic or irreligious, etc., the State will not form a nation.'

1808   The utopianist Charles Fourier theorises that 'esprit de corps is enough to eradicate the most shocking vices of the civilized populace'.

1809   'Esprit de corps' enters the British *Dictionary of Quotations in Most Frequent Use*.

1810   Napoleon's *Code pénal* forbids any association of more than twenty people without authorisation from the government.

1811   In Scotland, Walter Scott laments the 'cold and pettifogging esprit de corps' that governs most societies.

1815   Echoing a general sentiment, the poet and politician François-Auguste de Frénilly criticises the French Revolution for favouring the rise of individualism via its destruction of esprit de corps. In doing so he coins the term 'individuellism'.

1820   The German philosopher G. W. F Hegel praises the 'rectitude and esprit de corps of the universal man', servitor of the state.

1821   In England, Lord Byron wonders in a letter if one should write *esprit du corps* or *esprit de corps*.

1828   The essayist and politician Louis de Bonald writes a popular eulogy of esprit de corps: 'The esprit de corps is the general spirit of the whole body [. . .] The esprit de corps unites and strengthens, and one can say that a body without esprit de corps is a body without a soul.'

1833   Labour strikes in France. Some workers demand the right to associate and organise themselves in *syndicats*.

1836   The political theorist Alexis de Tocqueville explains to John Stuart Mill and his Westminster friends that French aristocrats lost their esprit de corps in the seventeenth century with Louis XIV, which led to the Revolution. In *Democracy in America*, he laments that democracies hinder both our capacity for esprit de corps and for individuation, which for him are codependent.

1850   In the UK, an investigation into the University of Oxford commissioned by Queen Victoria concludes that the lack of esprit de corps in top universities is highly damaging.

1863   William de Slane translates Ibn Khaldun's Arabic notion of *asabiyah* into French as *esprit de corps*.

1883   The writer Emile Zola defines esprit de corps as an 'instinct'.

1884   Labour unions (*syndicats*) become legal in France. In this, according to the politician Hubert Lagardelle, 'the corps of workers is recognised by the legislator as having a personal existence'.

1893   Emile Durkheim writes that 'the spirit of ensemble' and the related esprit de corps is a prophylactic form of professional solidarity.

1898   In his influential *J'accuse*, Emile Zola condemns the 'foolish' esprit de corps of the French army, which led to the Dreyfus affair.

1899   In the USA, James Mark Baldwin, professor at Princeton University, writes that 'national spirit is a form of natural esprit de corps'.

1899   The sociologist Gabriel Tarde distinguishes seven useful scales of esprit de corps, from the small family sphere to the large supranational sphere. The Nietzschean philosopher Georges Palante retorts that esprit de corps is but one form of 'social insincerity'.

1901   US President Benjamin Harrison celebrates the 'esprit de corps of the American soldier'.

1904   Peter Traub, a US captain of the cavalry, compares esprit de corps to a divine 'vital force'.

1907   The American activist Jane Addams calls for more esprit de corps in factories, defined as a 'playful and triumphant buoyancy'.

1913   Nietzsche's *Genealogy of Morals* is translated into English, celebrating 'the chronic and despotic esprit de corps and fundamental instinct of a higher dominant race'.

1914   In *Training Soldiers for War*, British officer John Fuller writes: 'What race pride is to the Empire, so should esprit de corps be to the regiment.'

1917   The entrepreneur Henri Fayol writes that the legal 'union of the employees' is an important principle of management. A mistranslation of Fayol's principle as 'esprit de corps', suppressing the trade union aspect, would become highly popular in English business studies.

1920   W. B. Barber, a British military officer, records a 'cult of esprit de corps' during the First World War. He adds that in times of peace '*esprit de corps* is a very good antidote to Bolshevism'.

1921   Publication in the USA of *The Management of Men: A Handbook on the Systematic Development of Morale and the Control of Human Behavior*. In it the phrase 'esprit de corps' appears 43 times, defined as 'a mental state making for cohesion of an organization, as necessary to commercial success as it is to military efficiency'.

1922   Nobel Prize laureate Anatole France explains that 'esprit de corps is the intelligence of those who have none'.

1929   A handbook of rhetoric published in Shangai defines esprit de corps as the 'spirit of the collective body'.

1929   The American businessman John Rowe calls esprit de corps a 'happy phrase' and a 'universal sentiment', 'the essence of co-operation'.

1930   In his autobiography, Winston Churchill equates esprit de corps with the ethics and 'honourable behaviour' he learned when he was young.

1931   In *Last and First Men*, British science-fiction writer and Freud reader Olaf Stapledon speculates about the human 'very special loyalty toward the whole group, a peculiar sexually toned esprit de corps unparalleled in other species'.

1932   The philosopher Henri Bergson compares esprit de corps to a 'feeling of honour' and a civilisational 'fabulation' creative of a 'virtual instinct'.

1934   The future war hero and French president Charles de Gaulle explains how the military can foster a well-organised local and national esprit de corps.

1942   The US national Office of Civilian Defense publishes *The Control System of the Citizens' Defense Corps*, a manual to foster 'esprit de corps among citizens', defined as 'instantaneous and unquestioned obedience'.

1943   The USA army advertises in magazines to find new recruits: 'In the army they call it esprit de corps – the stuff that builds champion teams and victorious armies in which each man is doing the job he does best.'

1949   The analytic philosopher Gilbert Ryle, in *The Concept of Mind*, insists that esprit de corps is an unreal 'ghost in the machine': 'I do not see whose role it is to exercise *esprit de corps*.'

1950   Rex D. Hopper, head of sociology at Brooklyn College, writes in the journal *Social Forces* that 'esprit de corps is a means of social control'.

1956   In the USA, the university field of Small-Group Studies publishes quantitative measures of esprit de corps.

1956   The Pentagon hires Rex D. Hopper, the academic specialist of 'esprit de corps as social control', to direct a counter-insurgency programme that would interfere in South American politics in the 1960s under the name of 'Project Camelot'.

1957   The American entrepreneur Conrad Hilton publishes his autobiography, in which he explains that the success of his chain of hotels is based on the systematic application of the techniques of esprit de corps he learned during the First World War.

1958   De Gaulle declares in a public speech: 'We are at the age of effectiveness, efficiency. We are at the time of ensembles.'

1961   In *Life* magazine, the author and diplomat Romain Gary compares esprit de corps to a collective 'mystique of self-adoration'.

1971   Irving L. Janis publishes an article that coins the term 'groupthink', defined as a collective loss of critical thinking, a perversion of 'amiability and esprit de corps' likely 'to result in irrational and dehumanizing actions directed against outgroups'.

1980   The philosophers Gilles Deleuze and Félix Guattari publish a laudatory reappraisal of 'nomadic esprit de corps' in *Mille plateaux*, which they associate with Ibn Khaldun's *asabiyah*.

1989   The French sociologist Pierre Bourdieu defines esprit de corps as a 'symbolic violence' and compares it to a 'magical possession'.

1993   The *Journal of Institutional and Theoretical Economics* publishes a paper in which esprit de corps, abbreviated as 'e', is a mathematical variable within a complex equation measuring 'organizational effectiveness'.

2002   US President George W. Bush creates the US Freedom Corps initiative to enable civilians to find ways to serve 'their community, their country, or the world'. Citizen Corps is a component of the Freedom Corps that 'creates opportunities for individuals to volunteer and respond to emergencies'.

2002   In Canada, Gilles Barbot founds the Groupe Esprit de Corps, a business consulting and team-building corporation.

2011   The French nationalist politician Marine Le Pen declares in a public speech: 'I solemnly call for the esprit de corps, the innate sense of duty and of sacrifice manifested by those who have incorporated the love of the fatherland.'

2013   The *Harvard Business Review* recommends that corporations should develop esprit de corps as military-inspired camaraderie-in-arms 'to push for hard work'.

2015   A review in the *Wall Street Journal* praises the 'girl power esprit de corps' of the movie *Pitch Perfect*.

2015   The future American president Donald Trump declares in a press conference that the USA needs 'spirit, esprit de corps'.

2016   David Davis, the future British Secretary of State for Exiting the European Union, writes that too much immigration hinders the 'national esprit de corps'.

2018   President Donald Trump, in a public speech at the White House, declares: 'There's tremendous spirit in our country right now [. . .] Esprit de corps . . .'

Introduction: A Thousand Platoons –
The Enduring Importance of Esprit de Corps

'You need spirit, esprit de corps', presidential candidate Donald Trump responded evasively at a news conference in 2015 when asked about his 'plan to improve race relations' in the USA.[1] In 2018, in a public speech at the White House given during a celebration of the Made in America label, the now President Trump declared:

> Every time a new factory opens, every time jobs are returned to our shores, every time we buy a product made by our own American neighbors, we are renewing the bonds of love and loyalty that link us all together as Americans. There's tremendous spirit in our country right now, sometimes you don't see it but there is. And you are producers, you produce like nobody else, and the spirit is incredible. Esprit de corps![2]

Why does the US president repetitively insist on this exotic French phrase? The answer is far from superficial, as we will discover by embarking on an eye-opening, three-centuries-long journey. Donald Trump is by no means the first person to invoke the cult of esprit de corps. Since the eighteenth century, sophisticated minds have pondered it: Montesquieu, d'Alembert, Voltaire, Rousseau, Kant, Bentham, the Founding Fathers, Sieyès, Mirabeau, Hegel, Tocqueville, Durkheim, Bergson, Churchill, Orwell, Bourdieu, Deleuze and many others.

As we will see, incantations about esprit de corps are never innocent. The signifier 'esprit de corps' is today a leitmotif of meta-military capitalism and managerial discourse, designating the zeal, collective *élan* and quasi-alchemical loyalty that entrepreneurs are looking for among their employees. The US president might be aware that, according to a Gallup study, 'disengagement in American organizations accounts for more than $450 billion in lost productivity annually', with less than a third of employees 'actively engaged' in their work.[3] In 2012, US companies spent $46 billion on team-building firms, and some observers are speaking of an 'economy of esprit de corps': 'Esprit de corps is a concept powerful enough to make soldiers go into battle knowing their odds of survival are slim: think how powerful it can be if harnessed in your marketing organization!'[4]

But Americans have forgotten that team spirit is only one meaning of esprit

de corps among many others, including negative ones. A strong attachment and
dedication among the members of a community of practice or a body politic,
esprit de corps can be perceived as a beneficial cohesion or a detrimental form
of groupthink. As a polemical signifier, the phrase has played a significant role
in cultural, political and economic history since the 1700s. It was influential and
was debated during the European secularisation of education in the eighteenth
century. The *Philosophes* considered esprit de corps to be the fierce enemy of a
republic. The Gallicism was uttered passionately in parliamentary debates during
the French Revolution. It was an *idée-force* in the process of the United States
achieving independence. It became one of the pillar values of the Bonapartist
Empire. It was subsequently praised by British colonialists and French sociologists, and emphasised during the world wars. Esprit de corps was instrumental
during the rise of administrative nation-states and the triumph of American
capitalism. The phrase is today a keyword in the revival of nationalist and
protectionist discourses.

Reflecting on the importance of ethics, Winston Churchill wrote in his autobiography that he thought it must mean 'esprit de corps, honourable behaviour,
patriotism, and the like'.[5] Over the last three centuries the phrase has been so
influential that one may wonder: is esprit de corps the very engine of history?

Team Spirits: Twenty-First Century Uses of Esprit de Corps

The twenty-first-century ubiquity in English of the originally French phrase *esprit
de corps* is the point of departure of this book, a source of the kind of wonder
that has long been said to be the impetus of thought.[6] Indeed, another cause for
surprise is the combination in this enduring international phrase of two often
opposed and semantically rich words, mind and body. Equally intriguing is the
difference in denotation between French and English uses of esprit de corps, the
former often pejorative, the latter often laudatory. This in itself would justify a
transnational investigation.

The French uses of esprit de corps are often sociopolitical and suggest a form
of cognitive uniformity generated by a more or less conscious adherence to a collective body. This idea of the automation – or at least control – by a group of our
thoughts, behaviour and emotions is a well-known modern preoccupation and
a challenging question for our global, digital and neuro-technological epoch.[7]
Because esprit de corps is a global idea that expresses both our desire for belonging and our fear of being alienated, it is an intriguing metonymy for the question
of identity. Moreover, the fact that its negative connotations are often buried
under a shiny discourse of team spirit and corporate or national camaraderie is
certainly a matter for inquiry. The *élan* of feeling *all for one and one for all* seems
sometimes to count for more than any critical understanding about the *one* at
stake. Mass-produced individualism and egotism often transform the idea of team
spirit into a desirable but ephemeral performance. To reflect on esprit de corps
is to consider how contradictory we might be when caught between these two
stools: our belonging and our self-importance.

But what exactly *is* esprit de corps? This is a question that we should refrain from answering dogmatically before carefully analysing the different and agonistic uses of the term in recent centuries. Esprit de corps is an evolving idea, a web of beliefs in process. The variety and disparity of modern uses of the phrase not only suggest that a prudent approach to a definition is well advised, but also that it would be foolish to try and add yet another definition. In this case as in many others, the game of definitions is not what ultimately matters, but what the historical and intellectual evolution of that game allows us to understand or speculate about our collective and individual destinies. Yet for such speculation to be sound, we do need to look very carefully at the empirical manifestations of an invariant spine made of 13 bones, *e-s-p-r-i-t-d-e-c-o-r-p-s*.

Between 2014 and 2017, I experimented with an 'Esprit de Corps Pointer', which recorded day by day a few hundred online contemporary occurrences of 'esprit de corps' in diverse contexts.[8] This was a sort of taxonomy, for which my main criteria of selection were any phrase containing explicitly the signifier 'esprit de corps', the variety of intended meanings, the self-definitional quality of the occurrence in its context and importance of the medium by readership audience. This experiment demonstrated that 'esprit de corps' is a thriving expression in several discourses, mostly in English-language contexts. Surveying online uses of 'esprit de corps' during those three years made it easier to sense that the phrase is nowadays much more used in English than in any other language, including French. The alert tool I used might be slightly biased towards more visited online pages,[9] but it did not exclude less expected sources, for example Indian journals, remote blogs, or niche French-language publications in Africa.

The kind of team spirit suggested in English by the phrase esprit de corps is one that can supposedly be reproduced, engineered or standardised, while in French it has durably meant either a distorted partisanship or the particular style of a particular group, indeed something unique and inimitable. The biography of esprit de corps in the present book tells the story of the slow vanishing of the French connotation, even in France, and the progressive triumph of a reductive, more customary and reproducible team-spirit connotation. Is it a complete triumph? I don't believe so: other meanings were produced across the centuries which remain somewhat active or dormant until a potential revival, related for example to the idea of collective intelligence or a hive mind. A mystique of esprit de corps is in fact still alive: it is a somewhat alchemical ideal, as argued by Deleuze and Guattari in our penultimate chapter.

Before we dive into the past, let's take a closer look at the twenty-first century. To manifest the contemporary diversity of uses of esprit de corps, I organised the online Pointer with a menu of categories, such as Nationalism, Religion, Politics, Economics, Military, etc. For example, under the category Nationalism, we find that in April 2016 *The Wall Street Journal* published a reader's opinion piece, 'Obama May Offend on Brexit, but He's Right': the article asserted that 'the Stateless, faceless EU is a weak, ineffectual opponent, lacking the courage and esprit de corps that only a national entity and strong, elected leadership can provide'.[10] On this idea of a national esprit de corps, we must also quote David

Davis, who, a few months before he was chosen to be the British Secretary of State for Exiting the European Union, wrote:

> We are proud to be a famously tolerant country. When people arrive in the UK the general response is one of welcome, certainly where those arrivals embrace our national values of freedom under the law and mutual tolerance. Newcomers can be successfully absorbed, but it does take time to build this national 'esprit de corps'. The scale of immigration means that integration doesn't happen. Or it doesn't happen fast enough. And without it, community cohesion suffers. And that feeds the double headed monster of extremism and intolerance.[11]

This casual association of esprit de corps with national spirit was also made in 2011 by the French Front National leader Marine Le Pen: 'I solemnly call for the esprit de corps, the innate sense of duty and of sacrifice manifested by those who have incorporated the love of the fatherland.'[12] Davis's and Le Pen's nationalist appeals demonstrate blatantly why a thorough transnational genealogy of esprit de corps is needed today. We may ask, without being accused of anti-populism, how many of their followers are aware that the association of the quality of esprit de corps with a nation-state is a denotation that was introduced into political discourse by French philosophers and politicians in the second half of the eighteenth century. How and why this happened, and with what consequences, is one important thread of the present book.

National esprit de corps is but one active meaning of the phrase, among many. Under the category Education of our online Pointer, for example, we are directed to an article published by *Times Higher Education*, in which Craig Brandist, Professor of Cultural Theory and Intellectual History at the University of Sheffield, discussed what he called the current 'risk of Soviet-style managerialism in UK universities':

> Something resembling a game of blind man's bluff that would have been recognisable to Soviet workers [. . .] now takes place on a daily basis. Senior management intervenes to ensure that key targets are met [. . .] Members of staff respond by ingratiating themselves with their superiors (*blat*), and cover for each other in order to defend themselves from scrutiny (*krugovaia porukha: esprit de corps*).[13]

At least three brief observations can be made here. First, proof that the term 'esprit de corps' is supposed to be known by at least literate English readers is indicated by the choice of translation from Russian into English solely via the French loan phrase. Secondly, the equation between esprit de corps and corporatism or professional bias (members or workers covering for each other) also became prominent in the second half of eighteenth-century France, as we will see in our first two chapters. Thirdly, this particular usage was well known in British and American English in the eighteenth and early nineteenth centuries, but became quite rare in the twentieth century, where, once again, esprit de corps was dominantly referred to as a form of beneficial group cohesion that employees *should* build, a quality associated with efficiency and productivity. This evolution, and its evolutive contrast with more pejorative French-language meanings, is also examined in depth in the present book.

Some francophone uses can be less pejorative. One interesting contemporary example comes from the newspaper *La Vérité* [*Truth*], published in the Republic of Madagascar, in which a recent editorial labelled 'Esprit de Groupe' explained that in our global world, 'the power of money slowly undermines the esprit de corps'.[14] In this text originally published in one of France's former African colonies, esprit de corps was equated with social solidarity and opposed to both individualism and capitalism.

Our introductory survey of the contemporary polysemy of our phrase leads us to discover that in 2016 a *New York Times* article described Morgan Stanley, a global financial company, as 'a firm long unified by a special esprit de corps'.[15] The once pleonastic formula 'special esprit de corps' confirms that English users are not necessarily aware that the early French origin of the expression, *esprit du corps* (rather than *de*), implied that the *esprit* of a *corps* was a phenomenon that pertained specifically to a given group, like a collective style or manner. Most corps, societies or institutions, as we will analyse, were thought by some authors, chief among them the encyclopaedist Jean le Rond d'Alembert, to possess their own unique (good or bad) character: 'Les sociétés ont [. . .] un *caractère* particulier, qu'on appelle *esprit du corps*.'[16] In a recent English academic translation of the *Encyclopédie*, this is translated by replacing the preposition *du* with the more idiomatic *de*: 'Societies [. . .] have a special quality, sometimes referred to as *esprit de corps*.'[17] Again, this is not superficial and the devil is in the detail: the slip between the two prepositions, *du* and *de*, distinguishes in French a difference between specificity and generality. Nevertheless, the French philosophers, and in particular d'Alembert, are also responsible for the connotations of automation and conformism – as opposed to style and originality – that esprit de corps might convey. And, conversely, the current team-spirit anglophone uses of the phrase do not always completely obliterate the idea of a special group identity. Esprit de corps is perhaps what the anthropologist Lévi-Strauss called a 'floating signifier',[18] a symbol apt to be charged with almost infinite intentions. This creative polysemy might be explained in part by the fact that the phrase itself combines two opposite or dialectical words, the primary dichotomy between mind and body, spirit and matter. And in English, the baroque strangeness of the Gallicism imbues it with a sense of vague and exquisite ancestral power.

Is there a reason for the notional evolution, in the last three centuries, from *esprit du corps* as designating the specific character of a given group, each well-organised society nurturing a different personality, to a notion of *esprit de corps* as a generic quality of strong body cohesion? In English, 'esprit de corps' is still often used to designate a standard of collective efficiency. A well-driven group, in capitalist discourse, is deemed capable of *creating* esprit de corps for itself, usually with the help of a leader: enthusiastic cohesion, effective cooperation, rather than distinct character or style; emphasis on a nearly mechanical idea of *corps* rather than on the complex aspects of *esprit*. Esprit de corps is often mentioned with approval in English, as if it were a familiar alchemy, the reified universal quality of goal-oriented solidarity, a general abstract quality of group dynamics that would apply to any human ensemble. A recent *Fortune* article claimed to reveal 'the secret to how the best employers can inspire workers': by 'put[ting] real work into sustaining environments where people can count on candor, respect and the esprit de corps necessary for the open, fruitful exchange of ideas'.[19] This corporate optimism creates a version of esprit de corps that is quite at odds with what the notion meant in the eighteenth century: for the *Philosophes*, esprit de corps was an antonym of open-mindedness.

Esprit de corps can be used as an unquestioned marketing buzzword within the team-building industry. Even nation-states experience managerial quandaries. In 2016, an article in the *Telegraph* explained what the British Secretary of State for International Trade should do as a team builder:

> There are two patterns we could follow. The European Commission's Directorate General for Trade has staff who expect to spend their career there. They have incredible expertise and esprit de corps. In contrast, the Office of the US Trade Representative has a smaller permanent cadre, with more movements between the rest of government and the private sector. We should try for the best of both. We will need core expertise, but should use plenty of outsiders to keep up connections with the world of business.[20]

This glissando from *corps* to *core* is striking but, as we will see, not unprecedented. The idea of the esprit de corps of a given group as being rich in discipline and expertise, but potentially poor in connections with – and openness to – the outside world and its state of perpetual change, is a recurrent pattern in the biography of the notion. The simple question behind it – *is esprit de corps good or bad?* – was central to the rhetorical debates that the phrase engendered across fields and centuries. Sometimes strongly defended, sometimes considered abominable, sometimes seen as a Janus-faced ambivalent phenomenon, esprit de corps could be categorised as an 'essentially contested concept',[21] on which more below.

The present book will also demonstrate that esprit de corps has an original historical locus in military discourse, although the idea of a single or prototypical origin for a complex notion would be fallacious, and an intellectual genealogy should always speak of origins with precaution, as famously advised by Foucault.[22] The venerable martial branch of the phrase is still producing leaves. Recently, for example, a major Canadian newspaper quoted Canada's defence minister on the advantages of insignias: 'The restoration of these historical features will encourage the esprit de corps of our soldiers.'[23] A *corps* here is a military unit of soldiers. *All for one and one for all*: we will analyse how the adventures of esprit de corps are partly rooted in the military organisation of the *Ancien Régime*, although the early modern influence of a more religious or even alchemical discourse is not to be ignored.

In the context of the military, esprit de corps is often equated with morale. In the British edition of the *Huffington Post*, a junior doctor compared the National Health Service to a crumbling army:

In military circles, 'morale', or a unit's 'esprit de corps', is often defined more precisely as the capacity of a group's members to maintain their belief in an institution or goal, particularly in the face of opposition or hardship. If a unit's morale is depleted, they are at risk of cracking and surrendering. An American General by the rather magnificent name of Knickerbocker gave a stirring definition of 'morale' during the Second World War. Morale was high, he said, 'when a soldier thinks his army is the best in the world, his regiment the best in the army, his company the best in the regiment, his squad the best in the company, and that he himself is the best blankety-blank soldier man in the outfit.'[24]

Here the connotation of esprit de corps as corporatism meets the military meaning to highlight the idea, not only of survival and integrity in the face of hardship, but also pride: esprit de corps as a supercilious attachment to a collective, to a task that develops individual self-importance. This is related to what the sociologist Pierre Bourdieu called an extended 'love of self in others, and in the entire group, favoured by the prolonged gathering of fellows'.[25] Is esprit de corps about love or *agape* among insiders? If so, it might also be said that hate or indifference for outsiders is never too far away.

Brotherhood or camaraderie are among the frequent quasi-synonyms of esprit de corps in corporate metaphors, but also in the discourse of sport. For instance, *The Times* described the Portuguese football team in the following terms: 'It was a display of camaraderie, the esprit de corps that had made them champions of Europe – a triumph of the collective over the individual.'[26] In the USA, a Colorado newspaper quotes John Wooden, a celebrated basketball player and coach:

The coach sums up team spirit like this: 'A genuine consideration for others. An eagerness to sacrifice personal interests of glory for the welfare of all.' Coach Wooden preferred the use of the word 'eagerness' in place of 'willingness.' He felt that willingness conveyed a sense of obligation and duty, a sense that if it had to be done it would be done. To him, eagerness conveyed a high sense of esprit de corps, a spirit of this is how we do it, not how we must do it. It was more cultural and ingrained in the individual.[27]

How can a spiritual quality be at the same time more cultural and more ingrained in the individual? This conundrum, to which Tocqueville proposed a solution that we detail in Chapter 5, explains why the modern debate about esprit de corps mattered for many intellectuals and still matters at a time of tension between individualism and communitarianism. Nuances between eagerness and willingness, duty and drive might seem abstract, but they are not irrelevant historically and politically.

Esprit de corps is clearly a remarkably enduring Gallicism and transnational idea, occasionally read or heard in a few other languages, such as for example Spanish, but dominantly used in the new lingua franca of globalisation. I will not insist further in this introduction on contemporary examples, since the reader can browse through my online Esprit de Corps Pointer. Despite a tendency to reduce the meaning of the phrase to team spirit and camaraderie, the Pointer demonstrates that the signifier is still active within a rich semantic field of meanings: 'cooperation', 'joint ownership of projects in the workplace', 'togetherness in combat', 'common consciousness', 'common sense of purpose', 'sport's greatest appeal', 'collective genius', 'patriotism', 'anti-cronyism', 'community spirit', 'nepotism', 'shared rituals', 'uniformity', 'commitment to the in-group identity', 'friendship at work', 'goodwill', 'high level of integration', 'joint-decision making', 'insiders' connection', 'commitment to service', 'platoon-like devotion to a cause', 'pillow-fight spirit', 'tradition', 'common trust', 'warrior spirit', 'employees' long-term focus', 'unquantifiable team cohesion', 'sense of inclusion and belonging', 'solidarity', 'obedience', 'girl power', 'corporate culture', 'looking out for one another', 'identification with a collective', 'devotion', 'gratitude to others' and 'being part of something bigger than the self'. It is probable that there is no such thing as a core universal and well-defined ahistorical concept designated by 'esprit de corps', upon which everyone would agree. If there were, it could lead to the formulation of speculative definitions that are abundant in philosophical literature on collective intentionality, social ontology or group agency.

To historicise notions such as esprit de corps is imperative in order to avoid the pitfalls of essentialism regarding the nature of collective consciousness. As I will explain in more detail in what follows, I did not feel that by taking a so-called analytic philosophical perspective on collective intelligence I could contribute with anything less partial or disembodied than the average substance realism. My method is not purely analytical in the sense that I am not trying to isolate a fixed law, privileged definition or universal model of esprit de corps. My method is not purely dialectical in the sense that it would isolate one systematic, historical narrative in which contradictory meanings would be sublated both rationally and agonistically towards the realisation of a higher version of esprit de corps. My perspective was inspired by Deleuze and Guattari's repetitive evocation of esprit de corps in *Mille plateaux*,[28] until now understudied. Complex concepts are not produced in a vacuum of mechanical truth but emerge and evolve from a creative multiplicity of virtual and actual experiences, in which a totalising unification is but an asymptotic horizon. My approach to intellectual history could be called 'hyperdialectical'[29] or 'crealectical'[30] in the sense that, as I will show empirically, it embraces both the analytical care in the distinction of significant parts to manifest a whole, and the dialectical perspective in which negations are moments in a dynamic and processual becoming, to show eventually that a creative overflow cannot be avoided in the unfolding and understanding of social phenomena. Some signifiers, such as esprit de corps, function as a portal or point of projection between virtual and experiential multiplicities or parallel worlds. Here esprit de corps is not only an object of study, but also a metonymy that evokes processes of emergence and embodiment in which spirit, structure and flesh are constantly changing places.

Knowledge Expansion: Academic Literature on Esprit de Corps

You are reading the first comprehensive intellectual history of esprit de corps. The literature on the idea has until now been scarce, fragmentary and insufficiently aware of the cultural importance of the phrase. In 2015, Cambridge University Press published a volume on the intellectual history of the notion of 'general will' under the title *The General Will: The Evolution of a Concept.*[31] Although several uses of the notion of esprit de corps pertain to the same semantic field as the idea of general will, the phrase 'esprit de corps' does not appear once in that book. This is not exceptional: esprit de corps is a polemical phrase that has been ignored or neglected as an object of neutral study.

In the chapters that follow I will try to avoid falling into the usual trap of taking sides: is esprit de corps good or bad? Is it necessary or avoidable? Any answer involving human matters is a contextual decision. The present systematic study is a contribution to knowledge and informed decisions. It will also throw light on current debates on agonistic pluralism.[32] According to Deleuze and Guattari, autonomous groups need to foster their own esprit de corps following an ancestral and alchemical collective practice, in order to become independent and territorialise their values and ethos.[33] One way of looking at the history of modernity is to observe that the professional spirit of competitiveness has been, over the last three hundred years, *downsized* from groups to individuals, each person becoming potentially the opponent of everyone else on a global capitalist battlefield in which self-development is the last utopia. In the meantime, some forms of communal, corporate, collective personality, group solidarity, labour or craft communities were weakened or perceived as weakened. Even for those who consider that organised groups can create some peace and security, at least internally, the modern narrative of emancipation of the individual from the tyranny of groups is still interpreted as beneficial, a liberation from discipline as coercion, cognitive subjugation and groupthink. The idea of discipline has not played positively over the last, Foucault-inspired academic decades. Historically and psychologically, intellectuals tend to be individualists at heart even when preoccupied with solidarity. The present book will help nuance and re-evaluate the idea of discipline as a liberating collective device. We will see how modernity has been construed as a deep and multifarious debate on group belonging in the name of various discourses (rational individualism, nationalism, socialism, Nietzscheanism, sociologism, capitalism, communism, communitarianism, individualism, etc.).

Despite a few mentions and interesting sketches here and there, political theorists, historians, philosophers and sociologists have never undertaken a comprehensive study of the various aspects of esprit de corps. The few significant contributions in the last decades were all written in French and I will examine them in detail: first, Bourdieu's *La Noblesse d'État*, in which he deals with a particular aspect of educational esprit de corps; secondly, Deleuze and Guattari's surprising political eulogy of esprit de corps; thirdly, an article published in 2005 by a French economist that I will save for the conclusion;[34] and last but not least, *Esprit de corps, démocratie et espace public*, the proceedings of a colloquium on esprit de corps organised in 2003 at the Sorbonne.[35] The explicit goal of the latter, a transdisciplinary collection of papers, was to 'shed light on the manifestations, ambiguities and consequences of esprit de corps and its use in social groups'.[36] This is the only existing book dedicated to various valences of the notion of esprit de corps, but it remains Franco-French, oblivious of the transnational nature of the phrase. Moreover, it is an interesting but disorganised collection of disparate views which are often sociological, psychological or speculative, but rarely historicised.

The editors start by quoting Émile Durkheim on what is implicitly presented as a definition of the positive outcomes of esprit de corps, taken from the preface of the second edition of *De la division du travail social*:

> What we see above all in the professional group is a moral power capable of containing individual egoisms, of maintaining in the workers' hearts a stronger feeling of their common solidarity, of preventing the law of the strongest from applying too brutally to industrial and commercial relations [. . .] When individuals with common interests form an association, it is not only to defend these interests, it is indeed to associate, to no longer feel lost in the midst of adversaries, to feel the pleasure of communion, to form a unity out of many, that is to say, ultimately, to lead together the same moral existence.[37]

This optimistic conception was essential to Durkheim, as we will examine in Chapter 5. In the second half of the nineteenth century, the French sociologist, partly inspired by his studies on Catholic groups, thought of esprit de corps as a form of solidarity that protected the workers from the violence of economic laissez-faire. For Durkheim, esprit de corps was not only a defensive strategy against the cold spirit of bookkeeping, it was about world-forming and world-keeping, an element of social creation, the ingredient of an industrious and healthy life in a community of practice, an organic form of belonging opposed to distressed and unhealthy isolation.

It is rare to read in French a definition of esprit de corps that does not mention cons along with pros, and the 2003 Sorbonne colloquium was not an exception. Favourable or neutral definitions were less numerous than critical ones: 'The esprit de corps is first of all a nucleus of collective beliefs and repetitive stereotypes that constitute a fund of doctrine and ideals common to members of the same body.'[38] The relation between the body politic and esprit de corps is problematic, because the latter can conflict with the ideals of equality and liberty.[39] This rhetoric, as we will see, was typical of French revolutionary language in 1789, a year when the signifier *esprit de corps* reached a peak in print. Since then, in France, esprit de corps has sometimes been perceived as creating stable pockets of social protection, even favouring the intersubjective individuation of each member, a cohesive common life that is 'necessary to bring man to surpass himself'.[40] But more often than not, Durkheimian optimism is tempered with a Weberian suspicion of the cult of leaders in iron-caged groups, and the fact that self-transcendence or self-improvement can turn into a de-personifying and intolerant fusion with the groupthink: 'The esprit de corps can lead to mistakes, be the source of excluding behaviour inspired by compliance.'[41]

In the introduction to *Esprit de corps*, the political theorist Lucien Sfez explains that esprit de corps is 'power in the body', an inner 'code' of conduct:

> Inside the group, the esprit de corps is totalitarian. Its empire ends where other bodies begin, where associations, groups can resist, where administrations and parties watch [. . .] Esprit de corps can be effectually criticised by individuals belonging to a body only if they have been placed in political, historical, administrative or technical situations that allow them to read several codes at once.[42]

We will see in our first chapter how the political meaning of esprit de corps was initiated by d'Alembert, Diderot and Voltaire in the *Encyclopédie*. The *Philosophes* presented themselves as the kind of enlightened interstitial community suggested by Sfez, protected from partisanship by the power of reasoning and by their attachment to the idea of a republican nation. Another idea suggested by Sfez is that, while the critical elite is supposedly gifted with multi-literacy in terms of code-deciphering, there is, in a given nation, a constant antagonism of different groups and plural forms of esprit de corps.[43] For example, the eighteenth-century French philosophers rose to prominence in part thanks to their opposition to the Jesuits, who had a monopoly on academic education. This is, as we will see, a striking example of how the three words we are studying worked as a polemical weapon with real social and cultural implications: the supposed esprit de corps of the Society of Jesus led to their banishment and liberated hundreds of teaching jobs at the Sorbonne, to be taken up by the secular bourgeoisie.

Still worthy of note from the *Esprit de corps* symposium of 2003 are the literary ideas of 'communauté seconde' (Georges Bataille) or 'communauté inavouable' (Maurice Blanchot),[44] according to which the members of a group are looking to fulfil collectively a deeply human desire for spiritual eternity:

> The group erases arbitrariness from their lives. On the contrary, they exist under the seal of a double legitimation: the individual finds fulfilment in the group which, by welcoming the individual, legitimises its existence. In return, the group is legitimised to the extent that it promotes in everyone what Rousseau called 'the sentiment of existence'.[45]

It is common knowledge that in his *Reveries* Rousseau connects happiness with the Heraclitean feeling of peace generated by the lone contemplation of our natural being, generally favoured by promenades on islands, or next to lakes, rivers and other entities that cannot talk back. How this sentiment can be felt in a human community is a profound mystery for a modern individual. Democracy creates the psychology of the independence-driven self and at the same time the alterity of other selves who equally aspire to independence, everyone restricting everyone else's independence. Even the idea of the social contract could be seen as an immature desire to fuse all selves into one gigantic uterine ego, and thus eliminate contradiction as in domesticated nature. The dialectical idea that an individual can only blossom within a supporting community has been key to the debate on esprit de corps since the eighteenth-century defence of the notion in religious discourse. An organised group can be a social machine producing a form of spiritual health, grounded in what the philosopher Castoriadis called its 'instituting imaginary' [imaginaire instituant],[46] following a process that Bergson called *fabulation*, of which more in Chapter 6.

The metaphor of the machine is slippery. The political theorist Paul Zawadzki considers – thus reproducing a typical Enlightenment discourse – that esprit de corps is mostly about mechanical obedience: 'Hypersocialised or dominated individuals act as puppets, or as mere cogs in a machinery called esprit de corps.'[47] During the French Revolution, Joseph-Antoine Cerutti, a deputy of the Assemblée nationale législative, claimed that monastery life in the *Ancien Régime* was not one of brotherhood: 'Cloisters forbid any special friendship; they only wanted members devoted to esprit de corps, uncommunicative rows of automatons, like Prussian soldiers.'[48] Is esprit de corps a mix of flesh and automation, a kind of collective anthropo-robot or *anthrobot*? We will come back to this timely idea in our conclusion.

The most intriguing and historically minded paper from the *Esprit de corps* Sorbonne symposium is by philosophers of law Thomas Berns and Benoît Frydman, who start by noting that in medieval times, a common juridical term for private or public associations was the Latin word *universitas*:

> In the middle of 13th century [. . .], we see Innocent IV assert that a community *fingitur una persona*, that it is [as] a person [. . .] This fiction of legal personality makes it possible to evoke the unity of multiplicity in what can henceforth be called a 'mystical body'.[49]

However, according to the authors, these medieval bodies were often incarnated in the figure of a leader:

> It is only the idea of incarnation that makes it possible to accomplish the incorporation: the abstraction of the *universitas* takes form and life when it is embodied in a person, the chief, the head, the one who represents it. It is not only a matter of incorporation in the strict sense (association in the hierarchy, association of the various members, subjects and leader in a single body), but it is also and always a matter of incarnation, by which this association is truly personified, and as such cannot suggest the question of esprit de corps.[50]

This seems to suggest *a contrario* that esprit de corps is a cohesion without a personified leader. Esprit de corps would only emerge once the group as a whole can be considered as a collective mind. The problem with such a logical schematisation is that historically, as we will see, esprit de corps, even after the eighteenth century, seems rarely to have been a leader-independent phenomenon. Or is it that the human leaders are less influential than it seems? Our current big data profiling of social clusters, which can be said to manifest our invisible group belongings via our digital traces, seems indeed to suggest that inspirational volition is less instrumental than we would like to believe. This is Bourdieu's thesis, addressed in Chapter 6.

In France, continue Berns and Frydman, the idea that absolute sovereign power was embodied by the king – as per Kantorowicz's classic study[51] – remained dominant until the second half of the eighteenth century, when its public questioning became one of the strong pre-revolutionary discursive acts. We will see how revolutionary figures proposed to inflate the feeling of esprit de corps to the limits of the entire nation. To build a *bodyfying* nation, '[qui] *fait corps*',[52] became an 'obsession' of the French Revolution.[53] Simultaneously, 'the Revolution seems to wish to expel or destroy intermediary bodies by considering them as parasitic or hostile bodies estranged from that of the nation'.[54] The great sovereign body of the state devoured the traditional social bodies, but did not digest them completely: some subsisted or reappeared in the nineteenth century, but with a different status; in Chapter 4, we will examine Napoleon's building of a national order via the production and regulation of a state-engineered esprit de corps, based on the emulation of military protocol.

Berns and Frydman locate the intellectual prehistory of the partnership between the modern nation and state-controlled esprit de corps in the work of the sixteenth-century political philosopher Jean Bodin:[55]

> The sovereignty proper to the political community is defined by the need to be radically different from any other body [. . .] Bodin directly confronts the question of 'whether it is good to eliminate or strengthen bodies and colleges'. In a finalist fashion, the bodies and intermediary societies are justified by the fact that they maintain the friendship which is at the very foundation of the Republic, 'such friendship as can only be maintained by alliances, societies, estates, communities, fellowships, bodies [*corps*] and colleges'.[56]

Bodin is, of course, not talking about the neoliberal idea of friendship, what we could call, in the vein of Hannah Arendt,[57] a domestic relationship between binomes of biologised individuals, a micro-solidarity often fetishised as unique, perhaps by analogy with private property. Intermediary bodies were seen by Bodin as socialising circles that produced the necessary collective solidarity that he thought would be difficult to produce at the sole level of the state. On the other hand, and here Bodin anticipated the French Revolution discourse on esprit de corps, 'ill-adjusted communities' [*communautez mal reiglees*] could create monopolies, factions, seditions, and partisanship [*partialitez*] that would endanger the sovereignty of the nation. A strong state was necessary as a regulator of com-munities. Such advice is still worthy of consideration in discussing the current politics of communitarianism.

Consistent with Bodin's perspective was Thomas Hobbes's chapter XXII of *Leviathan*, where, following a bodily metaphor, Hobbes defined 'systems' as human groups 'joined in one interest, or one business', which he compared to the 'parts, or muscles of a body natural' that should be 'subordinate to a sovereign power' or 'commonwealth'.[58] For Hobbes, intermediary societies can sometimes be unlawful, like factions, secret cabals, and then they are akin to 'evil humours' and diseases.[59] When lawful and regular, they resemble a family – yet even in families, law should be above the power of the patriarch.[60] Here one could ask: isn't the notion of esprit de corps precisely related to the idea that a strong intermediary group develops its own code of law, an ideological and behavioural uniform in which the national rule of law or the general will may not apply? Such was the main argument of the *Philosophes*, and in this they were followers of Bodin and Hobbes.

But the power of the state itself was not necessarily virtuous. For Berns and Frydman, the biased excesses of the *Terreur* reinforced the idea that the nation itself needed to institutionalise counter-powers to avoid being taken over by a pseudo-nationalist faction. Universal reason could be hijacked. A tempering of power, the attempt to protect the public power from itself and by itself, supposes the institution of a multitude of distinct and specialised bodies, inspired by the British 'checks and balances system'.[61] I will show in detail how the Jacobins' reign was rapidly interpreted as a proof that esprit de corps could neither be eradicated, nor extended to the sole level of national loyalty, an expansion that was one of the Revolution's ideals. If there would always be intermediary forms of esprit de corps, the right question was how docile they were towards the state, and how this docility could be produced and controlled via a system of rewards and promotions, as advocated efficiently by the Bonapartists.

Berns and Frydman's thought-provoking sketch of a genealogy of esprit de corps ignores the nineteenth and twentieth centuries and does not consider English uses of the phrase. Their main thesis is that the idea of esprit de corps appeared when modern intermediary bodies, societies and corporations started to be seen as an artificial problem, when they lost their apparent natural or divine legitimacy:

> Contrary to the 'natural' bodies of the *Ancien Régime*, these are only artificial creations, legal or administrative, purely abstract entities [. . .] But if these bodies do not rest on a substratum, on an identifiable component of the population, on a specific solidarity that unites its members, *what* is it that *will hold them together?* It is precisely here that the question of esprit de corps arises, which, in the modern sense of the term, designates the bond which unites the members of a body or a company.[62]

Did our occidental modernity start speaking of esprit de corps as a quality we should eradicate or recreate in organisations because social groups lost their 'natural' foundation? This suggests that pre- or early modern societies were more authentic, and that democracy lost something fundamental with regard to human bonding. This serious claim was at the heart of Tocqueville's pessimistic political philosophy. He regretted the loss of esprit de corps because this not only undermined our capacity for authentic group belonging, but also jeopardised our capacity to attain real self-realisation, as we will explain.

Berns and Frydman, and all the authors in the Sorbonne conference proceedings, overlooked the military origin of esprit de corps and the military or even 'metamilitary'[63] discourses on esprit de corps of the last three centuries. This is an omission that the present book will rectify.

To complete our overview of the French *Esprit de corps* symposium, it is worth mentioning the sociologist Pierre Ansart, who quotes Voltaire's entry on 'Esprit' in the *Encyclopédie* (1755):

> We must not forget here in how many different senses the word *esprit* is employed; it is not a defect of language, it is, on the contrary, an advantage to have roots thus ramifying out into several branches. *Esprit d'un corps*, of a society, to express the uses, the way of thinking, of behaving, the prejudices of a body. *Esprit de parti*, which is to esprit de corps what the passions are to ordinary feelings.[64]

Historically, the phrase *esprit de parti* was probably of earlier use than *esprit de corps*. We find it in print as early as 1701, in the gazette *L'Esprit des cours de l'Europe*, with the meaning of bias or partisanship, and in contradistinction from the Cartesian rational ego: 'I say it as I think and without partisanship' [*Je le dis comme je le pense et sans esprit de parti*].[65] It is possible that the notion of *esprit d'un corps* or *esprit du corps* evolved towards a more idiomatic *esprit de corps* under the influence of the expression *esprit de parti*, combined with the influence of the military use of *esprit de corps*, which, as we will see, predated the publication of the *Encyclopédie*. *Esprit de corps* started to be used in France in the second half of the eighteenth century to designate the *esprit de parti* of the members of a society defending the interests of their group. Voltaire's suggestion that the esprit de corps of a group was *ordinaire*, usual and not necessarily negative because not too passionate or extreme, was replaced – for example by Diderot and d'Alembert – by the idea that esprit de corps was necessarily abusive, restrictively antagonistic, representing a petty party *against* another. As we will show in our chapter on the early voyage of the phrase from France to the anglophone zone, Voltaire's more moderate view would in the long term, partly thanks to his friend Lord Chesterfield, be more influential in the UK and the USA than the less nuanced revolutionary view.

Abstract Universalism: The Problem of a Philosophical Perspective When Studying Esprit de Corps

Consider the above-mentioned book on the intellectual history of general will, subtitled *The Evolution of a Concept*. Is esprit de corps a concept? I prefer to speak of notions rather than concepts to designate ideas with unsettled and arguable definitions. While the signifier 'esprit de corps' has remained invariant in the last three centuries and across geo-cultural zones, the ideas that it has designated, its *signifieds*, have differed significantly. It is common knowledge that *signifier* and *signified*, a distinction operated by the linguist Ferdinand de Saussure, differentiate the material signs serving as vehicle from the meaning itself.[66] Mark Bevir explains in *The Logic of the History of Ideas*:

> Saussure [. . .] argues that the bond between signifiers and signifieds, words and concepts, is an arbitrary one. The bond is set up by social conventions, where the sole constraint on these conventions is that our signifiers must differ from each other.[67]

Bevir speaks of concepts to indicate something that is conceived, but not necessarily precise. Until a definite and consensual signified is globally established for the signifier 'esprit de corps', which seems unlikely, esprit de corps is rather an ambiguous *notion* that floats in a field of more or less related ideas. This is not a weakness in terms of thriving. After all, human beings are perhaps the most ambiguous species on earth and also the dominant one. It is the difference between, on the one hand, the transnational, transcultural, translingual and transepochal invariance of the signifier 'esprit de corps' and, on the other hand, the local, temporal and contextual variability of its connotations that makes its rigorous study possible and fecund.

According to the *Oxford English Dictionary*, esprit de corps is a 'phraseological combination' that designates 'the regard entertained by the members of a body for the honour and interests of the body as a whole, and of each other as belonging to it'.[68] This is a somewhat complicated definition that tries to synthesise the individual and the group in a *soi-disant* 'win-win' configuration. The American *Merriam-Webster Dictionary* proposes both a 'simple' and a 'full' definition of esprit de corps. The simple one is: 'Feelings of loyalty, enthusiasm, and devotion to a group among people who are members of the group.'[69] The full definition abandons *loyalty* and replaces it with *honour*: 'The common spirit existing in the members of a group and inspiring enthusiasm, devotion, and strong regard for the honor of a group.'[70] Common spirit, regard, feelings, loyalty, devotion, enthusiasm, honour: a philosopher's unifying perspective could posit that this all equates to a subjective attachment to the unity of a group, to the point that the group itself seems to possess a form of agency. Can we speak of the *honour of a group* as if a social body as a whole could be personified? This question is much debated in philosophy under the labels of 'shared intention', 'joint action', 'the plural subject', 'collective intentionality', 'team agency' etc.[71] Can groups be persons?[72] Too often, analytic philosophers omit to consider that such a problem is not devoid of ideological, cultural and historical aspects. For instance, Benito Mussolini wrote in 'The Doctrine of Fascism' (1932) that the state was both a living organism and the 'highest and most powerful form of personality'.[73] Is it reasonable to ignore the sociopolitics of such a claim? The influential *Philosophy of Right* proposed by G. W. F. Hegel in the nineteenth century also referred to the state as a superior spirit.[74] A consequence of this type of view is, of course, that discrete individuals – citizens, inhabitants, immigrants – might be more or less considered to be second-rate persons compared to the super-individual that is the state or the organised society:

> The very existence of individual citizens becomes tied into the ends of the group organism. They have no independent lives outside the group. Their very liberty must be defined in terms of the group. [When] the group becomes an end in itself [. . .] a corollary of this is that human units could become means to an end.[75]

Esprit de corps, once again, was often articulated in France in opposition to ideals of individual liberty. A peer-reviewed paper published in 1899 in the *Revue philosophique de la France et de l'étranger* subscribed to the Enlightenment's general suspicion of biased collectives: 'In our opinion, esprit de corps is a collective egoism, solely concerned with collective ends, and disdainful of the individual and of individual qualities.'[76] From this perspective, collective intentionality is a monstrosity. In fact, both in the individualist critique and in the praise of collective minds, the shadow of the ideology of laissez-faire capitalism cannot be ignored.

Research on esprit de corps could be tempted to answer questions such as is esprit de corps socially desirable or does individualism produce more harmonious effects in the long term? Is cooperation more effective for civilisational progress than competition? These general questions are interesting, but potentially misleading if they are abstractly universalised rather than contextualised by comparing different historical periods, geographical situations and contexts. To avoid participating in the battlefield of truth-aspiring definitions, polemical notions gain from being historicised in a discursive genealogy rather than generally defined. In this sense, esprit de corps can be compared to contested notions such as freedom or justice:

> The idea that it would be possible and meaningful, for example, to seek an adequate concept of justice, or of freedom, is confused. There are societies, human groups that have produced conceptions of justice, but the identity of the vocabulary does not imply the identity of the concepts and does not guarantee that we are talking about the same 'object'.[77]

A pure analytic description of political and social notions might be a chimera:

An analytic proposition cannot be true simply by virtue of definitions and the laws of formal logic since how we define something must depend on our other beliefs, where these other beliefs might alter as a result of further empirical investigations. All of our knowledge arises, therefore, in the context of our particular web of beliefs.[78]

Because there is no clear definition of what esprit de corps is, and, for example, no agreement on the possibility of a collective body manifesting its own personality, a genealogical approach to esprit de corps seems well advised before we engage in wild speculation. Hence the need to look at the uses that have been made of the signifying emblem that is esprit de corps, in what historical, social, discursive and rhetorical contexts, and within which webs of belief. The pertinence of a cultural and sociological notion must be examined as a 'speech act' situated in a certain social 'language context',[79] even when it points to an all-encompassing truth. Michel Foucault defined genealogy, following Nietzsche's considerations, as a historico-philosophical method that considers discursive utterances as signs in a larger structure or discourse to be unveiled:

> Following the complex path of provenance is [. . .] to maintain what has happened in the dispersion that is peculiar to it: it is to identify the accidents, the minute deviations – or on the contrary the complete reversals – the errors, the mistakes of appreciation, the bad calculations which gave birth to what exists and is valid for us.[80]

Of esprit de corps, we could repeat what David Armitage wrote in his long-term examination of the formula 'civil war': 'It has been reinterpreted and redeployed in multiple contexts for multiple purposes throughout the centuries. It may look descriptive, but it is firmly normative, expressing values and interpretations more than any stable identity.'[81] This does not signify that we should completely abandon the possibility of meta-narrative insights or hypotheses encompassing webs of belief that are interconnected across regions and times. We must avoid a historical and notional relativism – indeed a nihilism – in which general human evolution would be 'a tale told by an idiot, full of sound and fury, signifying nothing'.[82]

As Far as We Can Tell: A *longue durée* Intellectual History of the Uses of Esprit de Corps

Because of their imprecision and polysemy, a sensible approach to sociopolitical notions is to contextualise them historically. We want to draw lines and connections between different webs of belief and distinguish significant epochal patterns. A mind–body emblem such as the signifier 'esprit de corps' is particularly interesting because it is transcultural or transdiscursive (used in several social fields and normative discourses), transnational (used in several languages and geopolitical zones) and transtemporal (used across centuries). Because esprit de corps can emblematise different meanings with laudatory or pejorative valences, it is pertinent to study what strategies are at stake behind the enunciations of the phrase. Looking at history to understand notions goes along with looking at notions to understand history, or, as the historian Richard Whatmore puts it:

> Intellectual historians accept that ideas matter as first-order information about social phenomena and as directly revealing facts about our world that cannot be described except by reference to ideas. As such ideas are social forces. They may be shaped by other forces but they themselves, in turn, always influence the human world.[83]

The notion that ideas are social forces is, of course, not self-evident and has its own polemical history. It does not mean necessarily that ideas have a life of their own, as suggested by Alfred Fouillée's nineteenth-century notion of '*idée-force*', influenced by Darwinism: ideas as active principles that, once formulated, participate in their progressive social realisation through successive embodied approximations.[84] Despite fascinating attempts to isolate universal unit ideas, it is probably safer to consider that ideas cannot be separated from the argumentative uses that human groups make of them.[85] At the political and social level, arguments between humans and groups do take at times a turn that influences significant historical events. If something really universal could be said about human nature, it would be that we have been up to now an argumentative species with agonistic worldviews.[86] In their book *The Enigma of Reason: A New Theory of Human Understanding*, Hugo Mercier and Dan Sperber argue that 'reason has two main functions: that of producing reasons for justifying oneself, and that of producing arguments to convince others'.[87] This seems to justify the orthodox approach to intellectual history and genealogy championed by Quentin Skinner:

> There cannot be a history of unit ideas as such, but only a history of the various uses to which they have been put by different agents at different times [. . .] Our concepts not only alter over time, but are incapable of providing us with anything more than a series of changing perspectives on the world in which we live and have our being. Our concepts form part of what we bring to the world in our efforts to understand it [. . .] We need to treat our normative concepts less as statements about the world than as tools and weapons of debate.[88]

This view is representative of what has been called the Cambridge school of intellectual history, according to which 'we need to grasp not merely the meaning of what is said', but also what the enunciation is 'doing'.[89]

Notions are 'language acts' which follow certain 'assumptions', taking place in 'complex normative systems', where 'facts, values and roles and intricately and ambiguously related', and where 'the conveying of information may have complex normative and political consequences'.[90] Pocock calls these argumentative fields 'languages'. This is related to what Foucault called discourse, a violence that we inflict on things, a practice that we impose on them according to the rules of a certain society, web of belief, profession or institution:[91] 'In any society, the production of discourse is at the same time controlled, selected, organised and redistributed by a certain number of procedures.'[92]

Now, can we challenge the idea that our concepts are incapable of providing us in the long run with anything more than a series of changing perspectives on the world? Under certain conditions, I agree with Armitage that we should not be too reluctant to try and propose an interpretative meta-narrative, one or a few 'big ideas' that encompass meaningfully and coherently the long-term battlefield of ideas.[93] Conversely, because a language or discourse is localised in a certain period and a certain sociocultural field, we can wonder if it makes sense to interpret the destiny of a notion over a long period of time. Even if d'Alembert in 1751 and *The Wall Street Journal* in 2016 used the same signifier 'esprit de corps', how do we know that there is a fecund correlation to be found between their signifieds? Can there be a meaningful and robust meta-history of a phrase across different centuries and nations leading to a synthetic discovery? This book is an attempt to answer this type of question, recently revived by the use of digital corpuses.

The term *longue durée* has been used for the historical practice of surveying long periods of time, typically of more – and often much more – than a few decades.[94] To establish a genealogy of speech acts conveyed by the uses of esprit de corps from the eighteenth century up to the twenty-first is a long-term history that focuses on what we have learned to call modern times, a supposedly coherent occidental epoch.[95] The question of *longue durée* has been reconsidered recently because we now have access to relatively powerful digital tools that allow one researcher to consider the written use of terms much more exhaustively, with the help of large databases of texts and automatic search engines. This approach is part of what is called *digital humanities*:

> The promise of the digital humanities for transforming the work of intellectual historians is immense [. . .] And with ever greater flexibility for searching and recovering contextual information, we can discover more precisely and persuasively moments of rupture as well as stretches of continuity. In short, we now have both the methodological tools and the technological means to overcome most, if not all, of the traditional objections to the marriage of intellectual history with the *longue durée*. We can at last get back to studying big ideas in a big way.[96]

I sympathise with this enthusiasm to a certain extent, although I will explain why I think it is preferable, given the amount of data now at our disposal, to study, rather than 'big ideas in a big way', *small* ideas in a big way, an approach I have called *histosophy*.[97]

David Armitage, in his last opus on the *longue durée* intellectual history of civil war, seems himself reluctant to propose a big unifying idea.[98] His insistence on the antagonism of interpretations regarding the notion of civil war is closer to Skinner's or Pocock's modesty than might be expected. The reason for this caution, despite the above-mentioned enthusiasm, might be that a satisfactory practice of *longue-durée* history cannot propose all-encompassing interpretations without becoming somewhat speculative. Provided that one is clear that they pertain to philosophy, even on historical bases, speculative leaps remain interesting precisely because they are rarely fully convincing. Ideally, long-term historical genealogists should not just make a list of different 'webs of belief' regarding an idea and completely shy away from the ambition of synthesising these into a significant narrative: a meaningful approach to *longue durée* should avoid becoming a *longue purée*, a mashed potato of disparate enunciations that are put together without a general thread. Nevertheless, the modesty of historians compared to philosophers comes from their sensitivity to discourse and contingency. In the present book I shall advocate a middle way: a rigid argument will not be imposed on the reader, but enough synthetic interpretation will be provided, induced from data, to specify two or three overarching narratives or logics regarding the importance of esprit de corps to understanding our times.

Due to my continental philosophical training, I am inclined to share Armitage's bold aspiration, expressed in the *History Manifesto*, that we should 'think about the past in order to see the future'.[99] On another hand, the more data we have, the more interpretation, deduction and narrative synthesis are needed to structure it, which cannot be performed by machines. I believe long-term intellectual historians should dare to reflect on our global problems and challenges by identifying ideological patterns in the study of long, transnational periods, but such an approach should be careful, if possible, to avoid the pitfalls of 'epochalism', the reifying speculative tendency to attribute big-picture meanings to large periods of time, and the tendency to believe that these constructions are the real ontology of history.[100] The subsequent chapters will be as 'neutral' as possible in presenting the results of the genealogy and the dialectics of esprit de corps, in order for the reader to be able to establish her own synthetic reading. But here and there, as well as in the conclusion of this book, modest speculative leaps will be performed.

Surveying Large Issues Within a Small Compass: Digital Genealogy and Histosophy

It is certain that the 'return to *longue durée*', if there is such a thing, 'has a new relationship to the abounding sources of big data available in our time'.[101] The current book was written using digital tools to unveil the genealogy of esprit de corps in a specific manner. In our century, automated and digitised archives allow us to use computational software to search for a word or phrase in large corpora across centuries and genres. Data mining does not replace the work of analysis, synthesis and interpretation, but it does facilitate a more exhaustive look into available data.

I chose to focus on primary sources, texts and documents that are not necessarily canonical, but that all have a common point: they explicitly contain the signifier 'esprit de corps'. This does not mean that I neglected related notions, such as for instance 'group feeling', 'fellowship', 'zeal', 'partisanship', 'corporatism', 'code of honour', etc. However, for the sake of systematicity, I preferred to encounter them formulated in contexts where esprit de corps was explicitly mentioned, instead of assuming the conceptual field *a priori*. This empirical rule proved to be a safe strategy to avoid a personal bias regarding the meaning of esprit de corps. Esprit de corps is often located in a rich context of metaphors, and it would be ineffective to start by chasing down every analogue to the phrase one could think of; hence the need to focus on evidenced historical discourse regarding the syntactic space as well as the semantic space of esprit de corps.

To dig into French texts, I partly used the Frantext database, among other sources.[102] The ARTFL implementation of the database (formerly the *Trésor de la langue française*) 'consists of over 2900 texts, ranging from classic works of French literature to various kinds of non-fiction prose and technical writing. The eight-eenth-, nineteenth-, and twentieth centuries are about equally represented.'[103] In English as in French, I also used century-specific databases that will be referenced as the chapters unfold. To conclude this introduction, I will focus briefly on the main search tool I used, known as the Ngram Viewer, in order to offer a general understanding of the procedure I followed.

In 2011, a group of researchers connected with the Harvard Cultural Observatory published an article in *Science* to propose a digital tool that was meant to extend the boundaries of word- or phrase-searching to corpora of mil-lions of books in several languages, a data source produced by Google's effort to digitise as many books as possible in the last decade.[104] In their terminology, a 1-gram is either a word or a punctuation mark. 'Esprit de corps', for example, is a 3-gram. The search engine presents occurrences of the required n-gram in print, chronologically, within a time range that can be adapted manually. It is then often possible to explore the content of each book and read the environing pages in which the n-gram is used in order to understand the context of use. Because I have tried as far as possible to quote from first editions, and because the Ngram Viewer does not systematically offer the possibility of reading all the pages of a chosen book, I also used, as mentioned earlier, other digital archives, for example Gallica (from the Bibliothèque Nationale de France)[105] and the Internet Archive for English books (mostly UK and North America).[106] In other cases I had to look for an edition of a book in a library or in the second-hand market, but in these cases also I was often digitally pointed to such and such a document where I knew I would find the phrase 'esprit de corps'. This approach to the examination of sources is quantitatively more exhaustive compared to what intellectual histori-ans could achieve only a decade ago.

The type of results that the Ngram Viewer retrieves depends on the chosen chronological range. It is, for example, possible to search between 1895 and 1899 in French or English documents, or to choose longer scales. The suc-cession of texts is generally chronological, but not without a relative disorder and sometimes dating mistakes that must be resolved by human analysis. As of October 2015, the number of books scanned by Google Books – to which the Ngram retrieval engine is connected – was 25 million (English, French, Russian, Chinese, Italian, Hebrew and Spanish are represented, which of course reflects a form of cultural hegemony), while their estimate of all book titles ever published was 130 million.[107]

Let us look, for example, at a random retrieved result, the *Compte rendu des débats du Grand Conseil du canton de Vaud sur le projet de loi ecclésiastique* (1839), which contains two occurrences of esprit de corps, the first being the following:

> I did not mention anyone in particular; I only referred to esprit de corps in general. Now, it is in the nature of things and of men that every corporation which deals only with an object seeks to seize it exclusively; it is the propension of bodies [*l'esprit des corps*] to extend their attributions, their power [. . .] It can be said that as soon as a young man has completed his theological studies, he becomes part of a powerful corporation, which, more than any other, possesses an important leverage, the power it exerts over consciences, a weapon stronger than the civil power. Everywhere the priests' corps have had a tendency to rise above the civil authority and to dominate. This is the story of all times [. . .] I have, I repeat, no intention to refer to anyone in particular. I merely recall a historical fact. Nature is in the nineteenth century as it has been everywhere, in the Middle Ages and in all ages.[108]

Here the work of the robotic search engine must stop, and human exegesis is needed. We need to look beyond a particular enunciation of 'esprit de corps' in order to understand who the author of the text is, in what context the speech act was uttered, what rhetorical strategy was deployed, and to what other synchronic and diachronic uses it is related. The above example is a generalising consideration of esprit de corps, presented as a universal natural law of human groups and human nature. The claim is that whether individuals in the group like it or not, a specialised society or corporation will aspire to form a monopoly and expand at the expense of the outside world. We will in the following chapters meet other examples of such a naturalistic view of esprit de corps.

But who is affirming this and according to what rhetorical strategy? The title of the document gives us a clue via the word *ecclésiastique*, and so does its location, a Swiss region under strong historical French influence. Further research revealed the existence of a debate in Switzerland, at that time, regarding the separation of Church and state.[109] The author was a Doctor of Law, the président du Conseil d'État Emmanuel de la Harpe (1782–1842), brother of a former officer in the Napoleonic army.[110] This excerpt unfolds as a defence of the balance between the power of the state and the power of the Church. It is a secularist claim for the protection of citizens from an excessive religious authority. It is probable that the author wished to defend the primary power of the state, since he represented the public administration, but he used the tactical mask of an impartial or enlightened philosopher. The esprit de corps of the Church is diplomatically presented as dangerous not because it is evil, but because it is hegemonic by nature, as are all forms of organised power. The rhetorical strategy is to assert that this is not a case of *argumentum ad hominem* against such or such representative of the Church, not even against the power of the Church, but a moderate and benevolent exposition of a universal human law that calls for a counteractive mitigation. Any power must be controlled by counter-powers because the esprit de corps of societies tends to be a conquering force. Religious societies in particular can be overly influential because of their power over conscience. Nowadays this could be recategorised as a debate on 'cultural engineering'.[111]

De la Harpe's argumentation was a pastiche of the Enlightenment discourse, in the style of the *Encyclopédie*. We will see how the *Encyclopédistes* accelerated the use of the esprit de corps notion against religious groups, and how they succeeded in undermining the strong religious and educational power of the Jesuits, while the latter tried to defend themselves by presenting a eulogy of esprit de corps. Notions such as esprit de corps could be called 'combat concepts', as they are polemical notions used as power weapons by different 'cultural-political factions'.[112] A critic could argue that, by suggesting that human history is the history of combat notions used by antagonistic groups – as well as the history of the concrete consequences of such arguments – we are perhaps being as essentialising as Emmanuel de la Harpe in the above-mentioned example. But even if history demonstrates that esprit de corps has been universal and central until now, nothing authorises us to posit that a conflictual will to hegemony will forever be the essence of human or group relations, even if common sense or experience suggests that this is likely.

Much more could be said to analyse our prototypical *Canton de Vaud* example. This illustrates both the force and the limitations of my methodology. Its force is that by having access to hundreds of texts from the early eighteenth century to today, in which the signifier 'esprit de corps' can be spotted in context, I was able to operate a horizontal, comparative and diachronic analysis of the uses of the notion to form a long-term, insightful narrative. The limitation is that I will not be able to perform simultaneously, within the space, time and individual authorship of a single book, an exhaustive vertical and synchronic form of intellectual history as an approach that would look in detail at the precise context and micro-history of each enunciation in which esprit de corps has been performative. One could spend much more time trying to understand the nuances of the history of the relationship between Church and state in Switzerland in the 1830s, and there are probably different layers of understanding regarding de la Harpe's above-mentioned speech. However, it is evident that I have tried something different in this book: even had I not excluded selected and simplified micro-histories, the exhaustive vertical or synchronic study of a particular use of esprit de corps in a local context and within a relatively limited period of human history was never my intention. I hope that thorough specialists of such or such a period or of a given author will forgive the occasional schematisation.

Another limitation that calls for further research is that I will be mainly looking at French (mostly from France) and English (mostly from the UK and the USA) uses, although other languages have used the Gallicism 'esprit de corps', and at times (Spanish and German for example) still use it. But I found that the use of the signifier in languages other than English or French is much more sporadic and difficult to trace. The focus on English is justified by the fact that it is today the language that uses esprit de corps globally, and with much more frequency than any other. The choice of French is self-evident, as the language of origin of the phrase. When esprit de corps emerged as a signifier, French was the occidental lingua franca, a position now occupied by English. Transnational in the present book presupposes a comparative approach to different cultures in more or less intensive correspondence, alternatively local, national and global.

Only organised teamwork could help to expand my results by looking at other languages and at each period in more detail. It would be tempting but too simple to claim that each language carries a specific spirit or intellectual worldview that influences the individuals who use it dominantly, an *esprit de corpus*, so to speak. The dominant transnational force in modern global history, capitalism, is an ideology that changes the valence of human values over time and across borders as it itself evolves.

In the end, the chapters that follow might not be an example of orthodox history, nor are they an exercise in analytic or universalistic philosophy. But failing in 'pure history' and 'pure philosophy' – if purity can ever exist in any discipline – is my conscious premise, since my goal is to contribute to a form of genealogy that could be called histosophy, 'the art of surveying large issues within a small compass'.[113] Of course, doing history philosophically or doing philosophy historically is not new,[114] and the histosophical approach has been practised by others under other labels. The small compass of esprit de corps proved to be an effectual notion to study in the long term and across cultures, something I would not have dared with overused notions such as 'freedom' or even 'individualism'. The large issues addressed by the uses of esprit de corps are, for example, the political tension between particularism and universalism; the antagonism between freedom of thought and collectivism; questions of group identity, community, collective consciousness, nationalism, self-determination, corporatism, groupthink and freedom of speech; the idea that humans are social automata rather than free-will individuals, or the converse; the notion that history itself is a consequence of antagonisms between communities of interest; the impact of the capitalist ideology on our schemes of thought; the modern avatars of the long human history of disembodiment and contempt towards the bodily realm; and last but not least, what – as an open conclusion to my research on esprit de corps – I propose to call *ensemblance*, the fact that human ensembles, like all realities, never become totally one, for better or worse. We live in a universe of quasi-unities and quasi-multiplicities. Forgetting that full totality is a myth can be very dangerous, for example historically. Forgetting that full multiplicity is not real can be equally damaging, for instance individually.

But enough said: an answer to the enigma of esprit de corps must slowly emerge from the empirical and sympathetic interpretation of the data. And if I appear reluctant, even in my conclusion, to cut the theoretical Gordian knot, the reader might be tempted to borrow my sword.

Notes

1. Jeremy W. Peters, 'Donald Trump Defines His Style: Deal-Making Flexibility', *The New York Times*, 11 August 2015, <https://nyti.ms/1WgFYyr> (accessed 19 September 2019).

2. 'Donald Trump Hosts a Made in America Event at The White House – July 23, 2018', Factbase Videos, YouTube, <https://youtu.be/d0fp_X4MVP8> (accessed 19 September 2019).

3. Roger Van Scyoc, 'College of Arts and Architecture staff build team spirit outside the office', *Centre Daily Times*, 11 May 2017, <https://www.centredaily.com/news/local/education/penn-state/article150080217.html#storylink=cpy> (accessed 19 September 2019).

4. Thomas E. Boyt, Robert F. Lusch and Drue K. Schuler, 'Fostering Esprit de Corps in Marketing', *Marketing Management* 6.1 (1997), p. 21.

5. John Perry, *Winston Churchill* (New York: Thomas Nelson, 2010), p. 43.

6. Michael Funk Deckard and Péter Losonczi (eds), *Philosophy Begins in Wonder: An Introduction to Early Modern Philosophy, Theology, and Science* (Cambridge: James Clarke, 2011), p. 91.

7. Jan Christoph Bublitz and Reinhard Merkel, 'Crimes Against Minds: On Mental Manipulations, Harms and a Human Right to Mental Self-Determination', *Criminal Law and Philosophy* 8.1 (2014), pp. 51–77.

8. *The Esprit de Corps Pointer*, <https://researchonespritdecorps.wordpress.com> (accessed 19 September 2019).

9. Elad Segev, *Google and the Digital Divide: The Bias of Online Knowledge* (Oxford: Chandos, 2010), p. 54.

10. Ken Davenport, 'Obama May Offend on Brexit, but He's Right', *The Wall Street Journal*, 29 April 2016, <https://www.wsj.com/articles/obama-may-offend-on-brexit-but-hes-right-1461946482> (accessed 19 September 2019).

11. David Davis, 'With the EU Referendum Looming, the Government Must Give Us Reliable Immigration Figures', *ConservativeHome*, 2 March 2016, <https://www.conservativehome.com/thetorydiary/2016/03/david-davis-with-the-eu-referendum-looming-the-government-must-give-us-reliable-immigration-figures.html> (accessed 19 September 2019).

12. 'J'en appelle solennellement à l'esprit de corps, au sens inné du devoir et du sacrifice de ceux qui comme vous, ont l'amour de la patrie chevillé au corps'; 'Devant ses jeunes, Marine Le Pen decline ses fondamentaux', *Le Parisien*, 9 September 2011, <https://www.lepoint.fr/societe/devant-ses-jeunes-marine-le-pen-decline-ses-fondamentaux-09-09-2011-1371678_23.php> (accessed 19 September 2019).

13. Craig Brandist, 'The Risks of Soviet-Style Managerialism in UK Universities', *Times Higher Education*, 5 May 2016, <https://www.timeshighereducation.com/comment/the-risks-of-soviet-style-managerialism-in-united-kingdom-universities> (accessed 19 September 2019).

14. 'le pouvoir de l'argent sape peu à peu l'esprit de corps'; Ndrianaivo, 'Esprit de groupe', *La Vérité*, 31 May 2016, <https://researchonespritdecorps.wordpress.com/2016/06/01/solidarity-madagascar/> (accessed 19 September 2019).

15. Robert D. McFadden, 'Robert H. B. Baldwin, Transformer of Morgan Stanley, Dies at 95', *The New York Times*, 6 January 2016, <https://www.nytimes.com/2016/01/07/business/dealbook/robert-hb-baldwin-transformer-of-morgan-stanley-dies-at-95.html> (accessed 19 September 2019).

16. Jean-Baptiste le Rond d'Alembert, 'Caractère des sociétés ou corps particuliers', in Denis Diderot and Jean le Rond d'Alembert (eds), *Encyclopédie ou dictionnaire raisonné des sciences, des arts et des métiers* (Paris: Briasson, David, Le Breton and Durand, 1751–65), vol. II (1752), p. 666.

17. Jean-Baptiste le Rond d'Alembert, 'Character of Societies and Particular Groups', *The Encyclopedia of Diderot & d'Alembert Collaborative Translation Project* (2003), trans. Nelly S. Hoyt and Thomas Cassirer, University of Michigan Library, <https://quod.lib.umich.edu/d/did/did2222.0000.352/--character-of-societies-and-particular-groups?rgn=main;view=fulltext;q1=character+of+societies> (accessed 19 September 2019).

18. Jeffrey Mehlman, 'The "Floating Signifier": From Lévi-Strauss to Lacan', *Yale French Studies* 48 (1972), pp. 10–37.

19. Ed Frauenheim and Kim Peters, 'Here's the Secret to How the Best Employers Inspire Workers', *Fortune*, 22 August 2016, <https://www.greatplacetowork.com/resources/articles/here-s-the-secret-to-how-the-best-employers-inspire-workers> (accessed 19 September 2019).

20. David Frost, 'Liam Fox May Be a Virtual Minister – but He's Vital to Britain's Future Success', *The Telegraph*, 27 July 2016, <https://www.telegraph.co.uk/news/2016/07/27/fox-may-be-a-virtual-minister--but-hes-vital-to-britains-future/> (accessed 19 September 2019).

21. Walter Bryce Gallie, 'Essentially Contested Concepts', *Proceedings of the Aristotelian Society* 56 (1956), pp. 167–98.

22. Michel Foucault, 'Nietzsche, la généalogie, l'histoire', in *Hommage à Jean Hyppolite* (Paris: Presses Universitaires de France, 1971), p. 146.

23. David Pugliese, 'Canadian Army Generals to Get Maple Leaf Insignias Back', *National Post*, 1 April 2016, <https://nationalpost.com/news/canada/canadian-army-generals-to-get-maple-leaf-insignias-back> (accessed 19 September 2019).

24. Rachel Clarke, 'The Moral in "Morale" Is, Take it Seriously, Mr Hunt', *The Huffington Post*, 29 February 2016, <https://www.huffingtonpost.co.uk/rachel-clarke/the-moral-in-morale-is-ta_b_9341244.html> (accessed 19 September 2019).

25. 'l'amour de soi dans les autres et dans le groupe tout entier que favorise le rassemblement prolongé des semblables'; Pierre Bourdieu, *La Noblesse d'État. Grandes écoles et esprit de corps* (Paris: Minuit, 1989), p. 254.

26. Oliver Kay, 'Ronaldo Revels in his New Image as Ultimate Team Man', *The Times*, 12 July 2016, <https://www.thetimes.co.uk/article/ronaldo-takes-glory-in-his-finest-hour-as-first-among-equals-5fv3pgc8t> (accessed 19 September 2019).

27. John Benjamin, 'Are You Making Sure Your Team is Set for Success', *The Greeley Tribune*, 9 April 2016.

28. Gilles Deleuze and Félix Guattari, *Mille plateaux* (Paris: Minuit, 1980), pp. 434–527.

29. Jacques Taminiaux and Robert Crease, 'Merleau-Ponty: From Dialectic to Hyperdialectic', *Research in Phenomenology* 10 (1980), pp. 58–76.

30. Luis de Miranda, 'On the Concept of Creal: The Politico-Ethical Horizon of a Creative Absolute', in Paulo de Assis and Paolo Giudici (eds), *The Dark Precursor: Deleuze and Artistic Research* (Louvain: Leuven University Press, 2017), pp. 510–16.

31. James Farr and David Lay Williams (eds), *The General Will: The Evolution of a Concept* (Cambridge: Cambridge University Press, 2015).

32. Chantal Mouffe, *Agonistics: Thinking the World Politically* (London: Verso, 2013).

33. Deleuze and Guattari, *Mille plateaux*, pp. 434–527.

34. Jean Vauvilliers, 'Pour une théorie générale de l'esprit de corps', *Revue administrative* 347–8 (2005), pp. 489–98, 589–96.

35. Gilles J. Guglielmi and Claudine Haroche (eds), *Esprit de corps, démocratie et espace public* (Paris: Presses Universitaires de France, 2005).

36. 'éclairer les manifestations, les ambiguïtés et les conséquences de l'esprit de corps et de son usage dans les groupes sociaux'; Gilles J. Guglielmi and Claudine Haroche, 'Préface', in Guglielmi and Haroche (eds), *Esprit de corps*, p. 5.

37. 'Ce que nous voyons avant tout dans le groupe professionnel, c'est un pouvoir moral capable de contenir les égoïsmes individuels, d'entretenir dans le cœur des travailleurs un plus vif sentiment de leur solidarité commune, d'empêcher la loi du plus fort de s'appliquer aussi brutalement aux relations industrielles et commerciales [. . .] Quand des individus se trouvant avoir des intérêts communs s'associent, ce n'est pas seulement pour défendre ces intérêts, c'est pour s'associer, pour ne plus se sentir perdus au milieu d'adversaires, pour avoir le plaisir de communier, de ne faire qu'un avec plusieurs, c'est-à-dire, en définitive, pour mener ensemble une même vie morale.' Émile Durkheim, preface to the second edition, *De la division du travail social* (Paris: Félix Alcan, 1897), in Guglielmi and Haroche (eds), *Esprit de corps*, p. 5.

38. 'L'esprit de corps est tout d'abord constitué par un noyau de croyances collectives et de stéréotypes répétitifs qui constituent un fonds de doctrine et d'idéaux communs aux membres d'un même corps.' Claudine Haroche, 'L'Esprit de corps dans les grands corps de l'État en France', in Guglielmi and Haroche (eds), *Esprit de corps*, p. 289.

39. Haroche and Guglielmi, 'Préface', p. 11.

40. 'nécessaire pour amener l'homme à se dépasser lui-même'; Claudine Haroche, 'Modes de comportement et types d'aspiration dans les mouvements de jeunesse en Allemagne (1918–1933)', in Guglielmi and Haroche (eds), *Esprit de corps*, p. 53.

41. 'L'esprit de corps peut conduire à des errements, être à la source de comportements d'exclusion inspirés par la conformité.' Guglielmi and Haroche (eds), *Esprit de corps*, p. 8.

42. 'Dedans, l'esprit de corps est totalitaire. Il arrête son empire là où d'autres corps existent, là où des associations, des groupes peuvent y résister, où des administrations, des partis veillent [. . .] L'esprit de corps peut être critiqué avec efficience par les individus issus d'un corps qui ont été placés dans des situations politiques ou historiques, administratives ou techniques qui leur permettent de lire plusieurs codes à la fois.' Lucien Sfez, 'Introduction', in Guglielmi and Haroche (eds), *Esprit de corps*, pp. 22, 23.

43. This is related to Chantal Mouffe's idea of 'agonistic pluralism', developed for example in *Agonistics: Thinking the World Politically*.

44. Eugène Enriquez, 'Le Ravissement du corps, croyances et mécanismes de défense dans les communautés', in Guglielmi and Haroche (eds), *Esprit de corps*, p. 31.

45. 'Le groupe efface l'arbitraire de leur vie. Au contraire, ils existent sous le sceau d'une double légitimation: l'individu trouve son épanouissement dans le groupe qui, en l'accueillant, légitime son existence. En retour, le groupe est légitimé dans la mesure où il favorise chez chacun ce que Rousseau nommait "le sentiment d'existence".' Ibid., p. 32.

46. Ibid., p. 33.

47. 'Des individus supposés hypersocialisés ou dominés agissent comme des marionnettes, ou comme de simples rouages d'une machinerie nommée esprit de corps.' Paul Zawadzki, '"Un homme, ça s'empêche": sentiment moral et dimensions de la désobéissance', in Guglielmi and Haroche (eds), *Esprit de corps*, p. 119.

48. 'On interdisait dans les cloîtres toute amitié particulière: on ne voulait que des membres dévoués à l'esprit de corps, des automates serrés et muets entre eux, comme des soldats prussiens.' Joseph-Antoine Cerutti, *Œuvres diverses, ou Recueil de pièces composées avant et depuis la Révolution* (Paris: Desenne, 1792), vol. II, p. 35.

49. 'Dès le milieu du XIIIe siècle [. . .], on voit Innocent IV affirmer que la collectivité *fingitur una persona*, qu'elle est [comme] une personne [. . .] Cette fiction de la personnalité juridique permet de dire l'unité de la multiplicité dans ce qui peut désormais s'appeler un "corps mystique".' Thomas Berns and Benoît Frydman, 'Généalogie de l'esprit de corps', in Guglielmi and Haroche (eds), *Esprit de corps*, p. 163.

50. 'C'est seulement l'idée d'incarnation qui permet d'accomplir l'incorporation: l'abstraction de l'*universitas* prend d'abord vie et sens lorsqu'elle est incarnée dans une personne, le chef, la tête, celui qui la représente. Il ne s'agit pas seulement donc d'incorporation au sens strict: association dans la hiérarchie, association des divers membres, des sujets et du chef dans un seul corps, mais toujours aussi d'une incarnation, par laquelle cette association est véritablement personnifiée, et à ce titre ne peut pas poser la question de l'esprit de corps.' Berns and Frydman, 'Généalogie de l'esprit de corps', p. 169.

51. Ernst H. Kantorowicz, *The King's Two Bodies* (Princeton: Princeton University Press, 1958).

52. Marcel Gauchet, *La Révolution des droits de l'homme* (Paris: Gallimard, 1989), p. xviii.

53. Berns and Frydman, 'Généalogie de l'esprit de corps', p. 177.

54. 'la Révolution semble vouloir expulser ou détruire les corps partiels comme autant de corps étrangers à celui de la nation, parasites ou hostiles'; ibid., p. 159.

55. Jean Bodin, *Les six Livres de la République* (Paris: Jacques du Puys, 1576).

56. 'La souveraineté propre à la communauté politique se définit par la nécessité de se distinguer radicalement de tout autre corps [. . .] Bodin affronte directement la question de savoir "s'il est bon d'oster ou d'endurcir les corps et colleges." De manière finaliste, les corps et collèges se justifient par le fait qu'ils maintiennent l'amitié qui est au fondement même de la République, "laquelle amitié ne peut se maintenir que par alliances, societez, estats, communautez, confrairies, corps et colleges".' Berns and Frydman, 'Généalogie de l'esprit de corps', p. 168.

57. Hannah Arendt, *The Human Condition* (Chicago: University of Chicago Press, 1998 [1958]).

58. Thomas Hobbes, 'Of Systemes Subject, Political, and Private', in *Leviathan* (Oxford: Clarendon Press, 1909), p. 171.

59. Ibid., pp. 182–3.

60. Ibid., p. 180.

61. Berns and Frydman, 'Généalogie de l'esprit de corps', p. 178.

62. 'À l'inverse des corps "naturels" de l'Ancien Régime, il ne s'agit que de créations artificielles, juridiques ou administratives, d'entités purement abstraites [. . .] Or si ces corps ne reposent pas sur un substrat, sur une composante identifiable de la population, sur une solidarité spécifique qui unisse ses membres, *qu'est-ce donc qui les tiendra ensemble?* C'est ici précisément que se pose la question de l'esprit de corps, lequel désigne, dans le sens moderne de l'expression, le lien qui unit les membres d'un corps ou d'une compagnie.' Ibid., p. 177.

63. Peter Calvocoressi, *World Politics Since 1945* (Harlow: Pearson, 2009 [1968]), p. 272.

64. 'Il ne faut pas oublier ici en combien de sens différents le mot d'*esprit* s'emploie; ce

n'est point un défaut de la langue, c'est au contraire un avantage d'avoir ainsi des racines qui se ramifient en plusieurs branches. *Esprit d'un corps, d'une société*, pour exprimer les usages, la manière de penser, de se conduire, les préjugés d'un corps. *Esprit de parti*, qui est à l'esprit d'un corps ce que sont les passions aux sentiments ordinaires.' Voltaire, 'Esprit (Philos. & Belles-Lettr.)', in Denis Diderot and Jean le Rond d'Alembert (eds), *Encyclopédie ou dictionnaire raisonné des sciences, des arts et des métiers* (Paris: Briasson, David, Le Breton and Durand, 1751–65), vol. V (1755), p. 975, quoted by Pierre Ansart, 'L'Esprit de corps: réflexions épistémologiques', Guglielmi and Haroche (eds), *Esprit de corps*, p. 119.

65. Nicolas Gueudeville, *L'Esprit des cours de l'Europe* (The Hague: Étienne Foulque, 1701), p. 208.

66. Ferdinand de Saussure, *Cours de linguistique générale* (Paris: Payot, 1995 [1916]).

67. Mark Bevir, *The Logic of the History of Ideas* (Cambridge: Cambridge University Press, 1999), p. 56.

68. 'Esprit de corps, n.', *OED Online*, Oxford University Press, <http://oxforddictionaries.com/definition/english/esprit-de-corps> (accessed 19 September 2019).

69. 'Esprit de corps', *Merriam-Webster Dictionary*, <https://www.merriam-webster.com/dictionary/esprit%20de%20corps> (accessed 19 September 2019).

70. Ibid.

71. Facundo Alonso, 'Shared Intention, Reliance, and Interpersonal Obligations', *Ethics* 119.3 (2009), pp. 444–75; Ulrich Baltzer, 'Joint Action of Large Groups', in George Meggle (ed.), *Social Facts and Intentionality* (Frankfurt: Hänsel-Hohenhausen, 2002), pp. 1–18; Boudewijn de Bruin, 'We and the Plural Subject', *Philosophy of the Social Sciences* 39 (2009), pp. 235–59; John Searle, 'Collective Intentions and Actions', in Philip R. Cohen, Jerry Morgan and Martha E. Pollack (eds), *Intentions in Communication* (Cambridge: Bradford Books, 1990), pp. 401–16; Natalie Gold and Robert Sugden, 'Collective Intentions and Team Agency', *The Journal of Philosophy* 104.3 (2007), pp. 109–37.

72. Andrew Vincent, 'Can Groups be Persons?', *Review of Metaphysics* 42 (1989), pp. 687–715; Marie-Hélène Roberge, Qiumei Jane Xu and Denise M. Rousseau, 'Collective Personality Effects on Group Citizenship Behavior?', *Small Group Research* 43.4 (2012), pp. 410–42; Antony Taubman, 'Is There a Right to Collective Personality', *European Intellectual Property Review* 28.9 (2006), pp. 485–92.

73. Benito Mussolini, 'The Doctrine of Fascism', quoted in Michael J. Oakeshott, *The Social and Political Doctrines of Contemporary Europe* (Cambridge: Cambridge University Press, 1939), pp. 164–8.

74. G. W. F. Hegel, *Philosophy of Right*, trans. Thomas Malcolm Knox (Oxford: Oxford University Press, 1971 [1820]), section 321, p. 208.

75. Vincent, 'Can Groups be Persons?', p. 690.

76. 'L'esprit de corps est, selon nous, un égoïsme collectif, uniquement préoccupé des fins collectives, et dédaigneux de l'individu et des qualités individuelles.' Georges Palante, 'L'Esprit de corps', *Revue philosophique de la France et de l'étranger* 48 (1899), pp. 135–45 (p. 141).

77. 'L'idée qu'il serait par exemple possible et doué de sens de chercher une conception adéquate de la justice, ou de la liberté, est confuse. Il y a des sociétés, des groupes humains qui ont produit des conceptions de la justice, mais l'identité du vocabulaire ne signifie pas celle des concepts et ne garantit pas qu'il soit question du même "objet".' Jean-Fabien Spitz, 'Quentin Skinner', *Revue française d'histoire des idées politiques* 40 (2014), pp. 347–77.

78. Bevir, *The Logic of the History of Ideas*, p. 5.
79. John Greville Agard Pocock, 'The History of Political Thought: A Methodological Enquiry', in P. Laslett and W. Runciman (eds), *Philosophy, Politics and Society* (Oxford: Basil Blackwell, 1962), pp. 183–202.
80. 'Suivre la filière complexe de la provenance, c'est [. . .] maintenir ce qui s'est passé dans la dispersion qui lui est propre: c'est repérer les accidents, les infimes déviations – ou au contraire les retournements complets – les erreurs, les fautes d'appréciation, les mauvais calculs qui ont donné naissance à ce qui existe et vaut pour nous; c'est découvrir qu'à la racine de ce que nous connaissons et de ce que nous sommes – il n'y a point la vérité et l'être.' Foucault, 'Nietzsche, la généalogie, l'histoire', p. 152.
81. David Armitage, *Civil Wars: A History in Ideas* (New York: Knopf, 2017), p. 18.
82. William Shakespeare, *The Tragedy of Macbeth*, Act V, scene v.
83. Richard Whatmore, *What is Intellectual History?* (Cambridge: Polity, 2016), p. 9.
84. Alfred Fouillée, *L'Évolutionisme des idées-forces* (Paris: Alcan, 1890).
85. Arthur O. Lovejoy, *The Great Chain of Being. A Study in the History of an Idea* (Cambridge, MA: Harvard University Press, 1936).
86. Hugo Mercier and Dan Sperber, 'Why Do Humans Reason? Arguments for an Argumentative Theory', *Behavioral and Brain Sciences* 34 (2011), pp. 57–111.
87. Hugo Mercier and Dan Sperber, *The Enigma of Reason: A New Theory of Human Understanding* (London: Penguin Random House, 2018), p. 8.
88. Quentin Skinner, 'Rhetoric and Conceptual Change', in Margrit Pernau and Dominic Sachsenmaier (eds), *Global Conceptual History, a Reader* (London: Bloomsbury, 2016), pp. 136–7. Originally published in *Finnish Yearbook of Political Thought* (Helsinki: SoPhi, 1999).
89. Quentin Skinner, 'Meaning and Understanding in the History of Ideas', *Visions of Politics. Vol. I: Regarding Method* (Cambridge: Cambridge University Press, 2002), p. 82.
90. John Greville Agard Pocock, *Political Thought and History: Essays on Theory and Method* (Cambridge: Cambridge University Press, 2009), pp. viii, 70.
91. 'une violence que nous faisons aux choses', 'une pratique que nous leur imposons'; Michel Foucault, *L'ordre du discours* (Paris: Gallimard, 1971), p. 50.
92. 'Dans toute société, la production du discours est à la fois contrôlée, sélectionnée, organisée et redistribuée par un certain nombre de procédures.' Ibid., pp. 10–13.
93. David Armitage, 'What's the Big Idea? Intellectual History and the *Longue Durée*', *History of European Ideas* 38.4 (2012), pp. 493–507.
94. Fernand Braudel, 'Histoire et sciences sociales. La longue durée', *Annales* 13.4 (1958), pp. 725–53.
95. Modernity is itself a polemical notion, but this cannot be examined in this book.
96. Armitage, 'What's the Big Idea?', p. 507.
97. Luis de Miranda and Emile Chabal, 'Big Data, Small Concepts: Histosophy as an Approach to *longue-durée* History', *Global Intellectual History* (2019), <https://www.tandfonline.com/doi/full/10.1080/23801883.2019.1592871> (accessed 19 September 2019).
98. Armitage, *Civil Wars*, p. 18.
99. David Armitage and Jo Guldi, *The History Manifesto* (Cambridge: Cambridge University Press, 2014), p. 4.
100. Fran Osrecki, 'Constructing Epochs: The Argumentative Structures of Sociological Epochalisms', *Cultural Sociology* 9.2 (2015), pp. 131–46.
101. Armitage and Guldi, *The History Manifesto*, p. 9.

102. The ARTFL-Frantext Project, <https://artfl-project.uchicago.edu/content/art fl-frantext> (accessed 19 September 2019).

103. The ARTFL-Frantext Project, <https://artfl-project.uchicago.edu/node/83> (acc-essed 19 September 2019).

104. Jean-Baptiste Michel et al., 'Quantitative Analysis of Culture Using Millions of Digitized Books', *Science* 311 (2011), pp. 176–82.

105. BNF Gallica, <http://gallica.bnf.fr> (accessed 19 September 2019).

106. Internet Archive, <https://archive.org> (accessed 19 September 2019).

107. Google Books Search, <http://blog.google/products/search> (accessed 19 September 2019).

108. 'Je n'ai parlé de personne en particulier; je n'ai fait allusion qu'à l'esprit de corps en général. Or, il est dans la nature des choses et des hommes que chaque corporation qui ne s'occupe que d'un objet cherche à s'en emparer exclusivement; il est dans l'esprit des corps d'étendre leurs attributions, leur pouvoir [. . .] On peut dire que dès l'instant qu'un jeune homme a achevé ses études théologiques, il fait partie d'une corporation puissante, qui plus qu'aucune autre a un levier immense, le pouvoir qu'il exerce sur les consciences; arme plus forte que le pouvoir civil. Partout les corps de prêtres ont eu une tendance à s'élever au-dessus de l'autorité civile et à dominer. C'est l'histoire de tous les temps.' 'M. de la Harpe, président du Conseil d'État', in *Compte rendu des débats du Grand Conseil du canton de Vaud sur le projet de loi ecclési-astique, ou recueil des discours qui ont été prononcés* (Lausanne: Dépôt Bibliographique, 1839), p. 147.

109. James F. Maclear (ed.), *Church and State in the Modern Age: A Documentary History* (Oxford: Oxford University Press, 1995), p. 229.

110. Dictionaire historique de la Suisse, <http://www.hls-dhs-dss.ch> (accessed 19 September 2019).

111. Magoroh Maruyama, 'Cultural Engineering Toward Mental Health: Individual, Intracultural and Transcultural Solutions', *Zeitschrift für Ethnologie* 90.2 (1965), pp. 282–92.

112. Ian Hunter, 'Secularization: The Birth of a Modern Combat Concept', *Modern Intellectual History* 12.1 (2015), pp. 1–32 (p. 1).

113. Walker, David, '*Holy Virility: The Social Construction of Masculinity*, by Emmanuel Reynaud', book review, *Labour History* 48 (1985), p. 121.

114. Robert Piercey, *The Uses of the Past from Heidegger to Rorty: Doing Philosophy Historically* (Cambridge: Cambridge University Press, 2009).

1

Musketeers and Jesuits: The French Birth of Esprit de Corps in the Eighteenth Century

Not Only in the Military: First Occurrences of the Phrase in Print

The idiomatic phrase *esprit de corps* first appeared in print several decades earlier than was generally believed when I started my research. A French reference dictionary, the *Trésor de la langue française*, in its etymological and historical entry on the word *corps*, indicated: '1771 *esprit de corps* (Turgot, *Œuvres*, éd. G. Schelle, t. 3, p. 521)'.[1] The nineteenth-century major dictionary *Littré* quoted nothing older than Rousseau's *L'Émile* (1762): 'It is not only in the military that one acquires the esprit de corps',[2] unarguably an important quote, of which more below. A recent source refers imprecisely to Voltaire (1767).[3] Although it is difficult to identify with precision the birth of an old locution, what follows in this chapter offers new and significant information.

Before *esprit de corps* became idiomatic, between 1730 and 1762, the phrase *esprit du corps* appeared in Montesquieu's *Lettres persanes*, published in 1721.[4] This immediately famous epistolary fiction of *moeurs* was seen as the epitome of a literary genre probably invented by Jean-Paul Marana[5] and imitated thereafter.[6] It consisted in the technique of depicting the mores and manners of a society or nation through the eyes of a fictitious stranger. This literary vogue allowed the then immense francophone readership to discover the signifier 'esprit de corps', perhaps for the first time in print in 1732, in an imitation of the *Lettres persanes*, of which more below.

The narrative context of Montesquieu's reference to esprit de corps was a conversation between two ambitious Parisians in search of intellectual power by way of cunning rather than talent. Their strategy was to appear in high-society salons armed with rehearsed elements of wit, meant to be uttered as if brilliantly improvised:

> Let us team up and work together to develop our wit [*esprit*] [. . .] Do what I tell you, and I promise you a seat in the *Académie* within six months; see, we won't have to work for long, for once elected you will be able to abandon your practice of the art; you will be a man of wit [*homme d'esprit*] even if you don't

have any. It's been noticed in France that as soon as a man joins a society [*compagnie*], he promptly acquires what is called the *esprit du corps*: you will experience it; and I predict to you only the embarrassment of applause.[7]

This implicit definition of esprit de corps was a clear-cut standard for future polemical uses of the notion, in which *esprit* did not designate a form of independent thinking, but rather suggested a cognitive template, an imitative mindset, a form of intellectual automatism favouring the social reproduction of a biased elite. The wide international readership of the *Lettres persanes* and the contagiously humorous definitional quality of the passage suggest that this text was probably one of the strongest early contributions to the dissemination of the phrase.

Montesquieu suggested that *l'esprit du corps* was a common social trait in France at least, implying that he was not innovating in proposing this verbal expression. However, this might have been a rhetorical formula. I believe he was a pioneer in using the expression politically to criticise a powerful society with perpetual members. It was witty to play with the word *esprit* to satirise the Académie Française, which had been since 1635 a society of self-proclaimed *Immortels* endogenously elected from within the aristocracy to formulate the proper rules of the French language, as well as the correct definition of words in their official dictionary.[8] The *Dictionnaire de l'Académie française* had contained since 1694, under the word *esprit*, a reference to 'esprit d'une compagnie'.[9] Montesquieu was very likely to have been familiar with this, as he was personally close to some academicians. In spite of his irony, he became an elected member himself in 1728.

The two variants *esprit du corps* and *esprit de corps* were used more or less until the 1770s, after which the notion crystallised idiomatically and the more general formula *esprit de corps* became significantly dominant, as we will see in more detail.[10] A non-idiomatic version of the phrase attached to a specific corps was older in print: in 1652, an anonymous pamphlet entitled *L'Esprit de la vérité* suggested the existence of an '*esprit du Corps d'Etat*':

It is necessary to philosophise of the Body of State [*Corps d'État*] as of the human body. [The latter] is composed of several parts animated by the same soul as is a Body of State by the same spirit under the same laws [. . .] Such is the spirit of the Body of State [*l'esprit du Corps d'Etat*], that it is not so much enclosed in one organ but rather must be communicated to all parts, so that each one does its work as every part of the human body fulfils its function.[11]

This analogy between the laws of the state and the unifying soul of a body already pointed, before the phrase became idiomatic, to the notion of esprit de corps in its larger nationalist use, a theme that would become important anew in French revolutionary discourse. The above occurrence suggests that it is worth looking briefly at the seventeenth-century prehistory of esprit de corps, and in particular at the tradition of comparison between the human body and the body politic, of which more below.

In the *Persian Letters*, Montesquieu did not speak of esprit de corps on a national level. He wrote of it as produced by an organised and specific group of men. *Compagnie* in French could designate a military unit but also any form of relatively small society. I cannot assert with certainty that Montesquieu was influenced by an antecedent military use of the notion, but there are reasons to think that a less metaphorical oral usage of esprit de corps in the French army, neither ironical nor negative, was a logical precursor. In the first half of the eighteenth century, for reasons that we will examine, most *corps d'armée* and French armed *companies* had the habit of distinguishing themselves from the others with demonstrations of pride or contempt, what we would call today a superiority complex. Rousseau indeed wrote: 'It is not only in the military that one acquires the esprit de corps, and its effects are not always good.'[12] This implies that the French army context was an important source and model to the idea of esprit de corps.

Esprit de corps or *esprit du corps* was used in military discourse to characterise a cohesive and proud formation of soldiers. Louis de Rouvroy, duc de Saint-Simon, foregrounds the phrase in his *Mémoires* of the year 1717, probably written after 1740.[13] He meant to describe the *compagnies* of the *gendarmerie*, one of the most aristocratic corps of the French army:

> All this is supported by an esprit de corps (one would not dare say of a small republic, by this numerous swarm of officers [. . .] each competing to evidence at the highest degree what they call the honour of the corps).[14]

There are at least four interesting ideas in Saint-Simon's assertion. First, esprit de corps was strongly connected to honour and pride: it was a feeling, an emotion, not a mainly rational attitude. Secondly, esprit de corps was not incompatible with the ideas of a human hive and animal or insect swarm behaviour – yet this aspect did not seem to completely dissolve egotism, perhaps because of the feeling of honour, compatible both with self-effacement and self-aggrandisement. Thirdly, esprit de corps created an atmosphere of contest and competitive emulation between peers. And finally, it could be associated with the political idea of republican spirit, perhaps to emphasise the importance of equality or peer-to-peer relationships in the corps, at least among the officers, and also because of the common cause of each corps, oblivious of national unity as small independentist republics could be.

Before Saint-Simon, the first author to refer to esprit de corps in print as a military term was perhaps Germain-François Poullain de Saint-Foix in 1732, in a widely read pastiche of the *Lettres persanes* and therefore as a probable rectification of Montesquieu's irony regarding esprit de corps. Poullain de Saint-Foix had been a musketeer in the French royal infantry and served with the cavalry.[15] He later retired to become a popular Parisian writer and playwright, as well as a compulsive duellist.[16] He published his imitation of Montesquieu anonymously, and the *Lettres turques*, also known as *Lettres de Nedim Coggia*, were successful enough to be included for years as the accompanying text of some editions of the *Lettres persanes*.[17]

In the third letter, addressed to a Grand Vizier, the fictional emissary Nedim Coggia finds himself in Paris, admiring the parading royal army:

> Different companies of men in blue clothes trimmed with silver, were aligned on both sides of the street. Our march was opened by the Grenadiers on horse-back, a troop as commendable for the piety and regularity of its manners, as by its valour. I was told that after a battle, the late King Louis XIV asked one of the Chiefs of this Company, where it was, and that officer replied, *Sire, it [elle] is killed.* This word expresses well the complete defeat of a body [*corps*] of brave people that the same virtue, the same spirit [*esprit*], the same bravery animates.[18]

Here military esprit de corps was implicitly defined and contextualised a few lines before the signifier was explicitly introduced. We are told that the royal cavalry was not only grand but also homogeneous and unified as one person in the face of danger. According to the narrator, soldiers became one by sharing the same valour, and the cohesion of the corps was so strong that when the *compagnie* was decimated, one could say, in a macabre *bon mot*, that *she* was killed as if it were one person.

While Parisians were depicted by Saint-Foix as often vain, mostly preoccupied with ostentation and gossip, the various corps of the French army were presented as most righteous: in a significant change of tone, the satire ceased to be satirical. The description of the different *compagnies* culminated in the admiration of the *mousquetaires*, who had been since 1622 the king's *gardes du corps*:

> The Guards on foot formed a hedge along the Gardens up to the vestibule of the Castle. They are handsome men, well dressed, whom the jealousy of the soldiers of the other regiments would always be very quick to attack, if they suffered any setback.[19]

Even within the same royal army, esprit de corps could be partisan and agonistic: pride and jealousy were connected, as Saint-Simon also suggested. Esprit de corps was a manifestation of what some would call today an androcentric superiority complex.[20] More simply, this was called honour, a term that is semantically connected to esprit de corps in many texts.

How did military esprit de corps persist over time? Senior musketeers were expected to nurture it among younger recruits by transmitting knowledge and a sense of tradition:

> Since for some time France has no longer been at war, they fondly oppose the retirement of the old soldiers; they are exempted from certain services, and their pay increased; they are only required, so to speak, to die in the Regiment. They recount the sieges and battles in which they found themselves; they animate and maintain among the youth that honour and esprit de corps which otherwise would perhaps be lost imperceptibly during such a long peace and after an almost complete renewal of militia.[21]

The repeated celebration and memory of an edifying past developed the *esprit*, and this was necessitated by the replacement of one generation of soldiers by the next. A correlation between war and esprit de corps is established, as if there could be no esprit de corps without a common enemy, actual or narrated, an idea that was often expressed more or less explicitly over the centuries.

Because Poullain de Saint-Foix had been a musketeer and a soldier in the cavalry corps, he had first-hand knowledge of the French military. He was probably not neutral when he praised the *gardes du roi* and the *mousquetaires*, but neither did he forge their fame: the picaresque *Mémoires de Mr. d'Artagnan*, for example, published in 1700, was a popular book.[22] The association of ideas connecting a tight-knit fight club and the *mousquetaires* seems to have grown steadily from the creation of the *Régiment* in 1622 up until Alexandre Dumas's revival of the myth via the apocryphal motto *All for one! One for all!* [*Tous pour un! Un pour tous!*], a striking slogan for any form of esprit de corps.[23]

In a historical essay published in 1766, 'Les deux compagnies des Mousquetaires', the same Saint-Foix suggested, speaking of Louis XIII (1601–43), 'that what always pleased him in his Musketeers, was this expeditious gaiety, with which they advanced on whatever they were told to attack'.[24] This gives another important indication about what esprit de corps meant in a military context: not only a dynamic momentum that allowed each individual who was part of the corps to summon supra-individual courage, but also an uncritical collective *élan* in obeying the orders.

The Head of the World: A Short Prehistory of the Phrase *esprit de corps*

Since the idiomatic phrase *esprit de corps* first appeared in print in the eighteenth century, the seventeenth century can be called its pre-historical gestation period. I will now indicate a few significant genealogical elements that are helpful to understand the semantic ground of esprit de corps.

The form *esprit de*, designating a disposition of character, a *manière*, a principle of action, a typical aspect or a stubborn style, was definitely known in seventeenth-century French. The first *Dictionnaire de l'Académie française* (1694) stated:

> *Esprit* is sometimes taken for the principle, the motive, the conduct, the manner of acting. *Esprit of charity, esprit of peace, esprit of revenge, of faction, of lawsuits, such is not the esprit of this society* [*Esprit de charité, esprit de paix, etc.*].[25]

Here we see that *esprit de* could relate equally to an approbatory ('charity') or pejorative ('faction') meaning. Since a faction designates a small, organised, dissenting group within a larger one, *esprit de faction* announces the later pejorative use of *esprit de corps* by the Encyclopedists, for whom the two expressions would be nearly synonymous.

The title *L'Esprit d'intérêt* was used for an anonymous *Mazarinade* published in 1652, a pamphlet in which the author declared that because Mazarin and the Prince (Louis XIV) were following their own selfish interests, so should the people of Paris:

> It is a general principle to act for oneself, and with a view to one's satisfaction and contentment, it is a law necessary for the conservation of the species and individuals: it is the centre where all our actions converge [. . .] People, believe me: [. . .] follow your interest or renounce your being. But you may ask, what is this interest? It is your tranquillity, it is commerce re-established, it is high prices banished from within your walls and from your neighbourhood.[26]

This pamphlet, written in a moment of civil war and contested absolutism in France, and influenced by English debates regarding the separation of powers,[27] revealed an antagonism between the particular *esprit d'intérêt* of a few powerful rulers and the common interest of the people, a tension that was to become an important theme of the French Enlightenment.

The grammatical form *esprit de* was in fact very common and widespread in the second half of the French seventeenth century, at least among the literate class. For example, a Parisian theatre staged a play entitled *L'Esprit de contradiction*.[28] Some time between 1656 and 1659, Blaise Pascal wrote the famed *Différence entre l'esprit de géometrie et l'esprit de finesse*.[29] In 1662, the rhetorician and historiographer René Bary published *L'Esprit de cour*. For this adviser of Louis XIV, *esprit de cour* designated the *délicatesse* that distinguished the aristocratic *bel esprit* from those who lacked refined minds and manners.[30] To give an idea of the persistence over time of the form *esprit de* in French, and of its capacity to be both laudatory and pejorative, it is worth noting that *De l'esprit de cour* is also the title of a political pamphlet published in 2010 by a former prime minister, accusing the French presidential regime of being a monarchy in disguise.[31]

In the early seventeenth century, the use of the form *esprit de* could still be tinted with chemical or even alchemical connotation, designating the quintessence, the active principle of a physical element, for instance 'esprit de nitre' for nitric acid, 'esprit-de-vin' for alcohol.[32] In 1614, we find for instance a reference to immortal elementary spirits: 'The spirit of elements, as a spirit [*esprit*] of immortal bodies [*corps*], communicates the art of divination [. . .] There are substantial powers from which we obtain by various sacrifices some words of presage.'[33] Descartes mentioned in *Passions de l'âme* (1649) the subtle organic spirits (*esprits animaux*) that were thought to keep human bodies active.[34] The analogy between *esprit* and an inner immutable core must be kept in mind, since the effective togetherness implied by esprit de corps is still perceived today, mostly in English, as something mysterious, a kind of magic force – hence perhaps the use of a French loan phrase to emphasise the impression that the phenomenon is subtle and sophisticated.

The widespread use of the metaphor of the body in labour or political discourse during the *Ancien Régime* is another semantic seedbed for the subsequent propagation of the notion of esprit de corps. Numerous professional guilds were called *corps de métiers* or *corporations* and played a visible role in the structuration of society, as we will analyse. We need not recall in too much detail the long tradition of comparisons between collectives, the body politic and the human body before the eighteenth century: the history of this metaphor is well studied,[35] and here we will simply evoke a few themes that were part of the intellectual background of the eighteenth-century intellectual elite.

Education in France until the middle of the eighteenth century was very largely dominated by the Jesuits, who proposed a curriculum that was not only based on religious texts, but also on Greek and Latin classics.[36] Plato for example was often studied. He famously compared the city to a human body:

> Just as a sickly body needs only a slight push from outside to become ill, and sometimes even without any external influence becomes divided by factions within itself, so too doesn't a city that is in the same kind of condition as that body, on a small pretext [. . .] fall sick and do battle with itself, and sometimes even without any external influence become divided by faction?[37]

In Aristotle, French students of the late seventeenth century and the early eighteenth century found the idea that political groups precede their members ontologically or 'by nature', in the same manner as the human body exists before its parts, as a final cause:

> The city-state is prior in nature to the household and to each of us individually. For the whole must necessarily be prior to the part; since when the whole body is destroyed, foot or hand will not exist except in an equivocal sense [. . .] It is clear therefore that the state is also prior by nature to the individual.[38]

Cicero was another key cultural reference.[39] The capital of the Roman Empire named itself *Caput mundi*, the head of the world. Pupils could find in Cicero a comparison between societies and the human body, taught by the Jesuits to emphasise the Christian idea of a necessary solidarity in social life:

> Injustice is fatal to social life and fellowship between man and man. For, if we are so disposed that each, to gain some personal profit, will defraud or injure his neighbour, then those bonds of human society, which are most in accord with Nature's laws, must of necessity be broken. Suppose, by way of comparison, that each one of our bodily members should conceive this idea and imagine that it could be strong and well if it should draw off to itself the health and strength of its neighbouring member, the whole body would necessarily be enfeebled and die.[40]

The idea that an assembly of men could be *as one* and gain a unique voice was, of course, present in the Bible, still the main book of reference: 'And all the people arose as one man, saying: We will not any of us go to his tent, neither will we any of us turn into his house.'[41] In St Augustine's *Sermons*, a classic of the study of rhetoric in Jesuit education,[42] one could read: 'Wonder, rejoice, for we are made Christ! If He is the Head, and we the members, then together He and we are the whole man.'[43]

In short, the rhetorical identification of a group of humans with a natural or metaphorical body was for the educated class a *lieu commun*, 'borrowed from Catholicism'[44] as well as from Greco-Roman antiquity, and much echoed by Bacon, Machiavelli, Hobbes, Spinoza, Locke, Pascal, etc.[45]

One Hundred and Fifty: A Quantification of Esprit de Corps?

The idea of measuring esprit de corps is, as we will see in Chapter 7, typically a twentieth-century preoccupation, but the question of the size of groups is an underlying theme in discourses on esprit de corps from the eighteenth century onwards. Early uses of the phrase suggest that posterior attempts to conceive a *national esprit de corps* without intermediary bodies or mediating communities might be flawed by a scale error or too ambitious in size.

It should be clear by now that in the military context, esprit de corps was mostly a desirable quality: the soldiers' commitment to their unit, a proud feeling of belonging to a hegemonic group, a collective sense of honour, so strong as to induce reckless behaviour. This group feeling, capable of obliterating the fear of death, was more likely to be felt on the battlefield, but, as we have seen, elderly members could also nurture it through edifying storytelling in times of peace. Members of a company should not be renewed too often, in order for the solidarity of camaraderie to hold firm.[46] Saint-Foix not only suggested that the quality named esprit de corps could vanish without a defined enemy, he also indicated that the unity of a company could be threatened if additional recruitment were too frequent and the retirement of wiser warriors were premature.

An echo of this idea could be found in Diderot's *D'Alembert's Dream*, a manuscript in which the *esprit du corps* of religious orders was compared to a persistent pattern of collective intention, as in a swarm of bees:

> Mademoiselle de l'Espinasse – In the cluster of bees, there would not be one who had time to acquire the esprit de corps.
> D'Alembert – What are you saying?
> Mademoiselle de l'Espinasse – I say that the monastic spirit is preserved because the monastery is gradually being reshapen, and when a new monk enters, he finds a hundred old ones who lead him to think and feel like them. When a bee goes away, another replaces it in the cluster who soon learns.[47]

Diderot suggested that what held the group together was the memory of its identity, nourished by the information given by those who have been in the cluster for a longer time. The metaphor of esprit de corps here characterised the unifying direction in a group that could be composed of contradictory desires. Memory, as well as the slow pace of experience, was seen as an important element of centralisation. A number was indicated by Mademoiselle de l'Espinasse: about a hundred well-informed old members (as opposed to newcomers) seemed to be needed to maintain the integrity of a group and counterbalance the potential destabilisation from newcomers. If newcomers needed to be a minority in the group compared to the more informed ones, the total members of the persistent monastic order described by Diderot should perhaps be no more than one hundred and fifty individuals.

Coincidentally, when Saint-Foix published his *Turkish Letters*, there existed in France two corps of Mousquetaires du Roi, officially counting no more than 150 musketeers each (more or less the same number as in 1657).[48] Between 1622 and 1732, the average number of musketeers in each *régiment* oscillated between 100 and 200.[49] For the sake of speculation, we can also contemplate the fact that the seventeen volumes of the *Encyclopédie* were written by an average of 150 contributors (scholars have argued that the real number of authors was somewhere between 139 and 196).[50] Is anywhere between 130 and 170 members the upper limit for a particular group of peers to experience a really cohesive, effective and self-aware esprit de corps?

According to the anthropologist and evolutionary psychologist Robin Dunbar, who based his argument on the size of the human neocortex and the study of social networks, the ideal equilibrium size for a social group is in fact around 150 members.[51] Such a claim is controversial, but what is certain is that we find throughout the biography of esprit de corps the idea that size matters for the cohesiveness of a group. Researchers in social identity dynamics and psychobiology have tried to model the optimal size of a solidary human group, and most results seem to disfavour overly large groups:

> Minority groups tend, on average, to provide sufficient inclusiveness within the group for individuals to feel a sense of inclusion and belonging and, at the same time, provide sufficient differentiation between the in-group and out-group to allow for feelings of distinctiveness to emerge. Preferences for modestly-sized groups may constitute a biologically or culturally evolved heuristic for simultaneously maximizing successful group cooperation.[52]

If the equilibrium of esprit de corps were related to clusters of less than two hundred individuals, any attempt to build a strong 'national esprit de corps' might end up in an official monstrosity, producing what Judith Butler called 'a spectral doubling of universality', in which the portion of the population that the rulers count legally as the universal, free, equal or brotherly class carries 'the trace of the excluded in spectral form as an internal disruption of its own formalism'.[53]

What about leadership and hierarchy in the peer group? According to Saint-Foix, most of the *mousquetaires* were about twenty years old, which probably reinforced their feeling of belonging.[54] They were of aristocratic descent, a fact that is likely to have induced a form of class solidarity.[55] The *Mousquetaires du Roi* emerged as a specialisation within the *garde du corps*, which was the senior formation of the King of France's household cavalry: they were meant to protect the life and body of the head of the nation. A specialist on French administrative elites, Marie-Christine Kessler, suggests that: 'Each corps can differentiate itself from others by its organisation, its customs, its interests. But all these bodies [*corps*] proceed from the same essence: they combine internal solidarities and a submission to the orders of a head.'[56] If that assertion is correct, a group might not be able to develop a strong esprit de corps if an active leader – or a symbolic principle? – does not maintain its unity.

Bad Grafts: Critical Uses of Esprit de Corps in the *Encyclopédie*

In the second half of the eighteenth century, the notion of esprit de corps developed into a fierce critical weapon, indeed a 'combat concept'.[57] First targeting religious groups, chief among them the Jesuits, it would later, in the name of national interest, aim at various social groups perceived as privileged and biased. This political meaning of esprit de corps blossomed in the first volumes of the *Encyclopédie* of Denis Diderot and Jean le Rond d'Alembert, in different articles published between 1751 and 1755.

The most significant was the article entitled 'Caractère des sociétés ou corps particuliers'.[58] Although the other articles in the *Encyclopédie* used the generic form *esprit de corps*, d'Alembert's entry still referred to *esprit du corps*. Yet in subsequent editions, quotations from or copies of d'Alembert's article, the preposition *du* was often changed into *de*.[59] Moreover, the more idiomatic form *esprit de corps* soon became part of d'Alembert's own vocabulary: in a letter to Voltaire infused with criticism of the Jesuits and against religious censorship at the Sorbonne, we learn that 'esprit de corps brings bad luck to the best minds' [*L'esprit de corps porte malheur aux meilleurs esprits*].[60] In 1752 d'Alembert seems to hesitate between *l'esprit d'un corps* as the acquired character or singular ethos of a specific group, and esprit de corps as a generic trait of dependency that would be indifferently present in any organised faction.

Compared to the satirical badinage of Montesquieu in the *Lettres persanes*, d'Alembert's political intention was clearer: esprit de corps was a micro-national and even anti-national quality, comparable to a potentially viral graft implanted on the republican tree:

> Societies, or particular bodies [*corps*] in the midst of a people, are in some way little nations surrounded by a larger one; it is a kind of graft, good or bad, upon a great trunk; moreover, societies usually have a special character, which is called *esprit du corps*.[61]

Even if the graft is not necessarily bad, this definition presupposed that the higher body of the nation was natural and ontologically prior to its intermediate bodies, a perspective that we have already encountered in Aristotle regarding the Greek cities. As grafts, specific societies are secondary, if not artificial: their legitimacy is weaker than that of the nation. The comparison between the nation and a large tree is suggestive of robustness, and etymologically *robustus* meant both *strength* and *oak tree*. This naturalistic vegetal metaphor was a variation on the equally common naturalistic metaphor of the human body to designate the body politic. Here d'Alembert is reminiscent of Hobbes's *Leviathan*: 'Another infirmity of a Commonwealth is [. . .] the great number of corporations, which are as it were many lesser Commonwealths in the bowels of a greater, like worms in the entrails of a natural man.'[62]

If a group of humans can possess a specific unified character, could an entire nation manifest a personality, if not a form of supra-esprit de corps? This was moderately believed by French philosophers in the eighteenth century.[63] We read, for example, in a previous segment written by d'Alembert and entitled 'Caractère des nations':

> The character of a nation consists in a certain habitual disposition of the soul, which is more common in one nation than in another, although this disposition is not found in all the members of the nation.[64]

Because the character of a smaller society is compared to a little nation, we are led to deduce that *l'esprit du corps* is the soul of a group. Conversely, a strongly unified nation could perhaps use the natural glue, the sap of a good and vast esprit de corps, to build cohesion between its citizens. There is a difference between 'the essentialist move of identifying a nation with a particular quality or "character" on the one hand, and the implication that the image is descriptive of a true state of affairs on the other'.[65] But the proximity in the *Encyclopédie* of the notions of esprit de corps and of the soul of a nation was not innocent or devoid of consequences. One of the main French projects of the second half of the eighteenth century was to confer on the nation a cohesion comparable, on a grander scale, to the robust strength of a group united by esprit de corps. Up until Napoleon and including the Bonapartists, as we will see, the efficient brotherhood of the Jesuits would be both a hated and envied model for the solidarity and equality of secular citizens.

A source of clarification to intuit what d'Alembert meant by esprit de corps is the *Discours préliminaire* of the *Encyclopédie*, where he opposed *esprit de système* and *esprit systématique*, the former being considered as a dogmatic version of the latter. D'Alembert recommended the practice of a 'true systematic spirit that we must be careful not to confuse with the *esprit de système*, with which it does not always coincide'.[66] *Esprit de système* meant that rigid beliefs could become the enemy of experimental observation by creating a form of epistemic self-deception, in which empirical counter-results become invisible or distorted by the inertia of a dogma. *Esprit systématique* meant that 'd'Alembert, one of the great mathematicians of his time [. . .] proclaimed the end of the great philosophical systems without renouncing the idea of a fundamental unity of nature'.[67] Inspired by British natural philosophy, he believed that the principal law that governed physical bodies was the *force d'inertie*: 'Like Mr. Newton, I call *force of inertia* the property of bodies to remain in the state in which they are.'[68] Analogically, esprit de corps could mean that a human group resisted change under the influence of its own inertia, thus becoming the blind enemy of evolution and independent reasoning. But if esprit de corps was a sort of law of inertia, could it ever be avoided?

It was probably to avoid such a dilemma that d'Alembert's *Encyclopédie* article on *l'esprit du corps* did not develop a scientific analogy. The image of the graft was agricultural, and therefore both natural and cultural, suggestive of a horticultor, a human agency and will. It also implied a naturalisation of the idea of nation, of which more in Chapter 2. This register is confirmed by d'Alembert's reminiscence of Montesquieu's use of *esprit du corps*. Probably referring to Montesquieu's anecdote in the *Persian Letters*, d'Alembert commented: 'For example, according the remark of a man of wit [*esprit*], it would be necessary that literary societies were *pedantic*.'[69] Some forms of esprit de corps might be a necessary element of the social game, like the snobbery of the Académie française, which d'Alembert, like Montesquieu, seemed to tolerate, if sarcastically. At least for the moment, there were more serious enemies.

An important difference between the *Encyclopédie* and Montesquieu is that the latter, in *De l'esprit des Lois*, defended the political necessity of intermediary bodies as a principle of subsidiarity. Montesquieu's ideal society was constituted by several *rangs intermédiaires*, chief among them the aristocratic body.[70] 'Montesquieu held that common interest is easier to see in a smaller setting.'[71] And bodies ended up contributing to the common good by following their own esprit de corps, which was implicitly defined by Montesquieu as a form of honour: 'Honour moves all parts of the body politic; it binds them by its very action; and eventually everyone moves towards the common good while believing in the pursuit of particular interests.'[72] The idea of a state-supervised esprit de corps with semi-autonomous intermediary bodies would become a systematic reality with Napoleon, but it was seriously challenged in the second half of the eighteenth century. For Diderot, d'Alembert, Voltaire, Rousseau and their followers, honour and esprit de corps were more often than not self-deceitful and citizenship might have sufficed to foster healthy belongingness.

In d'Alembert's article, the metaphor of esprit de corps was both psychological (the collective body is a person) and naturalistic (a graft on to a tree). The use of the notion of character was also a metaphor, from the letter or the inscription to the idea of personality. Ancestral humans are said to have created typographical characters to designate all beings: 'It was necessary for them to represent these beings in the ear, so to speak, by sounds, but also to represent them in some way to the eyes, by agreeing on certain marks which designated them.'[73] Characters are a slicing of the material realm: 'The character separates, divides, compartmentalises the world; it transforms the continuum of matter into a succession of differentiated objects, capable of being arranged, classified, and thereby of signifying. Character is the semiotic break.'[74] The character of a group was an artificial break that could interfere with the general or national order of things and create a normative island.

To compare the personality of a corporation or group with the character of a single person was not an innocent analogy. This comparison had been the subject of ongoing debate since the medieval quarrel of universals, in particular regarding corporate legal personality:

For example, the 'fiction' theory of the personality of corporate bodies, or *universitates*, was promulgated if not originated, by Pope Innocent IV (1243–1254) [. . .] In outward form the doctrine that corporate bodies are *personae fictae* was directed at ecclesiastic bodies. The doctrine was stated as the reason an ecclesiastic *collegium* or *universitas*, or *capitulum* could not be excommunicated, or be guilty of a delict [. . .] They have neither a body nor a will.[75]

The *Encyclopédie*'s definitions of esprit de corps followed the opposite strategy: to attribute to religious societies a body and a will and therefore legal responsibilities. This proved effective – a convincing case study on how strong speech acts can affect history, as we will see. After his lenient note on pedantic literary academies, d'Alembert targeted the Jesuits with increased criticism, thus participating in, if not initiating, a political and ideological campaign that would rapidly become a national matter and culminate in 1764 with the official eviction from France of the religious order.

D'Alembert proceeded craftily from the general (good or bad grafts) to the particular (the Jesuits, a bad graft), clearly positioning esprit de corps as a political matter: 'In some societies [*compagnies*], for example, the general character is the spirit of subordination; in others the spirit of equality.'[76] The use of the term *compagnie* to designate human associations was tactical: the French name of the Society of Jesus was *Compagnie de Jésus*.[77] From here the article moved swiftly to a patent condemnation of the Jesuits:

> Often the character of a society is very different from that of the nation, where it is, so to speak, transplanted. Bodies [*corps*], for example, which in a monarchy would make a vow of fidelity to another prince rather than to their legitimate sovereign, ought naturally to have less attachment to that sovereign than the rest of the nation [. . .] 'The religious whose chiefs reside in Rome, says the celebrated M. de Voltaire in his admirable Essay on the Century of Louis XIV, are all immediate subjects of the pope spread throughout all states [. . .] The spirit of agitation, the misfortune of our times, have too often carried entire religious orders to serve Rome against their homeland'.[78]

The then recent book on the reign of Louis XIV by Voltaire[79] served as an authoritative reference to highlight the supposedly conspiratorial and antipatriotic spirit of religious societies that had made a vow of fidelity to the pope, chief among them the Jesuits (founded in 1534), who were sometimes categorised as soldiers of the Catholic Church, the spiritual army of Rome. Their founder, Ignatius of Loyola, was a former soldier who, to generate and nurture group cohesion, introduced daily spiritual exercises, dark minimalistic uniforms, and the official title of *General* for the leadership of his masculine order. Historian Michel Leroy adds: 'Religion was treated by Ignatius Loyola as a war machine, and morality as a mechanism [. . .] Transforming man into an automaton is a secret that Ignatius drew from military art.'[80]

Voltaire did not refer explicitly to esprit de corps in that particular book, but he made use five times of *l'esprit de parti*, which we saw had a similar or aggravated meaning for him, designating unreasonable partisanship:

> [Before Louis XIV], partisanship [*l'esprit de parti*] tore apart and debased France; and the *esprit de société*, which today makes this nation so famous and so amiable, was absolutely unknown. Nowhere did people of merit gather to communicate their ideas.[81]

This represents a rhetorical battlefield of words and nuances for the monopoly of the right *spirit*: *esprit de société* referred to the positive ideal of open-mindedness and communication in the Republic of Letters, ideally based on the values of reason, intellectual dialogue and literate tolerance.[82]

The two other articles that mentioned esprit de corps in the first volumes of the *Encyclopédie* were an illustration of the opposition between rational knowledge and the will to power. In the article entitled 'Encyclopédie', Diderot wrote:

> The *Encyclopedie* can easily be improved [. . .] But the danger we must principally obviate, and which we shall have foreseen, is that the oversight of subsequent editions should be abandoned to the despotism of a society, a company, whatever it may be. We have proclaimed, as our contemporaries and posterity will admit, that the inconvenience that could follow would be that essential things should be suppressed; that the number and the volume of articles that should indeed be suppressed were in fact multiplied; that the esprit de corps, which is ordinarily petty, jealous, and concentrated, infected the overall mass of the work.[83]

Esprit de corps lost its ambivalence: the phrase now manifested an unambiguous critical denotation, both cultural and political. Compare the above use of *ordinairement* by Diderot with Voltaire's contemporary use of *ordinaire* in his article 'Esprit'.[84] For Voltaire, esprit de corps could still be at times moderate, less negative than *esprit de parti*. For Diderot, esprit de corps was always excessive and despotic.

Etymologically, the despot is the master of the house. A despotic society is under the influence of an authoritarian leader or of an ideology that plays the role of a tyrant. Esprit de corps was, for Diderot, the negative and irrational, tight grouping of members in a company, society or institution devoted to a master man or master plan. The spirit of faction was a disease, an infection in any collective project meant to serve the greater good. The suspicion of groups induced the hope that esprit de corps could be eradicated at a national level and that objectivity could be attained in republican matters. But even the enlightened *esprit de société* of an intellectual enterprise such as the *Encyclopédie* could degenerate into esprit de corps by a ruse of reason hiding 'the philosophers' resignation to do no more than find a place for themselves in the world'.[85]

Let us now consider another occurrence of esprit de corps in the *Encyclopédie*, the 1751 anti-clerical entry 'Aristotélisme', in which the abbé Claude Yvon denounced:

the obsession that various orders have in defending the systems that someone of their order has found [. . .] It is evident first of all that not only does this delay the progress of Theology, but even that it stops it; it is not possible to think better than Molina among the Jesuits, since one must think like him [. . .] Thank God, the rules of hydrostatics, hydraulics, and the other sciences, have not been abandoned to the esprit de corps.[86]

The unbiased objectivity of science against the partiality of dogmas: esprit de corps was not only a social, cultural or political problem, but also an epistemic one, and even on this front the public enemy number one was the *Compagnie de Jésus*. We start discerning here an anticipation of the *modern atomising trio*: science, citizenship and capitalism as effectors of individualism.

Was the combat of the *Encyclopédistes* against the Jesuits and their esprit de corps governed by respect for rational objectivity, republican neutrality or even a form of disinterested humanity? Already in the eighteenth century, intellectual voices were being raised to unmask the intentions of the *Lumières*, for instance in the religious-friendly *Encyclopédie méthodique*:

By destroying the esprit de corps, we replace it with selfishness, the most pernicious character and the most opposed to the general interest [. . .] The purported humanity of our cosmopolitan philosophers is but a mask of hypocrisy under which they hide their selfishness.[87]

Was the original *Encyclopédie* – under the guise of universalism – a bourgeois war machine aimed towards a storming of the Sorbonne?

It would be reductive to portray the exercise of philosophy, erudition or intellectual abstraction, in any century, as a mere tactic for social promotion. However, one of the consequences of the combat of the *Philosophes* was that the Sorbonne faculty, still a fortress of Jesuit epistemocracy in the 1750s, became a secular corps in 1766 after the Jesuits were banned. From then on, it represented a continuous flow of appointment opportunities, with hundreds of new positions offered to non-Jesuits. The Jesuits lost the battle of education against the philosophers. This fierce combat of factions was evident for contemporary observers such as Joseph de Maistre:

The whole universe has heard of the Jesuits [. . .] Ignatius Loyola, a simple Spanish gentleman, a soldier without fortune and without knowledge [. . .] resolved, in the sixteenth century, to establish an Order entirely devoted to the education of youth [. . .] No founder achieved his goal better, no one succeeded more perfectly in the annihilation of particular wills in order to establish the general will and that common reason which is the generating and conservative principle of every institution, large or small: because the esprit de corps is simply a smaller form of public spirit, just as patriotism is only enlarged esprit de corps. If we wish to form an idea of the inner strength of the activity and influence of this Order, it suffices to reflect upon the implacable and truly furious hate with which it was honoured by philosophism.[88]

Beyond the antagonistic rhetoric, this was a manifestation of the emergence of a critique of individualism in the name of public spirit which would flourish in the early nineteenth century, when the Bonapartists tried to restore the idea that esprit de corps was a necessary link between individuals and the nation.

De Maistre was considered a pro-Catholic and royalist, but the critique of the *Philosophes* would later be pursued by Marxist historians, who tended to consider that the *Encyclopédie* was a weaponisation of the ideology of the rising bourgeois intellectual subclass. The latter were seen as having spent the 1750–1900 period distancing themselves from the Church so as to gain autonomous social status and sustainable positions within a state-financed educational system:

> [In France] the state became a major instrument of private appropriation for a growing class of office-holders, in ways and degrees unmatched elsewhere in Europe [. . .] Much of the debate surrounding the French monarchy concerned precisely this: the relation between public and private and who could claim to represent the public principle against the many private interests and jurisdictions that composed the polity of France [. . .] For all their cosmopolitanism and inclusive ambitions, 'Enlightenment' reformers in France were still addressing specifically French questions about the proprietary state, patronage, taxation, and venal offices. As the state continued to be a major resource, even beyond the Revolution and Napoleon, complaints were often directed less at the inherent evils of the state as an instrument of appropriation than at the inequalities of opportunity blocking access to its fruits.[89]

It is a fact that the Jesuits still held in the first half of the eighteenth century a dominant position in teaching, all over Catholic Europe, in over six hundred schools, universities and colleges.[90] Their quasi-monopoly over education – somewhat at odds with the development of experimental science – seemed a valid reason for the *Encyclopédistes* to defy them.

Little more than a decade separated the publication of the first *Encyclopédie* volumes and the official banning of the Jesuit corps in 1764. Shortly after, the Parisian university was driven by the Parlement de Paris to organise the first *concours de l'agrégation*, a public competition to recruit lecturers in all disciplines to the Sorbonne, since about six hundred of the previous teachers and professors had been dismissed for being Jesuits.[91] From then on, teaching in France could, at least in theory, be rooted in reason rather than faith, as the *Encyclopédistes* had openly wished. The anti-dogmatic, scientific and republican spirit of the *Lumières* identified esprit de corps with the obscurantism of the religious orders, and soon with any privileged social group.

The French nation was seen as a natural body that should not tolerate any disease within it. The revolutionaries considered the Church and the aristocratic body as offshoots that ought to be torn out, like poor plants or infections of the body politic. The ideal of a unified body of the nation would encourage the decapitation of privileged, parasitic sub-nations and *corps intermédiaires*. The case against the Jesuits was a real-life rehearsal, a social and political experiment that inspired the realisation that powerful groups could be defeated. Their robustness was an illusion compared to the robustness of the republican myth.

Too Zealous to be Honest? The Trial of the Jesuits

The European case against the Society of Jesus in the decades 1750–70 was a major step towards the secularisation of education and the prototype of revolutionary fights against elites. According to the historian Christine Vogel, it contributed to the polarisation and politicisation of the public sphere in the age of Enlightenment:

> When Portugal's minister [. . .] began his assault on the most powerful Christian religious order in 1759, the echo was heard all over Europe, both in Catholic and Protestant states. This momentous event prompted journalists, authors and translators, engravers, anthologists and editors to comment on the affair, thus fuelling a transnational debate that soon turned into a battle of fundamental ideas about state, society and religion.[92]

The Jesuits were expelled from Portugal in September 1759, accused of having instigated a plot against the king's life and of having seized royal territory to develop an independent 'Jesuit Republic' in South America.[93] In 1761, a controversy involving a financially corrupt Jesuit missionary in the French Caribbean, Père Lavalette, caused public attention to shift to France. The details of the case are too intricate to be developed here; the principal factor is that Lavalette, while in Martinique, engaged in speculative commercial affairs which failed and generated debt. The *Compagnie de Jésus* refused to admit its corporate responsibility by repaying the debt, claiming that Lavalette was a deviant individual, previously forbidden to be commercially active by the religious order itself, and that he should be condemned as an individual. Was a corps to be held responsible for the misbehaviour of one of its members? Less than ten years after the *Encyclopédie*'s criticism, the French *parlements* used this polemic to launch a general campaign against the French branch of the global religious order.

In 1762, an *Arrêt du parlement de Provence* denounced the submission of the Jesuits to the foreign authority of the pope, contrary to the values of individual freedom and reason. In it, the Avocat Général du Roi, André le Blanc de Castillon, in a tone that for a twenty-first century reader might be reminiscent of pleas against the influence of cults on their followers, claimed to be defending the supposedly vulnerable average Jesuit recruit against the influence of the *Compagnie de Jésus* as a whole. A worried Castillon asked if, among the Jesuits, 'constraint, seduction, the esprit de corps, the prestige of fanaticism [. . .] could not alter the equilibrium of reason and deceive the simplicity of the heart'.[94] In other words, each Jesuit was individually a victim who had been forced to renounce his freedom and belongings, not knowing that he would become a puppet in a deceitful scheme.

The Jesuits refuted the accusation, thus amplifying the use of esprit de corps as a combat concept. Already in the second half of the 1750s, shortly after the publication of the *Encyclopédie*, there had been several references to esprit de corps in the *Mémoires pour l'histoire des sciences et des beaux-arts*, known as *Mémoires de Trévoux*, an influential journal whose authors were almost all Jesuits.[95] In January 1756, the editors had published a defence of the virtue of esprit de corps, described as a form of respect for the general interest:

> It is a kind of patriotism which sets in motion all the springs of the soul, and gives it that activity which makes for triumph over all obstacles: under the impression of this general interest, private interests become meaningless [. . .] This esprit de corps is, if you will, only a being of imagination; but when we know how to make use of it, this being of imagination produces the most brilliant actions. Do we not see that the most illustrious and distinguished Societies degenerate if they neglect to maintain this general interest, this esprit de corps? In the great days of their Republic, Roman soldiers were occupied only with the dignity and majesty of their Empire. This brilliant image accompanied them everywhere and communicated to them this intrepid courage, and this warmth which is a form of enthusiasm.[96]

Without mentioning them directly, this text was an answer to the *Philosophes*. The Jesuits sensed that the growing critique of esprit de corps was not purely intellectual, but political and dangerous for their integrity. Ironically, as we will see in the next chapter, the revolutionaries would a few decades later use the same Jesuitical arguments to defend their idea of national esprit de corps.

In 1762, things were getting worse for the *Compagnie de Jésus*. André-Christophe Balbany, another Jesuit voice, decided to address the question of esprit de corps in more depth, using the art of rhetoric to suggest that esprit de corps was the essential quality that made humans social:

> What is then this esprit de corps of the Jesuits, which is so dreaded and so hated? Is it, as has been said, a spirit that tends *to make the members of the Society flexible to all kinds of crimes*? Is it a spirit of brigandage, which associates scoundrels to a reckless leader, to conquer the riches of the citizens, to disturb their rest and to sow terror and fear on all sides? Is it a spirit of fanaticism armed against the authority of laws [. . .]? Is it a spirit of independence and revolt, which under imposing names, precious titles, works secretly to undermine the supports of the throne, to weaken its defenders, to prepare revolutions [. . .]? What do you really mean by *this esprit de corps* which is so often reproached and so odiously represented? Do you mean it is that spirit of zeal, of work, of science which [. . .] defines [the Jesuits] everywhere, which everywhere makes them indefatigable in their tasks, irreproachable in their customs, invariable in their faith, unshakable in their duties, submitted to the Sovereigns, and therefore

detestable everywhere to heretics, envy, debauchery, revolt, impiety? Do you mean that spirit of union which binds them closely together, which creates a mutual interest among each of them, shelters their Houses from hatred, envy, unrest, dissension, and preserves among them precious models of the charity which should unite all states, all conditions, all men? It is not yet this, would you tell me, that is meant by the *esprit de corps* reproached in the Jesuits [. . .] Do you then mean the zeal and dedication one notices among the Jesuits for the glory and benefit of their Corps? [. . .] What! Would it really be a crime for the Jesuits to be attached to their mission, to uphold its glory, to perform its duties, to defend its interests, to confound its enemies? If such an attachment is described as a crime, it is a crime, in any case, which would be common to many guilty parties: [. . .] it is the crime of all the Clergy [. . .] It is the crime of the military. What is greater for them than the glory of combat? It is the crime of the Magistracy. Will we judge that the spirit of Laws is incompatible with esprit de corps? Esprit de corps is the crime of all men. Or shall we ever find men who live completely isolated, who form a separate class, who do not belong to a society?[97]

In this hyperbolic enunciation, a lyrical mix of irony and common sense, the possibilities allowed by esprit de corps were described as almost infinite because universally linked to human nature. Balbany could not possibly imagine a nation without intermediary groups of belonging, and therefore could not envision a world without esprit de corps. The idea of a self-standing rational individual was inept. Whether we liked it or not, esprit de corps was constitutive of what made us a social species. In fact, the *Philosophes* and the Jesuits implicitly agreed on one point: esprit de corps was not an anecdotal phrase, it was an embodied and socially active idea, and a major one. Esprit de corps was an important catalyst in the debates that led to the French Revolution.

The Jesuit author concluded his pleading by deducing, via an appeal-to-nature argument, that esprit de corps should not be disparaged but rather encouraged in all orders of the kingdom, thus clearly defending the status quo of the *Ancien Régime*:

How would it be possible to form, regulate, direct a body if the parts that compose it do not all contribute to the common and general end? It is the crime of nature, which has engraved in the hearts of all men a love of themselves, a love therefore, of all that relates to themselves; the consequent love of a Body [*Corps*], of an estate of which they themselves are a portion. Is it not from this source that the love of one's family, one's state, one's profession, one's country derives? [. . .] Those who consider esprit de corps in general as a crime have never analysed the idea that they form of this term [. . .] This esprit de corps, such as it is present among the Jesuits, far from being attacked, should be encouraged, revived in all estates, in all the orders of the Kingdom [. . .] by reviving in all hearts a noble emulation, it would revive intrepidness in the Military, the study of the Law among the Magistrates, zeal among the

Ecclesiastics, piety in the Religious Orders, love of the Fatherland among Citizens, and it would thereby become an inexhaustible source of resources for the Church and for the State.[98]

In other words, the *Philosophes* were not rational enough in their critique of esprit de corps, because a good analysis should include our emotional need for belonging. By claiming that the phenomenon of esprit de corps was universally distributed and natural, ingrained in self-esteem, the author was perpetuating the naturalisation of a society of organised divisions, states, corporations and classes, a society of *corps* with different *esprits*, and in which the Church was given a central ordinating role. This speech act suggested that there was no such thing as a self which would be independent of any group, and that the love of self anticipated the love for a group of peers. This debate announced the critique of individualism that would flourish in France after 1800.

The notion of esprit de corps became highly ambivalent as soon as it was imported into political discourse, and its semantic ambiguity probably partly explains the polemical dissemination of the signifier. Is esprit de corps a charm or a harm, a natural and protective necessity or an unnatural and dangerous alien-ation? The pendulum effect between laudatory and pejorative meanings of esprit de corps was not a superficial or ephemeral phenomenon. The phrase 'esprit de corps' crystallises a long-term debate between collectiveness and autonomy, national spirit versus individual spirit, and about the character of social bodies. This political discussion was spectacularly initiated in the conflicting dialogue between the *Philosophes* and the Jesuits, but was reactivated under different forms in other historical epochs and geopolitical spheres.

In the second half of the eighteenth century, the phrase *esprit de corps* started to spread in print like a virus. The curve of its relative frequency rose exponentially, while, at the same time, the independent use of the words *esprit* and *corps* taken in isolation did not vary in French publications between 1752 and 1789.[99] Once the Jesuits were neutralised, new groups of power could be targeted.

Notes

1. Trésor de la langue française informatisé <http://atilf.atilf.fr> (accessed 19 September 2019).
2. 'Ce n'est pas seulement dans le militaire que l'on prend l'esprit de corps.' Emile Littré, *Dictionnaire de la langue française* (Paris: Hachette, 1872), vol. I, p. 817.
3. Berns and Frydman, 'Généalogie de l'esprit de corps', p. 180.
4. Charles-Louis de Secondat, baron de la Brède et de Montesquieu, *Lettres persanes*, 2 vols (Amsterdam: Brunel, 1721).
5. Jean-Paul Marana, *L'espion du Grand-Seigneur et ses relations secrètes envoyées à Constantinople* (Paris: Barbin, 1686).
6. Gustave Leopold Van Roosbroeck, *Persian Letters before Montesquieu* (New York: The Institute of French Studies, 1932).
7. 'Travaillons de concert à nous donner de l'esprit; associons-nous pour cela [. . .] Fais ce que je te dirai, et je te promets avant six mois une place à l'Académie; c'est pour te

dire que le travail ne sera pas long: car pour lors tu pourras renoncer à ton art; tu seras homme d'esprit, malgré que tu en aies. On remarque en France que, dès qu'un homme entre dans une compagnie, il prend d'abord ce qu'on appelle l'esprit du corps: tu seras de même; et je ne crains pour toi que l'embarras des applaudissements.' Montesquieu, *Lettres persanes*, vol. I, Lettre LII, pp. 219–22.

8. Pierre Gaxotte, *L'Académie française* (Paris: Hachette, 1965), p. 49.

9. 'Esprit', in *Dictionnaire de l'Académie française* (1694), ARTFL-Frantext, <http://portail.atilf.fr/cgi-bin/getobject_?p.4:66./var/artfla/dicos/ACAD_1694/IMAGE/> (accessed 19 September 2019).

10. Google Book n-gram viewer, <https://books.google.com/ngrams> (accessed 19 September 2019).

11. 'Il faut philosopher du corps d'État comme du corps humain. [Celui-ci] est composé de plusieurs parties animées par une même âme comme un Corps d'Etat par un même esprit sous mêmes lois [. . .] Ainsi en est-il de l'esprit du Corps d'État, qui n'est point tellement enclos en une partie qu'il ne se doive communiquer à toutes, afin que chacune fasse sa charge comme chaque partie du Corps fait sa fonction.' Claude Du Bosc de Montandré, *L'esprit de la vérité, Représentant nuëment la Puissance et l'Authorité du Roy* (Paris, 1652), p. 11.

12. 'Ce n'est pas seulement dans le militaire que l'on prend l'esprit de corps, et ce n'est pas toujours en bien que ses effets se font sentir.' Jean-Jacques Rousseau, *Émile ou de l'Éducation*, in *Collection complète des oeuvres*, 4 vols (Geneva: Société Typographique, 1782 [1762]), vol. IV, p. 173.

13. Christian Biet, 'Mémoires, Saint-Simon', *Encyclopædia Universalis* (2014), <https://www.universalis.fr/encyclopedie/memoires-saint-simon/> (accessed 19 September 2019).

14. 'Tout cela est soutenu par un esprit de corps (on n'oserait dire de petite république, par ce nombreux essaim d'officiers [. . .], dont chacun se pique à qui soutiendra plus haut ce qu'ils appellent l'honneur du corps).' Saint-Simon, *Mémoires complets et authentiques du duc de Saint-Simon*, 21 vols (Paris: Sautelet, 1830), vol. XV, p. 170.

15. 'Germain-François Poullain de Saint-Foix', in Louis-Gabriel Michaud (ed.), *Biographie universelle ancienne et moderne*, 52 vols (Paris: Michaud, 1811–28), vol. XXXIX (1825), p. 573.

16. Joseph La Valine, 'Memoir of G. F. Poullain de Saint-Foix', *Gentleman's Magazine* 19 (1843), p. 37.

17. A 1744 edition was auctioned in 2013 with this description: 'This scarce edition contains the two volumes of Montesquieu's satiric novel [and] Poullain de St.-Foix's *Lettres Turques* with the same imprint. The added title is in the same vein as the *Persian Letters*.' <https://www.nationalbookauctions.com/11032013/3november135.htm> (accessed 19 September 2019).

18. 'Différentes compagnies d'hommes avec des habits bleus galonnés en argent, bordaient les rues des deux côtés. Notre marche s'ouvrit par les Grenadiers à cheval, troupe aussi recommandable par la piété et la régularité de ses mœurs, que par la valeur. On m'a dit qu'après une bataille, le feu Roi Louis XIV demandant à un des Chefs de cette Compagnie, où elle était, cet Officier lui répondit, *Sire, elle est tuée*. Ce mot exprime bien la défaite entière d'un corps de braves gens qu'une même vertu, qu'un même esprit, qu'une même bravoure anime.' Germain Poullain de Saint-Foix, *Lettres de Nedim Coggia, Secrétaire de l'Ambassade de Mehemet Effendi à la Cour de France* (Amsterdam: Pierre Mortier, 1732), pp. 15–16.

19. 'Les Gardes à pied étaient en haie le long des Jardins jusqu'au vestibule du Château. Ce sont des grands hommes bien faits, bien vêtus, et que la jalousie des soldats des autres régiments serait toujours très-prompte à attaquer, s'il leur arrivait le moindre échec.' Ibid., pp. 17–18.

20. April H. Bailey and Marianne LaFrance, 'Who Counts as Human? Antecedents to Androcentric Behaviour', *Sex Roles* 76.11–12 (2016), pp. 682–93, <https://link. springer.com/article/10.1007/s11199-016-0648-4> (accessed 19 September 2019).

21. 'Comme il y a même déjà quelques années que la France n'est plus en guerre, on s'oppose avec affection à la retraite des vieux militaires; on les dispense de certain service, on augmente leur paie; on n'exige, pour ainsi dire, d'eux que de mourir au Régiment. Ils y font le récit des sièges et des batailles où ils se sont trouvés; ils animent et entretiennent parmi les jeunes cet honneur et cet esprit de corps qui se perdrait peut-être insensiblement pendant une si longue paix, et dans un renouvellement presque entier de milice.' Saint-Foix, *Lettres de Nedim Coggia*, pp. 18–19.

22. Gatien de Courtilz de Sandras, *Mémoires de Mr. d'Artagnan, Capitaine Lieutenant de la première Compagnie des Mousquetaires du Roi* (Cologne: Marteau, 1700).

23. Alexandre Dumas, *Les Trois Mousquetaires* (Paris: Baudry, 1844).

24. 'Que ce qui lui plaisait toujours dans ses Mousquetaires, c'était cette gaîté célère, avec laquelle ils marchaient à tout ce qu'on leur disait d'attaquer.' Germain Poullain de Saint-Foix, 'Les deux companies des Mousquetaires', in *Essais historiques sur Paris*, 5 vols (London: Duchesne, 1766), vol. II, pp. 304–32.

25. 'Esprit se prend quelquefois pour le principe, le motif, la conduite, la manière d'agir. *Esprit de charité, esprit de paix, esprit de vengeance, de faction, de procès, ce n'est pas là l'esprit de cette compagnie*'; 'Esprit', *Dictionnaire de l'Académie française*, ARTFL-Frantext, <http://artfl-project.uchicago.edu>.

26. 'C'est une loi commune d'agir pour soi, et en vue de sa satisfaction et de son contentement, c'est une loi nécessaire à la conservation de l'espèce et des individus: c'est le centre où se rapportent toutes nos actions. [. . .] Peuple, crois-moi: [. . .] suis ton intérêt ou renonce à toi-même. Quel est-il, me diras-tu? C'est ton repos, c'est le commerce rétabli, c'est la cherté bannie de l'enceinte de tes murailles et de ton voisinage.' Anonymous, *L'Esprit d'intérêt, ou la censure des deux libelles intitulés l'Esprit de paix, et l'Esprit de guerre* (Paris: Nicolas Guérard, 1652), pp. 12–14.

27. Philip A. Knachel, *England and the Fronde. The Impact of the English Civil War and Revolution on France* (Ithaca: Cornell University Press, 1967).

28. Charles Rivière Dufresny, *L'Esprit de contradiction, comédie* (Paris: Barbin, 1700).

29. Christian Biet, 'Pensées, livre de Blaise Pascal', *Encyclopædia Universalis* (2014), <https://www.universalis.fr/encyclopedie/pensees/> (accessed 19 September 2019).

30. René Bary, *L'Esprit de cour, ou les conversations galantes. Divisées en cent dialogues dédiés au Roi* (Paris: Charles de Sercy, 1662), pp. 403–5.

31. Dominique de Villepin, *De l'esprit de cour: La malédiction française* (Paris: Perrin, 2010).

32. Pierre Thibaut, *Cours de Chimie* (Paris: Iolly, 1667), p. 53.

33. 'L'esprit des éléments comme esprit de corps qui sont immortels nous communique l'art de deviner [. . .] Il y a des puissances substantielles desquelles on obtient par divers sacrifices des paroles de présage.' Nicolas Coeffeteau, *Réponse au livre intitulé: Le Mystère d'iniquité, du Sieur du Plessis* (Paris: Cramoisy, 1614), p. 166.

34. A. Goffart, 'Les esprits animaux', *Revue néo-scolastique* 26 (1900), pp. 153–72.

35. Nanine Charbonnel, *Comme un seul homme: corps politique et corps mystique* (Lons Le Saunier: Aréopage, 2010).

36. François de Dainville, *L'Éducation des Jésuites*, XVIe–XVIIIe siècles (Paris: Minuit, 1978).

37. Plato, *Republic*, trans. Allan Bloom (New York: Basic Books, 1991), vol. VIII, 556e, p. 235.

38. Aristotle, *Politics*, in *Aristotle*, trans. Horace Rackham, 23 vols (Cambridge, MA: Harvard University Press, 1944), vol. XXI, 1253a.

39. Cinthia Gannett and John C. Brereton (eds), *Traditions of Eloquence, The Jesuits and Modern Rhetorical Studies* (New York: Fordham University Press, 2016), p. 61.

40. Cicero, *De Officiis*, trans. Walter Miller (Cambridge, MA: Harvard University Press, 1913), p. 290.

41. Judges 20:8 (King James Version).

42. Edmund P. Cueva, Shannon N. Byrne and Frederik Benda (eds), *Jesuit Education and the Classics* (Newcastle: Cambridge Scholars Publishing, 2009), p. 129.

43. Augustine, *Sermons*, in Emile Mersch, *The Whole Christ* (London: Dobson, 1962), p. 415.

44. Naomi Schor, 'The Crisis of French Universalism', *Yale French Studies* 100 (2001), pp. 43–64 (p. 43).

45. Charbonnel, *Comme un seul homme*, p. 13.

46. Saint-Foix, *Lettres de Nedim Coggia*, pp. 17–19.

47. 'Mademoiselle de l'Espinasse – Dans la grappe d'abeilles, il n'y en aurait pas une qui eût eu le temps de prendre l'esprit du corps. D'Alembert – Qu'est-ce que vous dites-là? Mademoiselle de l'Espinasse – Je dis que l'esprit monastique se conserve parce que le monastère se refait peu à peu, et quand il entre un moine nouveau, il en trouve une centaine de vieux qui l'entraînent à penser et à sentir comme eux. Une abeille s'en va, il en succède dans la grappe une autre qui se met bientôt au courant.' Denis Diderot, *Mémoires, correspondance et ouvrages inédits de Diderot, publiés d'après les manuscrits confiés, en mourant, par l'auteur à Grimm* (Paris: Paulin, 1834), vol. IV, p. 190.

48. Stéphane Thion, *Les armées françaises de la guerre de Trente Ans* (Auzielle: LRT, 2008), p. 89.

49. Louis Susane, *La Maison du Roi, Histoire de la cavalerie Française* (Paris: Hetzel, 1874), vol. I, p. 133.

50. Frank A. Kafker and Serena L. Kafker, *The Encyclopédistes as Individuals: A Biographical Dictionary of the Authors of the Encyclopédie* (Oxford: Voltaire Foundation, 1988); Louis-Philippe May, 'Note sur les origines maçonniques de l'Encyclopédie suivie de la liste des encyclopédistes', *Revue de synthèse* 58 (1939), pp. 5–110.

51. Robin Dunbar, 'Coevolution of Neocortical Size, Group Size and Language in Humans', *Behavioral and Brain Sciences* 16 (1993), pp. 681–735 (p. 687).

52. Paul Smaldino, Cynthia Pickett, Jeffrey Sherman and Jeffrey Schank, 'An Agent-Based Model of Social Identity Dynamics', *Journal of Artificial Societies and Social Simulation* 15.4 (2012), <http://jasss.soc.surrey.ac.uk/15/4/7.html> (accessed 19 September 2019).

53. Judith Butler, 'Competing Universalities', in Judith Butler, Ernesto Laclau and Slavoj Žižek, *Contingency, Hegemony, Universality: Contemporary Dialogues on the Left* (London: Verso, 2000), p. 167.

54. Germain Poullain de Saint-Foix, *Œuvres complètes de M. de Saint-Foix*, 5 vols (Paris: Duchesne, 1778), vol. V, p. 371.

55. Ibid., p. 373.

56. 'Chaque corps peut se différencier des autres par son organisation, ses coutumes, ses intérêts. Mais tous les corps procèdent d'une même essence: ils allient des solidarités

internes à la soumission aux ordres d'une tête.' Marie-Christine Kessler, 'L'esprit de corps dans les grands corps de l'État en France', in *Esprit de corps, démocratie et espace public* (Paris: PUF, 2005), p. 277.

57. Hunter, 'Secularization: The Birth of a Modern Combat Concept'.

58. D'Alembert, 'Caractère des sociétés ou corps particuliers', p. 666.

59. Simon Bourlet de Vauxcelles, *L'esprit de l'Encyclopédie* (Paris: Fauvelle et Sagnier, 1798).

60. 'D'Alembert to Voltaire, 14 July 1767', Oxford: Electronic Enlightenment Project, Bodleian Libraries, 2008–14, <http://www.e-enlightenment.com/item/voltfrVF1160202a1c/?letters=decade&s=1760&r=14802> (accessed 19 September 2019).

61. 'Les sociétés ou corps particuliers au milieu d'un peuple, sont en quelque manière de petites nations entourées d'une plus grande: c'est une espèce de greffe bonne ou mauvaise, entée sur un grand tronc; aussi les sociétés ont-elles pour l'ordinaire un *caractère* particulier, qu'on appelle *esprit du corps*.' D'Alembert, 'Caractère des sociétés ou corps particuliers', p. 666.

62. Thomas Hobbes, *Leviathan*, XXIX, §21, rev. ed. A.P. Martinich and Brian Battiste (Petterborough, Ont.: Broadview, 2010), p. 285.

63. Pauline Ka, 'The Concept of National Character in Eighteenth-Century France', *Cromohs*, 7 (2002), pp. 1–6, <http://www.fupress.net/index.php/cromohs/article/view/15716/14605> (accessed 19 September 2019).

64. 'Le caractère d'une nation consiste dans une certaine disposition habituelle de l'âme, qui est plus commune chez une nation que chez une autre, quoique cette disposition ne se rencontre pas dans tous les membres qui composent la nation.' D'Alembert, 'Caractère des sociétés ou corps particuliers', p. 666.

65. Schor, 'The Crisis of French Universalism', p. 43.

66. 'le véritable esprit systématique qu'il faut bien se garder de prendre pour l'esprit de système, avec lequel il ne se rencontre pas toujours'; D'Alembert, 'Discours préliminaire des éditeurs', in *Encyclopédie*, ed. Robert Morrissey, ARTFL Encyclopédie, University of Chicago (2013), <https://artflsrv03.uchicago.edu/philologic4/encyclopedie1117/navigate/1/3/> (accessed 19 September 2019).

67. Prosper Schroeder, *La loi de la gravitation universelle, Newton, Euler et Laplace* (Paris: Springer, 2007), pp. 248–9.

68. 'J'appelle avec M. Newton *force d'inertie*, la propriété qu'ont les corps de rester dans l'état où ils sont.' Jean le Rond D'Alembert, *Traité de Dynamique* (Paris: David, 1758), p. 3.

69. 'Il serait nécessaire, par exemple, suivant la remarque d'un homme d'esprit, que les compagnies littéraires fussent *pédantes*.' D'Alembert, 'Caractère des sociétés ou corps particuliers', p. 666.

70. Charles-Louis de Secondat, Baron de Montesquieu, *De l'esprit des lois* (London: Nourse, 1772), vol. I, p. 20.

71. Andreas Follesdal, 'The Principle of Subsidiarity as a Constitutional Principle in International Law', *Global Constitutionalism* 2.1 (2013), pp. 37–62 (p. 43).

72. 'L'honneur fait mouvoir toutes les parties du corps politique; il les lie par son action même; et il se trouve que chacun va au bien commun, croyant aller à ses intérêts particuliers.' Montesquieu, *De l'Esprit des Loix, ou du rapport que les Loix doivent avoir avec la Constitution de chaque Gouvernement, les Mœurs, le Climat, la Religion, le Commerce, &c.*, 2 vols (Geneva: Barillot, 1748), vol. I, p. 39.

73. 'Il leur était nécessaire de représenter, pour ainsi dire, ces êtres à l'oreille par des sons, mais de les représenter aussi en quelque manière aux yeux, en convenant de

certaines marques qui les désignassent.' D'Alembert, 'Caractère des sociétés ou corps particuliers', p. 645.

74. 'Le caractère sépare, divise, compartimente le monde; il transforme le *continuum* de la matière en succession d'objets différenciés, susceptibles d'être rangés, classés et, par là, de signifier. Le caractère constitue par là la coupure sémiotique.' Stéphane Lojkine, 'Le décentrement matérialiste du champ des connaissances dans l'Encyclopédie', *Recherches sur Diderot et sur l'Encyclopédie* 26 (1999), <http://rde.revues.org/1041> (accessed 19 September 2019).

75. John Dewey, 'The Historic Background of Corporate Legal Personality', *Yale Law Journal* 35.6 (1926), pp. 655–73 (p. 666).

76. 'Dans certaines compagnies, par exemple, le *caractère* général est l'esprit de subordination; dans d'autres l'esprit d'égalité.' D'Alembert, 'Caractère des sociétés ou corps particuliers', p. 666.

77. Alain Guillermou, *Saint Ignace de Loyola et la Compagnie de Jésus* (Paris: Seuil, 1960).

78. 'Souvent le *caractère* d'une société est très différent de celui de la nation, où elle se trouve pour ainsi dire transplantée. Des corps, par exemple, qui dans une monarchie feraient vœu de fidélité à un autre prince qu'à leur souverain légitime, devraient naturellement avoir moins d'attachement pour ce souverain que le reste de la nation [. . .] "Les religieux, dont les chefs résident à Rome, dit le célèbre M. de Voltaire, dans son admirable *Essai sur le siècle de Louis XIV* sont autant de sujets immédiats du pape répandus dans tous les états [. . .] L'esprit de trouble, le malheur des temps, n'ont que trop souvent porté des ordres entiers de religieux à servir Rome contre leur patrie."' D'Alembert, 'Caractère des sociétés ou corps particuliers', p. 666.

79. Voltaire, *Le Siècle de Louis XIV* (Berlin: Henning, 1751).

80. 'La religion a été traitée par Ignace de Loyola en machine de guerre, et la morale comme une mécanique [. . .] Transformer l'homme en automate est un secret qu'Ignace a tiré de l'art militaire.' Michel Leroy, *Le Mythe jésuite: de Béranger à Michelet* (Paris: Presses Universitaires de France, 1992), p. 231.

81. '[Avant Louis XIV], l'esprit de parti déchirait et avilissait la France; et l'esprit de société, qui rend aujourd'hui cette nation si célèbre et si aimable, étaient absolument inconnu. Point de maisons où les gens de mérite s'assemblassent pour se communiquer leurs lumières.' Voltaire, *Le Siècle de Louis XIV*, vol. I, p. 23

82. Dena Goodman, *The Republic of Letters: A Cultural History of the French Enlightenment* (Ithaca: Cornell University Press, 1994).

83. 'L'*Encyclopédie* peut aisément s'améliorer [. . .] Mais le danger auquel il faudra principalement obvier, et que nous aurons prévu, c'est que le soin des éditions subséquentes ne soit pas abandonné au despotisme d'une société, d'une compagnie, quelle qu'elle puisse être. Nous avons annoncé, et nous en attestons nos contemporains et la postérité, que le moindre inconvénient qui pût en arriver, ce serait qu'on supprimât des choses essentielles; qu'on multipliât à l'infini le nombre et le volume de celles qu'il faudrait supprimer; que l'esprit de corps, qui est ordinairement petit, jaloux, concentré, infectât la masse de l'ouvrage.' Denis Diderot, 'Encyclopédie', in Denis Diderot and Jean le Rond d'Alembert (eds), *Encyclopédie ou dictionnaire raisonné des sciences, des arts et des métiers* (Paris: Briasson, David, Le Breton and Durand, 1751–65), vol. V (1755), p. 649.

84. '*Esprit d'un corps, d'une société*, pour exprimer les usages, la manière de penser, de se conduire, les préjugés d'un corps. *Esprit de parti*, qui est à l'*esprit* d'un corps ce que sont les passions aux sentiments ordinaires.' Voltaire, 'Esprit (Philos. & Belles-Lettr.)', p. 975.

85. Hannah Arendt, 'Karl Marx and the Tradition of Western Political Thought', *Social Research* 69.2 (2002), pp. 273–319 (p. 317).

86. 'cette manie qu'ont les différents ordres de défendre les systèmes que quelqu'un de leur ordre a trouvés [. . .] Il est d'abord évident que non-seulement cela retarde les progrès de la Théologie, mais même les arrête; il n'est pas possible de penser mieux que Molina chez les Jésuites, puisqu'il faut penser comme lui [. . .] Grâces à Dieu, ce qui regarde l'hydrostatique, l'hydraulique, et les autres sciences, n'a point été livré à l'esprit de corps.' Claude Yvon, 'Aristotélisme', in Denis Diderot and Jean le Rond d'Alembert (eds), *Encyclopédie ou dictionnaire raisonné des sciences, des arts et des métiers* (Paris: Briasson, David, Le Breton and Durand, 1751–65), vol. I (1751), p. 654.

87. 'En détruisant l'esprit de corps, on lui substitue l'égoïsme, caractère le plus pernicieux et le plus opposé à l'intérêt général [. . .] L'humanité prétendue de nos philosophes cosmopolites n'est qu'un masque d'hypocrisie sous lequel ils cachent leur égoïsme.' Nicolas Sylvestre Bergier, 'Communautés ecclesiastiques', *Encyclopédie méthodique*, 26 vols (Paris: Panckoucke, 1782–1832), vol. XV (1789), p. 384.

88. 'Tout l'univers a entendu parler des Jésuites [. . .] Ignace de Loyola, simple gentilhomme espagnol, militaire sans fortune et sans connaissances [. . .] résolut, dans le XVIe siècle d'établir un Ordre entièrement dévoué à l'éducation de la jeunesse [. . .] Nul fondateur n'atteignit mieux son but, nul ne parvint plus parfaitement à l'anéantissement des volontés particulières pour établir la volonté générale et cette raison commune qui est le principe générateur et conservateur de toute institution quelconque, grande ou petite: car l'*esprit de corps* n'est que l'*esprit public* diminué, comme le patriotisme n'est que l'*esprit de corps* agrandi. Si l'on veut se former une idée de la force intérieure de l'activité et de l'influence de cet Ordre, il suffit de réfléchir à la haine implacable et réellement furieuse dont l'honor[a] constamment le philosophisme.' Joseph de Maistre, *Étude sur la souveraineté*, in *Œuvres complètes* (Lyons: Vitte, 1884 [1794]), pp. 388–90.

89. Ellen Meiksins Wood, *Liberty & Property: A Social History of Western Political Thought from Renaissance to Enlightenment* (New York: Verso, 2012), pp. 151–72.

90. According to the archives of the Society of Jesus, *Archivum Romanum Societatis Iesu*, <http://www.sjweb.info/arsi/>, confirmed for example by Agustin Udias, 'Jesuits', in David Gubbins and Emilio Herrero-Bervera (eds), *Encyclopedia of Geomagnetism and Paleomagnetism* (Dordrecht: Springer, 2007), p. 460.

91. Dominique Julia, 'Les professeurs, l'Eglise et l'État après l'expulsion des Jésuites', *Historical Reflections* 7.2–3 (1980), pp. 459–81; André Chervel and Marie-Madeleine Compère, 'Les candidats aux trois concours pour l'agrégation de l'Université de Paris (1766–1791)', *Ressources numériques en histoire de l'éducation* (2002), <http://rhe.ish-lyon.cnrs.fr/?q=agregar> (accessed 19 September 2019).

92. Christine Vogel, 'The Suppression of the Society of Jesus, 1758–1773', *European History Online* (2010), <http://www.ieg-ego.eu/vogelc-2010-en> (accessed 19 September 2019).

93. Ibid.

94. 'si la contrainte, la séduction, l'esprit de corps, les prestiges du fanatisme [. . .] n'y peuvent pas altérer l'équilibre de la raison, et tromper la simplicité du cœur'; André Le Blanc de Castillon, *Arrêt du parlement de Provence* (Aix en Provence, 1762), p. 15

95. Jack Censer, *The French Press in the Age of Enlightenment* (Oxford: Routledge, 1994), p. 101.

96. '[C'est] une espèce de patriotisme qui met en mouvement tous les ressorts de l'âme, et lui donne cette activité qui fait triompher de tous les obstacles: sous l'impression

de cet intérêt général, les intérêts particuliers sont comptés pour rien [. . .] Cet esprit de corps n'est, si l'on veut, qu'un être d'imagination; mais quand on sait en faire usage, cet être d'imagination produit les actions les plus éclatantes. Ne voyons-nous pas que les Sociétés les plus illustres et les plus distinguées dégénèrent à mesure qu'on néglige d'y maintenir cet intérêt général, cet esprit du corps? Dans les beaux jours de leur République, les soldats Romains n'étaient occupés que de la dignité et de la majesté de leur Empire. Cette image brillante les accompagnait partout et leur communiquait ce courage intrépide, et cette chaleur qui tient de l'enthousiasme.' Briasson et Chaubert, *Mémoires pour l'Histoire des sciences et des beaux-arts*, ARTFL-Frantext, pp. 118–20, <https://artfl-project.uchicago.edu/content/journal-de-trévoux> (accessed 19 September 2019).

97. 'Qu'est-ce donc cet esprit de corps si redouté, si détesté dans les Jésuites? Est-ce, comme on l'a dit, un esprit qui tende à *rendre les membres qui composent la Société flexibles à tous genres de crimes?* Un esprit de brigandage, qui associe des scélérats à un chef audacieux, pour envahir la fortune des Citoyens, troubler leur repos et semer de toute part la terreur et les alarmes? Est-ce un esprit de fanatisme armé contre l'autorité des lois [. . .]? Est-ce un esprit d'indépendance, et de révolte, qui sous des noms imposants, des titres précieux, travaille sourdement à saper les appuis du Trône, à affaiblir ses défenseurs, à préparer des révolutions [. . .]? Qu'entendez-vous donc par *cet esprit de corps* si souvent reproché, et si odieusement représenté? Entendriez-vous cet esprit de zèle, de travail, de science qui [. . .] caractérise partout [les Jésuites], qui partout les rend infatigables dans les travaux, irréprochables dans les mœurs, invariables dans la foi, inébranlables dans leurs devoirs, et dans la soumission aux Souverains, et par-là même détestables partout à l'hérésie, à l'envie, au libertinage, à la révolte, à l'impiété? Entendriez-vous cet esprit d'union qui les lie étroitement ensemble, qui les intéresse mutuellement les uns aux autres, met leurs Maisons à l'abri de la haine, de l'envie, des troubles, des dissensions, et conserve parmi eux des modèles précieux de cette charité, qui devrait unir tous les états, toutes les conditions, tous les hommes? Ce n'est pas encore là, me dites-vous, ce qu'on entend par l'*esprit de corps* reproché aux Jésuites [. . .] Entendriez-vous le zèle et l'attachement qu'on remarque parmi les Jésuites pour la gloire et l'avantage de leurs Corps? [. . .] Quoi! Voudrait-on sérieusement faire un crime aux Jésuites d'être attachés à leur état, d'en soutenir la gloire, d'en remplir les devoirs, d'en défendre les intérêts, d'en confondre les ennemis? Si cet attachement est qualifié de crime, c'est un crime, en tous cas, qui leur est commun avec bien des coupables: [. . .] c'est le crime de tout le Clergé [. . .] C'est le crime des gens de guerre. Que voient-ils de plus grand que la gloire acquise dans les combats? C'est le crime de la Magistrature. Jugera-t-on l'esprit des Lois incompatible avec l'esprit de corps? C'est le crime de tous les hommes. En trouvera-t-on qui soient entièrement isolés, qui forment une classe à part, qui ne soient pas dans un état [. . .]?' André-Christophe Balbany, *Acceptation du défi hazardé par l'auteur d'un libelle intitulé Réplique aux apologies des Jésuites* (Avignon, 1762), pp. 35–7.

98. 'Comment former, régler, diriger un corps sans que les parties qui le composent concourent toutes à la fin commune et générale? C'est le crime de la nature, qui a gravé dans le cœur de tous les hommes l'amour d'eux-mêmes, l'amour par conséquent de tout ce qui se rapporte à eux-mêmes; l'amour par conséquent d'un Corps, d'un état dont ils sont eux-mêmes une portion. N'est-ce pas de cette source que dérive l'amour de sa famille, de son état, de sa profession, de sa Patrie? [. . .] Ceux qui se font un crime de l'esprit de corps en général, n'ont jamais analysé l'idée qu'ils se forment de ce terme [. . .] Cet esprit de corps, tel qui est chez les Jésuites, bien loin d'être attaqué dans eux,

devrait être excité, ranimé dans tous les Etats, dans tous les ordres du Royaume; [. . .] en ranimant dans tous les cœurs une noble émulation, il ranimerait l'intrépidité dans les Soldats, l'étude des Lois dans les Magistrats, le zèle dans les Ecclésiastiques, la piété dans les Ordres Religieux, l'amour de la Patrie dans les Citoyens, et il deviendrait, par-là même un fond inépuisable de ressources pour l'Eglise et pour l'Etat.' Ibid., p. 44.

99. In a random sample of 11,345 printed books or *libelles* of all genres, accessed via Google Ngram viewer, <http://books.google.com/ngrams> (accessed 19 September 2019).

2

'Adunation' of the Nation: Towards a Republican Esprit de Corps

The Mask of Reason: The Dialectics of Particularism and Patriotism

Could actual personal merit be of greater value than centuries of noble ancestors? Such was the contention of Jean Soret in 1756, in his *Essai sur les mœurs*. He added that esprit de corps was a bad emotion:

> The esprit de corps, like the particular spirit [*l'esprit particulier*], ought only to be reason; but passions take the mask of reason, and enjoy its rights [. . .] Reason says that to be appreciated in society requires a sound judgment, a righteous heart, a solid merit, and above all great modesty. It is sad that reason is belied by experience.[1]

The intriguing hypothesis of a rational esprit de corps was here immediately dismissed as a rhetorical fiction. Societies were not rational, only a few people could be so. It was becoming common in the middle of the eighteenth century for an author to consider that individual reason was the highest human value while expressing moralistic contempt towards social mores. Because civilised humans were biased, there was much doubt regarding their collective capacity to act accordingly to reason instead of partisanship or pride.

Soret alluded to another important value of the century, experience, which confirmed that among human societies passions were more powerful than reason. In this context, what exactly was esprit de corps? 'Almost always a spirit of ambition, pride, illusion and vertigo. The esprit de corps is the mania of false spirits or weak spirits.'[2] This unnuanced claim represented another stage in the radicalisation of the critique against esprit de corps: not only a political critique but also a psychological one. Stubborn faithfulness to a group was likely to be a manifestation of self-deception. Behind apparently selfless attitudes such as dedication to a cause or discipline, the sceptical moralist detected irrational drives.

Yet a different idea was to become more influential before the French Revolution; it was a kind of synthesis between the national individualism of the *Philosophes* and the Jesuits' esprit de corps. This idea would claim that patriotism and devotion to the nation were an even healthier and grander form of esprit de corps than that encountered in smaller communities. François Le Prévost d'Exmes, a French former *garde du corps* of the king of Poland, published in 1756 one of the first eulogies of this kind of national esprit de corps that was, in his case, seen as a prolongation of more particular forms of the notion:[3]

> Explain to me, I beg you, said to me the other day a Stranger, how in a nation that cultivates honour, if I may say, to the point of madness; there may be people who practise vileness just as much [. . .] Your astonishment is under-standable, I replied, and I agree that this is the enigma of France. However, if one reflects upon the fact that the feeling of honour is often but a form of esprit de corps, which strongly strikes the imagination of each member, raises him above himself to participate in the glory of all; if we notice that the weakest soul then acquires a reinforcement of which it was not capable before, and which it owes principally to the eyes of its associates and its rivals fixed on it; it will be seen that it is consequent that a man thrown out of his social body [*corps*], if he finds himself freed from all ties of honour, if he looks upon the name of his country as a chimera, shall be returned from that moment to himself alone, and no longer fears being ignominious.[4]

An individual was likely to regress to a pre-civilised condition of animality if uncontrolled by the emulation game of group surveillance. Without the eyes of a collective body fixed on individual behaviour, without social monitoring, anyone could become ignominious, which etymologically means *ignorant of his name*. The lonely human being, hardly a human at all, was as if thrown out of his real body, that real body being the social corps and, encompassing it, the divine fatherland.

Le Prévost d'Exmes was not only a former member of the cavalry elite, he was also a devout Catholic.[5] For him, esprit de corps was a principle of civilisation and mutual elevation that manifested our social interdependence. It favoured the national development of an aggrandising imagined community.[6] The term *glory*, traditionally reserved to God, was now transposed to the body of the nation. The *Patrie*, the honourable corps *par excellence*, was not only an effective fiction, it was a necessity. The author did not openly condemn intermediary bodies, probably because of his Catholic sensibility. Soon, however, for less religiously minded pre-revolutionaries, the glory of the patriotic body was to imply ideologically the eradication or total subordination of intermediate corps.

During the 1760s, magistrates started referring insistently to the sovereignty of the nation; in the last four decades of the *Ancien Régime*, bitter feuds erupted between the parliaments of France and the Crown, and local parliaments trig-gered the process by which unitary sovereignty was transferred from the king to the nation.[7] Louis XV and his government, financially encumbered by the Seven Years War, which ended in 1763 with the loss of one-third of the North American territory, had just issued a set of *lettres patentes* to increase the taxes and the statute labour (*corvées*) imposed upon the regions via the coercive power of the judicial regional bodies (*parlements*).[8] The latter resisted and protested, partly because they anticipated the anger of the labourers, and partly to protect their own revenues and influence.

The remonstrance that the Parlement de Metz addressed to the king of France in 1765 defended what would turn to be one of the mottos of the Revolution: 'L'esprit de patriotisme est en grand ce qu'est en petit l'esprit de corps,'[9] a formula which meant that between esprit de corps and nationalism there was but a difference of scale, patriotism being the grander version of a smaller but necessary phenomenon. Here the rhetorical tactic contradicted the one developed by the same social group against the esprit de corps of the Jesuits only three years before. But the Jesuits considered that the highest authority after God was the pope in Rome; their esprit de corps could easily be accused of being an anti-patriotic partisan spirit. Conversely, parliamentary magistrates were trying to oppose an excessive royal intromission. They wished to protect the privileges they exercised in the administration of their regions and claimed this was for the greater good of the fatherland. The comparison between patriotism and esprit de corps was organic:

> The spirit of patriotism [l'esprit de patriotisme] is the grander version of esprit de corps [. . .] The first incorporates the citizen from birth into the glory acquired by our ancestors [. . .] The second strengthens the weapon temper of the one who is aggregated and puts before his eyes the reputation of a body of which he is a member, and of which he must uphold the honour.[10]

Nation, tradition, glory and honour. Aggregated magistrates were supposed to serve the higher interests of the people while living by the honourable rules of their semi-autonomous peer group. The familiar reference to honour, and the metaphor of the tempering of a weapon, pointed to the military connotation of esprit de corps. The text suggested indirectly that the magistrates could form a war machine by identifying with the soldier's pride and his character of steel.

The city of Metz was defying Louis XV, but in doing so it somewhat betrayed its particularism. If judicial bodies were asked to renounce some prerogatives and autonomy, they might lose their zeal in defending the Crown:

> The love of the fatherland depends on the advantages it procures; and these advantages are, Sire, the franchises and immunities of the Provinces. The general interest is the chain that binds all citizens; the rupture of this chain necessarily causes the dissolution of all the parts which form the State. Love of the Fatherland, general interest, national rights, these are synonymous words, or consequent ideas; since the love of the fatherland is born of the love of oneself; since the general interest is the art of the legislator, who unites the particular good with the greater good.[11]

This was an ambiguous speech. It defined the exemptions or privileges provided to the provincial administrations as a cause for patriotism. A chain of general interest was said to connect (detain?) all citizens, and the rupture of the chain was meant to be harmful to the national state. One could ask: what was a special prerogative enjoyed only by a specific group if not a break in national solidarity? The love of the nation was here said to have its origins in the love for one's self, suggesting that private interests were a deep reason for patriotism, more than selfless devotion to the general good.

This kind of ambivalent admonition might have sounded like a form of black-mail to the king's ears, and we will see below how Louis XV reacted. Such rhetorical juggling with both the interests of the nation and the interests of the magistrates partly explain why two decades later various pamphlets would accuse these *parlementaires*, all over France, of being in fact agents of the aristocratic party hiding behind the idea of general interest.[12] This boomerang effect would even hit the reputation of Montesquieu, who had served as a representative of Bordeaux:[13] the philosopher Helvetius is supposed to have written the following in a letter which some claim is apocryphal, but nevertheless reflects a view that became widespread before the Revolution:[14]

> The esprit de corps invades us from all sides. Under the name of corps, it is a power that is erected at the expense of the greater society. It is by hereditary usurpations that we are governed. Under the name of French there exists only corporations of individuals, and not a citizen who deserves this title [. . .] and our friend Montesquieu, stripped of his title of sage and legislator, is no more than a magistrate and a witty aristocrat. This is what afflicts me for him and for humanity.[15]

In such an attack, the equation between esprit de corps and corruption was unambiguous. How could hereditary power be fair if citizens were supposed to be equal? The king was naked. Helvetius also emphasised the lack of unity and cohesion within the French nation, a recurrent theme among revolutionaries.

One of the influential works of the Enlightenment,[16] *De l'Esprit* by Helvetius mentioned the phrase *intérêt général* thirty times, including in the first page of the preface: 'If I were wrong, and if, contrary to my expectation, some of my principles were not in the general interest, it would be an error of my mind, and not of my heart.'[17] According to Helvetius, the mind, *l'esprit*, collective or individual, was always driven by interest, gratification and pleasure. The metaphor of the heart was here used – somewhat rhetorically and in contra-diction with the main argument of the book – to designate a deeper form of authenticity, somewhere between the old (Christian) soul and the emerging (modern) self.[18]

In the second half of the eighteenth century, the notions of general interest and general will, related to the idea of people's sovereignty, began to play an increasing role in the documents that mentioned esprit de corps. In 1755, the Cour souveraine de Lorraine et Barrois asked: 'What would happen if a Sovereign Corporation were prevented from acting for the general interest?'[19] In the same text, *intérêt de l'Etat* and *intérêt public* were used four times as synonyms of *intérêt général*.[20] In 1766, Jean-Charles de Lavie, a former president of the Parlement de

Bordeaux, claimed that: 'It is necessary that what grounds the general interest thwarts the particular taste.'[21]

But 'interest' was also an ambivalent term. As Karl Marx would put it a century later: 'Every class which is struggling for mastery [. . .] must first conquer for itself political power in order to represent its interest in turn as the general interest.'[22] Interestingly, the phrase *intérêt général* did not appear once in Rousseau's *Du contrat social*. *Intérêt commun* was invoked eight times, while *volonté générale* appeared no less than fifty-eight times, often in opposition to *intérêt de corps* or *volonté particulière*:

> If it is not impossible that a particular will agrees on some point with the general will, it is impossible at least that this agreement is durable and constant; because the special will tends, by its nature, to preferences, and the general will tends to equality.[23]

Rousseau's argument was that the general will ought to be considered not only as the sum of all particular aspirations, but as a specific emergent entity, a kind of political supra-self, generated somewhat mystically by social agreement or 'association', and fleshed out in the national body:

> Each one of us places his person and all his power under the common and supreme direction of the general will; and we receive in body [*corps*] each member as indivisible part of the whole. Immediately, instead of the particular person of each contractor, this act of association produces a moral and collective body, composed of as many members as the assembly has votes, and this new body receives from this same act its unity, its common self, its life and its will.[24]

Not unlike Christian embodiment, the unified life of the body politic was expected to be produced somewhat mystically and instantly by the social contract: it was endowed with a living sanctified self, 'la sainteté du contrat social'.[25] The idea of a collective personal mind defined as a common self was here clearly inspired by religious discourse,[26] but also redefined esprit de corps as national character, 'le corps du peuple'.[27]

For Rousseau, collective selfhood was democratic and co-created by a 'supreme direction of the general will'[28] rather than inherited from tradition. He thought the general will could produce a common national identity, a specific *esprit du corps du peuple*, although he was also critical of esprit de corps:

> There are functions which seem to modify the natural tendencies, and to transform, for better or worse, the men who occupy them. A coward becomes brave when he enters the Navarre regiment. It is not only in the military that one acquires the esprit de corps, and its effects are not always felt as good. I thought a hundred times with dread that if I had the misfortune to fill today such or such position in certain countries, tomorrow I would be almost

inevitably a tyrant, a torturer, destroyer of the people, harmful to the prince, enemy by estate of all humanity, of all fairness, of every kind of virtue.[29]

This was a violent, if not delirious, critique of esprit de corps and its second-nature effects in hierarchical and non-democratic regimes. Rousseau also seems to confirm here *en passant* that esprit de corps originated in military discourse. Was he suggesting that its essence was coercive by definition and that serving a stately function could generate, along with esprit de corps, a form of insensibility to and legitimation of criminal behaviour? Such questions would emerge again notoriously during the ethical debates that followed by the bureaucratic cruelty of the Nazis.[30]

Esprit de corps could perhaps produce good effects if generated by the political general will of an egalitarian nation, but then there would only be one real body, the democratic body politic. If produced within an unfair system, esprit de corps became a partisan machine doomed to control and influence any individual, even the best-intentioned leaders. Of course, Rousseau also revealed here, in his hyperbolic jubilation of picturing himself as a bloody tyrant, his irritation and paranoia in the face of humanity's disorders: the only way he could tolerate humans was as a hyper-unified unit, *one* like nature itself or like his solipsistic self. In this sense, as we will explain in more detail, Rousseau is the continuation of Descartes. *I think, I am*, but why does my so-called friend not think like me?

For Rousseau a good republic was comparable to a machine, and the legislator to its *mécanicien*.[31] This mechanical capacity to constrain the citizen, even in the name of freedom, was certainly ambiguous, although Rousseau did not seem to believe it was a problem to force citizens to be free:

So that the social pact is not a vain paper form, it tacitly contains a commitment which alone can give strength to other ones, that whoever refuses to obey the general will be forced to do so by the whole body: which does not mean anything else than being forced to be free; for such is the condition which by offering every Citizen to the Fatherland protects from personal dependence; a condition which constitutes the artifice and play of the political machine, and which alone renders legitimate civil engagements, which otherwise would be absurd, tyrannical, and subject to the most enormous abuses.[32]

The republican *corps* was a machine-like force that had to have predominance over particular interests. Being dependent on the state – as a sacrificial offering – allowed for a paradoxical freedom: the democratic nation was seen, implicitly, as a giant golden prison that protected its citizens from the bad influence of smaller enslavements, a rhetoric that would later inspire totalitarian governments – hence perhaps the popularity of Rousseau among communist leaders in the Soviet era.[33]

The mechanical metaphor cohabited with a more spiritual perspective in Rousseau, and the mechano-spiritual political ambivalence between freedom and coercion manifested the ambivalence of esprit de corps itself. Rousseau was indeed very Cartesian in his attempt to imagine the general will as a collective cogito. How?

Collective Cogito: The Nation as a Natural and Spiritual *Corps*

'In order for the law to be an expression of the general will, the body [*corps*] of the nation must exercise sovereignty', claimed a Parisian gazette in 1790.[34] This was the culmination of a spreading discourse, at least since the 1750s, against the artifices of intermediary esprit de corps. Such speech acts might have been a performative necessity towards the social creation of a unified national body, one that was more often than not compared to a natural willing body, still seen as a model of sovereignty in the modern nation-state.[35]

The naturalisation of the French nation in the eighteenth century has been widely studied. By naturalisation is meant a multi-voiced, discursive process that presents a political construct as a natural reality when it is in fact a socially created reality, where 'supposed "givens" are actually normative ideals'.[36] As explained by Bourdieu in his book on esprit de corps in French education, the process of naturalisation supposes to a certain extent a process of incorporation, a physical and psychological assimilation produced via language, regulation, discipline and recognition, in which the social construction tends to become second nature.[37] In such a process body and mind are intertwined: hence the tension around the idea of esprit de corps.

The naturalisation of the body politic was also a spiritualising discourse in Rousseau, both because of his Catholicism and his Cartesianism. Moreover, the political metaphor of the spiritual body was, as I have shown, a familiar cultural and cognitive trope in the eighteenth century. This was not just *conversation de salon*: Louis XV, in his speech pronounced before the Parlement de Paris in 1766, disputed the idea of an autonomous national body politic separated from his control: 'The rights and interests of the nation, of which some dare to make a body [*corps*] separate from the monarch, are necessarily united with mine and rest only in my hands.'[38] To reaffirm his sovereignty, the king immediately added that 'my people is one with me' [*mon peuple est un avec moi*].

But the *Lumières*' suspicion towards individual interest disguised as legitimate power, the roots of which went back at least to the *Mazarinades*, could not compromise for much longer with the idea of sovereignty concentrated in one particular person, suggestive of despotism. The royal speech of 1766 was ironically called *Discours de la flagellation* by his contemporaries; on that day, the Christian calendar celebrated the flagellation of the body of Christ, an episode narrated in the canonical gospels, usually followed by the *Ecce homo*, in which Jesus is presented by Pilate *as a mere human*.[39] The king Louis XV, whose divinity was suspect, appeared to be castigating the magistrates if not symbolically chastening them; or was his speech perhaps perceived by some as a desperate self-flagellation? This royal palaver of little binding force was already anachronistic. Not only did it have no immediate legal consequences, it also did not reinforce the royal authority – quite the contrary; it was perceived by some as the swansong of absolute monarchy.[40]

Before the end of the *Ancien Régime*, France was seen as a divided artificial entity in search of a natural and unifying identity that the king could no longer incarnate: 'The French, until now an instituted aggregation of disunited peoples', claimed Mirabeau to celebrate the Revolution.[41] The historian David Bell proposed the idea that 'the architects of nationalism in eighteenth-century France were attempting, in a serious way, to address one of the great problems of modernity: how to keep their community from tearing itself apart'.[42] But such a search was not only reactive, out of fear of dismemberment or, as in today's nations, out of resentment against globalisation, deregulation and immigration. It was also socially creative: it was about nation-building and producing the reality of the nation itself while defining its ideology.

As the doctor removed a disease from a body, or as a botanist pruned her trees, revolutionary minds felt it was necessary to diminish the influence of power- and autonomy-driven intermediary groups – religious orders, aristocratic circles, labour corporations – if a strong bond and loyalty to the greater body of the nation was to be created. If pre-revolutionary nationalist metaphors were often naturalistic, it was perhaps because political harmony was to be the reflection of a universal harmony:

> A river is swollen by the waters of smaller rivers, which are themselves formed by an infinity of small streams: a natural image of society, as it should be. A great river divided into an infinity of small streams fleeing from their source, that weaken it incessantly, and seem to make efforts never to return to the river: an all too faithful image of society as it is. The public good is the object of the praises of all individuals, and a prey to their greed. It is a centre where it is said that everything should converge, but towards which no one goes.[43]

The atmosphere of the Enlightenment was not idealistic about humans in society, who were often seen as driven by self-interest and cupidity, but it was hoped, somewhat irrationally, that the vices of small groups would be redeemed by the national cause and a rational form of patriotism. The public good – *res publica* – was presented as the most natural state of political affairs, and this rhetorical naturalisation of the nation was probably necessary to overthrow a regime based on the supernatural divinisation of monarchy.

In *Histoire des deux Indes*, first published in 1770 by Guillaume 'Abbé' Raynal with revisions by Diderot, d'Holbach and a handful of representatives of the French Enlightenment, the esprit de corps of selfish magistrates was opposed to the virtue of primitive tribes, thought to live closer to a natural form of rational honesty:

> Reason, who had not been, as among us, distorted by prejudices and violated by acts of force, played for them the role of our moral precepts and police orders. Concord and security were maintained without the intervention of

the government. Never were these two powerful instincts of nature wounded, the love of equality and of independence [. . .] Their public affairs are handled with a disinterestedness unknown in our governments, in which the good of the state is almost always done out of personal interest or out of esprit de corps. Among the savages, it is not uncommon to see an orator who received a majority of votes warn those who deferred to his counsel that another man is worthier of their trust.[44]

Such was the official discourse of French intellectuals before the Revolution: esprit de corps, associated with prejudice, violence, self-interest or group-interest, was contrasted with common decency, love of equality, honesty and disinterestedness. This was not a revolutionary discourse based only on scientific voluntarism, socio-technical innovation or creative destruction:[45] the insistence on nature and on the trope of the *bon sauvage* could even be interpreted as manifesting a form of conservatism or traditionalism, perhaps demonstrating the growing influence of Rousseau over the *Lumières*, for example via his *Discours sur l'origine et les fondements de l'inégalité*.[46]

Remembering Rousseau's metaphor of the social machine, one could claim that social disorder, for the *Philosophes*, was often the result of selfishness, unregulated ambition and corrupt esprit de corps, while nature in its totality was, more often than not, the model of a well-ordered system: a clock for Voltaire, a healthy and robust tree for D'Alembert, a powerful machine for La Mettrie.[47] True enough, as the century went by, the idea of nature became more equivocal.[48] The Lisbon earthquake of 1755, for instance, had an negative impact on the representation of nature as harmonious and orderly.[49] What is certain is that strong analogies were drawn between natural and human realms: 'Ties between an objective natural order and our own human order were widely popularized in the eighteenth century.'[50]

Conceptions of harmony eventually diverged: general order could be primeval (lost and to be rediscovered), or derivative from chaos. An example of social philosophy based on the scheme of *ordo ab chaos*, Mandeville's influential *Fable of the Bees* – 'la fameuse fable des abeilles',[51] according to Voltaire – justified the paradox of a global social order emerging from local and particular divergences.[52] Human vices and individual unbalances produced, indirectly, a form of societal harmony:

As Mandeville was well aware, pride manifests individuals' desire to distinguish themselves from others. To satisfy that very desire, though, proud individuals need those others, specifically their admiration. Hence the very passion that aims at nothing but glorification of the individual does actually socialize. That it does so, is not at all that passion's goal; rather it is a necessary condition for reaching its goal. There may be many things you can have all by yourself; not so, however, the peculiar thing called recognition.[53]

The creation of a well-balanced, socialised group could be defined as the product of the mere sum of individual interests rather than as the result of a collective will. Under such views, quite opposed to Rousseau's, phenomena such as esprit de corps were the natural and beneficial conjunction of particular interests in search for rewards.

Conversely, *désintéressement*[54] was the idea according to which an individual could place a collective self, a *moi commun*,[55] above (or inside) himself, and act accordingly. In 1782, a contemporary of Raynal and Rousseau, the mathematician Nicolas de Condorcet, in his reception speech at the Académie française, expressed very critical views regarding esprit de corps, a notion that he also opposed to *désintéressement* and to the interests of the nation:

> I know that Monsieur de Montesquieu was an apologist for venal offices, and that the authority of a great name is quite powerful, especially when it is a mistake that it supports: but how weak are his reasons for defending such prejudice! [. . .] The venality of offices soon makes them hereditary; Tribunals become filled with ignorant and vain men, who disdain work and leave it to those in need of a fortune [. . .] it is soon not enough to earn the better positions, you have to be rich enough to buy them. Men born in the Tribunals [. . .] maintain and even strengthen the esprit de corps, this spirit so powerful over weak heads, over small souls, over corrupted men, over all those who cannot have either an opinion or a strength of their own, over those who seek a pretext to cover their interested views, or whose vices need support: this esprit de corps, always separated from the interests of the Nation, becomes even more dangerous in a class of men whose first merit should be the purest disinterestedness.[56]

It is not a coincidence that such uncompromising criticism should come from a scientist. There was an echo here of Diderot's praise of rationality and epistemic vehemence against 'l'esprit de corps, qui est ordinairement petit, jaloux'.[57] Moreover, Condorcet's speech was pronounced before the very institutional Académie française: many members would have noticed the irony of referring to Montesquieu, who, as we have seen, was not only an *Académicien* until his death in 1755, but had indeed also satirised the esprit de corps of the Académie before his own election.[58]

As a researcher, Condorcet developed a decision-theory for the collective mind that is still much discussed today, some claiming that 'the Condorcet jury theorem accurately captures the basic ideas underlying Rousseau's notion of the general will'.[59] According to this probability theorem, the majority opinion on a yes/no question is, under certain conditions, 'almost certain to be the correct one'.[60] It is not my purpose to discuss the vast literature on Condorcet's theorem and its relation to political thought – we must note, however, that Condorcet's intention, 'to counter-balance the interests and passions of different societies [*corps*]',[61] echoed Rousseau's intuition, formulated in the following manner:

> If, when a sufficiently informed people deliberated, the Citizens had no communication between them, the great number of small differences would always

result in the general will, and the deliberation would always be good. But when cliques are organised, partial associations at the expense of the greatest union, the will of each of these associations becomes general with respect to its members, and particular with respect to the State; we can then say that there are not as many voters as men, but only as many voters as associations. The differences become fewer and give a less general result. Finally, when one of these associations is so large that it overrides all the others, you no longer have a sum of small differences, but a single difference; then there is no longer any general will, and the opinion that prevails is only a particular opinion. It is important, therefore, in order to determine the statement of the general will, that there is no partial society in the State, and that every citizen should only think according to himself.[62]

This was a rationalist explanation – apparently backed up by Condorcet's mathematical results – for the pre-revolutionary disapproval of esprit de corps. Rousseau showed that he was aware of the law of large numbers, known since the early eighteenth century,[63] and still discussed in current studies in collective intelligence.[64]

One should, however, refrain from equating a quantitative justification of democracy with Rousseau's ultimately qualitative defence of it. For him, 'the general will is distinct from the sum of private wills'.[65] Rousseau's choice of the notion of will posits the body politic on an intellectualist ground rather on quantitative results. Arguably, his association of the general will with a 'common me' suggests the postulation of a collective mind modelled on the personal self. In the Social Contract, the discovery of the general will 'seems to precede the body politic itself, a little as, in the Cartesian meditations, the discovery of the cogito preceded that of the existence of the ego, which discovers itself first and foremost as a disembodied spirit'.[66]

Descartes' cogito was a psycho-philosophical event in modern history: I am a 'thing that thinks', a spirit [esprit].[67] Rousseau seemed to believe that democracies needed to nurture a supra-Cartesian mind, an esprit du corps de l'État to prevent the factions of intermediary esprit de corps. Could a democracy be considered as a collective cogito? Democracy does hold at least an implicit belief in a form of general will, presupposed by the voting system: we generally agree or tolerate that a certain sum of voters create a percentage result that is not only, according to Austin's analytical terminology, a constative, but also a performative: 'To utter the sentence (in, of course, the appropriate circumstances) is not [. . .] to state that I am doing it: it is to do it.'[68] To vote is a collective speech act that can change the name of a president, the composition of a parliament, the management of polities. Modern democracies and their mass media commonly presuppose that a majority of citizens, the electoral body, can express the spirit of a nation, a sort of collective mind that becomes self-aware, once the ballots are counted, in the form of a personification: Scotland chooses such and such a politics, for instance.

Capitalism versus Esprit de Corps: The Suppression of the *corps de métiers*

The eighteenth-century discourse against non-national esprit de corps was part of a strong critique of dynastic and ecclesiastic principles, but it also had a deleterious social effect on labour guilds. In 1776, in an attempt to counter a financial crisis, Louis XVI, advised by his minister Turgot, a close friend of Condorcet,[69] decreed a royal edict that was intended to dismantle labour *corporations* in the name of laissez-faire, freedom of trade and a certain deregulation of production. In this official text, the esprit de corps of the *communautés d'arts et métiers*[70] was accused of generating monopolies, rigidities and autonomies that challenged the economic wealth and financial control of the kingdom. This initiated a process by which the *corporations* would eventually be abolished by the *décret d'Allarde* (1789) and the Le Chapelier law (1791):[71] 'The blow struck by Turgot had been fatal to the corporations [. . .] The esprit de corps had been broken in them. It could not wake up under Necker, under the Revolution, under the Empire, nor under the Restoration.'[72]

For centuries, the *corps de métiers* had been labour and trade communities with specific rights and duties. For instance, in Paris in 1585, wine sellers and innkeepers were involved in a dispute with vinegar makers. The latter criticised the converting of soured wine into cheap vinegar, a practice that competed with the sale of patented vinegar.[73] Since the official vinegar producers were organised as a *corps* protected by *lettres patentes* of the king, a royal privilege of exclusivity, they won the dispute. In response, the wine sellers and innkeepers, who were not a unified society yet, asked Henri III to institute them 'en corps, confrairie et communauté'.[74] The Communauté des marchands de vins à pots, taverniers, cabaretiers et hôteliers was thus initiated by the Parlement de Paris in 1587.[75] They could not make vinegar but enjoyed a privilege of distribution over wine, began to follow written rules of self-regulation, and agreed on standard working conditions, salaries, apprenticeships, protocols of production, protection of widows, etc. The economic aspect of esprit de corps was institutionally induced.

Trade fellowships protected by the king were a ubiquitous feature during the *Ancien Régime*.[76] The corporations included various types of artisans or merchants performing mechanical or artisanal crafts: drapers, grocers, mercers, furriers, hosiers, goldsmiths, shoemakers, carpenters, wine sellers and hotelkeepers.[77] Craftsmen who had undergone a certain period of apprenticeship operated in workshops, supervised by a master who was often assisted by his wife. These activities required sizeable capital investment in wages, tools, raw materials, stock, furnaces, ovens, forges and human muscle.[78] It was expected that the workers would remain faithful to their master or guild. In return, the work of the *gens de métier* implied a certain 'stability of employment, the sense of community, and a legal social standing'.[79]

The idea of labour was still linked with the traditional Christian connotations of pain, burden and penitence.[80] Following Arendt, we could understand the organisation of labour guilds as an attempt 'to eliminate [painful] labour and necessity altogether'.[81] A relative alleviation of distressing labour is, in Arendt's view, a condition for a civilised world: 'Absence of pain is no more than the bodily condition for experiencing the world; only if the body is not irritated and, through irritation, thrown back upon itself, can our bodily senses function normally, receive what is given to them.'[82] Being part of an organised social body might have been a dignifying step towards a partial liberation of the worker from a vulnerable state, a non-protected submissive state in which one was isolated, taxed and manipulated at will, 'taillable et corvéable à merci'.[83] Institutionalised bodies were a device that did not radically eliminate the vulnerability and pain inherent in work, but tended to lighten it by providing some peace of mind and a degree of comfort. We must be cautious not to idealise the pre-industrial era, yet it is likely that the *communautés d'arts et de métiers* allowed at least some of their members, if not all, to shift their existence from that of an *animal laborans* to that of a *homo faber*.[84] This is how Arendt approaches the idea of the 'body politic': politics and incorporated work, because they are collective and therefore do not die with the individual's death, confer a kind of symbolic immortality and set aside the ordeals of individual bodily needs and fears, allowing for socially constructive action instead of animal-like reaction and egocentric survival behaviour.

Collective bodies were from this perspective a sublation or sublimation of the individual body, and esprit de corps an overcoming of individual fragility. Monarchic corporations allowed for a partial human spiritualisation, some form of escape from the mortal and suffering processes of bare and deregulated life. Fierce competition was softened by the monopolies or oligopolies guaranteed by royal protection to the *corps de métiers*, even if this presupposed on the other hand the segregation and exclusion of those who did not belong to such a body. Because the king and the working *corps* were interdependent and formed one system, Louis XVI's desperate manoeuvre to suppress the *corporations* via his laissez-faire minister seems retrospectively suicidal. And indeed, it preceded the end of French royalty by little more than a decade.[85] Capitalism and traditional esprit de corps were at odds.

All had not been idyllic in the world of economic esprit de corps: labour and trade communities experienced much internal conflict and malfunction in the decades before they were suppressed. The relationship between apprentices and masters had become openly problematic and antagonistic.[86] The *corps de métiers* were simultaneously units of enduring solidarity and hierarchical, sometimes punitive, closed institutions:

> Nor was there anything paradoxical, in the culture and society of the old regime, about this combination of hierarchy, surveillance, particularism, and solidarity. The very word '*corps*', or body, which was used to designate a bewildering variety of institutions in seventeenth- and eighteenth-century France, necessarily implied all of these characteristics [. . .] Each body was distinct from every other, with its own will, its own interests, its own internal order, and its own esprit de corps.[87]

External and internal competition, if softened by cooperation and regulation, was not eradicated by a somewhat antagonistic system of *corporations*. The private laws of the *corps de métiers* generated privileges and submissions – *privilegium* in Latin derives from *private* and *law*. One had to play by the rules, and those could be opaque and difficult for those situated at the bottom of the ladder.

In 1791, the *décret d'Allarde* officially designated the royal *corporations* as ene-mies of the Revolution and commercial freedom: 'It will be possible for any person to trade in anything or to have any profession, art or craft as desired; but one will be required to comply [. . .] with present or future police regulations.'[88] The mention of police control was significant, and one may conclude: 'The Revolution left the individual face to face with the State, unprotected by inter-mediary corporate bodies – the buffering institutions.'[89]

Common Good: Revolution and the 'Adunation' of Society

In the two last decades of the eighteenth century, the ambivalence that charac-terised the notion of esprit de corps was accentuated. Never in French history was the phrase *esprit de corps* more heard than in 1789 and the surrounding years. The phenomenon was deemed detestable when it qualified privileged and autonomous communities, but desirable when these communities served the general interest of the republican state:

> Of all the passions, one of the most violent is that which is called *intérêt de corps, esprit de corps*; and as it is a property of extreme things to do much good or bad, the esprit de corps, in relation to the general society, is the best or the worst principle. Is a body so constituted that its interests are in accord with the interests of other bodies and the entire state? The esprit de corps is then an excellent thing. Does it have a contrary constitution? The esprit de corps is then detestable.[90]

France's new nation was an 'imagined community' and one of its ideals was national or 'official' esprit de corps, 'i.e. something emanating from the state and serving the interests of the state first and foremost'.[91] The source of esprit de corps was now identified as a passion rather than a habit or strategy.

Several publications prove that French revolutionary discourse used the phrase *esprit de corps* not only as something that should be avoided in the pejorative sense created by the *Philosophes*, but with growing faith regarding its cohesive potential, a view that was explicitly related to the military denotation of the phrase, and more implicitly to its religious aura. In 1788, Jean-Paul Rabaut Saint-Étienne, soon to be a third-estate deputy of the États généraux,[92] wrote:

> We all have a self-esteem that seeks to expand its relations to take ownership of everything it can pretend to achieve. It swells from all the glories that enter into the sphere in which it is placed, and prides itself with all that is other, but with some relation with the self. It is this self-esteem which is called esprit de

corps [. . .] When all these self-loves tend to a common good, the later acquires great strength: it is thus that, in our armies, the esprit de corps of the various regiments makes them perform miracles in a day of combat: but if the esprit de corps is in contradiction with the general interest, one sees only a confused clash of interests against interests, which shall end in plunder.[93]

Equated with the ambivalent virtue of *amour-propre*, somewhere between self-esteem, pride, self-interest and vainglory, esprit de corps was here presented as an unavoidable natural feature of the human psyche that ought to be channelled by a large common goal rather than eradicated. *Intérêt général* designated a national level of cohesion, and the reference to the military suggested this national esprit de corps was a combat asset against other nations, protective or offensive.

The idea that esprit de corps could be valuable in consolidating the power of the state was slowly gaining momentum. In 1789, in an open letter, Mirabeau insisted that esprit de corps, when observed in a society that was 'mal unie avec l'État', ill-adjusted with the state, diverged from the public spirit,[94] but he also implied that there could be a good, official esprit de corps. Within the new Assemblée nationale, the former kind of autonomist esprit de corps of privileged groups was often mentioned as the dangerous 'ennemi de l'esprit public',[95] but a new value of universalist, in the sense of national, esprit de corps was articulated. Synthesising the dialectical revolutionary views, Guillaume Grivel, a lawyer, wrote in 1789:

In the logic of bodies, everything that tends to reunion is useful, and all that leads to separation is harmful [. . .] The soldier must be welded and united. It is good that he should have an esprit de corps, which makes obedience honourable and prompt, command fair and careful, and authority modest and generous [. . .] The civil body is something else [. . .] if it has an esprit de corps, such spirit must be justice. If it allows itself to admit an unjust esprit de corps, it might [. . .] fall into arbitrariness and corruption [. . .] We believe we must confine ourselves to declaring that every esprit de corps is precious [. . .] but that it is very important that any particular esprit de corps be subordinated to the national spirit, which [is] the common and social spirit [. . .] It is essential that the various bodies established in the State, to ensure education, public safety and convenience, are all determined to cooperate in the union.[96]

Esprit de corps could be just if national, because 'union' was the new national necessity and republican incantation. An influential theorist and agent of the Revolution, Emmanuel Joseph Sieyès fervently called it 'adunation', 'the act of uniting and linking non-constituted fragments into one whole'.[97]

In his pamphlet *Qu'est-ce que le Tiers-État?*, the Abbé Sieyès called for a 'science of social order' and compared it to an art in which France should challenge the English, then still admired for their Bill of Rights.[98] Fifty years before Auguste Comte, Sieyès called this desired sociopolitical science 'sociologie', 'socionomie' or even 'socialisme'.[99] The idea of sociability, a human capacity

to cohabit harmoniously with other fellow humans, was already present in seventeenth-century French via the adjective *sociable*,[100] and the conception of a
somewhat mystical social body, of the unity of human societies considered as
a whole – different in quality from the sum of its members – was indeed not an
invention of the eighteenth century, but, as we have seen, a borrowing from
Christology and the classical Greek and Roman corpus. The notion of national
esprit de corps was a variation on the theme of social union.

In 1621, *Les oeuvres spirituelles*, a religious text on the triumph of 'social love'
[*l'amour social*],[101] identified three kinds of love: *conjugal*, *paternal* and *social*.
Social love was presented as the highest form of love because it reflected the idea
of 'infinite charity' and suggested a strong, family-like link among people.[102] As
early as the sixteenth century, the adjective *social* could be used in French in a
context that blended political and religious meanings.[103] The expression *corps
social* was most likely a Christian-influenced political concept, representing a
Catholic ideal, as evidenced by this religious text from 1612:

> The body of which Saint Gregory speaks when he says, *We are made a body of
> the Lord*, is not the essential body of Christ, but the body politic [*corps politique*]
> and Ecclesiastical of Christ, that is to say his Church, which is made the social
> and political body of Christ, by the participation that it has in its real and
> essential body, according to this sentence of Saint Paul, *We are several a same
> bread and the same body which partakes of a bread*.[104]

Much has been written on the political and humanist quality of Christianism.
In 1590, the Dominican monk Louis of Granada declared, in a variation on
Aristotle, that 'Man is a political, social and human animal' [*l'homme est un
animal politique, social et humain*].[105] In 1587, *Le Jardin de plaisir et récréation spirituelle* referred to the 'commune société des hommes', the common social nature of
man, and even suggested the possibility of a collective will:[106]

> [The envious is a] man [who] shows himself as distorted, and worse than ani-
> mals, which have a natural society, and do not envy one another: the man who
> is born social should love everything he sees in his companion [. . .] Because
> since we all tend to the same end by various ways, our will should be consistent
> in helping each other.[107]

In short, social cohesion could be thought of as both natural and divine, and a
'socialist' nation, to use Sieyès' new word, was not alien to the Christian ideal,
even if many revolutionaries, chief among them Sieyès himself, who was a Roman
Catholic abbé, would have proclaimed their anti-clericalism. 'At the beginning
French universalism derives from its relationship to the Church; it is, as it were,
borrowed from Catholicism (from the Greek *Katholikos*, "universal").'[108]

But because the new spirit of liberty also meant more individualism, deregulation and competition, it was not clear for all that there could be a national form
of esprit de corps without intermediary bodies, which would foster fraternity.

Hence for instance the warning published in the *Encyclopédie méthodique* as early as 1789:

> By destroying the esprit de corps, we replace it with selfishness, which is the most pernicious character and the most opposed to the general interest, as well as to the spirit of Christianity, which is a spirit of charity and fraternity.[109]

In theory, religious common interest is transnational in its horizon, indeed cosmological. But could one conceive of an esprit de corps of humanity? Some wondered if the new universalistic humanism was compatible with patriotism.

The *Déclaration des droits de l'homme et du citoyen* seemed like the pinnacle of the idea that a republican adunation of the French nation was led by a faith in society seen as a vast and in theory extensible human unit, in opposition to the social clusters of the *Ancien Régime*:

> Universalism, and never more so than its Enlightenment incarnation, was grounded in the belief that human nature, that is, rational human nature, was a universal impervious to cultural and historical differences. Transcultural, transhistorical human nature was posited as identical, beyond particularisms [. . .] *The Declaration of the Rights of Man and the Citizen* [. . .] articulated Frenchness onto universalism.[110]

Was this humanism or neo-colonialism? Rousseau had already sensed the modern discrepancy between cosmopolitanism and patriotism. He did appear to praise the 'great cosmopolitan souls, who cross the imaginary barriers which separate peoples, and who, like the sovereign being who created them, embrace the whole human race in their benevolence'.[111] But Rousseau did not think that humanity could be a practical political concept for the government of a nation – perhaps because of the perceived bellicose threat of other sovereignties. Transnational love was apparently not heroic enough to rule the world:

> The love of humanity gives many virtues, such as gentleness, equity, moderation, indulgence; but it does not inspire courage or firmness, etc. and does not give these virtues that surplus of energy which they receive from the love of the country, which elevates them to heroism.[112]

Universality was, for Rousseau, the prerogative of the religion of Christ, which dealt with *les hommes* rather than *les citoyens*:

> Perfect Christianity is the universal social institution [. . .] The science of salvation and the science of government are very different; to want the first one to embrace everything is a fanaticism of small-mindedness. Patriotism and humanity are two incompatible virtues [. . .] The legislator who wants them both will get neither one nor the other.[113]

In other words, Church and state should probably be separated. If humanism was, for Rousseau, a weak political project, this could perhaps be read – but was not at the time by the majority of the revolutionaries – as a condemnation by anticipation of the *Déclaration des droits* of 1789, applied uniformly to citizens and to *Man*, thus operating a fusion between natural law and civil law – not to mention the absence of *la femme* in these rights, criticised as early as 1791 by Olympe de Gouges.[114]

Some revolutionaries were passionate cosmopolitans 'with missionary fervour. Liberty, Equality, Fraternity were to be France's gifts to the world.'[115] The ambiguity of such universalism became concretely visible for example when the Assemblée debated the possibility of conferring honorary citizenship on foreigners:

> This proposal leads us to consider the coming National Convention as an assembly of legislators of the Universe [. . .] However, to belong to the French sovereign body remains the condition to be fulfilled to be eligible in such an assembly. [This] leads to the conception of the French sovereign as the body that permits the assimilation and giving of voice to the cosmopolites.[116]

During that debate, which would eventually clarify the legal possibility of a French nationality of honour, deputy Pierre Victurnien Vergniaud claimed triumphantly: 'It is not for us alone, it is not for this part of the globe that is called France, that we have conquered liberty.'[117] In other words, France was seen as the centre of the universe, a nation above nations. Premonitory of Napoleonic imperialism was the will of a part of the universe to legislate the entirety of it.

Notes

1. 'L'esprit de corps, comme l'esprit particulier, ne devrait être que la raison; mais les passions prennent le masque de la raison, et jouissent de ses droits [. . .] La raison dit que pour plaire dans la société, il faudrait un jugement sain, un cœur droit, un mérite solide, et surtout une grande modestie. Il est triste que la raison soit démentie par l'expérience.' Jean Soret, *Essai sur les mœurs* (Brussels, 1756), pp. 129, 81.
2. 'Presque toujours un esprit d'ambition, d'orgueil, d'illusion et de vertige. L'esprit de corps est la manie des esprits faux ou des esprits faibles.' Ibid., p. 80.
3. Pierre Peyronnet, 'François Le Prévost d'Exmes', in *Dictionnaire des journalistes 1600–1789*, <http://dictionnaire-journalistes.gazettes18e.fr/journaliste/499-francois-le-prevost-dexmes> (accessed 19 September 2019).
4. 'Expliquez-moi, je vous prie, me disait l'autre jour un Etranger, comment chez une Nation qui porte le point d'honneur (permettez-moi le terme) jusqu'à la folie; il peut se trouver des gens qui portent la bassesse tout aussi loin [. . .] Votre étonnement est à sa place, lui répondis-je, et je conviens que c'est là l'énigme de la France. Cependant si l'on fait réflexion que le point d'honneur n'est souvent qu'un esprit de corps, qui frappant vivement l'imagination de chaque membre, l'élève au-dessus de lui-même pour participer à la gloire de tous; si on remarque que l'âme la plus faible acquiert un renfort dont elle n'était pas capable auparavant, et qu'elle doit

principalement aux regards de ses associés et de ses rivaux fixés sur elle; on verra qu'il est conséquent qu'un homme jeté hors de son corps, s'il se trouve affranchi de tout lien d'honneur, s'il regarde le nom de patrie comme une chimère, soit rendu dès ce moment à lui-même, et ne craigne plus l'ignominie.' François Le Prévost d'Exmes, *La revue des feuilles de Mr. Fréron, Lettres à Madame de **** (London, 1756), pp. 181–3.

5. Peyronnet, 'François Le Prévost d'Exmes'.

6. Benedict Anderson, *Imagined Communities: Reflections on the Origin and Spread of Nationalism* (London: Verso, 1991).

7. Matthew Levinger, 'La rhétorique protestataire du Parlement de Rouen (1753–1763)', *Annales: Économies, Sociétés, Civilisations* 3 (1990), pp. 589–613 (p. 596).

8. Hamish Scott, 'The Seven Years War and Europe's *Ancien Régime*', *War in History* 18.4 (2011), pp. 419–55.

9. 'Remontrances du parlement de Metz au sujet de ce qui s'est passé en Bretagne, 15 Mai 1765', in *La clef du cabinet des Princes de l'Europe* (Luxembourg: Chevalier, 1765), vol. CXXIII, p. 22.

10. 'L'esprit de patriotisme est en grand ce qu'est en petit l'esprit de corps. [. . .] Le premier incorpore le citoyen dès sa naissance à la gloire acquise par les ancêtres [. . .]. Le second renforce la trempe d'arme de celui qui est agrégé, et lui met devant les yeux la réputation d'un corps dont il devient membre, et dont il doit soutenir l'honneur.' Ibid., p. 22.

11. 'L'amour de la patrie tient aux avantages qu'elle procure; et ces avantages sont, Sire, les franchises et immunités des Provinces. L'intérêt général est la chaîne qui lie tous les citoyens; la rupture de cette chaîne cause nécessairement la dissolution de toutes les parties qui forment l'État. Amour de la Patrie, intérêt général, droits nationaux, mots synonymes, ou idées conséquentes; puisque l'amour de la patrie est né de l'amour de soi-même; puisque l'intérêt général est l'art du législateur, qui réunit le bien particulier au bien général.' Ibid., p. 24.

12. Jean Egret, *La pré-Révolution française, 1787–1788* (Paris: Presses Universitaires de France, 1962), pp. 338–51.

13. Rebecca Kingston, *Montesquieu and the Parlement de Bordeaux* (Geneva: Droz, 1996).

14. Richard Koebner, 'The Authenticity of the Letters on the *esprit des lois* attributed to Helvétius', *Historical Research* 24.69 (1951), pp. 19–43.

15. 'L'esprit de corps nous envahit de toutes parts. Sous le nom de corps, c'est un pouvoir qu'on érige aux dépens de la grande société. C'est par des usurpations héréditaires que nous sommes gouvernés. Sous le nom de Français il n'existe que des corporations d'individus, et pas un citoyen qui mérite ce titre [. . .] et notre ami Montesquieu, dépouillé de son titre de sage et de législateur, ne sera plus qu'homme de robe, gentilhomme et bel-esprit. Voilà ce qui m'afflige pour lui et pour l'humanité.' 'Lettre de Helvétius à Saurin', in *Œuvres complètes d'Helvétius*, 5 vols (Paris: Servière, 1795), vol. V, p. 219.

16. Richard Olson, *Science Deified and Science Defied: The Historical Significance of Science in Western Culture*, 2 vols (Berkeley: University of California Press, 1990), vol. I, p. 255.

17. 'Si je m'étais trompé, et si, contre mon attente, quelques-uns de mes principes n'étaient pas conformes à l'intérêt général, ce serait une erreur de mon esprit, et non pas de mon cœur.' Claude Adrien Helvétius, *De l'Esprit* (Paris: Durand, 1758), préface, p. ij.

18. John O. Lyons, *The Invention of the Self, The Hinge of Consciousness in the Eighteenth Century* (Carbondale, IL: Southern Illinois University Press, 1978).

19. 'De quelle conséquence ne serait-il pas qu'une Compagnie Souveraine fût empêchée d'agir pour l'intérêt général?' *Remontrances de la Cour Souveraine de Lorraine et Barrois au Roi* (Nancy: Charlot, 1755), p. 99.

20. Ibid., pp. 39–40, 99–100.

21. 'Il est nécessaire que ce qui fonde l'intérêt général contrarie le goût particulier.' Jean-Charles de Lavie, *Des corps politiques et de leurs gouvernements*, 3 vols (Lyons: Duplain, 1764–66), vol. III (1766), p. 165.

22. Karl Marx and Friedrich Engels, *The German Ideology*, trans. Richard Dixon and Clemens Dutt (Amherst, MA: Prometheus Books, 1976), p. 53.

23. 'S'il n'est pas impossible qu'une volonté particulière s'accorde sur quelque point avec la volonté générale, il est impossible au moins que cet accord soit durable et constant; car la volonté particulière tend, par sa nature, aux préférences, et la volonté générale à l'égalité.' Jean-Jacques Rousseau, *Du contrat social ou principes du droit politique* (Amsterdam: Rey, 1762), p. 48.

24. 'Chacun de nous met en commun sa personne et toute sa puissance sous la suprême direction de la volonté générale; et nous recevons en corps chaque membre comme partie indivisible du tout. À l'instant, au lieu de la personne particulière de chaque contractant, cet acte d'association produit un corps moral et collectif, composé d'autant de membres que l'assemblée a de voix, lequel reçoit de ce même acte son unité, son moi commun, sa vie et sa volonté.' Ibid., p. 29.

25. Ibid., p. 320.

26. Eric Desmons, 'Réflexions sur la politique et la religion, de Rousseau à Robespierre', *Revue française d'histoire des idées politiques* 1.29 (2009), pp. 77–93.

27. Rousseau, *Du contrat social*, p. 51.

28. Ibid., p. 29.

29. 'Il y a des états qui semblent changer la nature, et refondre, soit en mieux, soit en pis, les hommes qui les remplissent. Un poltron devient brave en entrant dans le régiment de Navarre. Ce n'est pas seulement dans le militaire que l'on prend l'esprit de corps, et ce n'est pas toujours en bien que ses effets se font sentir. J'ai pensé cent fois avec effroi que si j'avais le malheur de remplir aujourd'hui tel emploi que je pense en certains pays, demain je serais presque inévitablement tyran, concussionnaire, destructeur du peuple, nuisible au prince, ennemi par état de toute humanité, de toute équité, de toute espèce de vertu.' Rousseau, *Émile ou de l'Éducation*, p. 173.

30. Hannah Arendt, *Eichmann in Jerusalem: A Report on the Banality of Evil* (New York: Viking, 1963).

31. Rousseau, *Du contrat social*, p. 83.

32. 'Afin donc que le pacte social ne soit pas un vain formulaire, il renferme tacitement cet engagement qui seul peut donner de la force aux autres, que quiconque refusera d'obéir à la volonté générale y sera contraint par tout le corps: ce qui ne signifie autre chose sinon qu'on le forcera d'être libre; car telle est la condition qui donnant chaque Citoyen à la Patrie le garantit de toute dépendance personnelle; condition qui fait l'artifice et le jeu de la machine politique, et qui seule rend légitimes les engagements civils, lesquels sans cela seraient absurdes, tyranniques, et sujets aux plus énormes abus.' Ibid., p. 36.

33. Jacob Salmon, *The Origins of Totalitarian Democracy* (London: Mercury Books, 1919).

34. 'Pour que la loi puisse être l'expression de la volonté générale, il faut que le corps de

la nation exerce la souveraineté.' Anonymous, 'Du serment civique', *Révolutions de Paris, dédiées à la nation*, 27 (1790), p. 14.

35. Ayten Gündogdu, 'Potentialities of Second Nature: Agamben on Human Rights', in Crina Archer, Laura Ephraim and Lida Maxwell (eds), *Second Nature: Rethinking the Natural through Politics* (New York: Fordham University Press, 2013), p. 105.

36. Crina Archer, Laura Ephraim and Lida Maxwell, 'Politics in the Terrain of Second Nature', in Archer, Ephraim and Maxwell (eds), *Second Nature: Rethinking the Natural through Politics*, p. 14.

37. Bourdieu, *La Noblesse d'État*.

38. 'Les droits et les intérêts de la nation, dont on ose faire un corps séparé du monarque, sont nécessairement unis avec les miens et ne reposent qu'en mes mains.' 'Procès-verbal du lit de justice du 3 mars 1766', *Mercure historique de mars*, pp. 174–81, in Jean-Charles-Léonard Simonde de Sismondi, *Histoire des Français* (Paris: Treuttel and Würtz, 1842), vol. XXIX, pp. 360–4.

39. John 19:1, Mark 14:65, Matthew 27:26 (New Revised Standard Version).

40. Daniel Teysseire, 'Un modèle autoritaire: le discours de "la flagellation"', *Mots* 43.1 (1995), pp. 118–27 (p. 119).

41. 'Les Français, jusqu'alors agrégation instituée de peuples désunis.' Joseph Mérilhou, *Œuvres de Mirabeau, Discours et opinions*, vol. II (Paris: Dupont and Brissot-Thivars, 1825), p. 132.

42. David A. Bell, *The Cult of the Nation in France, Inventing Nationalism, 1680–1800* (Cambridge, MA: Harvard University Press, 2003), p. 21.

43. 'Un fleuve se grossit des eaux que lui portent les rivières, formées elles-mêmes d'une infinité de petits ruisseaux: image naturelle de la société, telle qu'elle doit être. Un grand fleuve divisé en une infinité de petits ruisseaux qui fuient loin de leur source, l'affaiblissent sans cesse, et semblent faire des efforts pour n'y jamais rentrer: image trop vraie de la société, telle qu'elle est. Le bien public est l'objet des éloges de tous les particuliers, et la proie de leur cupidité. C'est un centre où l'on dit bien que tout devrait aboutir, mais où personne ne tend.' Soret, *Essai sur les mœurs*, p. 79.

44. 'La raison, qui n'avait pas été comme parmi nous dénaturée par les préjugés et violée par des actes de force, leur tenait lieu de préceptes de morale, et d'ordonnances de police. La concorde et la sûreté se maintenaient sans l'entremise du gouvernement. Jamais il ne blessait ces deux puissants instincts de la nature, l'amour de l'égalité et celui de l'indépendance [. . .] Les affaires publiques y sont maniées avec un désin-téressement inconnu dans nos gouvernements, où le bien de l'état ne se fait presque jamais que par des vues personnelles ou par esprit de corps. Il n'est pas rare de voir un orateur sauvage qui était en possession des suffrages, avertir ceux qui déféraient à ses conseils, qu'un autre est plus digne de leur confiance.' Guillaume 'Abbé' Raynal, *Histoire philosophique et politique des établissements et du commerce des Européens dans les deux Indes* (La Haye, 1776), vol. VI, p. 20, ARTFL–Frantext, <http://artfl-project. uchicago.edu>.

45. Joseph Schumpeter, *Capitalism, Socialism, and Democracy* (New York: Harper and Brothers, 1942).

46. Jean-Jacques Rousseau, *Discours sur l'origine et les fondements de l'inégalité parmi les hommes* (Geneva: Rey, 1755).

47. 'L'univers m'embarrasse; et je ne puis songer | Que cette horloge existe, et n'ait point d'horloger.' Voltaire, 'Les Cabales', 1772, in *Oeuvres complètes de Voltaire* (Paris: Renouard, 1819), vol. XII, p. 219; D'Alembert, 'Caractère des sociétés ou

corps particuliers', p. 666; Julien Offray de La Mettrie, *L'Homme-machine*, in *Œuvres philosophiques*, ed. Francine Markovits, 2 vols (Paris: Fayard, 1987), vol. I.

48. Jacques Proust, 'L'idée de nature en France dans la première moité du XVIIIe siècle', *Annales Historiques de la Révolution Française* 178 (1964), pp. 478–88 (p. 480).

49. Theodore E. D. Braun and John B. Radner, *The Lisbon Earthquake of 1755: Representations and Reactions* (Oxford: Voltaire Foundation, 2006).

50. Andreas Dorschel, 'The Idea of Order: Enlightened Revisions', *Archiv für Rechts- und Sozialphilosophie* 98.2 (2012), pp. 185–96 (p. 185).

51. Voltaire, *Œuvres complètes* (Paris: Garnier, 1877–95), vol. XVII, p. 29.

52. Bernard Mandeville, *The Fable of the Bees, or, private vices, publick benefits* (London: Roberts, 1714).

53. Dorschel, 'The Idea of Order', p. 193.

54. Raynal, *Histoire des deux Indes*, p. 20.

55. Rousseau, *Du contrat social*, p. 29.

56. 'Je sais que la vénalité des Charges a eu Monsieur de Montesquieu pour apologiste, et que l'autorité d'un grand nom est bien puissante, surtout quand c'est une erreur qu'elle appuie: mais qu'elles sont faibles les raisons par lesquelles il défend ce préjugé! [. . .] La vénalité des Charges les rend bientôt héréditaires; les Tribunaux se remplissent d'hommes ignorants et vains, qui dédaignent l'étude et l'abandonnent à ceux qui ont leur fortune à faire [. . .] il ne suffit plus de mériter les premières places, il faut être assez riche pour les acheter. Les hommes nés dans les Tribunaux [. . .] y entretiennent, y renforcent même l'esprit de corps, cet esprit si puissant sur les têtes faibles, sur les petites âmes, sur les hommes corrompus, sur tous ceux qui ne peuvent avoir ni opinion ni force qui leur appartiennent, sur ceux qui cherchent un prétexte pour couvrir leurs vues intéressées, ou dont les vices ont besoin d'appui: cet esprit de corps, toujours séparé des intérêts de la Nation, devient plus dangereux encore dans une classe d'hommes dont le premier mérite devrait être le désintéressement le plus pur.' Nicolas de Condorcet, *Eloge de Michel de l'Hôpital, chancelier de France, discours présenté à l'Académie française en 1777* (Paris: Demonville, 1777), pp. 91–2.

57. Diderot, *Encyclopédie*, vol. V, p. 649.

58. Montesquieu, *Lettres persanes*, pp. 219–22.

59. Bernard Grofman and Scott L. Feld, 'Rousseau's General Will: A Condorcetian Perspective', *The American Political Science Review* 82.2 (1988), pp. 567–76 (p. 570).

60. Jason Wyckoff, 'Rousseau's General Will and the Condorcet Jury Theorem', *History of Political Thought* 32.1 (2011), pp. 49–62 (p. 51).

61. 'contre-balancer les intérêts et les passions des différents corps'; Condorcet, *Essai sur l'application de l'analyse à la probabilité des décisions rendues à la pluralité des voix* (Paris: Imprimerie Royale, 1785), p. iij.

62. 'Si, quand le peuple suffisamment informé délibère, les Citoyens n'avaient aucune communication entre eux, du grand nombre de petites différences résulterait toujours la volonté générale, et la délibération serait toujours bonne. Mais quand il se fait des brigues, des associations partielles aux dépends de la grande, la volonté de chacune de ces associations devient générale par rapport à ses membres, et particulière par rapport à l'Etat; on peut dire alors qu'il n'y a plus autant de votants que d'hommes, mais seulement autant que d'associations. Les différences deviennent moins nombreuses et donnent un résultat moins général. Enfin quand une de ces associations est si grande qu'elle l'emporte sur toutes les autres, vous n'avez plus pour résultat une somme de petites différences, mais une différence unique; alors il n'y a plus de volonté générale, et l'avis qui l'emporte n'est qu'un avis particulier. Il importe donc

pour avoir bien l'énoncé de la volonté générale qu'il n'y ait pas de société partielle dans l'Etat et que chaque Citoyen n'opine que d'après lui.' Rousseau, *Du contrat social*, pp. 58–9.

63. Ian Hacking, 'Jacques Bernoulli's *Art of Conjecturing*', *British Journal for the Philosophy of Science* 22.3 (1971), pp. 209–29.

64. Lu Hong and Scott E. Page, 'Groups of Diverse Problem Solvers Can Outperform Groups of High-ability Problem Solvers', *Proceedings of the National Academy of Sciences of the USA* 101.46 (2004), pp. 16385–9.

65. Wyckoff, 'Rousseau's General Will and the Condorcet Jury Theorem', p. 51.

66. 'semble précéder le corps politique lui-même, un peu à la manière dont, dans les *Méditations cartésiennes*, la découverte du *cogito* précédait celle de l'existence du moi, lequel se découvre d'ailleurs d'abord et avant tout comme esprit désincarné'; Berns and Frydman, 'Généalogie de l'esprit de corps', p. 179.

67. René Descartes, *Méditations métaphysiques* (Paris: Camusat & Petit, 1647), p. 22.

68. John Langshaw Austin, *How to Do Things with Words* (Cambridge, MA: Harvard University Press, 1975), p. 6.

69. Nicolas de Condorcet, *Vie de Monsieur Turgot* (Paris or London, 1786), p. 7.

70. Louis XVI, *Édit du Roi: portant suppression des communautés d'art & métiers ci-devant établies dans les villes du ressort du parlement de Paris* (Versailles: Imprimerie Royale, 1777).

71. Steven L. Kaplan, *La fin des corporations*, trans. Béatrice Vierne (Paris: Fayard, 2001); René de Lespinasse, *Les métiers et corporations de la ville de Paris du XIVe au XVIIIe siècle* (Paris: Imprimerie Nationale, 1886).

72. 'Le coup frappé par Turgot avait été mortel pour les corporations [. . .] L'esprit de corps avait été brisé en elles. Il n'a pu se réveiller ni sous Necker, ni sous la Révolution, ni sous l'Empire, ni sous la Restauration.' Léon Say, *Turgot* (Paris: Institut Coppet, 2014 [1887]), p. 142.

73. François Olivier-Martin, *L'organisation corporative de la France d'ancien Régime* (Paris: Sirey, 1938), pp. 205–10.

74. Luc Bihl-Wilette, *Des tavernes aux bistrots, une histoire des cafés, Lausanne* (Lausanne: L'Age d'Homme, 1997), p. 33.

75. *Dictionnaire Universel de Commerce* (Geneva: Cramer and Philibert, 1742), p. 1214.

76. William H. Sewell, Jr, *Work and Revolution in France: The Language of Labor from the Old Regime to 1848* (Cambridge: Cambridge University Press, 1980), p. 13.

77. Alfred Franklin, *Dictionnaire historique des arts, métiers et professions exercés dans Paris depuis le treizième siècle* (Paris: H. Welter, 1906), pp. 63–5, 211–13, 291–6, 520–2.

78. Sewell, *Work and Revolution in France*, p. 19.

79. Steven L. Kaplan, 'Réflexions sur la police du monde du travail, 1700–1815', *Revue Historique* 261 (1979), pp. 17–77 (p. 20).

80. 'Travail', *Dictionnaire de l'Académie française* (1694), ARTFL-Frantext, <https://artflsrv03.uchicago.edu/philologic4/publicdicos/navigate/4/8207/> (accessed 19 September 2019).

81. Arendt, *The Human Condition*, p. 87.

82. Ibid., p. 110.

83. Georges Lefranc, *Histoire du travail et des travailleurs* (Paris: Flammarion, 1957), p. 150.

84. Arendt, *The Human Condition*, p. 139.

85. Jean-Michel Gourden, *Gens de métiers et sans-culottes: Les artisans dans la Révolution* (Paris: Créaphis, 1988), p. 29.

86. Thierry Hamon, 'Corporations et compagnonnage en Bretagne d'Ancien Régime', *Mémoires de la Société d'Histoire et d'Archéologie de Bretagne* (Rennes: SHAB, 1999), vol. LXXVII, pp. 165–221.

87. Sewell, *Work and Revolution in France*, p. 36.

88. 'Il sera libre à toute personne de faire tel négoce ou d'exercer telle profession, art ou métier qu'elle trouvera bon; mais elle sera tenue de se [. . .] conformer aux règlements de police qui sont ou pourront être faits.' 'Décret portant suppression des maîtrises et jurandes, article 7, Séance à l'Assemblée du 2 mars 1791', *Archives parlementaires de 1787 à 1860*, ed. Jérôme Madival and Émile Laurent (Paris: Centre national de la Recherche Scientifique, 1961), vol. XXIII, p. 626.

89. William Rogers Brubaker, 'The French Revolution and the Invention of Citizenship', *French Politics and Society* 7.3 (1989), pp. 30–49 (p. 46).

90. 'De toutes les passions, l'une des plus violentes est celle qu'on appelle *intérêt de corps*, *esprit de corps*; et comme c'est le propre des choses extrêmes de faire beaucoup de bien ou beaucoup de mal, l'esprit de corps, par rapport à la société générale, est le meilleur ou le pire des principes. Un corps est-il constitué de telle sorte que ses intérêts s'accordent avec les intérêts des autres corps et de l'état entier? L'esprit de corps est une chose excellente. A-t-il une constitution contraire? L'esprit de corps est détestable.' Joseph-Michel-Antoine Servan, *Doutes d'un provincial* (Lyons: Prault, 1784), p. 99.

91. Anderson, *Imagined Communities*, p. 159.

92. August Wilhelm Rehberg, *Recherches sur la Révolution Française*, trans. Lukas K. Sosoe (Paris: Vrin, 1998), p. 124.

93. 'Nous avons tous un amour-propre qui cherche à étendre ses rapports pour s'approprier tout ce à quoi il peut atteindre. Il s'enfle de toutes les gloires qui entrent dans la sphère où il est placé, et s'honore de tout ce qui n'est pas lui, pourvu qu'il ait quelque rapport avec lui. C'est cet amour-propre que l'on appelle esprit de corps [. . .] Quand tous ces amours-propres tendent à un bien commun, il acquiert une très-grande force: c'est ainsi que, dans nos armées, l'esprit de corps des divers régiments leur fait faire des prodiges dans un jour de combat: mais si l'esprit de corps est en contradiction avec l'intérêt général, on ne voit plus qu'un choc confus d'intérêts contre intérêts, qui doit finir par le pillage.' Jean-Paul Rabaut Saint-Étienne, *Considérations trés-importantes sur les intérêts du Tiers-État, adressées au peuple des Provinces, par l'Auteur de l'Avis Important sur le Ministère et sur l'Assemblée prochaine des États-Généraux* (1788), p. 22.

94. Mirabeau, *Courrier de Provence* (Paris: François, 1789), p. 33.

95. *Journal des débats et décrets de l'Assemblée Nationale* (Paris: Baudoin, 1790).

96. 'Dans l'esprit des corps, tout ce qui tend à la réunion est utile, et tout ce qui mène à la séparation est nuisible [. . .] Le militaire doit être soudé et réuni. Il est bon qu'il ait l'esprit de corps, qui rend l'obéissance honorable et prompte, le commandement égal et soigneux, l'autorité modeste et généreuse [. . .] Le corps civil est autre chose [. . .] s'il a un esprit de corps, cet esprit doit être la justice. S'il se permet d'en admettre un autre, celui-ci court risque [. . .] de déchoir jusqu'à l'arbitraire et à la corruption [. . .] Nous croyons nous devoir borner à dire que tout esprit de corps est précieux [. . .] mais qu'il importe infiniment que cet esprit de corps particulier soit subordonné à l'esprit national, qui [est] l'esprit commun et social [. . .] Il est essentiel que les différents corps institués dans l'État, pour veiller à l'instruction, à la sûreté et à la commodité publique, soient tous déterminés à coopérer à l'union.' Guillaume Grivel, *Mélanges de philosophie et d'économie politique* (Paris: Briand, 1789), pp. 291–6.

97. 'l'acte d'unir, de lier en un tout des fragments inconstitués'; Antoine de Baecque, *Le*

corps de l'histoire. Métaphores et politique 1770–1800 (Paris: Calmann-Lévy, 1993), p. 123.

98. Emmanuel Joseph Sieyès, Qu'est-ce que le Tiers-État? (Paris: Boucher, 2002), p. 25.

99. Jacques Guilhaumou, 'Sieyès et le non-dit de la sociologie: du mot à la chose', Revue d'histoire des sciences humaines 15 (2006), pp. 117–34.

100. Yair Mintzker, '"A Word Newly Introduced into Language": The Appearance and Spread of "Social" in French Enlightened Thought, 1745–1765', History of European Ideas 34.4 (2008), pp. 500–13.

101. Jean Boucher, Les œuvres spirituelles (Paris: Moreau, 1621), p. 50.

102. Ibid., p. 56.

103. Jean de la Maison-Neuve, Colloque social de paix, justice, miséricorde, et vérité pour l'heureux accord des très augustes rois de France et d'Espagne, quoted in Jacques-Charles Brunet, Manuel du libraire et de l'amateur de livres (Paris: Sylvestre, 1843), p. 823, and Catalogus officinalis (Frankfurt: Kopf, 1610), p. 70.

104. 'Le corps dont Saint Grégoire parle lorsqu'il dit, Nous sommes faits un corps du Seigneur, n'est pas le corps essentiel du Christ, mais le corps politique et Ecclésiastique de Christ, c'est-à-dire son Église, qui est faite le corps social et politique de Christ, par la participation qu'elle a à son corps réel et essentiel, suivant cette sentence de Saint Paul, Nous sommes plusieurs un même pain et un même corps qui participons d'un pain.' Jacques Davy Duperron, Traité du Saint Sacrement de l'Eucharistie (Paris: Estiene, 1612), p. 627.

105. Louis of Granada, L'exercice spirituel pour tous les jours de la semaine, trans. François Primault du Mans (Lyons: Pillehotte, 1590), p. 277.

106. Pierre Crespet, Le Jardin de plaisir et récréation spirituelle (Paris: Nouë, 1587), vol. II, pp. 94, 187.

107. '[L'envieux est un] homme [qui] se montre comme dénaturé, et pire que les bêtes, lesquelles ont une société naturelle, et ne portent point d'envie les unes aux autres: l'homme aussi qui est né social, devrait aimer tout ce qu'il voit en son compagnon [. . .] Car puisque nous tendons tous à une même fin, par divers exercices, les volontés devraient être conformes, et s'entraider.' Crespet, Le Jardin de plaisir et récréation spirituelle, vol. I, p. 48.

108. Schor, 'The Crisis of French Universalism', p. 43.

109. 'En détruisant l'esprit de corps, on lui substitue l'égoïsme, caractère le plus pernicieux et le plus opposé à l'intérêt général, aussi bien qu'à l'esprit du Christianisme, qui est un esprit de charité et de fraternité.' Nicolas Sylvestre Bergier, 'Communautés ecclesiatiques', in Encyclopédie méthodique, 26 vols (Paris: Panckoucke, 1782–1832), vol. XV (1789), p. 384.

110. Schor, 'The Crisis of French Universalism', p. 44.

111. 'grandes âmes cosmopolites, qui franchissent les barrières imaginaires qui séparent les peuples, et qui, à l'exemple de l'être souverain qui les a créés, embrassent tout le genre humain dans leur bienveillance'; Rousseau, Discours sur l'origine et les fondements de l'inégalité, p. 139.

112. 'L'amour de l'humanité donne beaucoup de vertus, comme la douceur, l'équité, la modération, l'indulgence; mais il n'inspire point le courage ni la fermeté, etc. et ne leur donne point cette énergie qu'elles reçoivent de l'amour de la patrie qui les élève jusqu'à l'héroïsme.' Rousseau, 'De la patrie', in Œuvres complètes, 5 vols (Paris: Bibliothèque de la Pléiade, 1969), vol. III, p. 536.

113. 'Le parfait christianisme est l'institution sociale universelle [. . .] La science du salut et celle du gouvernement sont très différentes; vouloir que la première embrasse

tout est un fanatisme de petit esprit. Le patriotisme et l'humanité sont deux vertus incompatibles [. . .] Le législateur qui les voudra toutes deux n'obtiendra ni l'une ni l'autre.' Rousseau, *Lettres écrites de la montagne* (Amsterdam: Rey, 1764), p. 32.

114. Benoîte Groult, *Ainsi soit Olympe de Gouges: la déclamation des droits de la femme et autres textes politiques* (Paris: Grasset, 2013).

115. Brubaker, 'The French Revolution and the Invention of Citizenship', p. 41.

116. 'Cette proposition conduit à considérer la Convention nationale à venir comme une assemblée de législateurs de l'Univers [. . .] Cependant, appartenir au corps souverain français reste la condition à remplir pour être éligible dans une telle assemblée. [Ce qui] conduit à concevoir le souverain français comme le corps qui permet d'assimiler et de donner la parole aux cosmopolites.' Sophie Wahnich, *La Révolution Française* (Paris: Hachette, 2012), p. 254.

117. 'Ce n'est pas pour nous seuls, ce n'est pas pour cette partie du globe, qu'on appelle France, que nous avons fait la conquête de la liberté.' *Archives parlementaires de 1787 à 1860*, ed. Jérôme Madival and Émile Laurent (Paris: Centre national de la Recherche Scientifique, 1961), vol. XLVIII, p. 688.

3

'We Must Hang Together': The English Appropriation of Esprit de Corps in the Eighteenth and Nineteenth Centuries

Exotic Flavour and Distinction: Linguistic and Semantic Observations

The migration of words from French into English was not rare in the eighteenth century: 'From the mid sixteenth century onwards the proportion fluctuates either side of 5%, reaching its highest point in the second half of the eighteenth century [9%].'[1] French was still

> widely viewed as the language of humanity [. . .] By virtue of the doctrine of *translatio imperii et studii*, France was seen as the heir to the Roman Empire, and French was viewed as the legitimate successor to the ancient universal language, Latin.[2]

A detailed analysis of the early English uses of the Gallicism will provide a comparative and transnational perspective.

Esprit de corps is a particularly successful case: it rapidly and sustainably spread into several European languages. In most of these it was progressively domesticated and partly replaced in the nineteenth or twentieth centuries by local loanwords (for example *kåranda* in Swedish, *anda* meaning spirit and *kår* meaning corps; or *Korpsgeist* in German, on the same principle).[3] In English, however, the signifier persisted *talis qualis*, an exact importation from the donor language, morpheme by morpheme. It is an extreme version of a loanword, what linguists call a 'foreign idiom' because of its untranslatability.[4] Other examples of similar borrowings from modern French, more or less popular today in English, are *entrepreneur, avant-garde, laissez-faire, enfant terrible, raison d'être, joie de vivre* and *je-ne-sais-quoi*.[5] In the terminology of translation studies, a borrowed word can either be 'domesticated' or 'foreignized'.[6] While domestication implies that the word or expression is modified to suit the host language – for example 'career' for the French *carrière*, or 'account' for *compte* – foreignisation supposes a stricter fidelity to the donor language, perhaps 'in order to keep a kind of exotic flavour'.[7]

This linguistic exoticism is not only motivated by aesthetic preoccupations, but also by its capacity to convey a sense or effect of distinction:

One of the main incentives for borrowing words is the prestige of the donor culture. That is, words are borrowed not (only) for lack of the term in the borrowing language but in order to express expertise, educational standing, modernity, economic success, cultural superiority [. . .] Pronouncing a loan-word with its foreign sounds intact could indicate affiliation with the donor culture even more strongly.[8]

The feeling of distinction is clearly an important aspect of esprit de corps, along with duty, drive and discipline. I mentioned the fact that esprit de corps in English is often associated today with the idea of a mysterious alchemy in a group's cohesion. It is possible that the use of a now old French signifier helps to reinforce in English this impression of a semi-magical superior virtue carried by some human associations. It is also possible that the use of the Gallicism has been functional in preventing the reference to a more negative and reductive idea, such as *conformity*, for example.

In the nineteenth century, as we will see, esprit de corps became intertwined with imperialism and colonialism, and the visionary George Orwell was conscious of it, as shown by his reference to 'the five chief beatitudes of the pukka sahib' or 'true gentleman' in the novel *Burmese Days*:

> Keeping up our prestige
> The firm hand (without the velvet glove)
> We white men must hang together,
> Give them an inch and they'll take an ell, and
> *Esprit de Corps*.[9]

Burmese Days describes the white colonial society of Upper Burma, and it was an early prototype for the critical description of the ruling elite of Oceania in *Nineteen Eighty-Four*.[10] The colonisers were themselves to a certain extent mentally colonised:

> Imperialism's code was pervaded by the sense that no one was irreplaceable and by the belief that all whites must follow in the same way the same code of behaviour [. . .] Any deviation might encourage the ruled to question the infallibility of the rulers, and (more dangerously) cause the rulers to question their own infallibility. The assumption of replaceability, together with the mandatory *esprit de corps*, often created an overwhelmingly feeling of being totally submerged by a changeless conformity – even if one was only *slightly* deviant from the norm.[11]

'Code of behaviour', 'replaceability', 'conformity', 'mandatory', 'norm': this semantic field is related to what was named, after Max Weber, the 'iron cage', in which esprit de corps was a form of domestication that created an internal mental police, where each member of the group became interested and active in the regulation and control of the community to which they belonged, a form of alienation that is sometimes called 'institutional normative isomorphism'.[12]

Recent studies in cognitive sociolinguistics indicate that 'necessary' loanwords, filling a lexical gap, tend to persist more successfully over time than 'luxury' loanwords introduced as an alternative for an already lexicalised concept.[13] The persistence and success of esprit de corps in modern English would indicate that it is a necessary idiom with no exact or previous equivalent in the host language. It is also possible that the English equivalent may be somewhat enclosed within the French signifier: there is a phonetic identity between 'corps' and 'core', and one of the early modern meanings of 'core' in English was precisely 'a body of individuals', itself derived 'from French corps':[14]

> It [core] is used by Bacon for a body or collection (from *corps*, French; pronounced core.) *He was more doubtful of the raising of forces to resist the rebels, than of the resistance itself; for that he was in a core of people whose affections he suspected.* Bacon, Hen VII [1621].[15]

The 1828 edition of *Webster's Dictionary* gave 'a body' as a definition of core, but added in square brackets: 'not used': by then a more common use of core was 'the heart or inner part of a thing', perhaps under the influence of the French *cœur*.[16] Nevertheless, a simple Google search on the expression 'a core of people' still retrieves today hundreds of thousands of results in the sense of a group of people, often recent utterances. It would be reasonable to believe that the ambiguities of meaning heard in 'core' and 'corps' between body, group, platoon, heart and the idea of a central and foundational kernel partly explain the success of 'esprit de corps' in English. To this we can add the fact that *esprit* and *spirit* are not very distant orthographically, and therefore easily intuited by an averagely literate reader.

'Corps' was a familiar word in English in the eighteenth century. The rapid transnational dissemination of esprit de corps was perhaps facilitated by early modern usage of corps to designate a group of armed men. In 1598, a glossary of military terms published in London defined 'corps de guard' as 'the body of a watch, of a certain number of soldiers'.[17] 'Corps de guard' also appeared in seventeenth-century British dictionaries.[18] The military meaning of corps was elevated to the dignity of poetry when Joseph Addison celebrated in 1705 the English victories of John Churchill, Duke of Marlborough: 'In Heaps the Rolling Billows sweep away | And into Scythian Seas their bloated Corps convey.'[19]

To estimate with higher accuracy the level of integration of 'esprit de corps' into English lexis, we must ask precise questions regarding its currency: 'Is it used by the general population [. . .]? In which sorts of contexts is it found? Is it in general, everyday, unmarked use, or is it found only in formal or technical registers?'[20] As we will see, 'esprit de corps' belonged, in eighteenth-century English as in French, to what Olivia Smith called in *The Politics of Language* an 'intellectual vernacular language [. . .] an informal printed language capable of expressing political ideas'.[21] Informal did not mean vulgar:

Only the refined language was capable of expressing intellectual ideas and worthy sentiments, while the vulgar language was limited to the expression of the sensations and the passions [. . .] 'The vulgar and the refined', 'the particular and the general', 'the corrupt and the pure', 'the barbaric and the civilized', 'the primitive and the arbitrary', were socially pervasive terms that divided sensibility and culture according to linguistic categories.[22]

The notion of esprit de corps, even more so in English than in French, would become part of a specific social-class vocabulary: its enunciation proved an elitist affiliation and good education – even if it should not be reduced to such a function. To speak of esprit de corps was to take the perspective of the external rational analyst, the free-minded individual considering less individuated humans in groups. But it also betrays the expression of a nostalgia for a form of well-being relying on strong fellowship or like-mindedness, a *well-belonging*.

Bilingualism was a privileged vector for the migration of words or expressions: 'Bilinguals are typically assumed to be the agents of borrowing, the ones who use loanwords regularly and thus introduce them to the speech community.'[23] French was read *dans le texte* by a solid portion of the English literate population: from 1751 to 1800, there were almost as many editions of French-language manuals published in Great Britain (423) as in the rest of Europe (549 altogether for Germany, Italy, Spain, Flanders and Sweden).[24] One of these privileged bilinguals, among the first if not the first to refer to esprit de corps in an English document, was a friend of Voltaire, Lord Chesterfield.

Unavoidable Zeal: Early Propagation of Esprit de Corps in British English

On 26 June 1755, Philip Dormer Stanhope, 4th Earl of Chesterfield, wrote from Blackheath, near the Royal Observatory Greenwich, one of his regular letters to his friend Richard Chenevix, bishop of Waterford in Ireland. Referring to 'all churchmen of any religion', Chesterfield wrote:

> *Un esprit de corps* is too apt, though I believe often unperceived, to bias their conduct and inflame an honest, though too intemperate, zeal. It is the same in every society of men; for it is in human nature to be affected and warped by example and numbers.[25]

Esprit de corps was extreme zeal. Rather than an artificial graft, it was an inherent tendency of our social nature, the natural distension of individual minds produced by collective emulation. This essentialist and somewhat tolerant connotation of esprit de corps would become quite standard in English, with its implicit political consequences: if esprit de corps is natural, it cannot be eliminated. But it could be utilised. Chesterfield propagated a moderate, Voltairean idea of esprit de corps rather than the more unnerved version of d'Alembert or Diderot.

After his studies at Cambridge in the 1710s, Chesterfield travelled often, 'mainly in Paris. He was a great admirer of French manners, culture and taste [. . .] He was on familiar terms with [. . .] Voltaire.'[26] He 'frequented the society of men of letters in Paris'.[27] A proof of his close friendship with the author of *Candide* is a letter of 1771 that the older Voltaire sent to 'Milord Chesterfield' to offer him solace for his recent deafness: 'You have never been, in any activity, a charlatan or the fool of charlatans.'[28] It is probable that, before his letter of 1755, Chesterfield had read parts of the *Encyclopédie* and in particular its mentions of esprit de corps. As for Chenevix, understanding the phrase, even if it was the first time he had read it in print, was probably effortless: he 'was of French extraction, his parents having left their native country on the revocation of the Edict of Nantes'.[29]

If the anti-clerical sense of esprit de corps emigrated to England shortly after its French invention, it was in a more accommodating fashion, the religious context being different. Voltaire's influence on the migration of the term, including its initial variation between *de* and *du*, is confirmed in the 1759 English translation of his influential *Essai sur les mœurs*: 'There is what we call the *esprit du corps** that animates all societies.' The translator's footnote reads: 'The French give this name to that affection, which individuals have for the society, of which they are members.'[30] In this benign definition, esprit de corps became a pedestrian and universal group feeling, almost familial, felt by each individual, rather than the threatening quality of a corrupt group. This was consistent with Voltaire's entry on 'Esprit' in the *Encyclopédie*, in which esprit de corps was deemed ubiquitous and not as harmful as *esprit de parti*.

However, one should not conclude that early English uses were a unilaterally precocious orientation of the idea of esprit de corps towards the depoliticised, softened or apparently benevolent meanings that have become prevalent in today's global language. There were some decades of hesitation regarding the polarity of esprit de corps. The critical political uses were also known and practised in the second half of the eighteenth century on both English-speaking sides of the Atlantic, as we will see.

Perhaps the first clear and comprehensive English definition, still rather pessimistic, was proposed by Alexander Jardine, a British military lieutenant who visited France, Spain and Portugal in 1779:[31]

> Every society of human beings, be it a nation, a corporation, or a company, we know will act with a certain secret *esprit de corps*, or bias towards its own interests, against all mankind; and in a manner more unjust and unfeeling than individuals: and every corporate body, if not controlled, would tyrannize over all the rest. Hence the great difficulties of regulating the lesser bodies, of which the great one, the nation, consists; and of forming a system of government, wherein the different parts may not combine against the rest of the community.[32]

This eloquent definition not only confirms that the political version of esprit de corps was articulated in English soon after its French invention, it also combines the naturalistic point of view ('every society of human beings') with what we would call a holistic or emergent perspective, a view that considers that a group behaves in an autonomous way, different from the sum of its individual parts. This way could be mysterious or 'secret' – Chesterfield had already called it 'unperceived' – but more importantly it was recognised as potentially very cruel, more unjust and unfeeling than separated individuals.

Jardine, although he was an officer in the British army, did not define esprit de corps as a military device, but he did link it to an antagonistic tendency for conquest and violence, in a manner that echoed contemporary French debates. The author suggested that 'the best and most durable form of society is probably that which consists of the most complete system of mutual control'.[33] The author's model was the United Kingdom, in which a system of checks and balances, a plurality of reciprocally surveillant power groups, was considered the best rampart against tyranny. Although critical of esprit de corps even at a national level, Jardine did not propose its complete eradication, probably because esprit de corps was seen by him as not suppressible. This reflects the fact that in eighteenth-century English, intermediary bodies were often praised as the constituent elements of civil society and the condition of an active civic life. It is also an example of a cultural stereotype: Anglo-Saxon pragmatism and relativism versus French idealism and absolutism, the latter leading to what was infamously called 'nonsense upon stilts'.[34]

It is worth noting that in the last decades of the eighteenth century, in Prussia, Immanuel Kant was giving his lectures on ethics at the University of Königsberg, and his conception of esprit de corps was faithful to the critical spirit of the Encyclopédie:

There is a general love for every other person as such, for certain kinds of persons, and for the entire human race. Patriotism, the love of the fatherland, also belongs here, as does cosmopolitanism [. . .] Finally, there is also love for a particular group, or common obligation under a particular rule, to which there arises by custom a distinctive adherence [. . .] If we take the later association, it is obviously detrimental to the propensity for a general love of mankind; to the member thus associated, the class of men with whom he stands in no connection seems to become indifferent; he behaves as though he had separated himself from the generality of mankind, loses his allegiance thereto, and bends his moral endeavours solely in accordance with that Shibboleth to which he has subjected himself [. . .] Separatists and sectarians of every kind, clubbists, lodge-brothers, Herrenhuters and Pietists, are [. . .] destroyers of general goodwill and philanthropy; in brief a society may be aiming at a narrower bond, in regard to morals, politics or religion – its members' adherence to their sect, and the *esprit de corps* [in French in the German original][35] founded on this, make for an indifferentism towards the human race, which inhibits the dissemination of general human goodwill and prevents any communal participation for everyone. *Esprit de corps* leads the disposition away from objective moral principles, and reduces it merely to this subjective relationship as a foundation for one's actions; there comes to be prejudice in its favour and contempt for everything that is *profanum*.[36]

This is a severe criticism of esprit de corps, very much in the spirit of Diderot, d'Alembert or Condorcet. We will see that Hegel takes a more nuanced approach. There is some irony in Kant's suggestion, via the use of Latin, that the adherence group sees itself as sacred. There is also a form of reductive methodological individualism in supposing that esprit de corps is simply a subjective relationship. This can be seen as a contradiction, since the idea of 'general human goodwill' can itself proceed from an abstract sacralisation of humanity rather than empathy applied case-by-case: it has been often argued that Kant's objective, universalist moral principles could be unfair in concrete situations and make for indifferent-ism towards persons in the name of the abstract idea of the human race.[37] At any rate, Kant's puristic view would not be very influential in the nineteenth-century UK or USA, in which esprit de corps would be seen as a necessary evil, if an evil at all, a socially convenient middle way between individual isolation and idealistic universalism.

In the London of 1792 was published an early *History of the Revolution of France* which gave support to the idea that esprit de corps was unavoidable. It was a translation from Rabaut Saint-Etienne,[38] a leader of the French Protestants who would be guillotined in 1793.[39] In a chapter dealing with the États généraux of 1789, he wrote:

> Several of the members, the young magistrates particularly, had a real affection for liberty: they were sincere in demanding the convocation of the States-General: but the old magistrates had no other view in it, than the increase of their own power [. . .] None had really the public good at heart. It was necessary to save the State, and each was attentive to nothing but his own interest [. . .] Vain had been the hope [. . .] that this Assembly would assume the complexion of the national opinion: it was almost entirely composed of persons enjoying privileges. The *Esprit de Corps* presided in it, the *Esprit de Corps* prevailed in it.[40]

Such a dramatic personification of esprit de corps, enhanced by the capitalisation and the repetition, suggested that it was a powerful political and socio-natural force, if not the most powerful one. Yet the opposition between an idealistic lex-icon of feeling – 'real affection', 'sincere', 'heart' – versus the lexicon of effective agency – 'power', 'interest' and 'esprit de corps' – still suggested a Rousseauist ideal of politics.

English readers were exposed, if marginally, to the pessimistically lyrical French definitions of esprit de corps. An English translation of Mirabeau's *Des Lettres de cachet et des prisons d'État* urged in the name of liberty and 'public spirit': 'Let us steer clear of caprice, of envy, of the esprit de corps, that destructive bane of all sociality.'[41] Mirabeau explained that 'the esprit de corps, and the jealousy of different orders in the state support despotism'.[42] Esprit de corps for him was not purely natural, but cultural, produced by a specific political regime that followed a *divide and rule* strategy and that ought to be replaced by a really social republic.

London newspapers of the time sometimes hosted the phrase in its critical form, for example *The World* in 1788, or *The Oracle* in 1789: 'Some portion of an *Esprit de Corps*, some predilections for the privileges of their respective orders, might probably have infatuated the Nobles, the Clergy, and the Lawyers'[43] explained an article about the Austrian Netherlands. The critical political use of esprit de corps was also to be found across the British Empire, for example in newspapers such as the *Bombay Courier*.[44] In 1779, in Calcutta, a committee wrote a petition on behalf of the British inhabitants of Bengal, Bihar and Orissa: 'The *Esprit du Corps* which animates the Professors of the Law, and leads them to promote and maintain the Interests of the Profession in preference to all other Interests, is a Principle which may be prejudicial.'[45] Several sources correlated esprit de corps with the Bar, because 'success in this field was dependent upon some measure of patronage and favour'.[46] The lawyers' independence was regarded ambivalently, both internally and externally: 'Advancement to the elite was actually controlled by a combination of extra-professional patronage and aristocratic politics.'[47]

Was esprit de corps mostly a professional phenomenon? This was assumed by the philosopher Jeremy Bentham in 1789: 'The French expression, *esprit de corps*, for which as yet there seems to be scarcely any name in English, might be rendered [. . .] by the terms professional spirit, professional attachment, or professional zeal.'[48] However, the phrase also served to refer to the supposed superiority of a class or cast. The *Philosophical Reflections on the Late Revolution in France* metaphorically suggested in 1790 that 'the fighting *casts* are compelled to eat flesh [. . .] otherwise they would soon lose their courage and the *esprit de corps*, and merely degenerate into the tameness of mere citizens'.[49] The author, a former Irish officer in the British army and a Member of Parliament at Westminster, suggested that the French 'universal democracy' project, by destroying singular forms of esprit de corps, would create a domesticated and subservient population of fragile nationals. This very elitist view would be later shared by Alexis de Tocqueville and Friedrich Nietzsche in their critique of occidental democracies. For Kant and the like, esprit de corps was a backward state. For supercilious minds, it was democracy that was a regression, and esprit de corps the instinct of the dominant. Esprit de corps designated, for instance, the gentry's sense of superiority to the middle classes:

> There is, among the more elevated classes of society, a certain set of persons who are pleased exclusively to call themselves [. . .] *the fine world*. They have laws, immunities, privileges, and almost a language of their own; they form a kind of distinct *cast*, and with a sort of *esprit du corps* detach themselves from others, even in general society, by an affectation of distance and coldness; and only whisper and smile in their own little groups of the initiated; their confines are jealously guarded, and their privileges are incommunicable.[50]

This description was to be found in a book that presented itself as a manual on female education. It emphasised the use of *esprit du corps* rather than *esprit de corps* – not incorrect since the author was speaking of the specific style of a given social body – and the importance of verbal language and body language in the maintenance of class frontiers.

The ecclesiastical context of esprit de corps referred to by Chesterfield was nevertheless still remembered in England at the turn of the century, for example in a leisure magazine that offered a description of the alleged depravity of European Catholic monks:

> Let it be understood, that I speak of monks as a multitude, and acting in bodies. That there have been innumerable wise and virtuous individuals, who, secluded in cloisters, have devoted their lives and noble faculties to deep research and dignified labour, and to whom the human race will eternally remain indebted, every liberal-minded man will be proud to testify. But were these individuals satisfied with the scenes they witnessed? Did they approve the sloth, the sensualities, and the vices, by which they found themselves in some degree contaminated? Many of them, blinded by that *esprit de corps* of which the mind is so susceptible, acquiesced in silence.[51]

Beyond the commercial intention to entertain the reader by suggesting that Catholic monastic life had been a sort of restaging of Sodom and Gomorrah, the reference to esprit de corps here was faithful to the standard *Lumières* definition in opposing the spirit of individualist liberalism to the mental blinkers of subjugating collectives.

After 1800, critical uses of 'esprit de corps' in English became more rare. At the dawn of the nineteenth century, the phrase was to be found in novels in the more benign sense of peer-group complicity, for example gender solidarity in *Discipline* by the Scottish novelist Mary Brunton, the daughter of a British army officer:[52] '"Make yourself quite easy my dear Ellen," said Charlotte, with a provoking smile, "I have more esprit de corps than to tell a lady's secret."'[53] The expression amused writers such as Byron, who in a letter to fellow poet Thomas Moore asked for help, in the name of poets' solidarity, against a 'French lie' about him published in the *Gazette de France*:

> I won't bore you further now, than by begging you to comply with my request; and I presume the 'esprit du corps' (is it 'du' or 'de'? for this is more than I know) will sufficiently urge you, as one of '*ours*,' to set this affair in its real aspect.[54]

Us against them, and in this specific case the British poets against the French journalists, making it all the more exquisite to muse with the vocabulary of the enemy as a lexical weapon. Once again, Byron's literary instinct is right to hesitate between *du* and *de*, since in French *l'esprit de corps des poètes* would, in the spirit of the Enlightenment, designate their mimeticism, not a very poetical quality at all, while *l'esprit du corps des poètes* could refer, less idiomatically, to their specific values and dignity, such as the cult of singularity. But is it possible for an organised group to maintain creation and originality as their core value, or would it be a contradiction? In any case, the phrasing 'esprit de corps' was now widely preferred by English lexicographers, and became more and more twisted, in such a manner that its pejorative connotation became insignificant. In 1809, the *Dictionary of Quotations in Most Frequent Use* proposed the following definition: '*Esprit de Corps*. Fr. – "The spirit of the body." – that zeal for mutual honour which pervades every collective body, such as the gentlemen of the army, the bar, &c.'[55]

As for the more critical and political usage of the *Philosophes*, it was in the nineteenth century only remembered by an elite of authors, such as Walter Scott:

> Every step which a political adventurer makes in his advances into public life, convinces him how little unassisted and isolated talent is able to raise its possessor to the distinction of which he is laudably ambitious. At every turn a friend is to be acquired, or an enemy to be soothed and conciliated; the jealousy of party favours no man's views who does not place himself with entire devotion in its phalanx [. . .] This cold and pettifogging esprit de corps never disgusted us more than when the Spanish war has been the subject of discussion.[56]

The majestic plural *us* referred to Scott criticising the Whig writers of the *Edinburgh Review*, who had preached a policy of non-intervention against Napoleon.[57] The military metaphor of the phalanx suggested that social groups of influence were not unlike war machines. Scott was condemning partisanship and herd strategies with a hint of fatalism, but also to contrast them with independent and objective talent. Half a century after d'Alembert and Diderot, Scott saw himself as a defender of the life of the rational and republican spirit. More poignantly, like the famous Romantic character René created by Chateaubriand in 1802, he was realising that the hardly conquered intellectual liberty of the bourgeois intellectual could, if taken too seriously, mean loneliness and isolation in a modern world still governed by cliques and clans.

The Honour of a Nation: Official Debates about Esprit de Corps in the UK and the USA

In the eighteenth century, esprit de corps was a notion that infiltrated political debate at the highest level in both the British Empire and the emerging United States of America. In the House of Commons, references to esprit de corps were registered on several occasions; in 1777, Charles Lennox, Duke of Richmond and a military officer, declared in Parliament: 'I belong by much stronger ties to the nation, than to the army; and I hope the esprit de corps of an Englishman is still more prevalent in me.'[58] Two forms of esprit de corps were implicitly accepted: the military and the national. Lennox, who as Duke of Aubigny was also a French peer and had been British Ambassador Extraordinary in Paris in 1765,[59] meant that his defence of the withdrawal of British combat troops from America served the UK's interests. Even a military professional could understand the long-term benefits of peace and commerce.

In 1779, a general will aspect of esprit de corps was defended by MP James Martin in a speech in which the cronyism of the MPs was criticised:

> I may be allowed, Sir, to adopt a French military expression; I think we, as members of the British senate, want what they call l'esprit de corps; we have not that noble enthusiasm which should animate the representatives of the majesty of the people. Indeed, Sir, it is not to be wondered at that we should want that enthusiasm, if we consider the manner in which most of us are chosen into this assembly by every sort of undue influence, and with very little or no personal acquaintance with our constituents. But, Sir, a man in these days, who should profess that he seeks no private advantage by sitting in parliament, would be censured as hypocrite, or laughed at as a fool.[60]

Could the majesty of the people prevail over the majesty of George III? This was certainly an eccentric claim, although most fellow MPs could probably understand, at least theoretically, that the 'noble enthusiasm' of serving the nation should include self-sacrifice and prevail over the practice of politics for self-enrichment. Martin's glissando from military esprit de corps to national esprit de corps, the latter being equated with public spirit ('the interests of the public')[61] and opposed to the opportunism of the members of the parliament, is striking because it obliterates the idea of partisanship that the speech is nevertheless meant to criticise. In 1964, James Martin was described as 'one of the most conscientious and honest men who ever sat in Parliament [. . .] A diffident and portentous speaker, his frequent protestations of independence bored the House, and he was not always well heard.'[62] His idea of democratic esprit de corps was considered foolish and 'ludicrous'.[63]

Some MPs claimed more or less candidly that they were sufficiently diverse in opinions and origins, and therefore not biased. When a reform of Parliament inspired by the French Revolution was discussed in 1793 in the House of Commons, the following argument was registered:

> Suppose, that in that House there were only country gentlemen; they would not then be the representatives of the nation [. . .] Suppose there were in that House only commercial persons; they would not be the representatives of the nation, but the representatives of the commercial interest of the nation [. . .] However respectable those persons might be, an esprit de corps would naturally be found in all their proceedings [. . .] [But] the representatives of the people [. . .] have collectively no esprit de corps, because they are composed of persons in very different professions. They mix themselves with the landed and commercial interest, and prevent any esprit de corps, by this means, from affecting our proceedings.[64]

According to this view, one that equated esprit de corps with anti-public spirit, the British Parliament did not need to be further reformed, despite the claims of

The State of Representation of England and Wales,[65] a survey that demonstrated that members were elected by a very small portion of the population, property-owning men of a certain income who met religious and other very specific requirements. The so-called 'representatives of the people' were wealthy men often chosen from among the landed gentry to occupy the county seats, while rich merchants tended to occupy the borough seats.[66]

When in the first years of the nineteenth century, Thomas Robert Malthus claimed that 'all improvements in government must necessarily originate with persons of some education, and will of course be found among the people of property',[67] few voices were heard to claim the contrary. An isolated social critic, William Hazlitt, riposted ironically:

> The people of property and education have no vices of their own, which blind their understandings, no prejudices about royalty, or aristocracy, or church or state, no attachment to party [. . .] no connections, no privileges, no interest in the abuses of government, no pride, none of the *esprit de corps*, to hinder them from pronouncing sentence on the laws, institutions, uses, and abuses of society with the same calmness, disinterestedness, and wisdom, as they would upon cleaning a sewer, or paving a street.[68]

The author, an heir of the Enlightenment spirit, believed that disinterestedness was a new hypocritical attitude professed by the ruling class, one that had become most necessary in times of revolution and rationalism. In several European nations, the likelihood of popular insurrections seemed to be on the increase. Democratic representation was debated. The dominant classes had to sharpen their arguments and attitude to defend the idea that they were rational and enlightened enough to govern the people. Under the influence of the French Revolution, aristocratic arrogance and paternalism towards the masses would have to be progressively cross-dressed as nationalism, humanism, charity or a more capitalist survival-of-the-fittest ideology.

The military denotation of esprit de corps was less forgotten in English than in French. After the 1790s, the idea that the military and the political ought to be unified in any grand idea of a national esprit de corps became influential beyond the French borders. A military pamphlet written by the Vice-Lieutenant of Perthshire claimed that esprit de corps was a key factor for the success of the British Empire:

> The real patriotism and loyalty of the people induced them to join these corps with the utmost alacrity. Every individual [was convinced] that his own personal importance was not so great as he might have imagined; and the *esprit de corps* [. . .] was soon felt.[69]

The rhetorical chasm between what is real and what is less real is interesting: while individual importance was suggested to be rather imaginary, patriotism and loyalty to the British Empire were connected to a sense of reality. Other parts of this text contained assumptions regarding the building of esprit de corps, among which was the idea that a shared uniform and its ritualised public display was an efficient device to shape the minds of soldiers into uniformity, discipline and a self-sacrificial patriotic emotion.

An idealised and emotional belonging to a national culture ought to be the citizen's uniform:

> The early nationalists sought to create a new form of civic harmony and, in the course of a period marked by vertigo-inducing change, concluded that the solution lay in giving a large and disparate community what we would call a shared culture – common language, customs, beliefs, traditions . . .[70]

It is now common knowledge that in the nineteenth century, the social engineering of a national culture was implemented as an official ideology, for example in schools or history books. To the imperialists, it seemed that one unified body politic would be easier to govern than disparate associations and communities with specific interests. National esprit de corps could be a desired goal of the state, while a more autonomist form of esprit de corps could be its enemy. An early nineteenth-century comment on the government of the British West Indies considered the advantage of a universalist unite-and-conquer approach regarding the imperialist politics of population control:

> The Maroons, instead of being established into separate hordes or communities [. . .] should have been encouraged by all possible means to frequent the towns and to intermix with the negroes at large. All distinction between the Maroons and other free blacks would soon have been lost; for the greater number would have prevailed over the less; whereas the policy of keeping them a distinct people, continually inured to arms, introduced among them what the French call an *esprit de corps*, or community of sentiments and interests.[71]

For the English ruling class, the difficulty was to generate obedience and order within a heterogeneous empire without being compelled to claim that all men were equal citizens or that they could become full nationals by assimilation. The above recommendation to follow the French example was an isolated claim. In practice, this kind of anticipated critique of communitarianism in the name of aggregation was not systematically applied in the Commonwealth colonies. In the nineteenth-century United Kingdom, particular esprit de corps, as we will see, was encouraged among the ruling classes as a form of gilded and club-like rivalry. The imperial social club served as a distinctive sphere for the elites, 'a unique institution of colonial civil society that functioned in an intermediate zone between both metropolitan and indigenous public spheres'.[72]

In the newly born United States of America, the official discourse on esprit de corps at first reproduced the ambivalence of French utterances. The phrase could be employed pejoratively to qualify unfair partisanship and biased communities of interest, but independence efforts simultaneously called for a supra-esprit de corps, an all-American sense of honour, superiority and cohesion. In 1799, the *Philadelphia Review* explained that such national pride was not only inspired by 'the Roman Republic' as was the French Revolution, but was also a matter of domestic protection against 'foreign influence':

> It is impossible that the honor of a nation should be dear to its citizens, or be much respected by strangers, as long as the rights of citizenship are too easily obtained; wherever this *esprit de corps*, this national pride (however ridiculed by cosmopolites) is wanting, public spirit and the patriot virtues will be fought for in vain.[73]

This was written in 1799 but is often heard today. Cosmopolitanism was and still is a threatening idea for those who wanted to give 'the fact of being American a special salience in moral and political deliberation, and pride in a specifically American identity and a specifically American citizenship a special power among the motivations to political action'.[74]

Philadelphia was in 1787 the largest city in North America when it hosted a constitutional convention presided over by George Washington; this gathering of fifty-five men ended with the promulgation of the US Constitution. The briefings and records of the Convention show various mentions of esprit de corps; Charles Pinckney, a war veteran, a delegate of South Carolina and a member of the Federalist party, which advocated a strong national government,[75] said on 21 June 1787: 'There is an esprit de corps which has made heretofore every unfederal member of congress, after his election, become strictly federal, and this I presume will ever be the case in whatever manner they may be elected.'[76] Perhaps this 'becoming federal' was a reminiscence of Rousseau's instantaneous production of the body politic by the general will (and vice versa), since Pinckney was familiar with Rousseau's writings.[77] Conversely, Roger Sherman, delegate of Connecticut, thought that esprit de corps ought to be avoided:

> Our people are accustomed to annual elections. Should the members have a longer duration of service, and remain at the seat of government, they may forget their constituents, and perhaps imbibe the interest of the state in which they reside, or there may be danger of catching the esprit de corps.[78]

One year of common work before a renewal of elected members was considered an ideal limit to avoid the formation of in-group bias. Esprit de corps was, for Sherman, something a group could catch like a threatening and ineluctable virus.

Discussed at the highest official level during the Founding Era, esprit de corps was related to a semantic field of impartiality and partiality. Thomas Jefferson, while in office as president, also advocated in a letter to the Secretary of the Treasury the ethical principle of regular rotation in the nomination of bank directors: 'It breaks in upon the *esprit de corps*, so apt to prevail in permanent bodies; it gives a chance for the public eye penetrating into the sanctuary of those proceedings and practices.'[79] French ideals of republicanism were indeed familiar to the Founding Fathers and their collaborators. In 1794, Edmund Randolph, the new Secretary of State and former First Attorney General of the USA, published a pamphlet composed of thirteen political letters 'to the Citizens of the United States' – under the counter-intuitive pseudonym of 'Germanicus, a gentleman in Paris' – in which he called for popular meetings where 'the esprit de corps, which leads men, even in opposition to their particular sentiments, to espouse and enforce particular measures, will be an absolute stranger'.[80]

The idea that esprit de corps could be totally eliminated has always been proclaimed in idealistic contexts. But how could a nation-state then fabricate and maintain a homogeneous dedication among its servitors? One method was to claim that the nation was like a universal family.

The Natural Bond: Universalist and Familial Esprit de Corps

A new idea, connected with the notions of civil society and public service, was that the rights of a people – and sometimes of humanity altogether – were to be guarded by a 'universal class' of enlightened and educated officials. A philosophical justification of such an idea, directly inspired by the French Revolution,[81] was proposed in 1820 by the philosopher G. W. F. Hegel in relation to a state of mind that he called *Standesehre*, the honour and dignity of serving in a profession or estate, a word which was often translated in English as 'esprit de corps':

> A man actualises himself only in becoming something definite, i.e. something specifically particularised; this means restricting himself exclusively to one of the particular spheres of need. In this class-system, the ethical frame of mind therefore is rectitude and *esprit de corps*, i.e. the disposition to make oneself a member of one of the moments of civil society by one's own act, through one's energy, industry, and skill, to maintain oneself in this position, and to fend for oneself only through this process of mediating oneself with the universal, while in this way gaining recognition both in one's own eyes and in the eyes of others.[82]

Esprit de corps was not, for Hegel, a form of collective somnambulism, but rather an individual effort demanding dedication, energy, industry and skill, in order to keep up with the needs and standards of a given community of labour. Even a private corporation was ultimately serving the spiritual unity of the nation. Hegel's intellectual attempt to reconcile the 'universal' and the 'particular' in the synthesis of public service was inspired by his well-known historical procession of Spirit. The public and private sectors ought to collaborate for the spiritual glory of the state:

> In the *Philosophy of Right*, Hegel does offer a view of rectitude based on a less dichotomous relationship of public and private. This is particularly evident in his discussion of corporations and the other associations that citizens of large-scale states join to secure their private interests. Corporate membership

breeds corporate spirit, an *esprit de corps* or *Standesehre* rooted in genuine subjective sentiment. Individuals care for and assist those in distress, not out of obligation, but from a sense of 'benevolent inclination'. Indeed, it is precisely through *benevolence* that 'rectitude obtains its proper recognition and respect'. It is in the *esprit de corps* connected with group association that rectitude acquires 'ethical foundation'.[83]

A well-regulated national spirit allowed for a revival of intermediate esprit de corps, provided that the latter was functionally supervised by the nation-state, a recipe which, as we will examine in the next chapter, was efficiently achieved by Hegel's modern paragon of actualisation, Napoleon.

There would be more to say than space permits about Hegel's 'considerable influence' in Britain in the Victorian era,[84] or about the British concern for 'standards of official and professional conduct' in the nineteenth century.[85] A 'benevolent' moralist notion of universalised esprit de corps was compatible with the dominant British and American ethos of service, centred around the values of religion and family as pillars of the nation.

It is often argued that universalism is a typical French trait: 'Access to the universal, which at least since the French Revolution has defined France's singularity, its "exception", stubbornly remains a key phrase in France's discourse of national self-representation and identity.'[86] French universalism arose in part 'out of and in opposition to Christian systems of belief'.[87] In Protestant England, by contrast, 'the choice between God and Fatherland presented itself much less starkly, and religious universalism had far less resonance. The Church was a state church headed by the English king.'[88] Yet one can also argue that universalism's different avatars (family values, science and technology, standardisation, nationalism, commodification, etc.), are transnational features rather than being exclusively French. A well-studied perspective, for example, is how political universalism was internationally inspired by early modern science and its idea of natural laws.[89] A common point between different universalist discourses is that, when in a position of power, they tend to become hegemonic ideologies.[90]

Social control in nineteenth-century English-speaking geopolitical zones relied on religion and science to present a version of esprit de corps as a natural and familial quality. The clearest expression of this essentialist view, not devoid of Hegelian influence, was formulated in 1899 by one of the fathers of sociobiology and evolutionary psychology, James Mark Baldwin, professor at Princeton University:

The relationships of the family are [. . .] characterized by natural *esprit de corps*. The family *esprit de corps* has such a firm root in the breast of the individual that family action is necessary to him as action in his own private interest. The naturalness of such action from family *esprit de corps* is seen in the powerful place it has in animal life [. . .] A similar natural bond, which the historians of society trace back to the family, extends to the various natural aggregations into which the social body falls at different periods in its development from the family to the village community, then through the various stages of tribal and patriarchal organization [. . .] This *esprit de corps* shows itself also sentimentally in patriotism, race feeling, colour prejudice, etc. [. . .] National spirit is a form of natural *esprit de corps*.[91]

In reductionist fashion, all types of esprit de corps were given one unique origin: family instinct presented as an elemental bond under the vague authority of some 'historians of society'. For Baldwin, esprit de corps was wired into our cells and nerves and therefore never could or should be eradicated:

It is clear that in actions done from natural *esprit de corps*, the individual is acting simply and only from impulse. The fact that he does not reason, that he does not hesitate, nor ask even for ethical or social justification – these facts show that he is now in the region of just that form of compulsion which we called, in the consideration of his impulses, the sanction of 'necessity' [. . .] We have seen reasons, in our study, for the coincidence between this form of social sanction and that of the individual's impulsive nature. The instincts of natural affection, of natural *esprit de corps*, are engrained in the very nervous organization of man.[92]

We saw how such a naturalisation of esprit de corps started in the eighteenth century, for example with Chesterfield. But authors now dreamed of grounding the naturalist approach to esprit de corps on scientific rather than philosophical explanation. The latter was seen as too disputable. What had been considered by the *Philosophes* as the second nature of esprit de corps (a graft) was now presented as first nature. Such a sacralisation of family instinct was coherent with religious forms of social control and moralistic ideas of how a good, useful citizen was expected to behave. For Baldwin's nineteenth-century students, it would have been difficult to conceive that family spirit was a social construct.

The natural-bond paternalist discourse went hand in hand with Christian values. Pamphlets on public education published in England between 1840 and 1890 made general claims about how children should be trained accordingly. *On National Education*, for instance, written by an army officer and 'member of different scientific and literary societies at home and abroad', explained:

The general good demands the mutual esteem of all orders of the State, and their frank, cordial, and brotherly cooperation [. . .] No happiness or prosperity can be secured but on the most strictly moral principles, and as no code of morals can surpass that contained in the gospel, it follows that the *spirit* of the Christian religion must be the basis of the national education.[93]

From natural and patriarchal familial brotherhood to national esprit, via the spirit of Jesus, a continuous line was established. British university education and experience also drew on 'the ethos of Christian manliness'.[94] Such an ethos was not politically egalitarian:

The grand political principle [. . .] to be inculcated in a national education is not the false, or rather the perverted doctrine, that all men are equal, but, on the contrary, that inequality of rank is necessary to the stability of the social order; that each class is useful, and consequently, as such, each is entitled to the respect of every other.[95]

Esprit de corps had to do with perceived legitimacy, which created deference. In less than one hundred years, the English perception of esprit de corps had moved from the idea of a necessary evil to a necessary good. It was now rarely considered in the Anglo-Saxon semiosphere as an unnecessary evil, as d'Alembert or Diderot had viewed it. Moreover, the specificity indicated by the prototype formulation of the idiom, esprit du corps, meaning that each group had its character, was lost in translation: esprit de corps was now a generic term, the universal feature of any group attachment, as if there was only one standard way to adhere to a community, whether it was a family, a nation or a club.

To be fair, we could still find a few isolated examples of an understanding of esprit de corps as peculiarly different depending on the type of association or group. Some pamphlets of the Victorian era presented academic esprit de corps as a beneficial competitive game among elites in a class-divided system. In 1850, Edward Arthur Litton, late fellow of Oriel College, was asked by a royal commission 'to investigate the state of the university at Oxford'.[96] The result was an open letter to John Russell, then prime minister of the United Kingdom, in which the future of academia was believed to rely on more esprit de corps, seen as a form of dynamic agonism between different academic bodies:

The absence of intellectual society, of well stocked libraries, of the stimulating influence of example and rivalry, – in short, of all that constitutes the peculiar *esprit de corps* of a university, necessarily operates in depressing the energies.[97]

Example and rivalry, quasi-military virtues of esprit de corps, were presented as necessary to an excellent and enthusiastic education of 'men of the same class, of the same *esprit de corps*'.[98]

Two kinds of esprit de corps consolidated the social divide in the nineteenth century: on the one hand, an agonistic and self-aggrandising esprit de corps for the wealthy and protected, on the other, a self-humiliating religious or national esprit de corps for the middle or lower classes. 'Government help is needed', explained a British peer in 1880: 'Two or three million a year, so distributed as to form a monopoly of schools and a caste of teachers, is certain to create, not only a selfish interest, but an unselfish official *esprit de corps*.'[99]

The idea of a national training of the middle and poorer classes towards civil discipline was also common in the United States. An influential example was given by the psychologist John Dewey, in his *Introduction to the Principles and Practice of Education*:

Sympathy has its origin in the contagious character of feeling [. . .] Children are constantly manifesting such sympathy [. . .] The imitative sympathy is a factor which the teacher may largely rely upon [. . .] This feeling possessed by *groups* of persons may be disciplined, and then it becomes *esprit de corps* – as important a help to the teacher as to the officer.[100]

Dewey and McLellan called for the 'training' of a '*reflex* sympathy' among pupils, if necessary through 'punishment', not only to develop children's knowledge 'from the Vague to the Definite, and from the Particular to the Universal', but also to favour the child's 'emotional growth' towards 'moral feelings', and a family-like spiritual 'peace':[101]

The school is, both historically and philosophically, the expansion, the continuation of the family. It is the connecting link between the family and a higher ethical community, the general social order. Thus the school is, both historically and philosophically, the preparation for the community and the state.[102]

The unproven idea of a continuum of esprit de corps between the family and the state was presented as a means to a form of social engineering. Sympathy was natural and almost effortless, and therefore easier to manipulate via a hidden curriculum:[103]

The hidden curriculum is [. . .] a composite concept for the way in which a pedagogical legacy functions even today as a 'frozen ideology' in the school institution [. . .] Hidden phenomena such as *esprit de corps* and culture [. . .] remain as hidden and often unmentioned influences on school activity.[104]

From the middle of the nineteenth century onwards, the signifier 'esprit de corps' was so widespread in English that it became itself an object of teaching. Breen's renowned textbook on 'blemishes of modern English'[105] was then on many bookshelves and in university libraries, both in England and the USA – Mark Twain claimed to write with a copy nearby.[106] The textbook explained:

There is no word in the French language that requires such cautious handling as the word 'esprit'. It is as versatile and multifarious as the people whose mental characteristic it so aptly represents; and in proportion to its versatility is the ill-usage to which it is daily subjected by English writers of every degree. One of the numerous meanings of this word occurs in the phrase 'esprit de corps', frequently written 'esprit du corps', which if it means anything, means 'the spirit of the body'.[107]

The author's puzzlement could not find a better way out than irony and a deflated literal translation. Multifarious esprit de corps indeed, but by the end of the nineteenth century, the ambivalence of esprit de corps was no longer so obvious for English minds because the pejorative use of the phrase had tended to fade away. Laudatory and naturalised meanings were largely accepted, especially, as we have seen, to describe professional and public bodies as functional extensions of the familial kinship, in accordance with a certain 'romanticization of the family' and of national belonging.[108]

In the seventeenth and eighteenth centuries, professional esprit de corps often meant that one worked with one's biological family in the labour guild and practised the same skill as one's father, mother or brothers. But with the industrial revolution, workplaces became less and less familial environments. To maintain social peace and efficiency, the new capitalist owners hoped that a brotherly form of professional esprit de corps could alleviate the affliction of working with strangers in a mechanical and uninspiring atmosphere. A typical example of this new rhetoric as applied to the professions was displayed in *The British Architect* in 1887: '*Esprit de corps* makes for the general progress and well-being of any professional community.'[109]

As we shall see in Chapter 7, such corporate uses of the phrase would become dominant in the twentieth century with English as the new lingua franca. With the process of globalisation and the internationalisation of production and commerce, the idea of competition among corporations would be considered as a quasi-military endeavour. Brotherhood in arms is still today an idealised model for capitalist communities. But before we examine how American capitalism transformed esprit de corps into its slogan in the twentieth century, we need to learn from the most successful political transposers of military esprit de corps into the rest of society: the French Bonapartists.

Notes

1. Philip Durkin, *Borrowed Words: A History of Loanwords in English* (Oxford: Oxford University Press, 2014), p. 311.
2. Schor, 'The Crisis of French Universalism', p. 44.
3. *Kåranda* or *Korpsgeist* are each often translated into English as 'esprit de corps', *Glosbe: Multilingual Online Dictionary*, <https://glosbe.com>.
4. Durkin, *Borrowed Words*, p. 3.
5. A monograph similar to the present book, but on the transnational genealogy of the phrase *laissez-faire*, would be an interesting *histosophical* sequel.
6. Lawrence Venuti, *The Translator's Invisibility* (London: Routledge, 1995), p. 17.
7. Fade Wang, 'An Approach to Domestication and Foreignization from the Angle of Cultural Factors Translation', *Theory and Practice in Language Studies* 4.11 (2014), pp. 2423–7 (p. 2424).
8. Shiri Lev-Ari, Marcela San Giacomo and Sharon Peperkamp, 'The Effect of Domain Prestige and Interlocutors' Bilinguism on Loanword Adaptations', *Journal of Sociolinguistics* 18.5 (2014), pp. 658–84 (p. 662).
9. George Orwell, *Burmese Days* (London: Penguin, 1975), p. 181.
10. George Woodcock, *The Crystal Spirit: A Study of George Orwell* (Montreal: Black Rose, 2005), p. 62.
11. Ian Slater, *Orwell: The Road to Airstrip One* (Montreal and Kingston: McGill-Queen's University Press, 2003), p. 41.

12. Paul J. DiMaggio and Walter W. Powell, 'The Iron Cage Revisited: Institutional Isomorphism and Collective Rationality in Organizational Fields', *American Sociological Review* 48 (1983), pp. 147–60 (p. 152).

13. Eline Zenner, Dirk Speelman and Dirk Geeraerts, 'Cognitive Sociolinguistics Meets Loanword Research: Measuring Variation in the Success of Anglicisms in Dutch', *Cognitive Linguistics* 23 (2012), pp. 749–92 (p. 767).

14. *Webster's Dictionary* (1913), ARTFL Project, <http://machaut.uchicago.edu>.

15. Samuel Johnson, *A Dictionary of the English Language*, 5 vols (London: Longman, 1818), vol. I, p. 12.

16. *Webster's Dictionary* (1828), ARTFL Project, <http://machaut.uchicago.edu>.

17. Robert Barret, *The Theoric and Practic of Modern Wars* (London: Ponsonby, 1598).

18. Thomas Blount, *Glossographia or a Dictionary* (London: Newcomb, 1656).

19. Joseph Addison, *The Campaign: A Poem, To His Grace the Duke of Marlborough* (London: Tonson, 1705), p. 16.

20. Durkin, *Borrowed Words*, p. 401.

21. Olivia Smith, *The Politics of Language 1791–1819* (Oxford: Oxford University Press, 1986), p. x.

22. Smith, *The Politics of Language*, p. 3.

23. Lev-Ari, San Giacomo and Peperkamp, 'The Effect of Domain Prestige', p. 660.

24. André Chervel, *Histoire de l'enseignement du français du XVIIe au XXe siècle* (Paris: Retz, 2006), p. 137.

25. Lord Chesterfield, 'To Dr. Rev. Chenevix, Lord Bishop of Waterford, Blackheath (June 26, 1755)', *Miscellaneous Works of Lord Chesterfield*, 3 vols (Dublin: Maty, 1777), vol. III, p. 340.

26. 'Philip Dormer Stanhope, 4th earl of Chesterfield', *Encyclopædia Britannica Online* (2007), <https://www.britannica.com/biography/Philip-Dormer-Stanhope-4th-Earl-of-Chesterfield> (accessed 19 September 2019).

27. 'Philip Dormer Stanhope', *A Cambridge Alumni Database*, University of Cambridge <http://venn.lib.cam.ac.uk/cgi-bin/search-2018.pl?sur=Stanhope&suro=w&fir=&firo=c&cit=&cito=c&c=all&z=all&tex=&sye=&eye=&col=all&maxcount=50> (accessed 19 September 2019).

28. 'Vous n'avez jamais été, dans aucun genre, ni charlatan ni dupe des charlatans.' Voltaire, 'Lettre CCCIII à Milord Chesterfield (24 Sept. 1771)', in *Œuvres complètes de Voltaire* (Paris: Société Littéraire-Typographique, 1784), vol. LXVIII, p. 533.

29. Philip Stanhope, aka Lord Mahon (ed.), *The Letters of Philip Dormer Stanhope, Earl of Chesterfield*, 4 vols (London: Bentley, 1845), vol. III, p. 119.

30. Voltaire, *An Essay on Universal History, the Manners, and Spirit of Nations, from the Reign of Charlemeign to the Age of Lewis XIV*, trans. Thomas Nugent, 4 vols (London: Nourse, 1759), vol. III, p. 167.

31. Henry Manners Chichester, 'Jardine, Alexander', in *Dictionary of National Biography* (London: Smith, Elder, 1885–90), vol. XXIX (1892), p. 249.

32. Alexander Jardine, 'Letter III from Portugal to Friends in England', in *Letters from Barbary, France, Spain, Portugal, etc., by an English officer*, 2 vols (London: Cadell, 1788), vol. II, p. 425.

33. Ibid., p. 426.

34. Philip Schofield, 'Jeremy Bentham's "Nonsense upon Stilts"', *Utilitas* 15.1 (2003), pp. 1–26.

35. Immanuel Kant, *Vorlesungen über Moralphilosophie* (Berlin: de Gruyter, 1975), p. 674.

36. Immanuel Kant, *Lectures on Ethics*, trans. Peter Heath (Cambridge: Cambridge University Press, 1997), pp. 405–6.

37. Donald De Marco, 'Personalism vs Abstract Humanism', *The Linacre Quarterly* 45.3 (1978), pp. 258–63.

38. Jean-Paul Rabaut Saint-Étienne, *Précis historique de la Révolution Française* (Paris: Onfroy, 1792).

39. André Dupont, *Rabaut de Saint-Etienne, 1743–1793* (Geneva: Labor and Fidès, 1989).

40. Jean-Paul Rabaut de Saint-Etienne, *The History of the Revolution of France* (London: Debrett, 1792), p. 37–50.

41. Mirabeau, *Enquiries concerning Lettres de Cachet, the Consequences of Arbitrary Imprisonment and a History of the Inconveniences, Distresses, and Sufferings of State Prisoners*, 2 vols (London: Robinson, 1787), vol. I, p. 476.

42. Ibid., p. 457.

43. 'Austrian Netherlands', *Oracle*, 10 November 1789, in *The 17th and 18th Century Burney Collection*, <http://tinyurl.galegroup.com/tinyurl/PAZj0> (accessed 19 September 2019).

44. Eighteenth Century Journals, <http://www.18thcjournals.amdigital.co.uk>.

45. H. Cottrell, T. D. Pearse et al., *Remarks on the petition of the British inhabitants of Bengal, Bihar, and Orissa, to Parliament. By the gentlemen of the Committee at Calcutta, appointed to transmit the petition to England, and transact the business appertaining thereto* (London, 1780), p. 67.

46. David Lemmings, *Professors of the Law: Barristers and English Legal Culture in the Eighteenth Century* (Oxford: Oxford University Press, 2000), p. 110.

47. Ibid., p. 250.

48. Jeremy Bentham, *An Introduction to the Principles of Morals and Legislation* (London: Payne, 1789), p. 120.

49. John Courtenay, *Philosophical Reflections on the Late Revolution in France, and the Conduct of the Dissenters in England* (London: Becket, 1790), p. 63.

50. Hannah More, *Strictures on the Modern System of Female Education, with a view of the principles and conducts prevalent among women of rank and fortune*, 2 vols (London: Cadell and Davies, 1799), vol. II, p. 165.

51. Thomas Holcroft, 'A view of Amsterdam', *The Lady's Magazine, or Entertaining Companion for the Fair Sex; Appropriated Solely to their Use and Amusement* 35 (1804), p. 80.

52. Mary McKerrow, *Mary Brunton: The Forgotten Scottish Novelist* (Kirkwall: The Orcadian, 2001), pp. 40–7.

53. Mary Brunton, *Discipline* (Edinburgh: Ramsay, 1814), p. 259.

54. Byron, 'Letter CCCCXXVIII to Mr. Moore, May 20th, 1821', in Thomas More, *Life and Journals of Lord Byron*, 2 vols (Hamburg: Lebel, Truttel & Wrutz, 1831), vol. II, p. 324.

55. David Evans Macdonnel, *A Dictionary of Quotations in Most Frequent Use, Taken chiefly from the Latin and French, but comprising many from the Greek, Spanish, and Italian Languages* (London: Wilkie and Robinson, 1809), p. 89.

56. Walter Scott, 'On the present state of periodical criticism', *The Edinburgh Annual Register For 1809* (Edinburgh: Ballantyne, 1811), vol. II, p. 577.

57. Hesketh Pearson, *Sir Walter Scott: His Life and Personality* (New York: Harper, 1964), p. 82.

58. 'The Duke of Richmond', in *The Parliamentary register; or, History of the proceedings*

and debates of the House of Commons, 17 vols (London: Wilson, 1802), vol. X, p. 43.

59. 'Charles Lennox, Third Duke of Richmond', Encyclopaedia Britannica Online (2008), <https://www.britannica.com/biography/Charles-Lennox-3rd-duke-of-Richmond> (accessed 19 September 2019).

60. The Parliamentary History of England From the Earliest Period to the Year 1803 (London: Hansard, 1814), vol. XX, p. 119.

61. Ibid.

62. Lewis Namier and John Brooke, The History of Parliament: The House of Commons, 1754–1790 (London: Secker and Warburg, 1964), vol. III, p. 113.

63. Ibid.

64. 'Debate on Mr. Grey's motion for a Reform in Parliament', in The Parliamentary History of England (London: Hansard, 1817), vol. XXX, pp. 813–14.

65. The State of the Representation of England and Wales, delivered to the Society of the Friends of the People, associated for the Purpose of obtaining a Parliamentary Reform (London: Society of the Friends of the People, 1793).

66. Edward Porritt, The Unreformed House of Commons (Cambridge: Cambridge University Press, 1909), p. 296.

67. Thomas Robert Malthus, An Essay on The Principle of Population: Or a View of Its Past and Present Effects on Human Happiness (London: Bensley, 1803), p. 533.

68. William Hazlitt, A Reply to The Essay on Population by The Rev. T. R. Malthus (London: Longman, 1807), p. 356.

69. Alex Muir Mackenzie, General Observations upon the probable effects of any measures which have for their object the increase of the regular army (Edinburgh: Manners and Miller, 1807), pp. 60–1.

70. Bell, The Cult of the Nation, p. 21.

71. Bryan Edwards, The History, Civil and Commercial, of the British West Indies, 5 vols (London: Miller, 1819), vol. I, p. 537.

72. Mrinalini Sinha, 'Britishness, Clubbability, and the Colonial Public Sphere: The Genealogy of an Imperial Institution in Colonial India', Journal of British Studies 40.4 (2001), pp. 489–521 (p. 492).

73. 'Domestic Intelligence', The Philadelphia Magazine and Review; or, Monthly Repository of Information and Amusement, January 1799, vol. 1, p. 53.

74. Martha C. Nussbaum, 'Patriotism and Cosmopolitanism', Boston Review, 1 October 1994, <http://bostonreview.net/martha-nussbaum-patriotism-and-cosmopolitanism> (accessed 19 September 2019).

75. 'Charles Cotesworth Pinckney', Encyclopaedia Britannica Online (2009), <https://www.britannica.com/biography/Charles-Cotesworth-Pinckney> (accessed 19 September 2019).

76. 'Thursday, June 21, 1787', The Records of the Federal Convention of 1787, American Memory from the Library of Congress, <https://oll.libertyfund.org/titles/1057#lf0544-01_head_189> (accessed 19 September 2019).

77. Nicholas Michael Butler, Votaries of Apollo: The St. Cecilia Society and the Patronage of Concert Music in Charleston, South Carolina, 1766–1820 (Columbia: University of South Carolina Press, 2007), p. 214.

78. 'Thursday, June 21, 1787', The Records of the Federal Convention.

79. 'Thomas Jefferson to The Secretary of The Treasury Albert Gallatin, 13 December 1803', in The Works of Thomas Jefferson, ed. Paul Leicester Ford, 12 vols (New York and London: Putnam, 1904–5), vol. X, p. 56.

80. Edmund Randolph, *Germanicus* (Philadelphia, 1794), p. 20.
81. Joachim Ritter, *Hegel and the French Revolution* (Cambridge, MA: MIT Press, 1982).
82. Hegel, *Philosophy of Right*, § 207, p. 133.
83. Andrew Buchwalter, *Dialectics, Politics, and the Comtemporary Value of Hegel's Practical Philosophy* (New York: Routledge, 2012), p. 165.
84. Tibor Frank, 'Hegel in England: Victorian Thought Reconsidered', *Hungarian Studies in English* 13 (1980), pp. 49–58 (p. 49).
85. Gloria C. Clifton, *Professionalism, Patronage, and Public Service in Victorian London* (London: Bloomsbury, 2015), p. 154.
86. Schor, 'The Crisis of French Universalism', p. 48.
87. Bell, *The Cult of the Nation*, p. 7.
88. Ibid., p. 48.
89. Margaret C. Jacob, 'Newtonianism and the Origins of the Enlightenment', *Eighteenth-Century Studies* 11.1 (1977), pp. 1–25.
90. Chantal Mouffe, *On the Political* (London: Routledge, 2005), p. 18.
91. James Mark Baldwin, *Social and Ethical Interpretations in Mental Development: A Study in Social Psychology* (New York: Macmillan, 1899), pp. 407–9.
92. Ibid., pp. 409–10.
93. Colonel J. R. Jackson, *On National Education; With Remarks on Education in General* (London: Alexander and Co., 1840), pp. 16, 33.
94. Keith Vernon, *Universities and the State in England, 1850–1939* (London: Routledge, 2004), p. 217.
95. Jackson, *On National Education*, p. 34.
96. Timothy C. F. Stunt, 'Litton, Edward Arthur (1813–1897)', *Oxford Dictionary of National Biography*, <https://www.oxforddnb.com/view/10.1093/ref:odnb/9780198614128.001.0001/odnb-9780198614128-e-47639> (accessed 19 September 2019).
97. Edward Arthur Litton, *University Reform, A Letter to the Right Hon. Lord John Russel* (London: Hatchard, 1850), pp. 9–16.
98. Lyon Playfair, *On Teaching Universities and Examining Boards* (Dublin: Hodges, Foster, 1873), p. 30.
99. Earl Hugh Fortescue, *Public schools for the middle classes* (London: Ridgway, 1880), p. 19.
100. John Dewey and James Alexander McLellan, *Applied Psychology. An Introduction to the Principles and Practice of Education* (Boston: Educational Publishing Company, 1889), pp. 121–5.
101. Ibid., p. 77.
102. Ibid., pp. 123–5.
103. Philip W. Jackson, *Life in Classrooms* (New York: Holt, Rinehart and Wilson, 1968), p. 33.
104. Gunnar Berg, 'School Culture and Teachers' Esprit de Corps', in Éva Balazs, Fons van Wieringen and Leonard Watson (eds), *Quality and Educational Management* (Budapest: Wolters Kluwer, 2000), <https://www.ofi.hu/quality-and-educational-090617/school-culture-and> (accessed 19 September 2019).
105. Henry Hegart Breen, *Modern English Literature, Its Blemishes and Defects* (London: Longman, 1857).
106. Mark Twain, 'General Grant's Grammar', in *Mark Twain's Civil War*, ed. David Rachels (Lexington: University Press of Kentucky, 2007), p. 84.
107. Breen, *Modern English Literature*, p. 122.

108. Stephanie Coontz, *The Social Origins of Private Life: A History of American Families, 1600–1900* (London: Verso, 1988), p. 210.
109. Anonymous, 'Esprit de corps', *The British Architect: Journal of Architecture and the Accessory Arts* 27 (1887), p. 283.

4

The Way of Napoleon:
The Uniformisation of Esprit de Corps in
Early Nineteenth-Century France

Superiorly Normal: Renewal and Normalisation of Esprit de Corps

Around 1800, esprit de corps became a praised notion once more in France, provided that its manifestation was not only authorised but also controlled by the state. In the early nineteenth century, esprit de corps was nationally manufactured, and Napoleon was its first engineer. The phrase came to describe an institutionalised form of competition for social distinction, a new national sport, the expected prizes of which were individual prestige and collective order. This national production of esprit de corps became possible partly because of the generalised acceptance that humans have a natural tendency to form rivalling coteries: instead of trying in vain to crush intermediary groups, as attempted by the Revolution, a strong state was to organise, supervise and utilise them.

This programme was clearly theorised by Charles Maurice de Talleyrand, Bonaparte's minister of foreign affairs. In 1800, Talleyrand told the other members of the government that each branch of state administration should have its own subordinate 'esprit': 'This spirit [*esprit*] confers unity, uniformity, and a certain energy to the conducting of business; it transmits a tradition of duties' and 'binds the corps and its individual members to the Government', the latter being the 'goal and source of all consideration'.[1] Talleyrand advocated a system of promotions, rewards and advancements that became the basis of France's state bureaucracy.

The forging of the citizen's esprit de corps in the name of social order started early in life. *Lycées* and boarding schools became places of masculine friendship: 'The camaraderie of the schools and the strong esprit de corps that resulted [. . .] often delinquent within the internat [boarding school]'[2] was expected to produce disciplined servitors of the state afterwards. The elite offspring were given the opportunity to develop an elitist esprit de corps in the newly created *grandes écoles*, which are still today a pillar of French education. A student of the prestigious École polytéchnique in the years 1814–16, the philosopher Auguste Comte ecstatically described this higher education institution as a 'paradise, where the most perfect union existed among the students'.[3] His philosophy, popular among the elites after 1830 as we will see, could be interpreted as an attempt to expand this experience on a larger social scale.

The systematic critique of esprit de corps in the style of the *Encyclopédistes* and other revolutionaries was not forgotten fifty years after d'Alembert's charge against the Jesuits, but it tended to become an idiosyncrasy practised by some members of the artistic or literate class. Even there, the critique was now more nuanced, as for example in 'L'Académie et le Caveau', a song written and sung by Pierre-Jean de Béranger. Béranger was a renowned *chansonnier* who described, in contraposition with the pompous formality of the Académie française, the joyful spirit of the *goguette du Caveau modern*, a society where, from 1806 to 1817, writers and poets met for long musical dinners. Béranger's song describes his admission in the circle in 1813:

> Once admitted, will my spirit
> Become a mere esprit de corps?
> In the latter, one must say,
> Common sense turns into foolishness;
> But in your society
> Esprit de corps is merriment.
> Such a spirit is not a reign of tyranny.
> It is not like in the *Académie*.[4]

In fact, a few members of the Caveau were also *Académiciens*. It is probable that not only they, but most attendees, were familiar with Montesquieu's ironical attack on the esprit du corps of the Académie française in the now legendary *Lettres persanes*.

The song also suggests subtle parallels between solidarity/cheerfulness and tyranny/foolishness, which alluded to the duality of esprit de corps. The popular songwriter and his listeners knew that esprit de corps could be about subjugation as well as camaraderie. Béranger suggested that some societies could generate the latter without producing the former: a good esprit de corps was conceivable even from the perspective of the mocker. Even if he were simply flattering his audience, the fact that he chose to enter this elitist circle with a song on esprit de corps demonstrates how the notion was still on everyone's minds. Satire works better on epochal obsessions.

In the androcentric society of Napoleon, the phenomenon of esprit de corps met the need for virile companionship in various networks of power. Through the voice of one of her paternalist characters, the writer and musician Madame de Genlis exposed an ideological *lieu commun* of her time: 'There is no esprit de corps among women.'[5] Interestingly, the main reason given by the author to explain this alleged fact is that women are not interested in glory. This suggested that esprit de corps was a collective strategy to attain praise, recognition and renown, in a world where male domination was institutionalised.

Among the authors who proposed a reappraisal of esprit de corps, the most renowned was the writer François-René de Chateaubriand. In his *Génie du*

Christianisme, he conceded that esprit de corps could sometimes engender biased behaviour, but more importantly it contributed locally to the civilising virtue of belongingness: 'Esprit de corps, which can be bad in the whole, is always good in the part.'[6] This affirmation reversed the discourse of the French Revolution, for which esprit de corps was bad in intermediary groups, but desirable at the level of the national ensemble – Chateaubriand was a royalist and his brother had been guillotined in 1794.[7] What Chateaubriand meant in this context was that no matter how much we criticised the phenomenon of esprit de corps philosophically and generally, he was convinced that in practice most members of a religious society, when holding a public position and civic responsibility, behaved individually with righteousness, if only for the 'glory' of their religious order and because of the 'yoke' it imposed on them. In other words, esprit de corps was a good recipe to avoid social anarchy. This conviction was spreading among the renewed French dominant class.

By the end of the first half of the nineteenth century, the ideal of engineering esprit de corps in different parts of society was such that different social groups wanted their own cohesion formula. The Société royale de Médecine de Marseille, for instance, launched in 1842, and again in 1844, an essay contest with a 200-francs gold medal prize, on the following lines:

> Define 1) The advantages conferred by esprit de corps among medical doctors; 2) The most desirable ways to build this esprit de corps. Our Society wishes competitors to consider esprit de corps among practitioners not only in the interest of the medical corps, but also with the progress of science in mind, and for the good of suffering humanity.[8]

Several contestants preached the then fashionable positivism of Auguste Comte, a combination of scientism, religiosity and politics. An esprit de corps among doctors would facilitate, they explained, the development of a universal and messianic form of health: a doctor, 'at the cost of a complete reform of his education and practice, will then be incorporated to the priesthood of Humanity and devoted to the progressive reform of occidental institutions'.[9] For the positivists, esprit de corps was acceptable because the human reality was primarily social; it called for discipline and order. A strong desire for individualist freedom was a form of mental illness. Bodies and groups were everywhere, they functioned as biological organisms and had to follow a regulated regime. Disorder was the enemy of social progress.[10] Such was the new dominant idea in most power circles: esprit de corps brought order, and 'where there is no esprit de corps, there's only anarchy'.[11]

The signifier 'esprit de corps' was even featured in 1835 in the standard-setting *Dictionnaire de l'Académie française*: 'Esprit de corps, Attachment of the members of a corporation to the opinions, rights, and interests of the society.'[12] The French word *corporation* limited the definition to a professional context; in the same dictionary, *corporation* was defined as: 'Association authorised by public authorities, formed of various persons who live under a common policy in relation to their profession.'[13] The choice of the word 'attachment' was not innocent and had probably been much reflected upon by the *Académiciens* in charge of the diction-ary. *Attachement* in French can designate a bond or an emotional connection, as of affection or mutual longing. It was defined in the same volume as *sentiment*.[14] It could suggest dedication, or even, more subtly, the state of being tied up, deprived of freedom. But *sentiment* was the dominant meaning: what was described in this official definition of esprit de corps was an emotional form of loyalty to one's professional fellows, humanly understandable. This denotation reflected once more the new dominant perception of esprit de corps in France, more distant from the *Lumières*' critical definition than from the nineteenth-century English uses of the term.

How was this related to the important consequence of the French Revolution for labour, namely the end of the system of *corporations* as *corps de métiers* that was typical of the *Ancien Régime*?

Esprit de corporation: The Decline of Labour Communities and the Spread of Individualist Competition

In the eighteenth-century context of growing hostility towards the monopolistic power of *corporations*, the esprit de corps of opaque labour communities gained a derogatory connotation. Competition was to be moved to a general level of free trade. The different *corps de métiers*, sometimes burdened by excessive regulation, nepotism and deficient external control, were accused of creating artificial social divisions. An advocate of laissez-faire and commercial freedom, the influential merchant Vincent de Gournay wrote as early as 1752: 'The natural enemies of a community are all other communities.'[15] Such a critique was of course manifest in the *Encyclopédie*, in the words of François de Forbonnais, a translator of David Hume and a friend of de Gournay:

> These communities have particular laws, which are almost entirely opposed to the general good and to the views of the legislator. The first and most dangerous law is the one that sets barriers to industry by multiplying costs and formalities [. . .] Monopolies are contrary to the laws of reason [. . .] The first principle of commerce must be competition [*concurrence*]; it is only through it that craft perfects itself, that food abounds, that the State obtains superfluous goods to export [. . .] and in the end that the State fulfils its immediate purpose, which is to occupy and nourish the greatest possible number of men.[16]

In the fields of commerce, agriculture and industry, esprit de corps was in the second half of the eighteenth century often equated with harmful monopoly. The supposed affinity between reason and competition was a striking claim; today we have learned to unmask that defence of deregulated *concurrence* as a certain connivance between capitalism and the French Revolution spirit.[17] At least one hegemonic monopoly was nevertheless preserved for the partisans of laissez-faire: that of the state.

The Revolution discredited the *esprit de corporation*. By the end of the century, merchants and producers were often thankful for the republican defence of more competitive and less regulated entrepreneurship:

> This esprit de corps which distinguished different classes of workers [. . .] did not make the products more perfect [. . .] Masters who had acquired the right to make shoes were less worried about improving them, because through the coalition they formed among themselves and the esprit de corps they knew how to maintain, they did not fear the effects of competition.[18]

This was a deliberate reversal of the traditional argument according to which the communities of production and trade facilitated a better quality of the final product thanks to their expertise, craft and care.

We saw how the Jesuits were attacked for their esprit de corps, and how they defended themselves in vain. Labour communities also fought back soon after, and this time the debate lasted several decades. When the finance minister and Physiocrat Turgot, who admired de Gournay's ideas, attempted to eradicate the *corporations* in 1776 in the name of laissez-faire,[19] they attempted to legitimise their existence as a means not only of supervising product quality, but also of maintaining a form of social harmony and preventing economic chaos. The argument was that:

> Corporations were guarantors of morality and guardians of security. They thus worked as a double 'filter' to eliminate the incompetence that was imperceptibly transformed into corruption. The arrival of freedom, conversely, was the 'triumph of usury and deceit', of 'bad faith', 'brigandage', 'imperfection in works', 'indifference and negligence'. Without the criteria imposed by the corporations, without the esprit de corps and the control it performed, the market would be invaded by fraudulent goods and services.[20]

For the defenders of labour communities, the *philosophie moderne* of liberty and rationalism was the enemy of social cohesion. Some *corps de métiers* published eloquent pamphlets that turned the accusation of biased interest against the intellectual class. The guild of Fruits and Oranges, for example, claimed strikingly in 1776:

> The more we reflect upon our Modern Philosophy, the more convinced we are that the first and foremost of its principles is egoism. Freedom, property, these are the rallying cries. The idea of a common society was only introduced to ensure that freedom and property thrive, as if each individual owed nothing to society; he must attach himself to his personal interest only.[21]

The new atomic *individu* was an enemy of traditional solidarities. For sure, the word *individualisme* would only appear a few decades later in French,[22] but the idea of considering the individual consumer or producer as a valuable unit of the Republic was in the air even before the Revolution, not only among economists, but also among influential revolutionary voices, such as Mirabeau for instance.[23]

The new rejection of professional esprit de corps also emerged from within the French *corporations*. A few years before the Revolution, the visionary writer Louis-Sébastien Mercier, the son of an artisan, observed in Paris what he perceived to be a general atmosphere of popular intractability and insolence, a questioning of authority 'visible in the people for a few years and especially in the trades'.[24]

> Apprentices and masons want to show they are independent; they lack respect for the master [. . .] Nowadays the little people have come out of subordination to a point that I can predict that before long we will see the worst effects of this forgetfulness of all discipline.[25]

Was discipline about respect or coercion, craft or subjection? This is an important question raised by debates on esprit de corps. For the revolutionaries, individual freedom was presented as a protection against subjection or coercion. An intermediate body, with its system of internal hierarchy, could become the enemy of the nation and the common good by creating an abusive elitism. But as we will see, discipline as craft and care is the baby thrown out with the bathwater of discipline as subjection.

In 1791, the Le Chapelier law proclaimed that free trade and free working were the new economic standard by banning labour *corporations* as well as the right to gather and strike, presented as potentially reactionary because anti-national.[26] Individualised citizens were meant to work for the national common good, and the fatherland was expected to protect them better than monopolistic or oligopolistic guilds. This law was so crucial that it would only be modified in 1864, although one could argue that, in practice, labour communities and their less autocratic form known as *compagnonnage* (*associations ouvrières*)[27] did not completely disappear. They tried to reorganise themselves in the first half of the nineteenth century: there were then some 200,000 *compagnons* workers, who had to disguise themselves as religious or charity communities.[28] Their protective structure was severely weakened by the ideology of free trade, the progress of industrialisation, and state police surveillance – Napoleon's new *Code pénal* punished strike action with two to five years' imprisonment.[29]

In short, esprit de corps as solidarity was stolen from the labouring people to be used by the elites as coercive power, along the lines of an authoritarian and paternalist military model.

The Honour and Duty of the Soldier

In French military discourse, esprit de corps was a virtue of combative excellence. During the last century of the *Ancien Régime*, it was a sign of distinction within the army, differentiating each regiment (*corps d'armée*), and sometimes even triggering quarrels. However, the reasons for a soldier to feel the honour associated with esprit de corps changed along with the transformations of France. In 1793, the Revolution initiated an unprecedented process of generalised conscription via a *décret sur la levée en masse*. By 1798, the army was no longer a profession dominated by the aristocracy: it was a national duty that permeated most classes.

When monarchy was still strong, French military corps functioned as a set of semi-private companies ruled and managed by relatively powerful officers and recruiting largely within the aristocracy. In the mid-eighteenth century, captains of infantry as well as cavalry were still in charge of the recruitment and maintenance of their units in exchange for a certain amount of money, the actual expenses of captains often exceeding the sums granted to them.[30] In other words, a military *compagnie* was not unlike a French *corporation*, with its specific leadership and style: the army was far from homogenised. Every regiment believed it had a specific esprit *du* corps.

In the Régiment d'infanterie d'Auvergne, for instance, as in many other armed corps, soldiers belonged to the same families, villages or region.[31] This situation raised their *esprit de clocher*, a form of parochialism, and probably enhanced the military esprit de corps, a feeling of belongingness as well as an attitude of proud scorn towards other groups in the same profession. It was not rare to observe brawls and affrays between different military companies. Emotional manifestations of regimental distinction can still be observed today in the US army, as if the national scale were too wide for a proper esprit de corps, even in the army. This was strikingly analysed in Hutchins's *Cognition in the Wild*:

> These patterns of differentiation are present at all levels of organization in the military [. . .] Such effects are present to some degree in many social organizations, but they are highly elaborated in the military. Much of the establishment of identity is expressed in propositions like this: 'We are the fighting X's. We are proud of what we are and what we do. We are unlike any other group.'[32]

A good dialectic between national and regimental esprit de corps is vital in the military. Intermediary forms of esprit de corps were often tolerated and perhaps even encouraged in the French military, at least until the Revolution:

> The esprit de corps thus appears as a feeling conjugated on several levels, the action of which contributes to the definition of the army as an entanglement of communities that are both concurrent and competitive [. . .] As a source of inter-individual solidarity associated with the conviction of sharing a common honour, history and ideals, esprit de corps indeed contributed to the elevation of the military unit as an intermediary between the law and the individual [. . .] The esprit de corps thus appeared as a passion able to bind the individual interest to the general interest, thus being the expression of an art of necessitating individual heroic actions.[33]

Esprit de corps was an effectual feeling, with positive martial results. Its potential disrespect of the rule of law here and there was tolerated because the end – the sacrifice of the individual for the sake of national power – justified the means.

But not all officers or war theorists agreed that vainglorious competition between internal military units was good for the sake of the nation.

In 1762, after a series of French defeats, the clustered form of military esprit de corps was criticised and a reform was adopted. The management of French military corps became the responsibility of the royal administration, which now dealt with the recruiting and maintenance of the soldiers, including individual payments. This significant change prepared the ground for the Republican army, just as Turgot's royal attack on *corporations* prepared the ground for state capitalism. This military reform itself was much debated. A *capitaine* did not consider himself as a simple officer in the military hierarchy, but 'as the father of his soldiers, for whom he played the role of mediator vis-à-vis the requirements of the service'.[34] Until the Revolution, many memoirs promoted the re-establishment of the military profession as a 'family profession', where the officer would feel for his men and perhaps take fewer risks.[35] Small-scale esprit de corps in the army followed the 'rule of the father',[36] as did labour guilds, the royalist regime and religious autocracy. The *Ancien Régime* type of esprit de corps was structurally dependent on an embodied masculine figure of the master, the latter being often compared to a benevolent, protective and when needed severe paterfamilias.

Opposed to the familial and biased *feeling* of esprit de corps was the rational, mechanical figure of a well-regulated social machine, the clockwork ideal of the Enlightenment. After the reform, some *mémoires* on military discipline did advocate against the risk of a rationalised army of automata-soldiers (*soldats automates*), a reference to the mechanical techniques of the Prussian army. Passion was still needed, some French officers argued, and this was not incompatible with the national scale: 'The point of honour is not a chimera, as some false minds think, it is a national self-esteem produced by a secret satisfaction of doing well regardless of the reward.'[37] There was, as we have seen in the previous chapter, a common point on both sides of the debate: a growing tendency to favour the idea of a national level of esprit de corps. From this emerged the figure of the citizen-soldier: 'The question of the moral foundations of military obedience [. . .] is now associated with the requirement of conformity of discipline with the spirit of the nation.'[38] The duty to the regiment, its captain and one's brothers in arms was tentatively replaced by the more abstract ideal of duty to the fatherland.

Such evolution was not specific to France. The idea of national duty would also be emulated in Great Britain, as epitomised by the famous Nelson signal at the dawn of the nineteenth century: 'England expects that every man will do his duty.'[39] But esprit de corps was more than duty, or at least it intended to convey also the idea of enthusiasm. The production of a national esprit de corps was not only expected to reduce disorder and improve discipline and obedience, but also to increase ardour in combat. This increased the influence of the state over individuals without the interference of semi-autonomous brigades. The hope was that control by the supposedly more rational state would result in more efficiency.[40]

Deleuze, commenting on Foucault's views on discipline, described modern nation-states as societies where the liberty-and-equality discourse was a strategic way of maintaining forms of social conformity and internalised surveillance, 'un mécanisme de contrôle'.[41] In the next section, we will deepen our analysis of how Bonapartist politics organised society in accordance with a certain para- or meta-military notion of esprit de corps, where order and competitive agonism were incorporated in social institutions.

Defend Your Flag: Napoleonic Esprit de Corps

The army was for Napoleon the primary instrument of national cohesion, but which type of army? In the past, scholars have distinguished the 'army of virtue' of the Revolution and the 'army of honour' of the Empire:

> The Revolutionary government expected its soldiers to fight without concern for personal reward and to sacrifice for the good of the people and the state. On the other hand, Napoleon encouraged the personal interest of the soldier and strived to link it to that of the Empire by a system of awards and preferments.[42]

Expectations do not always become reality: the so-called army of virtuous citizen-soldiers was apparently short-lived, if it ever existed, although increased efforts were made during the Revolution to eradicate esprit de corps in the French military.

Honorific incentive was quickly re-established, as the call for virtue was considered insufficient to obtain the consent of soldiers conscripted more or less against their will and driven to fight further away from the national territory, in longer conflicts. Honour as a search for public recognition and official rewards, as opposed to honour as mere feeling, was seen by the ruling class as necessary, and loyalty was encouraged in particular by awards such as the *fusils d'honneur* distributed after 1796.[43] At the same time, an embodied top-down concept of authority and discipline appeared to be unavoidable. It was difficult for the French nation to function only as an abstract ideal; it had to manifest itself through material and symbolic recognition, and via human representatives. After the general conscription imposed by the *levée en masse*, which was reinforced by the *Loi Jourdan-Delbrel* in 1798, the recruiting of male citizens aged 20–25 became in theory compulsory. When they did not desert or could not afford a paid substitute, recruits were forced to fight and needed incentives.[44] Napoleon re-established an organised form of open competition between different corps, thus partly returning to the military esprit de corps of the *Ancien Régime*, although under a stricter form of state management.

This was a shift from the semi-mythical 'army of virtue' of the Revolution:

> The government of the Terror feared esprit de corps. Not surprisingly, revolutionary regimes in general tend to suspect this basic motivation, because it encourages the soldier to see himself primarily as a member of the armed forces. Such intense loyalty threatens the individual's identification with the revolution or the people. The Committee of Public Safety regarded the officer

corps as a threat and believed that loyalty to a regiment or battalion was a string by which officers might mislead their men.[45]

Esprit de corps in the eighteenth century, indeed an esprit *du* corps, was a subjective group quality seen by scientific minds as obsolete in a world where machines, rational and neutral protocols, were the new ideal, inspired by the idea that nature's harmony is itself mechanical.

In 1793, several *commissaires du pouvoir exécutif* advised Jean-Baptiste Bouchotte, the minister of war, to 'annihilate this esprit de corps which reproduces itself every day [. . .] the public spirit needs to be nurtured by the officers, who are generally preoccupied with their personal career rather than by the love of the fatherland [*patrie*]'.[46] Esprit de corps was associated with professional ambition: the pursuit of rank and distinctions. A certain revolutionary idealism was still wondering how this could be compatible with dedication to the nation. Napoleon would be more pragmatic and romantic: he knew that humans could not be persistently rational.

The very existence of officers tended to confirm that the military could not be devoid of hierarchy and the internal competition that it generates. An army that would function without orders, as a nationalist swarm of self-organising armed citizens, was deemed a fiction by critics of revolutionary idealism. Bertrand de Moleville, who worked in the Revolutionary government as a minister of the French marine corps before he emigrated to England, wrote in 1800:

> All the welfare that can be given to the soldiers is just and necessary; but there can be no army without officers and without discipline, and there will never be, as long as the soldiers think themselves entitled to judge the conduct of their leaders.[47]

In other words, in post-revolutionary France, hierarchy and paternalism was once more the key to military success: the authority of leaders should not be constantly questioned by egalitarian prattle.

Napoleon reintroduced and normalised the proud identification of the soldier with his combat unit, using for example regimental flags (*aigles*).[48] Soldiers would no longer take the vow to fight for 'Unité, indivisibilité de la République, liberté, égalité, fraternité ou la mort',[49] but instead take a pledge to defend their flag and regimental corps, and serve the emperor.[50] Competition, *émulation* and the quest for awards and recompense became important motives in an army driven by ambition, even if attitudes of self-sacrifice according to noble values were probably still present, as the exception that confirms the rule. The Consulat and the Empire used esprit de corps as a psychological force to bind French soldiers to the state's agenda:

> It is no accident that the final form of the inscription on the eagles makes no mention of the French people but ascribes the gift of the flag to Emperor Napoleon alone [. . .] In addition to the shift towards esprit de corps, the Army

of Honor required more emphasis on the self-interest of officers and soldiers alike. Certainly the self-interest of survival is a constant factor, but what is meant here is the desire for benefit and status [. . .] To be publicly chosen by your officers, acclaimed by your fellows, and rewarded by your Emperor not only honored the man promoted, but powerfully reinforced esprit de corps, primary group cohesion, and sense of closeness with, and love for, Napoleon.[51]

Napoleon created an army largely motivated by vainglory, *gloriole*, where anyone could collect either crumbs or slices of imperial glory.[52]

Under the Bonapartists, French society became a reflection of the military. Following the same strategy of constant ranking and competition, Napoleon and his ministers organised and disciplined the public service by reshaping the *grands corps de l'État*, the administrative chambers that still draw the outlines of the management of France (Conseil d'État, Cour de cassation, Cour des comptes, Corps préfectoral, Corps des mines, ponts et chaussées . . .). Under Bonapartism, the *grands corps* were consolidated. Official and solemn texts gave them a new legitimacy. They were instruments of centralisation, growing in influence along with the state, both parties taking advantage of each other.[53] As observed in military corps, the *grands corps d'État* developed a dual form of esprit de corps, serving the state and the interests of the particular corps in a constant tactical equilibrium. They reinforced the power of the state over its citizens, and they benefited from the official legitimacy given by the state to assert 'their domination over the administration and the administrated'.[54]

As official microcosms of masculine prestige and social promotion, the state corps contributed to the normalisation of administrative esprit de corps in France. Many of the members of the *grands corps* had been acquainted since their student years:

> The main mechanism for creating such an 'esprit' was in fact to establish institutions that became known as 'corps'. One often speaks of the English 'old-boy network' based on the 'school tie', but important as the tie may be in binding people later on in life, it can scarcely compare with a system that institutionalises the camaraderie of school days by ensuring that it continues during one's active life [. . .] There is no other country where the term 'esprit de corps' has such a literal meaning.[55]

This official normalisation and standardisation of esprit de corps relied on a inegalitarian social system, in which the elite who had access to the *grand* implied a majority confined to the *petit*. In the *grandes écoles*, with their admission exams [*concours*] organised as social funnels, and their diplomas which functioned as passes to mandarinates, a form of military order was merged with 'engineering rationality'.[56] The political theorist Marie-Christine Kessler suggests:

> These are barriers that stand between civil society and the administrative society and defend access to the Great Bodies [. . .] The Grandes écoles are

simultaneously born of the idea of selection and of a technological necessity. The notions of competition and selection were unknown in the old universities of France [. . .] The idea of selection is part of a general concern for rationality linked to the Enlightenment.[57]

Note the historical irony: while most eighteenth-century *Philosophes* advocated the eradication of esprit de corps in the name of rational merit and national spirit, post-revolutionary France offered to combine them. And this was possible because the French Revolution itself invented the idea of a 'national esprit de corps'.

The new and less religious philosophy of education, following an international tendency, valued science and engineering studies over letters and humanities, contrary to the dominant education formerly provided by the Jesuits. Napoleon amplified this movement and gave it a standardised structure. An archetypical manifestation of the new state-engineered form of esprit de corps was the aforementioned École polytéchnique, which offered both military and scientific education. Its students – exclusively male until 1972 – are still required today to possess a tailored military uniform and a sabre to be worn on special occasions. In combination with military-like discipline, the spirit of mathematics helped to create an ordered and normative society. Beyond being a tool for knowledge, mathematical science is believed to be a foundation of competence and becomes the instrument of distinction of the *polytéchnicien* within social and political elites. It produces the norms of rational judgement on which the technocratic action and the organisation of state bureaucracy are built.[58]

Strictly speaking, the *grands corps d'État* were not a spontaneous nineteenth-century invention: this form of governance had slowly matured since the centralisation process initiated by Louis XIV. Vauban created the Corps du génie (military engineering corps) in 1691 by bringing together royal engineers involved in constructing the kingdom's fortifications.[59] The Ponts et chaussées and its corps of engineers were institutionalised in 1716 to run public works throughout the country.[60] But in the last years of the eighteenth century, the distinction between civilian and military engineers was completely blurred, and the mission of the École nationale des ponts et chaussées, created in 1747, was extended to supply the army with technical experts. The unification and social engineering of a meta-military social order became systematic during Napoleon's administration, and this was reinforced by the schooling system.

The *lycée* teachers in secondary schools were to be trained with the same homogeneity of spirit and respect for – or fear of – the state. Where a military ethos could not prevail, the crypto-military fashion of the Jesuits was remembered. In the words of Napoleon Bonaparte himself, a 'corporation of education'[61] was to be created, in which the esprit de corps of the Jesuit schools ought to be emulated:

This body would have a spirit. The Emperor could protect its most distinguished members and raise them by his favours higher in opinion than were the priests when the priesthood was considered as a kind of nobility. Everyone felt the importance of the Jesuits; it would not be long before we saw the importance of the corporation of education, when one would see a man first educated in a *lycée*, called by his talents to become a teacher himself, to advance grade after grade, and to find himself at the close of his career in the first ranks of the State. Of all political questions, this one is perhaps of the first order. There will be no stable political state if there is not a teaching body [*corps enseignant*] with fixed principles. If we do not learn from childhood whether to be republican or monarchical, Catholic or irreligious, etc., the State will not form a nation; it will rest on uncertain and vague bases; it will be constantly exposed to disorder and change.[62]

This was a clear statement of Bonapartist ideology. The use of expressions such as *avancer de grade en grade* indicated that this was a military-inspired regime which promised a progressive ranking to its most deferential and zealous citizen-soldiers, trained to be competing and state-obedient citizens before they became adults. Education was unified in the name of social order around the idea of discipline, and positive disciplines related to calculus were encouraged. Scientific minds were considered more useful and less seditious than writers, artists or philosophers.

Technocracy was the new aristocracy. The *polytéchniciens* were called to administrate different prestigious official institutions:

> In all, twelve technical services recruited at least some of their future technical experts and top administrators at the École polytéchnique in the middle of the 19th century. Most of these senior executives were organised within a corps-based system [. . .] Within each department, there was a strong '*esprit de corps*'. Yet, the forces that bound all these technical departments together were much more powerful than those that drove them apart [. . .] By unifying the recruitment and training structures for state experts and developing a homogeneous professional culture, mainly based on mathematics and science [. . .] the reformers [. . .] transformed a disparate group of technical corps into a homogeneous bureaucratic universe.[63]

The two scales of esprit de corps, autonomous (corporate) and universal (national), often considered antinomic in the eighteenth century, were now intertwined around a conformative 'cultural capital'[64] that combined social privileges, technical power and officialised norms. The chaos, excesses and fears of the Revolution created a national religion of order, ideologically validated by the combined successes of science and imperialism. The French Empire – not unlike the British one – established a perennial technocratic esprit de corps as a foundation for the dominant class. The motto of the Polytéchnique, for example, was self-explanatory: *Pour la patrie, la science et la gloire.*

Today, L'École polytéchnique is still considered to be a world-class higher-education institution, providing private and public chief executives, high-profile managers, or docile financial brains that are appreciated by recruiters internationally. Students start their education with basic military and command training, a propaedeutic that is advertised on the school's website as 'leadership training [according to] methods that inspire the business world'.[65] Between 2008 and 2012, the Polytéchnique claims to have collected over 30 million euros from its alumni to develop the school's international ambition. A former student and donor recently said: 'It's my contribution to the esprit de corps of the school [. . .] If you had the chance to study at the Polytéchnique, it is natural to give back.'[66] Financing younger recruits, via the school, because they belong to the same body is not philanthropy: 'The *polytéchnicien* system [. . .] which was explicitly set up to provide the French State with technical personnel, formed a close-knit separate world.'[67] The institution serves as a status- and order-producing machine, and as long as the *polytéchniciens* are pursuing a better position, rank after rank, which is an effort that is meant to last most of their life, they have a vested interest in the ongoing reputation of the school.

A system of *internats* was also normalised by Napoleon, thanks to which more students were living and sleeping in the schools:

> An admirer of the organisation of army and church, he thought in terms of hierarchy, uniformity, and order. The *internat* or French boarding school, with its strict military and cloistered regime, moulded strong mutual bonds and an esprit de corps which carried over into professional life.[68]

This point reveals a fundamental aspect of the engineering of esprit de corps, the 'principle of enclosure', defined as follows by Foucault:

> Discipline sometimes requires enclosure, specifying a place that is heterogeneous to all others, closed on itself. The protected place of disciplinary monotony [. . .] Colleges: the convent model is slowly imposed; the boarding school appears as the most perfect education regime, if not the most frequent.[69]

An important word here again is 'discipline'. It is once again important to note that the historical polarity of esprit de corps is mirrored in the ambivalence of the notion of discipline, which can imply both coercion (authority by force) and know-how (*a* discipline, a skill, a craft, a careful and specialised domain of practice).

Normalisation and national-universalism were connected after the Revolution, but even more so in the nineteenth century. The prestigious École normale supérieure, a *grande école* founded in 1794, was reorganised by the Bonapartists with the intention of standardising higher education and research. State boarding schools where students were trained to be teachers were also called *écoles normales*:

> With the introduction of a standardized education and the establishment of the *Écoles normales*, the Normal is established as a principle of coercion. In a sense, normalization as a form of power forces homogeneity; but it individualizes the

members by allowing certain limited divergences, by determining a ranking, by fixing specific skills and producing useful differences and adjusting them to each other. We understand that the power of the norm operates efficiently within a system of formal equality: in accordance with the rule of homogeneity, it introduces a *dégradé* of individual differences as a useful and measured imperative.[70]

Competition, emulation, reward, order, normality, measure and ranking were key notions in the post-revolutionary state, a society in which everybody ought to serve the national machine, even if some well-supervised coteries were allowed to think of themselves as *superiorly normal*.

Napoleon created a 'noblesse d'État',[71] still largely operational in today's France. It could be argued that the universalisation of competitive conformity was not entirely negative for democracy: over the last two centuries, mostly in periods of economic growth, emulation and ordered rivalry allowed for some assimilation of differences and reduction of inequalities to a certain extent, in the name of the Republic. Official esprit de corps allowed some citizens to climb up the social ladder by playing the game of normalised agonism, the regulated fight for recognition. The various national corps and the official educational institutions attracted both the upper classes and the middle class, thus functioning as instruments both of social confirmation and social mobility.

In the nineteenth century, some boarding schools became a space of very relative – and dominantly masculine – social diversity, or *mixité sociale*. In the *écoles d'arts et métiers*, for instance:

> By the second half of the century [. . .] 28 percent [of the pupils] were the sons of industrialists, businessmen or company supervisors; 38 percent of skilled workers, artisans and foremen; and the remainder of small employees in business and industry, government clerks, and farmers. Seventy-one percent of graduates attained supervisory posts and a good number rose eventually to become factory managers, company directors and independent manufacturers.[72]

The debate as to whether French education is egalitarian or not is today less optimistic, as illustrated recently by the publication of an encyclopaedic dictionary of school inequalities (*Dictionnaire des inégalités scolaires*).[73] According to the historian Émile Chabal, France is a highly 'divided republic'.[74] The sociologist Louis Chauvel observes that for the new generations, the social lift is indefinitely out of order.[75]

The Cement of the Social Edifice: The Counter-Revolutionary Praise of Esprit de Corps

After 1800, unsympathetic histories of the French Revolution were published in France and became more or less popular among the ruling elite. In one of them, the aforementioned Bertrand de Moleville suggested sarcastically that if esprit de corps, a revolutionary derogatory trope, was to be taken as a negative phenomenon, then it was in fact epitomised during the *Terreur* by the Jacobins who pretended to be enemies of esprit de corps. They, more than any, were the biased power clique, a 'small minority of scoundrels who managed, by their audaciousness, to dominate France, and to cut its throat'.[76] The author mocked the so-called patriotism of the 'frenzied revolutionaries' [*forcenés*]: 'If there ever was an esprit de corps, dare I say a public spirit, it was among the members of this abominable sect [. . .] for the eternal shame of decent people.'[77] Esprit de corps was here sarcastically associated with *esprit public* because it had been the rhetoric of the Jacobins to claim that their acts were virtuously driven by the latter. When a minority wants to subjugate an entire nation, suggested Moleville, it pretends to combat particularism in the name of a form of universalism, so as to disguise its partisan politics.

Not unlike future Marxist interpreters of the French Revolution,[78] authors who were nostalgic for monarchy claimed that the systematic critique of esprit de corps had been produced by the *Philosophes* and the revolutionaries as an ideological bait, a sociopolitical tactic to disarm opposing groups, and eventually replace them. Esprit de corps was a rhetorical notion serving what Carl Schmitt would call the argumentative construction of a 'friend–enemy' distinction, for the sake of 'political actions and motives'.[79]

To understand through another example how the perception of esprit de corps evolved before and after the Revolution, we can compare two views on academia. In the first, defended in 1788, Mirabeau echoed the *Encyclopédie*'s derogatory use of esprit de corps to condemn universities and their monopoly on knowledge production. He accused higher-education institutions of misdirecting their *raison d'être* by creating spheres of power rather than producing an open and neutral form of knowledge:

> Universities [. . .] in addition to the ridiculous and harmful monopoly of knowledge that is accorded to them, produce an even greater evil by giving the men of letters who compose them an esprit de corps, which limits or dominates them, since they are obliged to conform to it, at least externally, either in what they teach or in what they publish.[80]

It should be clear by now that such equation of esprit de corps with monopoly and the corruption of thought, combined with an implicit and ambiguous defence of market competition, was a relatively orthodox Enlightenment discourse.

Conversely, it became accepted in the nineteenth century to assume that esprit de corps, in universities and elsewhere, if controlled by the state to limit its autonomous drive, could be 'excellent' and 'noble'.[81] During a speech in 1844, the statesman Victor de Broglie was cheerfully acclaimed when he declared before the upper house of Parliament (Chambre des pairs):

> The university is a body [*corps*]; she says it, she boasts of it, and she does well to boast of it. Yes, the university is a corporation. I am glad it is a corporation

[. . .] This body has a spirit, and such spirit is called esprit de corps. (Laughter in the audience). This is not an evil, it is good; it must be accepted, because it is good, and then, as being a corps comes with some disadvantages, it must be taken into account. (Signs of approval).[82]

The context of this speech was the introduction of a new law that was intended to confer more autonomy – under state control – to private educational institutions and therefore weaken the monopoly of the public university. Half a century after the Revolution, elitist esprit de corps, even if it could be said, for the sake of politics, to have 'some disadvantages', was no longer a real threat for the public power, which after the departure of Napoleon remained highly centralised and organised according to the same administrative principles of control. The patronising and self-confident words and humour of de Broglie suggested that all forms of education, public or private, were anyway under state surveillance; the autonomy of the university was a pretence from the point of view of the rulers.

After Napoleon, even autonomist forms of esprit de corps – if disciplined and contained – were encouraged. Institutional societies were authorised to cultivate a form of idiosyncrasy and relative oligopoly, as long as they continued to serve the state's interests. The consensus within the French dominant classes was that revolutionary hubris had gone too far; individual freedom and the myth of equality needed to be counter-balanced with norms and hierarchy. In the end, freedom of trade mattered more than liberty. In the words of the president of the École de médicine, Jean-Noël Hallé, who was also Napoleon's personal physician:[83]

When men are united in a society, two very different and often opposed spirits [esprits] are formed among them: one develops in all social institutions; it is the esprit de corps; the other animates these ardent men, whose authority mobilises and leads the general mass of people: it is the spirit of innovation. The first spirit wishes to conserve; the second to perfect through change [. . .] A good government makes use of the one and the other spirit: with the first one it cements the useful institutions and gives morals to men; with the other, the government improves and perfects without destroying.[84]

Esprit de corps, naturalised as ubiquitous and inevitable, was candidly presented as an instrument of social arrangement, far from the violent rebellious spirit of which the rulers of France were weary. Esprit de corps produced a sort of secular ethos that served social regulation and consent. In this official distinction between corps (for the many) and innovation (by the few), even creativity was seen as controlled by the government.

Hallé's text was considered important enough to be published in 1803 in the *Mercure de France*, one of the major echo chambers for the new kind of conservatism that pervaded the country. For the new rulers, innovation should not disturb order, the latter being justified as a collective and emotional need, again often by analogy with the idea of family and kinship: 'In families, there is an esprit de corps which, from degree to degree, meanders throughout the social edifice, of which it is the cement.'[85] This contributed to the view that considered esprit de corps as a dam against the excesses of freedom and equality. If the Revolution's attempt to create a unified and horizontal form of republican loyalty that would have prevailed over more specific corporatist attachments had failed, it was because the roots of esprit de corps were sentimental and natural.

In such a context, it is not surprising that religion was seen once more as the partner of the state. The most prominent advocate of the return to a disciplined social order under the influence of Christianism was Louis de Bonald. Upon returning to France after a decade of counter-revolutionary political exile, he collected year after year official distinctions of French prestige, culminating in his election in 1815–16 both to the Académie française and to the governing Assemblée nationale.[86] A regular writer for the *Mercure de France*, he published stark defences of the values of order, family and work, in which he praised esprit de corps as the natural glue of a virtuous Catholic society:

The true nature of man is society [. . .] The Christian religion regulates the state, the state regulates the bodies [*corps*], the bodies regulate the families, the family regulates the individual: everything tends to be a body in the social world; it is the force of adherence of the physical world [. . .] spirit of religion, spirit of homeland, esprit de corps, family spirit, public spirit ultimately, this soul of society, the principle of its life, of its strength and progress.[87]

Eighteenth-century oppositions between public spirit and esprit de corps were dismissed, in a sort of crypto-scientific theological discourse where the physical and the spiritual were interrelated. Many readers of the *Mercure* were probably familiar enough with Latin to know that *religion* meant, etymologically, *to tie, to bind* (*religare*).

Under the restored monarchy, de Bonald wrote *De l'esprit de corps et de l'esprit de parti*, a short but widely noticed pamphlet in which he defended hereditary and aristocratic representatives against elected ones. What the eighteenth-century spirit had criticised under the name of esprit de corps, he argued, should have never been ceased to be called *esprit de parti*:[88]

Esprit de corps and *esprit de parti* are two different and even opposite spirits. Party spirit is [. . .] the particular spirit of a part, of a fraction of a great whole; and religious or political parties are but fractions or sects of French society. The esprit de corps is the general spirit of the whole body. The *esprit de parti* divides and dissolves; the esprit de corps unites and strengthens, and one can say that a body without esprit de corps is a body without a soul [. . .] Nations also have their esprit de corps, which is called public spirit, the principle of their force of resistance and stability [. . .] There was a great deal of this public spirit in France before the Reformation, which divided it into two parties, religious and political.[89]

Decade after decade, the historical redefinition of esprit de corps continued, depending on the web of belief; here it was the universal beneficial soul of all collective bodies under the rule of a Catholic state. The Protestant spirit was, like the revolutionary spirit, a factor of social dissolution.

Another argument in favour of esprit de corps, according to de Bonald, was that its mode of transmission was, more often than not, hereditary. Members were therefore part of a potentially immortal, eternal body. In other words, esprit de corps was sacred, while *esprit de parti*, motivated by particular interests, was a secular and contingent road to perdition. Well-versed in the intellectual history of the eighteenth century, de Bonald dedicated several pages to the defence of the 'excellent' esprit de corps of the Jesuits, and only a few lines to the detestable *esprit de parti* of the *Encyclopédistes*, chief among them d'Alembert and Diderot. This counter-revolutionary view contended that social order was to be based on a society of bodies embedded in one another like nesting dolls decreasing in size: Church, state, corps and family. Individual freedom, if it were to be tolerated, had to come last and smallest. Indistinct masses of democratic individuals were a threat if led to believe in a regime in which 'government is by the crowd and is no longer by the state'.[90]

Despite his Catholic allegiance, de Bonald was at odds with the kind of cosmopolitan humanism exemplified by authors such as Bernardin de Saint-Pierre. The latter had claimed in 1788: 'I have attacked particular bodies to defend that of the fatherland, and, above all, the body of the human race. We are all but members of the latter.'[91] Internationalist humanistic views did not disappear in the nineteenth century, but they were not mainstream, as France was preoccupied with the rebuilding of its transnational hegemony and the avoidance of sedition, not only within the Hexagone but also, after 1830, in the new colonies.

I described how the Jesuits were banned from France in the 1760s. If it is true that the Society of Jesus was a paragon of effectual esprit de corps, their progressive return to France in the first half of the nineteenth century was symptomatic. Although some anti-Jesuitism remained present as the 'quintessence and core of anticlericalism',[92] the Jesuits did regain part of their power over the French Church. Napoleon himself considered them as an organisational model, in part because their corporation had since its origin been meta-military.

In a state interested in the institutionalisation of esprit de corps, the Jesuits' know-how was useful again:

> I know that their enemies have greatly criticised their esprit de corps, and that they have pretended that this is what made them so dangerous; but I also know that this esprit de corps is what worried their enemies the most [. . .] I would say that the Jesuits were like those brothers in arms among ancient knights, on whom the bonds of the closest friendship imposed the duty of marching towards combat equally, to attack together and defend each other.[93]

The idea of brotherhood in arms is often correlated with esprit de corps, and some are tempted to consider it as the core common denominator of most uses of the phrase, the 'original exemplar' of a 'contested concept'.[94] We have seen and will meet again conceptions of esprit de corps that do not seem to carry a combative denotation, but rather, for instance, the idea of familial love or natural sociality. Yet one could ask whether even in these contexts esprit de corps isn't an agonistic notion, one that implicitly suggests enmity towards outer groups. In the first half of the nineteenth century, esprit de corps was a large-scale *dispositif*, an apparatus to concentrate power in the hands of groups that should serve or appear to be serving the national order:[95] 'Here the *Grands corps* are filled with what is called esprit de corps.'[96] The ideological officialisation of esprit de corps was possible in part because forming coalitions was considered a trait of human nature, like egoism and the quest for individual glory: 'That esprit de corps, which is to societies, what egoism is to individuals.'[97] The 'power of esprit de corps'[98] was seen as an irreducible historical and social force.

In the meantime, a small constellation of intellectuals who still hoped for a more open society and considered esprit de corps to be surmountable or avoidable could only lament its social or discursive endurance. Reflecting on the influence of literature upon society, Madame de Staël criticised the post-revolutionary prominence of games of power over real freedom. She saw how the military spirit now influenced the entire society, to the detriment of liberty:

The excessive influence of the military spirit is also an imminent danger to free states [. . .] Discipline prevents individual opinions from being formed among the troops. In this respect, their esprit de corps has something to do with that of the priests; it equally excludes reasoning, admitting solely the will of the hierarchical leaders [. . .] By winning battles, one can subdue the enemies of liberty; but to diffuse the principles of such liberty within men, the military spirit must be obliterated; it is necessary that thought, united with warlike qualities, with courage, ardour, decision, should give rise in men's souls to something spontaneous.[99]

This was to a certain extent a revival of the view of the *Philosophes* regarding esprit de corps, but with the ambivalent suggestion of not abandoning a martial state of mind and 'warlike qualities', while associating them with the faculties of reason and a form of autonomous spontaneity. This idealistic combination of reason, ardour, fighting force of character and personal spontaneity was an ambitious and perhaps contradictory Romanticist ideal, an attempt to unite contraries as they seemed united in nature – or in Napoleon?

The writer Benjamin Constant, a close friend of de Staël,[100] explained less ambiguously that esprit de corps and *esprit de conquête* were synonymous, and opposed to the ideals of peace, liberty and humanism:

An exclusive and hostile esprit de corps always seizes associations that have a different purpose than the rest of men. In spite of the sweetness and purity of Christianity, the confederations of its priests have often formed separated states within states. Everywhere men gathered in army corps separate from the nation. They develop a kind of respect for the use of force, of which they are depositories.[101]

The idea of a state within a state was a reprise of d'Alembert's definition of esprit de corps as a nation within a nation. Both Constant and de Staël intuited that there was a disturbing connection between modernity and a more or less symbolic weaponisation of society, and that even churches were not devoid of this quasi-military spirit. This martial connotation would continue to crystallise around our signifier in the twentieth century, especially in American capitalist discourse.

What was this purpose of 'the rest of men' that Constant alluded to? He defended the new value of happiness, le bonheur,[102] the product of an equilibrium between the sociality of belongingness and the vigour of personal freedom. Such a balance was much discussed in the second half of the French nineteenth century: it became a major concern for both socialists and sociologists.

Notes

1. 'Dans tout État bien gouverné, il y a un esprit propre à chaque branche d'administration. Cet esprit donne de l'unité, de l'uniformité et une certaine énergie à la direction des affaires; il transmet la tradition des devoirs, il en perpétue le sentiment et l'observation; il attache et le corps, et les individus qui en sont membres, au Gouvernement, comme au but vers lequel toutes les émulations se dirigent, comme à la source de tous les degrés de considération dont on ambitionne de jouir.' Charles Maurice de Talleyrand, 'Rapport au Conseil d'État du 20 avril 1800', in Louis Bastide, Vie religieuse et politique de Talleyrand-Périgord, Prince de Bénévent (Paris: Faure, 1838), p. 229.

2. C. R. Day, 'Making Men and Training Technicians: Boarding Schools of the Ecoles d'Arts et Métiers during the Nineteenth Century', Historical Reflexions 7.2/3 (1980), pp. 381–96 (p. 395).

3. Mary Pickering, Auguste Comte: An Intellectual Biography, 2 vols (Cambridge: Cambridge University Press, 1993), vol. I, p. 25.

4. 'Admis enfin, aurais-je alors, / Pour tout esprit, l'esprit de corps? / Il rend le bon sens, quoi qu'on en dise, / Solidaire de la sottise; / Mais, dans votre société, / L'esprit de corps, c'est la gaîté. / Cet esprit-là règne sans tyrannie. / Non, non, ce n'est point comme à l'Académie.' Pierre-Jean de Béranger, 'L'Académie et le Caveau, Chanson de réception au Caveau Moderne', in Chansons complètes (Paris, 1832), pp. 7–8.

5. 'Il n'y a point d'esprit de corps parmi les femmes, et cela doit être. Formées par leur sensibilité, pour avoir une existence moins intéressante et moins égoïste, la gloire, à moins d'exceptions très rares, au lieu d'être pour elles une possession personnelle, n'est presque toujours qu'un bien relatif. Elles la trouvent dans les actions d'un père, d'un fils, d'un époux; elles l'empruntent et ne la donnent pas, et les lois, en cela, sont d'accord avec la nature.' Félicité de Genlis, 'La Femme Auteur', in Nouveaux Contes moraux et nouvelles historiques, 3 vols (Paris: Maradan, 1802), vol. III, p. 128.

6. 'L'esprit de corps, qui peut être mauvais dans l'ensemble, est toujours bon dans la partie.' François-René de Chateaubriand, Génie du Christianisme ou beautés de la religion chrétienne, 5 vols (Paris: Migneret, 1803), vol. IV, p. 393.

7. George F. Nafziger, Historical Dictionary of the Napoleonic Era (Lanham, MD: Scarecrow Press, 2002), p. 80.

8. 'Déterminer 1° Les avantages attachés à l'esprit de corps parmi les gens de l'art [medical doctors]; 2° les moyens d'établir cet esprit de corps de la manière la plus désirable. La société désire que les concurrents envisagent l'esprit de corps parmi

les gens de l'art, autant dans l'intérêt du corps médical lui-même, qu'en vue des progrès de la science et du bien de l'humanité souffrante.' *Journal de Médecine et de Chirurgie Pratique, à l'usage des médecins praticiens* (Paris: Crapelet, 1844), vol. XV, p. 322.

9. 'Au prix d'une réforme complète de son éducation et de sa pratique, [le médecin] sera en conséquence incorporé au sacerdoce de l'Humanité et voué à la réforme progressive des institutions occidentales.' Frédéric Dupin, 'Réformer la médecine par la littérature: l'éducation des médecins dans la philosophie positive d'auguste Comte', *Cahiers de Narratologie* 18 (2010), <https://journals.openedition.org/narra tologie/5981> (accessed 19 September 2019).

10. 'Tout trouble de l'ordre arrête le progrès.' Eugène Bourdet, *Principes d'éducation positive* (Paris: Germer-Baillière, 1877), p. xi.

11. 'Là où il n'y a pas d'esprit de corps, ce n'est qu'anarchie.' Nicolas Magon de la Gervaisais, *La péninsule en tutelle* (Paris: Pihan-Delaforest, 1828), p. 71.

12. 'Esprit se dit également de la disposition, de l'aptitude qu'on a à quelque chose; ou du principe, du motif, de l'intention, des vues par lesquelles on est dirigé dans sa conduite [. . .] *Esprit de corps*, Attachement des membres d'une corporation aux opinions, aux droits, aux intérêts de la compagnie.' *Dictionnaire de l'Académie française*, 2 vols (Paris: Firmin-Didot, 1835), vol. I, p. 679.

13. 'Association autorisée par la puissance publique, et formée de plusieurs personnes qui vivent sous une police commune relativement à leur profession.' Ibid., p. 412.

14. Ibid., p. 122.

15. 'Les ennemis naturels d'une communauté sont toutes les autres communautés.' Jacques Claude Vincent de Gournay, *Mémoire à la chambre de commerce de Lyon* (Lyons: Archives Municipales, 1752), p. 202.

16. 'En effet ces communautés ont des lois particulières, qui sont presque toutes opposées au bien général et aux vues du législateur. La première et la plus dangereuse est celle qui oppose des barrières à l'industrie, en multipliant les frais et les formalités [. . .] On ne voit qu'un monopole contraire aux lois de la raison [. . .] Le premier principe du Commerce est la concurrence; c'est par elle seule que les Arts se perfection-nent, que les denrées abondent, que l'[É]tat se procure un grand superflu à exporter [. . .] enfin qu'il remplit son objet immédiat d'occuper et de nourrir le plus grand nombre d'hommes qu'il lui est possible.' François Véron Duverger de Forbonnais, 'Communauté (commerce)', in Denis Diderot and Jean le Rond d'Alembert (eds), *Encyclopédie, ou dictionnaire raisonné des sciences, des arts et des métiers* (Paris: Briasson, David, Le Breton and Durand, 1751–65), vol. III (1753), p. 724.

17. Kenji Kawano, 'The French Revolution and the Progress of Capitalism', *Kyoto University Economic Review* 30.2 (1960), pp. 31–42; William H. Sewell Jr, 'Connecting Capitalism to the French Revolution: The Parisian Promenade and the Origins of Civic Equality in Eighteenth-Century France', *Critical Historical Studies* 1.1 (2014), pp. 5–46; William Scott, 'Commerce, Capitalism, and the Political Culture of the French Revolution', *History of European Ideas* 11 (1989), pp. 89–105; William M. Reddy, *The Rise of Market Culture: The Textile Trade and French Society, 1750–1914* (Cambridge: Cambridge University Press, 1984).

18. 'Ce n'est pas [. . .] cet esprit de corps qui distinguait les différentes classes d'ouvriers, moins encore le temps qu'on exigeait pour l'apprentissage, qui rendaient les produits plus parfaits [. . .] Les maîtres qui avaient acquis le droit de faire des souliers, étaient moins jaloux de les perfectionner, parce qu'au moyen de la coalition qu'ils formaient entre eux et de l'esprit de corps qu'ils savaient entretenir, ils craignaient peu les

effets de la concurrence.' Vital Roux, *De l'influence du gouvernement sur la prospérité du commerce* (Paris: Fayolle, 1800), pp. 262–4.

19. Liana Vardi, *The Physiocrats and the World of the Enlightenment* (New York: Cambridge University Press, 2012), p. 241.

20. 'Les corporations étaient les garantes de la moralité et les gardiennes de la sécurité. Elles faisaient doublement office de "filtre", afin d'éliminer l'incompétence qui se transformait imperceptiblement en corruption. L'arrivée de la liberté était "le triomphe de l'usure et de la tromperie", de la "mauvaise foi", du "brigandage", de "l'imperfection dans les ouvrages", de "l'indifférence et de la négligence". Sans les critères imposés par les corporations, sans l'esprit de corps et le contrôle des corporations, le marché allait être envahi de marchandises et de services frauduleux.' Kaplan, *La fin des corporations*, p. 89.

21. 'Plus on réfléchit sur notre Philosophie Moderne, plus on est convaincu que le premier de tous ses principes est l'égoïsme. Liberté, propriété, voilà les signes de ralliement. La Société n'a été introduite que pour en assurer la jouissance, chaque individu ne lui doit rien; c'est à son intérêt personnel qu'il doit uniquement s'attacher.' Anonymous, *Mémoire des fruitiers-orangers*, 1776, BNF, Coll. Joly 462, fol. 120–1, <http://gallica.bnf.fr>.

22. Marie-France Piguet, 'Individualisme: Origine et reception initiale du mot', *Œuvres et critiques* 33.1 (2008), pp. 39–60.

23. Michael Kwass, 'Consumption and the World of Ideas: Consumer Revolution and the Moral Economy of the Marquis de Mirabeau', *Eighteenth-Century Studies* 37.2 (2004), pp. 187–213.

24. 'visible dans le peuple depuis quelques années et surtout dans les métiers'; Louis Sébastien Mercier, *Tableau de Paris* (Amsterdam, 1782), vol. XII, p. 323.

25. 'Les apprentis et les maçons veulent se montrer indépendants; ils manquent du respect au maître [. . .] De nos jours le petit peuple est sorti de la subordination à un point que je puis prédire qu'avant peu on verra les plus mauvais effets de cet oubli de toute discipline.' Ibid., p. 324.

26. Kaplan, *La fin des corporations*, p. 560.

27. François Icher, *Le compagnonnage* (Paris: Gallimard, 1994).

28. Ibid., pp. 29–37.

29. Bernard Valade, 'Droit de grève (France)', *Encyclopaedia Universalis*, <https://www.universalis.fr/encyclopedie/droit-de-greve/> (accessed 19 September 2019).

30. Arnaud Guinier, *L'honneur du soldat: Éthique martiale et discipline guerrière dans la France des Lumières* (Paris: Champ Vallon, 2014), p. 292.

31. Ibid., p. 306.

32. Edwin Hutchins, *Cognition in the Wild* (Cambridge, MA: MIT Press, 1995), p. 9.

33. 'L'esprit de corps apparaît ainsi comme un sentiment décliné à plusieurs niveaux et dont l'action participe à la définition de l'armée comme un enchevêtrement de communautés à la fois concourantes et concurrentielles [. . .] Source de solidarités interindividuelles associées à la conviction de partager un honneur, une histoire et des idéaux communs, l'esprit de corps participait en effet à l'élévation de l'unité comme intermédiaire entre la loi et l'individu [. . .] L'esprit de corps apparaissait donc comme l'une des passions à même de lier l'intérêt individuel au général, s'inscrivant de ce fait à l'intérieur d'un art de nécessiter les hommes aux actions héroïques.' Guinier, *L'honneur du soldat*, p. 306.

34. Ibid., p. 318.

35. Ibid., p. 318.

36. Julia Adams, 'The Rule of the Father: Patriarchy and Patrimonialism in Early Modern Europe', in Charles Camic, Philip S. Gorski and David M. Trubek (eds), *Max Weber's Economy and Society* (Stanford: Stanford University Press, 2005), pp. 237–66.

37. 'Le point d'honneur n'est pas une chimère, comme quelques esprits faux le pensent, c'est un amour-propre national produit par une secrète satisfaction de bien faire sans égard à la récompense.' Anonymous, 'Observations sur le rétablissement de la discipline militaire', in *Manuscrits du Service historique de la défense* (1766), <http://www.servicehistorique.sga.defense.gouv.fr/?q=content/nos-ressources> (accessed 19 September 2019).

38. Guinier, *L'honneur du soldat*, p. 20.

39. David Howarth and Stephen Howarth, *Nelson: The Immortal Memory* (London: Conway Maritime Press, 2004), p. 371.

40. Guinier, *L'honneur du soldat*, p. 295.

41. Gilles Deleuze, 'Post-scriptum sur les sociétés de contrôle', in *Pourparlers* (Paris: Minuit, 1990), p. 242.

42. John A. Lynn, 'Toward an Army of Honor: The Moral Evolution of the French Army, 1789–1815', *French Historical Studies* 16.1 (1989), pp. 152–73.

43. Guinier, *L'honneur du soldat*, p. 365.

44. T. C. W. Banning, *The French Revolutionary Wars, 1787–1802* (London: Hodder Education, 1996), p. 111.

45. Lynn, 'Toward an Army of Honor', p. 164.

46. 'anéantir cet esprit de corps qui se reproduit journellement [car] l'esprit public a besoin d'être ranimé parmi les officiers qui, en général, sont plus occupés du calcul de leurs places que de l'amour de la patrie'; Camille Rousset, *Les Volontaires: 1791–1794* (Paris: Didier, 1870), p. 199.

47. 'Tout le bien-être qu'on peut donner aux soldats est juste et nécessaire; mais il ne peut y avoir d'armée sans officiers et sans discipline, et il n'y en aura jamais, tant que les soldats se croiront en droit de juger la conduite de leurs chefs.' Antoine François Bertrand de Moleville, *Annals of the French Revolution*, 4 vols (London: Cadell and Davies, 1800), vol. IV, p. 113.

48. Jean-Paul Bertaud, *La vie quotidienne des soldats de la Révolution, 1789–1799* (Paris: Hachette, 1985), pp. 113–15.

49. 'Unité, indivisibilité de la République, liberté, égalité, fraternité ou la mort', estampe (Paris: Basset, 1792).

50. Marcel Baldet, *La vie quotidienne dans les armées de Napoléon* (Paris: Hachette, 1964), pp. 127–8.

51. Lynn, 'Toward an Army of Honor', pp. 165–8.

52. Rory Muir, *Tactics and the Experience of Battle in the Age of Napoleon* (New Haven, CT: Yale University Press, 1998), p. 221.

53. Marie-Christine Kessler, 'Les grands corps de l'État', *La Revue administrative* 231 (1996), pp. 221–8 (p. 221).

54. Ibid., p. 222.

55. Ezra N. Suleiman, *Elites in French Society: The Politics of Survival* (Princeton: Princeton University Press, 1978), p. 97.

56. Yehouda Shenhav, *Manufacturing Rationality: The Engineering Foundations of the Managerial Revolution* (Oxford: Oxford University Press, 2002), p. 45.

57. 'Ce sont des barrières qui se dressent entre la société civile et la société administrative et défendent l'accès des Grands corps [. . .] Les Grandes écoles sont nées

d'une rencontre de l'idée de sélection et d'une nécessité technique. Les notions de compétition, de sélection étaient inconnues dans les vieilles universités de la France [. . .] L'idée de sélection s'intègre dans un souci général de rationalité lié au mouvement des Lumières.' Kessler, 'Les grands corps de l'État', p. 222.

58. Jean-Luc Chappey, 'La formation d'une technocratie. L'école polytéchnique et ses élèves de la Révolution au Second Empire', *Annales Historiques de la Révolution Française* 137 (2004), pp. 223–7 (p. 224).

59. Bruno Belhoste and Konstantinos Chatzis, 'From Technical Corps to Technocratic Power: French State Engineers and their Professional and Cultural Universe in the First Half of the 19th Century', *History and Technology* 23.3 (2007), pp. 209–25 (p. 211).

60. Ibid., p. 212.

61. Louis Bignon, *Histoire de France* (Brussels: Meline, Cans, 1839), vol. I, p. 402.

62. 'Ce corps aurait un esprit. L'Empereur pourrait en protéger les membres les plus distingués, et les élever par ses faveurs plus haut dans l'opinion que ne l'étaient les prêtres lorsqu'on considérait en eux le sacerdoce comme une sorte de noblesse. Tout le monde sentait l'importance des Jésuites; on ne tarderait pas à sentir l'importance de la corporation de l'enseignement, lorsqu'on verrait un homme d'abord élevé dans un lycée, appelé par ses talents à enseigner à son tour, avancer de grade en grade, et se trouver, avant de finir sa carrière, dans les premiers rangs de l'État. De toutes les questions politiques, celle-ci est peut-être de premier ordre. Il n'y aura pas d'état politique fixe s'il n'y a pas un corps enseignant avec des principes fixes. Tant qu'on n'apprendra pas dès l'enfance s'il faut être républicain ou monarchique, catholique ou irréligieux etc., l'État ne formera point une nation; il reposera sur des bases incertaines et vagues; il sera constamment exposé aux désordres et aux changements.' Napoléon Ier, 'Note sur les Lycées du 16 février 1805', in *Correspondance de Napoléon Ier*, 32 vols (Paris: Plon and Dumaine, 1858–70), vol. X, pp. 144–8.

63. Belhoste and Chatzis, 'From Technical Corps to Technocratic Power', p. 215.

64. Pierre Bourdieu, 'Les trois états du capital culturel', *Actes de la recherche en sciences sociales* 30 (1979), pp. 3–6.

65. École Polytéchnique online <https://www.polytechnique.edu/>.

66. 'C'est ma contribution à l'esprit de corps de l'école [. . .] Quand on a eu la chance de suivre des études à Polytéchnique, il est naturel de renvoyer l'ascenseur.' Sophie Blitman, 'Fundraising: Polytéchnique a levé 31,6 M€ en misant sur son réseau d'anciens', *L'étudiant*, 23 May 2012, <https://www.letudiant.fr/educpros/actualite/fundraising-polytechnique-a-leve-316-mEUR-et-ne-compte-pas-sarreter-la.html> (accessed 19 September 2019).

67. Belhoste and Chatzis, 'From Technical Corps to Technocratic Power', p. 221.

68. Day, 'Making Men and Training Technicians', p. 382.

69. 'La discipline parfois exige la clôture, la spécification d'un lieu hétérogène à tous les autres et fermé sur lui-même. Lieu protégé de la monotonie disciplinaire [. . .] Collèges: le modèle du couvent peu à peu s'impose; l'internat apparaît comme le régime d'éducation sinon le plus fréquent, du moins le plus parfait.' Michel Foucault, *Surveiller et punir* (Paris: Gallimard, 1975), p. 143.

70. 'Le Normal s'établit comme principe de coercition avec l'instauration d'une éducation standardisée et l'établissement des écoles normales. En un sens le pouvoir de normalisation contraint à l'homogénéité; mais il individualise en permettant de limiter les écarts, de déterminer les niveaux, de fixer les spécialités et de rendre les différences utiles en les ajustant les unes aux autres. On comprend que le pouvoir de

la norme fonctionne facilement à l'intérieur d'un système de l'égalité formelle, puis-que, à l'intérieur d'une homogénéité qui est la règle, il introduit, comme un impératif utile et le résultat d'une mesure, tout le dégradé des différences individuelles.' Ibid., p. 186.

71. Bourdieu, *La Noblesse d'État*.

72. Day, 'Making Men and Training Technicians', p. 387.

73. *Dictionnaire des inégalités scolaires*, ed. Jean-Michel Bareau (Issy-les-Moulineaux: ESF, 2007).

74. Emile Chabal, *A Divided Republic: Nation, State, and Citizenship in Contemporary France* (Cambridge: Cambridge University Press, 2015).

75. Louis Chauvel, 'Les nouvelles générations devant la panne prolongée de l'ascenseur social', *Revue de l'OFCE* 96.1 (2006), pp. 35–50.

76. 'Petite minorité de scélérats qui est parvenue, par son audace, à dominer la France, et à l'égorger.' Antoine François Bertrand de Moleville, *Histoire de la Révolution de France pendant les dernières années du règne de Louis XVI*, 10 vols (Paris: Giguet and Michaud, 1800), vol. V, p. 132.

77. 'Il n'y a eu véritablement d'esprit de corps, dirai-je d'esprit public, que parmi les membres de cette secte abominable [. . .] pour [. . .] la honte éternelle des honnêtes gens.' Ibid., p. 132.

78. François Furet, *Marx et la Révolution Française* (Paris: Flammarion, 1992).

79. Carl Schmitt, *The Concept of the Political*, trans. George Schwab (Chicago: University of Chicago Press, 1996), p. 26.

80. 'Les universités [. . .] outre le monopole ridicule et nuisible des sciences qui leur est accordé, produisent un mal plus grand en donnant aux gens de lettres qui les compo-sent un esprit de corps dont les uns sont rétrécis et les autres dominés, puisqu'on les oblige de s'y conformer, du moins extérieurement, soit dans ce qu'ils enseignent, soit dans ce qu'ils publient.' Mirabeau, *De la monarchie prussienne sous Frédéric Le Grand*, 8 vols (London: Brunel, 1788), vol. I, p. 222.

81. Anonymous, 'Organisation de la liberté d'enseignement', *Le Correspondant* (Paris: Sagnier & Bray, 1847), vol. XVII, p. 328.

82. 'L'université est un corps; elle le dit, elle s'en vante, et elle fait bien de s'en vanter. Oui, l'université est une corporation. Je suis bien aise qu'elle soit une corporation [. . .] Ce corps a un esprit, et cet esprit s'appelle de l'esprit de corps. (On rit). Ce n'est pas un mal, c'est un bien; il faut l'admettre, parce que c'est un bien, et ensuite, comme cela a quelques inconvénients, il faut en tenir compte. (Marques d'approba-tion).' 'M. Le Duc de Broglie', *Discussion de la loi sur l'instruction secondaire* (Paris: Moniteur Universel and Hachette, 1844), vol. I, p. 672.

83. Félix Madeline, *Jean-Noël Hallé (1754–1822): Médecin ordinaire de Napoléon* (Paris: Office Parisien, 2011).

84. 'Quand les hommes sont réunis en société, il se forme parmi eux deux esprits bien différents et souvent bien opposés: l'un se développe dans toutes les institutions sociales; c'est *l'esprit de corps*; l'autre anime ces hommes ardents, dont l'autorité soulève la masse générale et l'entraîne, c'est *l'esprit d'innovation*. Le premier a pour but de conserver; le second de perfectionner en changeant [. . .] Un bon gouverne-ment se sert de l'un et l'autre esprit: avec l'un il cimente les institutions utiles, et donne des mœurs aux hommes; avec l'autre, il améliore et perfectionne sans détru-ire.' C. Hallé, 'Discours prononcé dans la séance publique de l'École de Médecine, par le C. Hallé, président de l'École', in *Mercure de France, littéraire et politique*, vol. 11 (Paris: Mercure de France, 1803), p. 421.

85. 'Dans les familles, il est un esprit de corps qui, de degrés en degrés, serpente dans tout l'édifice social dont il est le ciment.' Bernard François Anne Fonvielle, *Situation de la France et de l'Angleterre à la fin du 18e siècle*, 2 vols (Paris, 1800), vol. II, p. 85.
86. 'Bonald, Louis Gabriel Ambroise, viscount de', *Encyclopædia Britannica Online*, <https://www.britannica.com/biography/Louis-Gabriel-Ambroise-vicomte-de-Bonald> (accessed 19 September 2019).
87. 'La vraie nature de l'homme est la société [. . .] La religion chrétienne règle les Etats, les Etats règlent les corps, les corps règlent les familles, la famille règle l'individu: tout tend à faire corps dans le monde social; c'est la force d'adhérence du monde physique [. . .] esprit de religion, esprit de patrie, esprit de corps, esprit de famille, esprit public enfin, âme de la société, principe de sa vie, de sa force et de ses progrès.' Louis Gabriel Ambroise de Bonald, *Législation primitive, considérée dans les derniers temps par les seules lumières de la Raison*, 3 vols (Paris: Le Clère, 1802), vol. III, pp. 63–79.
88. We have shown in the introduction that *esprit de parti* existed in a pejorative sense before the birth of the phrase *esprit de corps*.
89. 'L'esprit de corps et l'esprit de parti sont deux esprits différents et même opposés. L'esprit de parti est [. . .] l'esprit particulier d'une partie, d'une fraction d'un grand tout; et les partis religieux ou politiques ne sont que des fractions ou des *sectes* de la société. L'esprit de corps est l'esprit général du corps tout entier. L'esprit de parti divise et dissout; l'esprit de corps réunit et affermit, et l'on peut dire qu'un corps sans esprit de corps est un corps sans âme [. . .] Les nations ont aussi leur esprit de corps, qu'on appelle l'esprit public, principe de leur force de résistance et de leur stabilité [. . .] Il y avait beaucoup de cet esprit public en France avant la *réforme*, qui l'a divisée en deux partis, religieux et politique.' Louis Gabriel Ambroise de Bonald, *De l'esprit de corps et de l'esprit de parti* (Paris: Le Clère, 1828), pp. 7–10.
90. 'Le gouvernement est dans la foule et n'est plus dans l'État.' Ibid., p. 63.
91. 'J'ai attaqué les corps particuliers pour défendre celui de la patrie, et, par-dessus tout, le corps du genre humain. Nous ne sommes tous que les membres de celui-ci.' Jacques-Bernardin-Henri de Saint-Pierre, *Etudes de la nature*, 4 vols (Paris: Didot and Mequignon, 1788), vol. I, p. xxx.
92. Robert Tombs, *France: 1814–1914* (London: Routledge, 2014), p. 92.
93. 'Je sais que leurs ennemis leur ont beaucoup reproché cet esprit de corps, et qu'ils ont prétendu que c'est ce qui les rendait si dangereux; mais je sais aussi que cet esprit de corps est ce qui a le plus désespéré leurs ennemis [. . .] Je dirais qu'ils étaient comme ces frères d'armes parmi les anciens chevaliers, auxquels les liens de la plus étroite amitié imposaient le devoir de marcher d'un pas égal au combat, d'attaquer et de se défendre mutuellement.' Louis Abel de Bonafous, *Du rétablissement des Jésuites et de l'éducation publique* (Emmerick: Romen, 1800), p. 132.
94. Gallie, 'Essentially Contested Concepts', p. 180.
95. Tom Frost, 'The *Dispositif* between Foucault and Agamben', *Law, Culture and the Humanities* 15.1 (2015), pp. 157–71, <https://journals.sagepub.com/doi/abs/10.1177/1743872115571697> (accessed 19 September 2019).
96. 'Ici vous avez de grands corps qui sont tous remplis de ce qu'on appelle l'esprit de corps.' Jean-François de Saint Lambert, *Œuvres philosophiques*, 5 vols (Paris: Agasse, 1800), vol. V, p. 275.
97. 'Cet esprit de corps, qui est aux sociétés, ce que l'égoïsme est aux individus.' Antoine Etienne Nicolas Fantin-Désodoards, *Histoire philosophique de la Révolution de France*, 10 vols (Angers: Belin and Calixte, 1801), vol. V, p. 4.

98. 'Puissance de l'esprit de corps'; Pierre-Louis-Claude Gin, *Discours sur l'histoire universelle, depuis Charlemagne jusqu'à nos jours* (Paris: Bertrand-Pottier, 1802), vol. II, p. 12.

99. 'L'influence trop grande de l'esprit militaire est aussi un imminent danger pour les états libres [. . .] La discipline bannit toute espèce d'opinion parmi les troupes. À cet égard, leur esprit de corps a quelque rapport avec celui des prêtres; il exclut de même le raisonnement, en admettant pour unique règle la volonté des supérieurs [. . .] En gagnant des batailles, on peut soumettre les ennemis de la liberté; mais pour faire adopter dans l'intérieur les principes de cette liberté même, il faut que l'esprit militaire s'efface; il faut que la pensée, réunie à des qualités guerrières, au courage, à l'ardeur, à la décision, fasse naître dans l'âme des hommes quelque chose de spontané.' Anne-Louise-Germaine de Staël-Holstein, *De la littérature, considérée dans ses rapports avec les institutions sociales*, 2 vols (Paris: Maradan, 1800), vol. I, pp. 63–4.

100. Renee Winegarten, *Germaine de Staël and Benjamin Constant: A Dual Biography* (New Haven, CT: Yale University Press, 2008).

101. 'Un esprit de corps exclusif et hostile s'empare toujours des associations qui ont un autre but que le reste des hommes. Malgré la douceur et la pureté du christianisme, souvent les confédérations de ses prêtres ont formé dans l'état des états à part. Partout les hommes réunis en corps d'armée se séparent de la nation. Ils contractent pour l'emploi de la force, dont ils sont dépositaires, une sorte de respect.' Benjamin Constant, *De l'esprit de conquête et de l'usurpation, dans leurs rapports avec la civilisation européenne* (London: John Murray, 1814), p. 21.

102. Ibid., p. 53.

5

Collective Temperament: Esprit de Corps as Sociality and Individuation in the Second Half of the Nineteenth Century

Whose Norms? *Conformative* Esprit de Corps and *Autonomist* Esprit de Corps

Throughout the French nineteenth century explicit references to esprit de corps remained constant. Esprit de corps was considered a useful device in the process of state building and social engineering. 'Corporatisme d'État',[1] as is called by the historian Pierre Rosanvallon, was a centralising, standardising, state-controlled social form of administration.

I have begun to distinguish two aspects of esprit de corps, *conformative* and *autonomist*: conformative esprit de corps is the form of group cohesiveness that is primarily meant to reproduce procedures, beliefs, repetitions and protocols. It maintains a centralised form of power, and serves a higher entity, as for example the state, a church or a cause. The fact that French elites were organised according this esprit remained true after Napoleon. Quoting François Guizot, who was both an academic and a minister under the *Restauration* (1814–30), Rosanvallon helps us to define the conformative aspect of esprit de corps:

> The esprit de corps is no longer the enemy of generality, it becomes its servant: it is a 'principle of union and energy', which has only advantages when it brings together and connects individuals without separating them from the state.[2]

Conformative national esprit de corps was sometimes called pejoratively *jacobinisme*: '"Jacobinism" or the demon of centralisation [. . .] France has long been singled out by the pre-eminent role given to the public power in the organisation of collective life.'[3]

While a normative, state-ruled esprit de corps certainly became in the course of the nineteenth century France's style of governing and maintaining social order, we also observe at that time the slow peripheral growth of a utopian or sociological discourse regarding group autonomy that was not always congruous with state hegemony. The regulating and standardising national power was also challenged by formations which started as non-legal societies and sometimes engaged in seditious behaviour, for example during the revolutions of 1830 and 1848, and the Paris Commune of 1871. These movements defended a form of esprit de corps concerned, for example, with the independence of work *associations* and in particular the creation of *syndicats*. In this case, groups were thought of as existing to create a form of independence towards a dominant form of power, according to an autonomy-driven esprit de corps. Distinguishing autonomist esprit de corps from conformative esprit de corps is a theoretical division that is, of course, not as sharply delimited in reality, as bodies are in practice hybrid compounds exhibiting an ambivalent relation to conformity and autonomy. Some autonomist groups tend to become more conformative over time, for instance when the state integrates their logic in its all-encompassing system: it could be argued that this is what happened to a certain extent in France at the end of the nineteenth century, with the legalisation of labour unions (*syndicats*) and with the 1901 law on *associations*, of which more below.

Conversely, conformative groups can develop a certain degree of autonomy over time. French Jacobinism was not a totalitarianism: 'The French model has in fact always operated at a certain distance from itself, more pragmatic than its stated principles suggest.'[4] The notion of esprit de corps functioned in fact as one of the markers for the dialectical tension between a nationalist unifying programme and a continuous background of aspiration to decentralisation.[5] Autonomous forms of solidarity and fraternity remained an ideal within both popular and intellectual groups in society.

Importantly, in both the autonomist and the conformative aspects, individualism and lack of belonging were often perceived as a form of degeneration. A system tending to dissolve a nation into a mere sum of atomic individuals was often felt as a monstrous abuse,[6] or, as Baudelaire lamented:

> The absolute and divergent freedom of each person, the division of efforts and the splitting of the human will, did bring this weakness, this doubt and this poverty of invention; a few eccentrics, sublime and suffering, hardly make up for this mediocre swarming disorder. Individuality – this petty quality – has consumed collective originality.[7]

Baudelaire was referring in particular to the art world, in which master painters used to work collectively with a group of skilled assistants, but his observation had a larger scope. It reflected a general disapproval, contemporary with industrialisation, of disaggregated or 'mechanised'[8] individuals. The idea of 'collective originality', perhaps an optimistic reformulation of what d'Alembert had called the character of groups or 'esprit *du* corps', meant that social groups could still be seen – or remembered – as a mould for the individuation or sublimation of its members. This is an intuition we will meet again with Tocqueville's analyses of the risks of democracy.

'We who suffer': The Problematic Regulation of Solidarities

We must take as our point of departure the so-called *tabula rasa* of the French Revolution in order to better understand the creation of labour union solidarities at the end of the nineteenth century, which were interpreted by some as a regeneration of the corporative spirit: 'The establishment of the *syndicats* and their survival in the face of anticorporatist legislation is testimony to the strongly felt need for some kind of corporate structure, which persisted long after the disappearance of the guilds.'[9] As we will see, the unions were a continuation of Bonapartism as much as they were spaces of increased autonomy for the workers.

It is worth remembering that Le Chapelier, a main actor in the abolition of labour corporations and *corps de métiers*, triumphantly declared in 1791:

> There are no longer corporations in the state, there is only the particular interest of each individual and then the general interest. No one is allowed to inspire citizens with an intermediary interest, to separate them from the republic by a spirit of corporations.[10]

Within the type of labour guilds prevalent during the *Ancien Régime*, *esprit de corporations* was a synonym of professional esprit de corps: 'The old esprit de corps is the main accused.'[11] Sieyès had equated esprit de corps with the worst of evils, the unjust hegemony of a self-proclaimed elite: 'Social order demands [. . .] not to let ordinary citizens organise themselves in corporations [. . .] the esprit de corps degenerating into aristocracy.'[12] As we have seen, the revolutionary desire to eliminate esprit de corps from democratic republics would not eradicate elitism or state corporatism, but it weakened the working classes by jeopardising popular forms of solidarity among workers.

After 1800, along with the production of an administrative esprit de corps, the state regulation of work increased. Several professions, such as bakers, butchers, stockbrokers, physicians, pharmacists and midwives, now less protected by guilds, were subject to prefectural authorisation, police surveillance and standard regulation.[13] The trend towards increased state surveillance was sometimes accepted because of increasing fear of a new kind of deregulated economy, producing capitalistic monopolies, sometimes named 'Gargantuas of commerce'.[14] Merchants were concerned with the dangers of a deregulated and competitive market, in which individualism and freedom did not appear to go hand in hand. The critique of competition was expressed in political terms and related to the end of communities of esprit de corps:

> Let there be no mistaking it, the system which tends to dissolve a nation into individuals is one of the most fatal errors of the revolution; it is the greatest obstacle to the [. . .] strengthening of true freedom. Let us consult history; it teaches us that wherever despotism wants to establish itself, it isolates men, increases their individual weakness and subjugates them to the omnipotence of one government.[15]

In France, the new idea of individualism was met with scepticism by many: how could one single person, vulnerable and weak in isolation, protect herself from the hegemony of a political regime without the protecting esprit de corps of intermediary groups? While the state, especially after Napoleon's reordering, was perceived as all powerful, the individual citizen was seen as too weak – hence a progressive call, popular also among the labouring classes, for a return to associations of some kind as an intermediate form of professional solidarity.

It would take decades for associations to become a positive legal concept in France again, in part because of the long-term effects of the Le Chapelier law. Article 291 of the *Code pénal* of 1810 implied that all regular meetings of more than twenty people were subject to government approval, which seriously limited the freedom of *réunion*:

> No association of more than twenty people, whose purpose is to meet every day or on certain given days to deal with religious, literary, political or other matters, may be formed without the consent of the Government and under other conditions than those imposed on the society by public authority.[16]

In the context of state monopoly and administrative control of esprit de corps, non-official forms of autonomist solidarity were considered subversive by default. People were indeed thought to be better constrained by the government when divided.[17]

In order to convince the rulers that a renewed popular form of corporatism would not contribute to anarchy or sedition, a few political observers argued that an unofficial 'police du corps'[18] would self-regulate any group without the need of overarching supervision by the state police. This internal communal surveillance and policing was presented as a civilising and moralising factor, more humane than coercive external sanction. This suggested that an individual was better disciplined when belonging to an organised group with a social function. Outside of the protected elitist circles, which had their own official esprit de corps, post-revolutionary popular classes could even be seen as being deprived of sociality: 'Society is reduced to dust, because men are disassociated, because there is no bond between them, because man is foreign to man.'[19] The administration of esprit de corps by the Napoleonic state and its transformation into conformity was not functioning in a satisfactory manner for the lower classes. The idea that labour guilds could reorganise around legalised structures such as *associations* or *syndicats* met with much official resistance before it was officially accepted at the end of the nineteenth century. In the meantime, a strong movement of workers in favour of labour organisations emerged in the 1830s under the influence of the July Revolution.[20]

In 1833, Zael Efrahem, a cobbler and shoemaker, initiated a few illegal strikes and published *De l'association des ouvriers de tous les corps d'état*, a pamphlet that contained the following slogan: 'Union et Force'. Efrahem described the chaotic agitation that followed the republican uprising of June 1832, and proposed a solution:

We who suffer and count only on ourselves, we feel the evil, we seek an immediate and effective remedy; let's apply it. I think we will find it in the *association* [emphasis in original] [. . .] You all understand perfectly that the association has the double advantage of gathering all forces and of giving to this whole a direction. If we remain isolated, scattered, we are weak, so we will be easily diminished, and we will suffer the law of the master [. . .] We need a bond that unites us, an intelligence that governs us, we need an *association*. First, workers of the same profession must form a body [*corps*] among themselves.[21]

The associative structure was the intelligence, the *esprit* that was fit for a collective *corps* because it would provide a common direction and a frame to discontent, thus allowing for more effectual change. The author suggested that workers were not necessarily seditious and could respect the rule of the state if given a legal social status or recognised as an official class. Once again, the labouring individual is described as vulnerable and in a painful personal struggle for economic survival. Counting only on one's self was a source of dereliction.

The author of the pamphlet added, in anticipation of what the labour unions would be, that these associative *corps* of workers needed headquarters, a centralised administration and a ruling committee that would speak with one voice and negotiate coherently with the state. The idea seemed simple, but one should not overlook the rivalries that opposed different people in the *métiers*, the 'ridicules jalousies de corps': 'Let us not allow these different corporations to scatter and dissolve, let them not be spoiled by individualism and the selfishness of isolation. Let us join in amity with each other.'[22] The language of friendship suggested a sentimental factor which echoed the revolutionary ideal of fraternity. Another influence of the discourse of the Revolution was the fact that the *corps* were seen by the author both as negative and desirable, depending on their size, scale, unification and interrelations: suffering workers needed one larger united body that would sublimate corporatist or selfish quarrels – a decade later, this unifying ideal would become part of the intellectual signature of communism according to Marx and Engels.[23]

Some militants considered that the sentimental ideal of *amitié* was less important than legalism. The inconclusive benefits of the French Revolution for the working classes had generated some mistrust of abstract ideas such as fraternity. Socialists progressively proposed a more pragmatic conception of associated workers, united by concrete claims and legal aspirations rather than by only a vague feeling of communion. Reformists such as the philosopher Alfred Fouillée, the father of the concept of *idée-force*, claimed that social justice should be a legal duty rather than an abstraction of pathos: 'In order to counterbalance and limit individual rights, the Revolution did not proclaim a duty of social justice; or at least, under the name of *fraternity*, it was left in the vague form of sentiment, without any legal necessity.'[24] And what about equality? It concerned for Fouillée individual citizens rather than groups, but social justice should also preserve the rights of communities.

The esprit de corps of the proletariat did eventually get institutionalised.

Theorists and politicians slowly succeeded in establishing a recognised structure for professional and social cooperation. In 1866, for the first time in France, the association of shoemakers and cobblers called itself, albeit still illegally, a *syndicat*.[25] In 1884, labour syndicates became legal in France, partly because members of the ruling class expected after the Paris commune that socialist legalism would prevent revolutions and attenuate social divides. The major artisan of the official recognition of the unions of workers was minister Pierre Waldeck-Rousseau, who would explain sixteen years later in the Chambre des députés how much social order his reform created:

> The new phenomenon, the precious and consoling fact, is that trade unions do not just go on strike: they regularise the strikes, they discipline them. And this is the social progress that was born from the legislation of 1884. Do you think it is nothing to see that the first effort of these supervised, disciplined workers, having their leaders, is to seek negotiation, to initiate a debate?[26]

This is one more instance of official esprit de corps as social engineering, and it is an evidenced fact that strikes became less violent after the legal recognition of *syndicats*.[27] Politicians such as Waldeck-Rousseau considered unions as an expansion of the administrative and conformative esprit de corps, a way for the nation-state to control the proletariat. The economist Paul Leroy-Beaulieu commented in 1900:

> The corporation of the *Ancien Régime*, against which Turgot had fought and which the Revolution had suppressed, is absolutely resurrected and officially recognised [in the legalisation of the *syndicats*]. This is the most colossal change that has been made in France since 1789.[28]

Organised collectiveness was still expressed at the turn of the twentieth century in terms of *corps*. An early advocate of *syndicalisme*, Hubert Lagardelle, a socialist who would later become a fascist friend of Mussolini and work as minister of labour during the Vichy regime in 1942, noted in 1901: 'The conception of the "collective worker" begins to impose itself on the legislator, in lieu of the isolated worker. *The corps of workers is recognised as having a personal existence.*'[29] But there was a major difference between eighteenth-century *corporations* and the new *syndicats*: the bureaucracy and surveillance reach of the state was now much more efficient and ubiquitous via its organised administration, also called *fonction publique*.[30] The idea of *function* is both an organicist and mechanistic metaphor.

Esprit de Corps and the Spirit of Individuality: Tocqueville's Reminiscence

In the first decades of the nineteenth century, the new notion of individualism, seen as a by-product of the French Revolution, was immediately opposed to esprit de corps:

A single principle existed in France, individualism [*l'individuellisme*], this universal selfishness, a natural fruit of a time that had broken all bonds. No love of one's neighbour any more where there was no longer a religion to make a precept out of it [. . .] No more esprit de corps when bodies [*corps*] had ceased to exist.[31]

The poetic and ephemeral form *individuellisme* was suggestive of a constant *duel* between individuals, a systematic antagonism between humans. Once more a rhetorical association was made between emotional values such as social ties, fraternity and esprit de corps.

The political theorist Alexis de Tocqueville was an original nineteenth-century critic of individualism, one who did not treat group belonging and self-realisation as opposites. His defence of esprit de corps is worth highlighting:

> Considering the effects of the rise of democracy, Tocqueville is particularly interested in the future of what he calls 'corps pride' [*orgueil de corps*], 'corps will' [*volonté de corps*] [. . .] The expression 'esprit de corps' [. . .] cannot be found in his writings, but it is nevertheless of such a 'spirit' of solidarity but also of distinction existing between the members of the same 'social body' that Tocqueville speaks.[32]

In fact, the phase 'esprit de corps' did appear, and more than once, from Tocqueville's pen. In a text describing the *Ancien Régime*, commissioned by John Stuart Mill and published in French in the *London and Westminster Review*, Tocqueville explained in 1836:

> Noblemen enjoyed the exclusive right to provide officers to the army. This would doubtless have represented an important privilege if the nobles had retained a certain individual importance or a powerful esprit de corps. But having lost both, they became, in the army as everywhere else, passive instruments in the hands of the king.[33]

Individual importance or the lack thereof was here a collective class phenomenon. According to Tocqueville as well as more recent historians,[34] French aristocrats did exhibit a strong caste type and solidarity based on a certain idea of class merit more or less until Louis XIV. After that, absolutism, the politics of centralisation and the *esprit de cour*, a competition for royal attention, tended to dissolve the aristocratic esprit de corps: 'We observed within this great body [before the end of the seventeenth century] a certain homogeneous spirit. It obeyed fixed rules altogether, governed itself according to certain invariable usages, and maintained certain ideas common to all his members.'[35] Louis XIV's centralisation started what the French Revolution achieved: the dissolution of social castes in favour of one class without authentic esprit de corps, the capitalist bourgeoisie, of which the US democracy was the highest example.

Quite counter-intuitively, Tocqueville thought that this was a negative aspect of democracy, because class identity had been the source of a real and distinctive form of individuality:

> When citizens are divided into castes and classes [. . .] they have neither the taste nor the desire to resemble each other; on the contrary, everyone seeks more and more to keep his own opinions and habits intact, and to remain himself. The spirit of individuality [*l'esprit d'individualité*] is then very much alive. But when a people reaches a democratic social state, which means there are no more castes or classes in it, people [. . .] resemble each other, and moreover, they suffer somewhat if they do not do so.[36]

The new democratic form of so-called individualism was in fact, for Tocqueville, a process of de-individuation, a gradual loss of self-distinction and identity. Pre-democratic social distinctions as manifested in pre-modern times maintained a level of individuation that was not incompatible with belongingness, and implied, according to Tocqueville, less suffering. From an egalitarian perspective, this discourse might have appeared like a conservative legitimation of social inequalities expressed by a viscount whose family, the Clérel de Tocqueville, had been a part of the *noblesse* for several centuries.[37] His suppositions regarding *esprit de classe* could be considered problematic or naive if they neglected altogether the possibility of political discontent and aspiration to class mobility. One might doubt that the poor labourer wanted to remain a poor labourer. However, the intriguing idea here is that individual identity is understood as collective, a form of shared intentionality.

Tocqueville was not the only one to think that esprit de corps was a desirable individuating phenomenon. In an essay written in 1851, Paul de Flotte, a socialist revolutionary, explained that during the *Ancien Régime*, labour groups created 'a general habit of esprit de corps, which acted strongly on individuals, and brought them singularly close to the most perfect type of their profession'.[38] The form of individuality created by a community of production generated a sort of ideal-type that each individual could aspire to, which was not exactly synonymous with the idea of 'class for itself' or 'class consciousness' because it was a realisation of the individual within a collective ethos.[39] It offered a promise of autonomous individuality, an esprit *du* corps that could be reached through a shared practice of constant distinction, by imitating or co-creating human paragons, real individual models active in the group and for the group. This probably also implied symbolic scarecrows outside of the group of individuation, the idea that those who do not belong are not very respectable persons. One could call this type of peer-group attitude *co-excellence*, which has to do with autonomous esprit de corps.

An important rule in maintaining a strong esprit de corps seems to be the avoidance of standard universal language. In a chapter entitled 'How American Democracy Changed the English Language', Tocqueville explained that esprit de corps used to be maintained via a particular shared language: 'Each of these classes invariably takes and preserves intellectual habits that are unique to it, and favours certain words and terms that then pass from generation to generation as inheritances.'[40] Recent studies seem to give some credit to this claim. Group cohesiveness is said to suffer if a specific language is not adopted: 'Language diversity is negatively associated with group involvement.'[41] A given group's language will tend to become specific partly in order not to be fully understood by other groups, sometimes creating an *argot* or jargon, 'an artificial language, intended not to be understood by a certain class of people'.[42] The same could be said of accents and received pronunciations.

In Tocqueville's somewhat paternalistic view, any social group, even the lower classes, could feel the pride and dignity of belonging to an identified social caste. Modern democracies, conversely, tended to prevent even the privileged classes from developing a proper *esprit*: 'Today, we still see rich people, but they no longer form a compact and hereditary body [*corps*]; they could not adopt an *esprit*, persevere in it and make it penetrate all its ranks.'[43] A recent academic translation of this passage has replaced *esprit* with 'esprit de corps': 'Today, wealthy individuals still exist, but they have ceased to constitute a distinct and hereditary body capable of fostering and maintaining an *esprit de corps*, and instilling it in people of all ranks.'[44] The first English translation (1863) used the compound 'class spirit',[45] and added 'esprit de corps' in parentheses in another passage where once again Tocqueville used the word *esprit*:

> The will of the majority is the most general of laws, and it establishes certain habits to which everyone must then conform; the aggregate of these common habits is what is called the class spirit (esprit de corps) [*esprit*] of each profession; thus there is the class spirit of the bar, of the court, etc.[46]

For Tocqueville, esprit de corps was something of a pleonasm, since he believed individuation was a collective process, hence the frequent use of the sole word *esprit*. Democratic individuals can hardly form an *esprit*, which means that, etymologically speaking, they could be called 'idiots':

> How do people remain their own masters? By maintaining the kind of community that secures their liberty. Freedom and community are not opposing forces any more than pluribus and unum. We are free *so that* we can create a community life *so that*, in turn, we can be free. Tocqueville's singular contribution to our understanding of idiocy and citizenship is this notion that *idiots are idiotic precisely because they are indifferent to the conditions and contexts of their own freedom*. They fail to grasp the interdependence of liberty and community.[47]

Analysing the future of democracy, Tocqueville anticipated a dissolution of generational transmission and a degradation of social rituals. Playing with the polysemy of the term *corps*, he considered that modern societies were heading towards disintegration, as if by scientific fatalism, 'like those supposed elementary bodies within which modern chemistry encounters new separable particles as it looks at them ever more closely'.[48] The transnationalisation of mores in capitalist democracies meant that the tendency of modern global history was a universal standardisation of individuals condemned to be confused *dividuals* enjoying an abstract form of humanity, a sort of default configuration of humanhood:

> The human species loses its variety: the same ways of acting, thinking and feeling are found in every corner of the world. This does not come only from the fact that peoples have more commerce with each other and copy each other more faithfully, but it is due to the fact that in every country humans are moving away from ideas and feelings peculiar to a caste, to a profession, to a family, and get closer to what is nearest to the constitution of man, which is everywhere the same.[49]

The claim is that we become biological and cultural clones once we are deprived of a specific community spirit. Could we, however, hope for an internationalist form of esprit de corps? Not so for Tocqueville: 'In the common crowd [. . .] the spirit of individuality is nearly destroyed.'[50] In today's language, we are ghosts wandering in 'zombie democracies'.[51] Perhaps this narrative of zombification and need for social belonging explains the recent revival of communities in contemporary democracies.

Tocqueville's insistence on the virtues of us-versus-them class politics and the dangers of democracy was related to the expansion of French colonialism, for example the then recent conquest of Algeria. In 1863, an Arabic interpreter in the French North African army translated the work of the fourteenth-century Muslim historian Ibn Khaldun – which would be remembered in 1980 when Deleuze and Guattari defined esprit de corps as a tribal war machine, of which more in the next chapter. In *Les Prolégomènes d'Ibn Khaldoun*, the central notion of *asabiyah* was translated as *esprit de corps*, in a text with explicit imperialist and racist connotations:

> A family which has generated respect and fear out of its union and its esprit de corps, and which is composed of individuals belonging to a race whose blood is pure and reputation intact, is placed by this confraternity of sentiments, in a very advantageous position and obtains great success [. . .] This is how associations are formed, capable of subjugating other peoples and of conquering empires. To clarify this principle, we will observe that the esprit de corps in a tribe is like temperament in created beings [. . .] The esprit de corps, elevated in this manner to its highest degree of intensity, is only found in illustrious families who are accustomed to command. In such a house, one of the members must have the power to impose his will on others.[52]

Such discourse indicated a by then familiar 'isomorphism'[53] between family and state, thus justifying a patriarchal social order, but more strikingly it introduced a vocabulary of consanguinity into the semantics of esprit de corps, preparing the ground for dangerous associations between nation and blood.

The translator, William McGuckin de Slane, was born in Ireland, where he spent the first twenty years of his life, graduating from Trinity College in Dublin before moving to Paris to study oriental languages. It is reasonable to assume that a French intellectual would not have used the phrase *esprit de corps* to translate *asabiyah*, given the fact that such an equation between esprit de corps and natural family ties, rather than professional bias, was rather the way the English language transformed the notion. This reintroduction of esprit de corps into French as a form of collective temperament located in the blood of the imperialist group placed the emphasis on ideas of dominion. According to Ibn Khaldun via de Slane, effectual esprit de corps was an elitist strategy of conquest and needed a patriarchal commander in chief. Singular identity or collective temperament was generated by tight-knit association within a specific group, enhanced by the honour and incentive felt in shared influence, and through an identitarian and antagonistic distinction from other groups.

The result was supposedly a strong specificity of the kind defined by Tocqueville, whose disdain for egalitarianism was also influenced by the Anglo-Saxon naturalisation of esprit de corps. These authors compared the constitution of a group *esprit* with the formation of a new species: 'Each of these associations forms as it were a new species of the human race.'[54] For Tocqueville, the destruction of singular forms of esprit de corps in various social bodies was a political disaster because it could favour a global bureaucratic master rather than promoting real equality: 'Today's men who are so independent of one another are all more or less dependent on the administration.'[55] This bureaucratic dominion generated a new form of individualistic opportunism among state careerists: 'There are, today, many people who are very comfortable with this kind of compromise between administrative despotism and the sovereignty of the people.'[56]

Could administrative despotism mean that the esprit de corps of classes and castes was fully replaced by an esprit de corps of public administration? Such was the opinion of the specialist of administrative law Émile-Victor Foucart, a contemporary of Tocqueville. But this implied, in line with the French intellectual tradition, that esprit de corps was a socially-constructed perseverance rather than a natural given:

> If one understands esprit de corps as a systematic spirit which is firmly focused towards a legal and useful goal, we shall admit that this esprit de corps is essential to the administration, which can only achieve good results by the fixedness of its views and the constancy of its pace.[57]

The body of the public administration was like a mechanical animal, an inflexible and gigantic automaton, a sophistication of the famous artificial Leviathan described by Hobbes. This kind of stubborn esprit de corps announced the unstoppable bureaucracy of the twentieth century and perhaps also the artificial sovereignty of today's multinational digital companies such as Google, Facebook or Amazon.

The complex question of the political advantages and disadvantages of strong social cohesion, as well as the relationship between communities and the whole of the nation, were philosophical and sociological leitmotifs throughout the century. In France, a middle sociological way was invented between the English biologisation of esprit de corps and the Enlightenment's negative critique of it: Saint-Simon, Comte, Fourier, Durkheim and Tarde were among the intellectuals who attempted to think the notion of esprit de corps positively, simply because they believed that 'esprit de corps was the source of so many great things'.[58]

Esprit de Corps and the First French Sociologists: Fourier, Tarde, Durkheim

What if esprit de corps was less class-related than suggested by Tocqueville – an institutional matter, therefore not incompatible with democratic regimes? George Sand, in her autobiography, writing about the Jesuits, offered an elliptic and thought-provoking formula: 'esprit de corps, tendance d'institution'.[59] Institutionalisation would be the real driver of modern esprit de corps. The collective desire to become and remain an institution would both necessitate and generate esprit de corps in order to be effectual and durable.

The *corps de métiers* or *corps d'états* of the *Ancien Régime* were institutional *corps* because their privileges and functions were legally configured to last over a lifetime and sometimes even become hereditary.[60] Esprit de corps was an institutional shell generating a persistent community that would not exist without the formal and legal protection of the group. In France the need to be officially recognised by the state had always been an aspect of esprit de corps: even in the early eighteenth-century army, the musketeers, who were considered the champions of esprit de corps, were an institution. The Jesuits of course, as pointed out by Sand, had always actively tried to achieve official recognition. By disconnecting esprit de corps from institutionalisation, the English language had paved the way for narrowed corporate perceptions of esprit de corps as cohesive *team spirit*. Sand's suggestion leads to a somewhat speculative insight: perhaps esprit de corps is particularly strong in groups that are quasi-institutions as opposed to fully official ones, in the sense that the need for constant renewed official recognition might create the kind of pride and honour that is in fact an awareness of the fragility of power? Esprit de corps as a *collective being on the lookout* . . .

According to a new kind of French thinker in the nineteenth century, the *Sociologues*, to focus only on the legal aspect of institutions would be reductive: esprit de corps was also an emotional system of *solidarité*, and solidarity was not a simple legal notion any more. Certainly, in the eighteenth century, as attested by the *Encyclopédie méthodique* of 1787 or the 1798 *Dictionnaire de l'Académie française*,[61] *solidarité* – from *solidaire* – was used as a synonym of *solidité*, a juridical term designating the legal dependence of contractors.[62] In the second half of the nineteenth century, the ideas of solidarity and sociability became more emotional and theoretical, while semantically connected to esprit de corps.

In the journal dedicated to his 'science sociale', the utopianist Charles Fourier insisted that a theory of human groups was necessary, a 'group theory, of which our scientists have never deigned to write a study'.[63] Fourier did not think of himself as conservative, quite the contrary, yet he praised the sense of cohesiveness of ancient castes or ethnological groups. Esprit de corps was the traditional virtue *par excellence*:

> With regard to mores, we can see that in every tribe, poor as it may be, there reigns an esprit de corps, a jealousy for the honour of the Tribe [. . .] This esprit de corps is enough to eradicate the most shocking vices of the civilised populace, its rudeness, its uncleanliness, its vileness.[64]

Esprit de corps demanded manners. It was the original panacea for all ills, a moralising emotion. The ambition it fostered was socialising. Its dynamics, dividing and uniting at the same time, pertained to a socially elevating form of rivalry based on sentiment: 'Out of pride and esprit de corps, we want the corporation of which we are part to maintain a distinguished rank among rival corporations.'[65] Fourier did not wish to eradicate our natural tendency to agonism and conflict but to optimise it, to make it fruitful: he unambiguously called his ideal communities *phalanges* – a phalanx was a platoon formation practised by ancient Greek military corps.[66]

For Fourier, esprit de corps was highly related to ambition:

> Should it be called group of ambition, honour group, group of sectism, ascendant group, corporation group, I do not know which term to choose [. . .] Ambition is the passion whose growth is greatest in any civilised state, it alone now embraces the whole globe in its plans [. . .] If this passion is insatiable in individuals, it is even more so within corporations.[67]

Corporations were intensifiers of ambition. Because organised groups could survive the death of some of their members, their collectively distributed ambition was more sustainable. Fourier suggested a middle way between the ideas of esprit de corps as natural gregariousness and esprit de corps as artificial politics: it was an expansive conquering force that ought to be channelled. It was not inertia and it was not perversion: it was about growth. The passion of esprit de corps was a better social fuel than purely rational utilitarianism.

In an attempt to emulate scientific discourse, Fourier spoke of a 'spirit of universal influence' [*esprit d'influence universelle*],[68] a general tendency to impose a worldview or form of life. To channel it was to propose regulated activities 'in harmony with the human passions'.[69] In his *Théorie des quatre mouvements* (1808), Fourier explained that passions were the engine of civilisation and that they all obeyed the same universal law, which he called – since he imagined himself as a Newton of human nature – 'Passionate Attraction' [*Attraction passionnée*].[70] Passions were not mere individual phenomena but always intersubjective; social harmony and order could be reached by using the 'influence of the esprit de corps, in an ascending spiral'.[71] A spiral of emulation, desire and rivalry could create a happily ordered society, and we could understand the mechanisms of such ordering more scientifically.

Because he believed, not unlike Tocqueville, that the art or skills of esprit de corps were now almost lost among the masses, Fourier proposed to recreate them: society was to be scientifically divided into communities of craft and passion in such way that 'the products of their industry reach the perfection which we must expect from people who will work by passion, by esprit de corps and self-esteem, and by no means driven by need and profit'.[72] Far from seeing social agents as cold calculators, survival-focused rational beings, Fourier tried to understand our original needs for passion, ambition, pleasure, beauty, enthusiasm, agonism, shared ideals, and imagined a common society based on disparate individual drives. Although he was labelled an 'extravagant figure of Romanticism',[73] Fourier's insistence on esprit de corps as fecund ambition is still inspirational today, for example in the idea of 'agonistic pluralism',[74] a political theory advocating a society of distinct communities, each democratically competing for the expression and respect of their identity, none being allowed to become totally hegemonic: 'If we want people to be free we must always allow for the possibility that conflict may appear and to provide an arena where differences can be confronted.'[75]

A few decades later, the sociologist Émile Durkheim was also preoccupied, if in a more sober fashion, with the institutionalisation of a holistic and communal form of esprit de corps, which he called 'the spirit of ensemble or feeling of common solidarity'.[76] Once more, this spirit was termed a feeling rather than a rationale, even in its professional form, *l'esprit corporatif*.[77] Solidarity was emotional rather than merely contractual. Durkheim did not wish to create an opposition between the professional sphere and the public sphere – he considered that professional corporations were or should have remained the moral pillars of social life, in the name of 'common utility', *l'utilité commune*.[78]

Speaking of the Danish army, for example, he wrote: 'The esprit de corps, life in common, should have here the prophylactic influence it exerts elsewhere.'[79] A prophylactic influence was one that protected a physical body, prevented future deviance or illness. Durkheim used a medical word to refer to a moral benefit. Such a biological analogy was not a fortuitous metaphor. Durkheim also used the term 'immunity' to categorise groups that were less likely to favour the suicide of some of their members.[80] Well-being and what we could call *well-belonging* were correlated: there was a form of collective immunity protecting individuals, to a certain extent, from mental or moral dysfunctions. According to this vocabulary, derived from Pasteur's then influential findings, immunity was a psycho-physical protection against physical infection or disease.[81] Durkheim introduced the notion of 'constitution organico-psychique'[82] to indicate a close interdependence between body and mind. He defended a speculative form of isomorphism between biological organisms and social organisations: 'The law of division of labour applies to organisms as well as to societies.'[83] The physiology of organic activity offered a model to think society's order in holistic terms: 'Social differentiation can be pathological, just like cancer in the biological organism.'[84] Such a mode of thinking was already a trope in the eighteenth century, not the least with d'Alembert's comparison between esprit de corps and a bad graft. But for Durkheim, esprit de corps was more often than not a good graft; it was the soul of bodies, and bodies were the optimal manifestation of life.

In the vein of Tocqueville and Fourier, Durkheim observed that esprit de corps tended to disappear in modern nations, in which individualism was like a sickness. In protective traditional societies, consciousness was one: 'Originally the individual is absorbed in the group.'[85] At the start of this diachronic social narrative, we found the 'social protoplasm', 'a society, the cohesion of which [results] exclusively from similarities', 'an absolutely homogeneous mass', the 'primitive horde'.[86] The horde possessed a collective mind that bestowed its meanings on the environment, and vice versa: 'In a small society, as everyone is placed in essentially the same conditions of existence, the collective environment is essentially concrete [. . .] The states of consciousness that schematise it therefore have the same character.'[87] Modern times have left the tribal 'mechanical solidarity' behind, because in larger societies, a division of labour produced disparate forms of organic interdependence and psychism:

> As one climbs up the ladder of civilisation, a new distribution of individuals and activities takes place. A division of labour is progressively established, which engenders specialised organs, whose activity becomes more and more defined, with geometric lines increasingly clear and complex.[88]

Social links in modern societies are, for Durkheim, characterised by an 'organic solidarity that is produced by task specialisation'.[89] He suggested that a healthy nation should reintroduce a circulation of esprit de corps, for example in corporations or associations: specialisation should not mean isolation.

In 1899, a continuator of Durkheim, Gabriel Tarde, soon to be professor at the Collège de France,[90] gave a lecture with L'esprit de groupe as a headline, in which he explained:

> Group spirit, or, esprit de corps in the broadest sense of the word, includes several important varieties [. . .] 1. Crowd spirit [. . .] 2. Family spirit [. . .] 3. The spirit of profession [. . .] that is, esprit de corps proper, in the precise sense of the word. The latter is subdivided into as many species as there are categories of professions: clerical spirit, academic spirit, military spirit, judicial spirit, mercantile spirit. The spirit of profession gives birth to class spirit and caste spirit. 4. The spirit of party [. . .] 5. There is also the sectarian spirit. 6. There is above all these mentalities, and embracing them, the spirit of nation, patriotism, which is indeed an enlarged esprit de corps [. . .] 7. Finally, it seems necessary to indicate a place for a supranational group spirit, of a spirit of civilisation (which might perhaps be related to the spirit of religion)?[91]

The list was convoluted but provided an interesting piece of information: the generic idea of 'group spirit', which was the meaning that was preferred in English, was now important enough in French to become the title of Tarde's conference. Another inference we can make is that esprit de corps was a catalyst for the fact that the still largely unrecognised field of sociology was hindered in its early scientific ambition by its spiritual references:[92] the word esprit was here used twenty-one times in just a few lines, without ever being defined, as if the conference were an incantation. Apparently, different scales of esprit de corps could contain each other, as in nesting dolls, or perhaps be adjacent without communicating. Tarde's hope was that if all social groups were of a common essence, they could perhaps be described by laws.

In fact, Tarde and Durkheim saw esprit de corps as key to the central question of sociology: how and why do we become social and what happens when we do? It was a different notion from that of rational individuals assembling and disassembling out of free will. Humans did not join a group because they were conscious that they were of the same kind – rather, they felt they were of the same kind because they belonged to a persistent group. Solidarity was a feeling induced by praxis: 'This deep feeling that rises among us when, the more we see each other, the more we interact with each other, the more we reflect each other unwittingly or intentionally, we feel gradually bound by a close and intimate solidarity.'[93] Esprit de groupe emerged out of a process of bonding, through mutual imitation and shared activities. Tarde added that the formation of such an esprit de corps necessitated ceremonies, rituals, a boycott of those who are not part of the group and a relative ban on relationships with external individuals or bodies. A major feature of esprit de corps was costumes and similar modes of dress – some were blatantly distinct, as in professional clothing or school uniforms.[94]

Because of his nesting-dolls understanding, Tarde, contrary to Tocqueville or Fourier, did not think the phenomenon of esprit de corps was disappearing in democratised societies. The size of organised groups animated by the spirit was simply expanding:

> Esprit de corps, by the very fact that it has expanded, has changed [. . .] A spirit of intense solidarity between trades formerly at war has replaced the former exclusivism [. . .] The great workers' federations of the United States are now industrial armies [. . .] Imitative and assimilative sympathy, which constitutes sociability in action, is manifested by two contrary and alternative effects: first by the formation of a closed society, of a social enclosure in which the culture of sociability is practised; then [. . .] by deformation and breaching of these enclosures, the walls of which fall here to rise again, expanded, further out.[95]

There was for Tarde an expanding dialectic of esprit de corps: it was partly a tendency to exclusiveness and specificity, and partly an aspiration to incorporation and assimilation. This dynamic contradiction explains the military metaphor of industrial armies: esprit de corps was perhaps expanding in scale, but not losing its somewhat bellicose quality.

Self-Alienation: The Individualistic Critique of Esprit de Corps

At the dawn of the twentieth century, French secondary school pupils could read in a widely distributed philosophy textbook the following definition, which implied that state-controlled esprit de corps was now a clearly established paternalistic norm: 'Esprit de corps. – We thus call the inclination that leads us to form, in the large family that is called the State, more specific groups, more restricted associations [. . .] in short, corporations.'[96] The metaphor of the nation as family confirmed a web of belief with strong historical implications:[97] retrospectively, one could be tempted to say it prepared the ground for imperialist fascism and its diverse social phalanxes. But at that time, only isolated thinkers insisted that esprit de corps was a threat, and that individualism was altogether better for the sake of liberty.

Most critics preferred to insist on equality among social organs rather than advocate a full eradication of esprit de corps. When a society was divided into professional organs within the controlling body of the nation-state, some of these organs were considered superior to others, as the brain is considered superior to the hand in industrial and post-industrial societies: 'The creation of aristocracies, and, to speak more generally, the heredity of positions and the esprit de corps, are intended solely to favour the development of some social organs at the expense of others, thus breaking the equilibrium of the human organisation.'[98] The new form of esprit de corps by official specialisation was producing new inequalities: 'The public instinct is right: inequality or, better, the difference between rights and duties is indeed the only way of largely reconstituting the esprit de corps and the identification of humans with their profession.'[99] For socialists and communists, a fairer esprit de corps was needed.

A more radical and individualistic attack on esprit de corps came from the Nietzschean philosopher Georges Palante. In an influential academic journal, he started with a seemingly objective and neutral definition:

> In its broad sense, the expression 'esprit de corps' refers to the spirit of solidarity in general, considered not only in the occupational group, but in all social circles, whatever they may be (class, caste, sect, etc.), in which the individual feels more or less subordinated to the interests of the community.[100]

This solidarity came at a severe cost for Palante: the loss of personal freedom. Reminiscent of d'Alembert's use of the word *character*, which could designate both a signified and a signifier, Palante compared esprit de corps to an *estampille*,[101] an official mark, a stamp that gave validity and legitimacy to a document. This image of a tag implied a form of bureaucratic production, a process of reproduction and standardisation under the disciplinary influence of an overarching authority. Palante was quick to state his opinion: 'The moral and social discipline that [the body] imposes on its members is tight and forceful.'[102]

In 1899, what exactly was a *corps*? Palante went one step further than Durkheim or Tarde in the psychobiological personification of the group:

> A 'body' [*corps*] is a defined professional group with its own interests, its own will-to-live, that seeks to defend itself against all external or internal causes of destruction or diminution. If we now ask ourselves what are the goods for which a corps struggles, we understand that these are moral advantages: the

good reputation of the body, influence, consideration, credit. These moral advantages are doubtless but means to ensure the material prosperity of the body and of its members.[103]

Palante's simplified form of social Darwinism tinted with vitalism proposed that a social body was a collective strategy, a conspiracy of supra-individual desire. An avid reader of Nietzsche,[104] Palante believed competition and will-to-power to be the principal laws ruling the evolution of human societies. As we will see below, the idea of 'will-to-live' was also reminiscent of Schopenhauer's pessimistic philosophy.

Esprit de corps, in Palante's disenchanted view, was a tactical instinct that relied on humanity's art for deception: 'The special tactics by means of which a body conceals its deficiencies belong to the great general law of *social insincerity*.'[105] Imperfect and degenerated humans united in a deceitful group in order to become stronger, more efficient and hegemonic over some persecuted, exceptional but isolated individuals – this was the critique of social togetherness learned by Palante from Nietzsche's *Genealogy of Morals*, in which competition for power ruled the relations between different organised groups as well as their internal life: 'Competition is the great law that dominates the evolution of societies; it also dominates the life of the constituted bodies.'[106] Institutional groups tended to expel members by a process of social selection comparable to animal behaviour, 'as a barnyard attacks the sick fowl to finish it off'.[107] Simultaneous with this internal movement of exclusion was an outward movement of conquest: 'Esprit de corps tends to extend its sphere of influence as far as possible. It is essentially an invading trait.'[108]

This text was an attempt to define esprit de corps philosophically: the use of italics reinforced the aspiration to a conceptual definition. Citations served as an argument from authority:

> These few remarks on the comings and goings of esprit de corps allow us to see in it a particularly energetic manifestation of what Schopenhauer calls the will-to-live. A social body is, in fact just like any organised society, a form of *condensed human will-to-live*, carried to a degree of intensity that individual selfishness never attains.[109]

Unfortunately, this is where the demonstration becomes self-contradictory. If a societal *will* can be stronger and more condensed than a person's will, then shouldn't we redefine the scale of what an individual is? While trying to defend the individual as more radical, vital and real than the group, Palante also suggested that groups were stronger and more powerful individuals than single persons. In this case, shouldn't a consequent Nietzschean individualism defend and align with the more intense form of individuality, that is, living-and-willing unified groups, against less intense and dense forms of life, the subjugated individual?

Palante's idea of individuality was not clear. He sometimes seems opposed to the Tocquevillian idea that *esprit d'individualité* was a collective feature, and that some strong communities could co-create paragons of identity and individuation as the result of the internal co-excellence and effortful emulation of their members:

> What [the corps] requires of its members is [. . .] a certain posture, a certain perseverance in obedience to the moral code of the body. It is this perseverance in docility that, by some sort of confusion of language, we are sometimes pleased to call character. By this last word a body will by no means understand initiative in decision taking, or boldness in execution, nor any of the qualities of spontaneity and energy which make for a fine and forceful individuality.[110]

Behind the contradiction or theoretical hesitation that conferred a superior energy and individual intensity either on the group or on the individual, Palante was trying to reject the idea that belonging to a group enhanced the definition of character of its members. But his emphasis on notions of energy and conquest to define a superior form of life, instead of rationality, eventually weakened his critique of esprit de corps. The focus on the docility of the members is a partial view: it neglects to mention that most groups have their leaders, models, servants and inner hierarchy. It also forgets the sometimes difficult and active discipline of developing a *savoir-faire* by respecting the demanding standards of a community of practice.

Notes

1. Pierre Rosanvallon, *Le Modèle politique français, La société civile contre le jacobinisme de 1789 à nos jours* (Paris: Seuil, 2004), p. 397.
2. 'L'esprit de corps n'est plus l'ennemi de la généralité, il en devient le serviteur: il est un "principe d'union et d'énergie", qui n'a que des avantages lorsqu'il rapproche et lie entre eux les individus sans les séparer de l'État.' Ibid., p. 399.
3. 'Le "jacobinisme" ou le démon de la centralisation [. . .] La France s'est longtemps singularisée par le rôle prééminent accordé à la puissance publique dans l'organisation de la vie collective.' Ibid., p. 10.
4. 'Le modèle français a en fait toujours fonctionné à une certaine distance de lui-même, plus pragmatique que ne le laissent supposer les principes affichés.' Ibid., pp. 199, 307.
5. Ibid., p. 13.
6. Michael David Sibalis, 'Corporatism after the Corporations: The Debate on Restoring the Guilds under Napoleon I and the Restoration', *French Historical Studies* 15.4 (1988), pp. 718–30 (p. 721).
7. 'La liberté absolue et divergente de chacun, la division des efforts et le fractionnement de la volonté humaine ont amené cette faiblesse, ce doute et cette pauvreté d'invention; quelques excentriques, sublimes et souffrants, compensent mal ce désordre fourmillant de médiocrités. L'individualité, – cette petite propriété, – a mangé l'originalité collective.' Charles Baudelaire, 'Salon de 1846', in *Œuvres complètes de Charles Baudelaire*, 7 vols (Paris: Lévy, 1868), vol. II, p. 193.
8. 'Individus mécanisés', in Foucault, *Surveiller et punir*, p. 245.
9. Sibalis, 'Corporatism after the Corporations', p. 729.

10. 'Il n'y a plus de corporation dans l'État, il n'y a plus que l'intérêt particulier de chaque individu et l'intérêt général. Il n'est permis à personne d'inspirer aux citoyens un intérêt intermédiaire, de les séparer de la chose publique par un esprit de corporations.' Isaac René Guy Le Chapelier, 'Séance du mardi 14 juin 1791 à l'Assemblée nationale', *Archives parlementaires*, French Revolution Archive, <https://frda.stanford.edu/en/catalog/ph525xc1642_00_0203> (accessed 19 September 2019).

11. 'L'ancien esprit de corps est le principal accusé.' Rosanvallon, *Le Modèle politique français*, p. 26.

12. 'L'ordre social exige [. . .] de ne pas laisser les simples citoyens se disposer en corporations [. . .] l'esprit de corps dégénér[ant] en aristocratie.' Abbé Sieyès, *Qu'est-ce que le Tiers état?* (Paris: Correard, 1822), p. 207.

13. Rosanvallon, *Le Modèle politique français*, p. 136.

14. G. P. Legret, *Sur les corporations* (Paris: Scherff, 1818), p. 27.

15. 'Qu'on ne s'y trompe pas, le système qui tend à dissoudre une nation en individus est l'une des plus funestes erreurs de la révolution; c'est le plus grand obstacle [. . .] à l'affermissement d'une véritable liberté. Consultons l'histoire; elle nous apprend que partout où le despotisme veut s'établir, il isole les hommes et les place ainsi dans leur faiblesse individuelle en présence de la toute puissance du gouvernement.' Antoine Levacher-Duplessis, *Réponse des délégués des marchands en détail et des maîtres artisans de la ville de Paris aux Rapports et délibérations des conseils généraux du commerce et des manufactures établis auprès de Son Excellence le ministre de l'Intérieur* (Paris: Dondey-Dupré, 1821), p. 19.

16. 'Nulle association de plus de vingt personnes, dont le but sera de se réunir tous les jours ou certains jours marqués, pour s'occuper d'objets religieux, littéraires, politiques ou autres, ne pourra se former qu'avec l'agrément du Gouvernement, et sous les conditions qu'il plaira à l'autorité publique d'imposer à la société.' *Code des délits et des peines, servant de supplément au procès verbal des séances du corps législatif* (Paris: Hacquart, 1810), p. 86.

17. Rosanvallon, *Le Modèle politique français*, p. 402.

18. Pierre Soufflot de Merey, *Considérations sur le rétablissement des jurandes et maîtrises* (Paris: Marchant, 1805), p. 54.

19. 'La société est en poussière, parce que les hommes sont désassociés, parce qu'aucun lien ne les unit, parce que l'homme est étranger à l'homme.' Pierre Leroux, 'Religion. Aux philosophes', in *Revue Encylopédique, ou analyse raisonnée des productions les plus remarquables dans la littérature, les sciences et les arts* (Paris: Sédillot, 1831), vol. LI, p. 501.

20. William H. Sewell, Jr, 'La confraternité des prolétaires: conscience de classe sous la Monarchie de Juillet', *Annales. Histoire, Sciences Sociales* 4 (1981), pp. 650–71 (p. 651).

21. 'Nous qui souffrons, ne comptons que sur nous-mêmes, nous sentons le mal, nous cherchons un remède immédiat et efficace; appliquons-le. Je crois que nous le trouverons dans l'*association* [. . .] Vous comprenez tous parfaitement que l'association a le double avantage de rassembler toutes les forces et de donner à ce tout une direction. Si nous restons isolés, éparpillés, nous sommes faibles, nous serons donc facilement réduits et nous subirons la loi du maître [. . .] Il faut donc un lien qui nous unisse, une intelligence qui nous gouverne, il faut une *association*. D'abord les ouvriers du même état doivent former entre eux un corps.' Zael Efrahem, *De l'association des ouvriers de tous les corps d'état* (Paris: Mie, 1833), p. 1.

22. 'Ne laissons pas ces différentes corporations s'éparpiller et se dissoudre, ne les laissons

pas s'abîmer dans l'individualisme et l'égoïsme de l'isolement. Mettons-nous en rapport d'amitié les uns avec les autres.' Ibid., p. 3.

23. Karl Marx and Friedrich Engels, *Manifest der Kommunistischen Partei* (London: Burghard, 1848).

24. 'En face du droit individuel et pour le limiter, la Révolution ne proclama pas le devoir de justice sociale; ou du moins, sous le nom de *fraternité*, elle le laissa à l'état vague de sentiment, sans résultat juridique.' Alfred Fouillée, *La Démocratie politique et sociale en France* (Paris, 1900), p. 164

25. Rosanvallon, *Le Modèle politique français*, p. 283.

26. 'Le phénomène nouveau, la constatation précieuse et consolante, c'est que les syndicats ne font pas seulement les grèves: ils les régularisent, ils les disciplinent. Et c'est là le progrès social qui est né de la législation de 1884. Croyez-vous que ce ne soit rien de voir que le premier effort de ces ouvriers encadrés, disciplinés, ayant leurs chefs, c'est de rechercher la discussion, d'instituer un débat?' Pierre René Waldeck-Rousseau, 'Le droit de grève et le gouvernement (18 janvier 1900, Chambre des députés)', in Georges Pellissier (ed.), *Anthologie des prosateurs français contemporains*, 3 vols (Paris: Delagrave, 1910), vol. II, p. 427.

27. Edward Shorter and Charles Tilly, 'Le déclin de la grève violente en France de 1890 à 1835', *Le Mouvement social* 76 (1971), pp. 95–118.

28. 'C'est la corporation de l'Ancien Régime contre laquelle avait lutté Turgot et que la Révolution avait supprimée, absolument ressuscitée, reconnue officiellement [. . .] C'est le plus colossal changement qui ait été effectué en France depuis 1789.' Paul Leroy-Beaulieu, 'Un nouveau pas dans la voie du socialisme. Le syndicat obligatoire', *L'Économiste Français*, 29 September 1900, p. 423.

29. 'La conception du "travailleur collectif" commence à s'imposer au législateur, au lieu et place du travailleur isolé. *Le corps des travailleurs est reconnu comme ayant une existence personnelle.*' Hubert Lagardelle, *L'Évolution des syndicats ouvriers en France. De l'interdiction à l'obligation* (Paris: L'Émancipatrice, 1901), p. 181.

30. Guy Thuillier and Jean Tulard, *Histoire de l'administration française* (Paris: Presses Universitaires de France, 1994), p. 7.

31. 'Un seul principe existait en France, l'individuellisme, l'universel égoïsme, fruit naturel d'un temps qui avait brisé tous les liens. Plus d'amour du prochain là où il n'y avait plus de religion pour en faire un précepte [. . .] Plus d'esprit de corps là où tout corps avait cessé d'exister.' François-Auguste Faveau de Frénilly, *Considérations sur une année de l'histoire de France* (Paris: Chaumerot, 1815), p. 27.

32. 'Parmi les effets de l'avènement de la démocratie, Tocqueville est particulièrement attentif au devenir de ce qu'il appelle "l'orgueil de corps", la "volonté de corps" [. . .] Si l'expression "esprit de corps" [. . .] ne se retrouve pas dans ses écrits, c'est bien cependant de cet "esprit" de solidarité mais aussi de distinction existant entre les membres d'un même "corps social" dont parle Tocqueville.' Yves Déloye, 'Penser l'esprit de corps: L'actualité de l'anthropologie des corps et des esprits chez Alexis de Tocqueville', in Guglielmi and Haroche (eds), *L'esprit de corps*, pp. 201–2.

33. 'Les nobles jouissaient du droit exclusif de fournir des officiers à l'armée. C'eût été là sans doute un important privilège si les nobles eussent conservé une certaine importance individuelle ou un puissant esprit de corps. Mais n'ayant ni l'un ni l'autre, ils n'étaient à l'armée, comme partout ailleurs, que des instruments passifs dans les mains du roi.' Alexis de Tocqueville, *Mélanges, fragments historiques et notes sur l'ancien régime, la Révolution et l'empire* (Paris: Lévy, 1865), p. 9.

34. Jay M. Smith, *The Culture of Merit: Nobility, Royal Service, and the Making of Absolute*

Monarchy in France, 1600–1789 (Ann Arbor: University of Michigan Press, 1996).

35. 'On voyait régner [avant la fin du dix-septième siècle] au sein de ce grand corps un certain esprit homogène. Il obéissait tout entier à des règles fixes, se gouvernait d'après certains usages invariables, et entretenait certaines idées communes à tous ses membres.' Tocqueville, *Mélanges*, p. 5.

36. 'Lorsque les citoyens sont divisés en castes et en classes [. . .] ils n'ont ni le goût ni le désir de se ressembler; chacun cherche, au contraire, de plus en plus, à garder intactes ses opinions et ses habitudes propres, et à rester soi. L'esprit d'individualité est très vivace. Quand un peuple a un état social démocratique, c'est-à-dire qu'il n'existe plus dans son sein de castes ni de classes [. . .] les hommes se ressemblent, et de plus ils souffrent, en quelque sorte de ne pas se ressembler.' Alexis de Tocqueville, *De la démocratie en Amérique* (Paris: Gosselin, 1835–40), vol. IV, p. 243.

37. François-Alexandre de la Chenaye-Desbois and Jacques Badier, *Dictionaire de la Noblesse* (Paris: Schlesinger, 1865–67), vol. VII, p. 761; vol. X, p. 141.

38. 'une habitude générale de l'esprit de corps, qui agissait fortement sur les individus, et les rapprochait singulièrement du type le plus parfait de leur profession'; Paul de Flotte, *La Souveraineté du peuple: essais sur l'esprit de la Révolution* (Paris: Pagnerre, 1851), p. 417.

39. Georg Lukács, *History and Class Consciousness* (London: Merlin Press, 1971).

40. 'Chacune de ces classes prend et conserve invariablement des habitudes intellectuelles qui ne sont propres qu'à elle, et adopte de préférence certains mots et certains termes qui passent ensuite de génération en génération comme des héritages.' Tocqueville, *De la démocratie en Amérique*, vol. I, p. 130.

41. Jakob Lauring and Jan Selmer, 'Multicultural Organizations: Common Language and Group Cohesiveness', *International Journal of Cross Cultural Management* 10.3 (2010), pp. 267–84 (p. 271).

42. 'Une langue artificielle, destinée à ne pas être comprise par une certaine classe de gens.' Marcel Schwob and Georges Guieysse, *Études sur l'argot français* (Paris: Bouillon, 1889), p. 6.

43. 'Aujourd'hui, on voit encore des riches, mais ils ne forment plus un corps compact et héréditaire; ils n'ont pu adopter un esprit, y persévérer et le faire pénétrer dans tous les rangs.' Tocqueville, *De la démocratie en Amérique*, vol. II, p. 331.

44. Alexis de Tocqueville, *Democracy in America*, trans. Arthur Goldhammer (New York: Library of America, 2004), p. 403.

45. Alexis de Tocqueville, *Democracy in America*, trans. Henri Reeve (Cambridge: Sever and Francis, 1863), vol. I, p. 237.

46. Tocqueville, *Democracy in America*, trans. Reeve, p. 237.

47. Walter C. Parker, *Teaching Democracy: Unity and Diversity in Public Life* (New York: Teachers College Press, 2003), p. 4.

48. 'Il semble que le peuple français soit comme ces prétendus corps élémentaires dans lesquels la chimie moderne rencontre de nouvelles particules séparables à mesure qu'elle les regarde de près.' Alexis de Tocqueville, *L'Ancien régime et la Révolution* (Paris: Lévy, 1856), p. 168.

49. 'La variété disparaît du sein de l'espèce humaine: les mêmes manières d'agir, de penser et de sentir se retrouvent dans tous les coins du monde. Cela ne vient pas seulement de ce que tous les peuples se pratiquent davantage et se copient plus fidèlement, mais de ce qu'en chaque pays les hommes, s'écartant de plus en plus des idées et des sentiments particuliers à une caste, à une profession, à une famille,

arrivent simultanément à ce qui tient de plus près à la constitution de l'homme, qui est partout le même.' Tocqueville, *De la démocratie en Amérique*, vol. IV, p. 134.

50. 'Dans la masse commune [. . .] l'esprit d'individualité est presque détruit.' Ibid., p. 243.

51. Isaac Berk, 'The Walking Dead as a Critique of American Democracy', *Cineaction* 95 (2015), pp. 48–55.

52. 'Une famille qui s'est fait respecter et craindre par son union et par son esprit de corps, et qui se compose d'individus appartenant à une race dont le sang est pur et la réputation intacte, se place par cette confraternité de sentiments, dans une position très avantageuse et obtient de grands succès [. . .] C'est ainsi que se forment des associations capables de soumettre les autres peuples et de conquérir des empires. Pour éclaircir ce principe, nous ferons observer que l'esprit de corps dans une tribu est comme le tempérament dans les êtres créés [. . .] L'esprit de corps, porté de cette manière à son plus haut degré d'intensité, ne se trouve que dans les familles illustres qui ont l'habitude du commandement. Dans une telle maison, il faut qu'un des membres ait le pouvoir d'imposer ses volontés aux autres.' Ibn Khaldoun, *Les Prolégomènes d'Ibn Khaldoun*, trans. William de Slane (Paris: Imprimerie Impériale, 1863), pp. 341–97.

53. Mary Douglas, *How Institutions Think* (London: Routledge and Kegan Paul, 1987), p. 48.

54. 'Chacune de ces associations forme comme une espèce particulière dans le genre humain.' Tocqueville, *De la démocratie en Amérique*, vol. I, pp. 208–9.

55. 'Les hommes de nos jours qui sont si indépendants les uns des autres sont tous plus ou moins dépendants de l'administration.' Tocqueville, 'Lettre du 25 juin 1838 à Francisque de Corcelle', *Œuvres complètes*, 16 vols (Paris: Gallimard, 1983), vol. XV, p. 101.

56. 'Il y a, de nos jours, beaucoup de gens qui s'accommodent très aisément de cette espèce de compromis entre le despotisme administratif et la souveraineté du peuple.' Tocqueville, *De la démocratie en Amérique*, vol. I, p. 152.

57. 'Si l'on entend par esprit de corps un esprit systématique qui tend avec fermeté vers un but permis et utile, on conviendra que cet esprit de corps est essentiel à l'administration, qui ne peut arriver à de bons résultats que par la fixité de ses vues et la constance de sa marche.' Émile Victor Foucart, *Éléments de droit public et administratif*, 3 vols (Paris: Videcoq, 1843), vol. III, p. 253.

58. Esprit de corps was the 'source de tant de grandes choses'. Jean-Gustave Courcelle-Seneuil, *Dictionnaire politique, Encyclopédie du langage et de la science politiques, rédigé par une réunion de députés, de publicistes et de journalistes* (Paris: Pagnerre, 1842), p. 96.

59. George Sand, *Histoire de ma vie*, 10 vols (Paris: Lévy, 1893 [1856]), vol. III, p. 295.

60. Seneuil, *Dictionnaire politique*, p. 290.

61. *Dictionnaire de l'Académie française*, 2 vols (Paris: Smits, 1789), vol. II, p. 580, Dictionnaires d'Autrefois <http://portail.atilf.fr/>.

62. 'L'obligation est *solidaire* quand chacun des obligés peut être contraint pour le tout.' *Encyclopédie méthodique*, 210 vols (Paris, Panckoucke, 1787), vol. VII, p. 618.

63. 'théorie des groupes, dont jamais nos savants n'ont daigné faire aucune étude'; Charles Fourier, 'Le groupe hypermajeur', in *Manuscrits de Fourier* (Paris: Librairie Phalanstérienne, 1849), p. 562.

64. 'Relativement aux mœurs, on peut entrevoir que dans chaque Tribu, quelque pauvre qu'elle soit, il règne un esprit de corps, une jalousie de l'honneur de la Tribu [. . .] Cet esprit de corps suffit pour faire disparaître les vices les plus choquants de la populace

civilisée, sa grossièreté, sa malpropreté, sa bassesse.' Charles Fourier, *Théorie des quatre mouvements et des destinées générales* (Leipzig, 1808), p. 163.

65. 'Par amour-propre et esprit de corps, on veut que la corporation dont on fait partie tienne un rang distingué parmi les corporations rivales.' Ibid., p. 91.

66. Pierre Mercklé, 'La "science sociale" de Charles Fourier', *Revue d'Histoire des Sciences Humaines* 2 (2006), pp. 69–88 (p. 79).

67. 'Faut-il l'appeler groupe d'ambition, groupe d'honneur, groupe de sectisme, groupe d'ascendance, groupe de corporation, je ne sais lequel choisir [. . .] L'Ambition est la passion dont l'essor est le plus immense dans l'État civilisé, elle seule dès à présent embrasse le globe entier dans ses plans [. . .] Si cette passion est insatiable dans les individus, elle l'est bien plus encore dans les corporations.' Fourier, 'Le groupe hypermajeur', p. 551.

68. Ibid., p. 552.

69. Julian Eagles, 'Marxism, Anarchism, and the Situationist's Theory of Revolution', *Critical Sociology* 43.1 (2017), pp. 13–36 (p. 19).

70. Fourier, *Théorie des quatre mouvements*, p. 19.

71. 'l'influence de l'esprit de corps [par] entraînement ascendant'; Charles Pellarin, *Théorie sociétaire* (Paris: Librairie Phalanstérienne, 1850), p. 61.

72. 'les produits de leur industrie s'élèvent à la perfection que l'on doit attendre de gens qui travailleront par passion, par esprit de corps et amour-propre, et nullement par le véhicule du besoin et du bénéfice'; Fourier, *Théorie des quatre mouvements*, p. 417.

73. I. D. Loyd Jones, 'Charles Fourier: Faithful Pupil of the Enlightenment', in Peter Gilmour (ed.), *Philosophers of the Enlightenment* (Edinburgh: Edinburgh University Press, 1990), p. 151.

74. Chantal Mouffe, 'Hearts, Minds and Radical Democracy', interview, *Red Pepper*, <https://www.redpepper.org.uk/hearts-minds-and-radical-democracy/> (accessed 19 September 2019).

75. Ibid.

76. 'l'esprit d'ensemble ou le sentiment de la solidarité commune'; Émile Durkheim, *De la division du travail social* (Paris: Alcan, 1893), p. 404.

77. Ibid., p. 335.

78. Émile Durkheim, *De la division du travail social* (Paris: Alcan, 1897), preface, p. 11.

79. 'L'esprit de corps, la vie en commun, devrait avoir ici l'influence prophylactique qu'elle exerce ailleurs.' Émile Durkheim, *Le Suicide* (Paris: Alcan, 1897), p. 248.

80. Ibid., p. 400.

81. Max S. Marshall, 'The Concept of Immunity', *The Centennial Review of Arts and Science* 3.1 (1959), pp. 95–113 (p. 98).

82. Durkheim, *De la division du travail social* (1893), p. 451.

83. 'La loi de la division du travail s'applique aux organismes comme aux sociétés.' Ibid., p. 3.

84. 'Une différentiation sociale peut être pathologique, à l'image du cancer dans l'organisme biologique.' Dominique Guillo, 'La Place de la biologie dans les premiers textes de Durkheim: un paradigme oublié?', *Revue française de sociologie* 47.3 (2006), pp. 507–35 (p. 517).

85. 'À l'origine, l'individu est absorbé dans le groupe.' Durkheim, *De la division du travail social* (1893), pp. 317–18.

86. 'Une société dont la cohésion [résulte] exclusivement des ressemblances', 'une masse absolument homogène', 'la horde'; ibid., pp. 149–89.

87. 'Dans une petite société, comme tout le monde est placé sensiblement dans les mêmes conditions d'existence, le milieu collectif est essentiellement concret [. . .] Les états de conscience qui le représentent ont donc le même caractère.' Ibid., p. 318.

88. 'Lorsque l'on s'élève le long de l'échelle des sociétés, une nouvelle distribution des individus et des activités s'opère. Une division du travail s'installe progressivement, qui fait apparaître des organes spécialisés, à l'activité de plus en plus définie et aux lignes géométriques de plus en plus nettes et complexes.' Guillo, 'La Place de la biologie dans les premiers textes de Durkheim', p. 518.

89. Durkheim, *De la division du travail social* (1893), p. 133.

90. Gabriel Tarde, *On Communication and Social Influence: Selected Papers*, ed. Terry N. Clark (Chicago: University of Chicago Press, 1969), p. 7.

91. 'L'*esprit de groupe*, ou, dans le sens le plus large du mot, l'*esprit de corps*, comprend plusieurs variétés importantes [. . .] 1° L'*esprit de foule* [. . .] 2° L'*esprit de famille* [. . .] 3° L'*esprit de métier* [. . .] ou, dans le sens précis du mot, l'*esprit de corps* proprement dit. Il se subdivise en autant d'espèces qu'il y a de catégories de professions: *esprit sacerdotal, esprit universitaire, esprit militaire, esprit judiciaire, esprit mercantile.* L'esprit de métier donne naissance à l'*esprit de classe* et à l'*esprit de caste.* 4° L'*esprit de parti* [. . .] 5° Il y a aussi l'esprit de secte religieuse. 6° Il y a au-dessus de tous ces esprits-là, et les comprenant, l'*esprit de nation*, le *patriotisme*, qui n'est en effet qu'un esprit de corps agrandi [. . .] 7° Enfin, n'y a-t-il pas à indiquer la place d'un *esprit de groupe supra-national*, d'un *esprit de civilisation* (ou aussi bien de *religion*)?' Gabriel Tarde, *L'esprit de groupe, Conférence faite au Collège Libre des Sciences Sociales le 6 Novembre 1899* (Lyons: Storck, 1900), pp. 1–24 (p. 1)

92. Johan Heilbron, *French Sociology* (Ithaca: Cornell Unversity Press, 2015), p. 152.

93. 'Ce sentiment profond qui naît entre nous quand, à force de nous voir, de frayer ensemble, de nous entre-refléter à notre insu ou volontairement, nous nous sentons peu à peu liés par une solidarité étroite et intime.' Tarde, *L'esprit de groupe*, p. 3.

94. Ibid., p. 7.

95. 'L'esprit de corps, par le fait même qu'il s'est amplifié, s'est modifié [. . .] Un esprit de solidarité intense entre corps de métiers jadis en guerre a succédé à l'exclusivisme [. . .] Les grandes fédérations ouvrières des Etats-Unis sont des armées industrielles [. . .] La sympathie imitatrice et assimilatrice, qui constitue la sociabilité en action, se manifeste par deux effets contraires et alternatifs: d'abord par la formation d'une société close, d'un enclos social où la culture intensive de la sociabilité est pratiquée; puis [. . .] par la déformation et l'ébrèchement de ces enclos, dont les murs tombent, mais pour se relever plus loin, en s'élargissant.' Ibid., p. 18.

96. '*Esprit de corps.* – On appelle ainsi l'inclination qui nous porte à former dans la grande famille qu'on appelle État des groupes plus particuliers, des associations plus restreintes [. . .] en un mot des corporations.' Paul Janet, *Traité élémentaire de philosophie à l'usage des classes* (Paris: Delagrave, 1899), p. 264.

97. George Lakoff, *Moral Politics: How Liberals and Conservatives Think* (Chicago: University of Chicago Press, 2002), p. 3.

98. 'La création des aristocraties, et, pour parler d'une manière plus générale, l'hérédité des fonctions et l'esprit de corps n'ont pour but que d'obtenir ce développement de quelques organes aux dépens de quelques autres, et de rompre ainsi l'équilibre de l'organisation humaine.' Flotte, *La Souveraineté du peuple*, p. 418.

99. 'L'instinct public ne se trompe pas, l'inégalité ou pour mieux dire la différence des

droits et devoirs est en effet le seul moyen de reconstituer largement l'esprit de corps et l'identification de l'homme avec sa profession.' Ibid., pp. 420–1.

100. 'Au sens large, l'expression "esprit de corps" désigne l'esprit de solidarité en général, envisagé non plus seulement dans le groupe professionnel, mais dans tous les cercles sociaux, quels qu'ils soient (classe, caste, secte, etc.), dans lesquels l'individu se sent plus ou moins subordonné aux intérêts de la collectivité.' Georges Palante, 'L'esprit de corps', *Revue philosophique de la France et de l'étranger* 48 (1899), pp. 135–45 (p. 135).

101. Ibid., p. 136.

102. 'La discipline morale et sociale qu'il [le corps] impose à ses membres est étroite et énergique.' Ibid., p. 137.

103. 'Un "corps" est un groupe professionnel défini qui a ses intérêts propres, son vouloir-vivre propre et qui cherche à se défendre contre toutes les causes extérieures ou intérieures de destruction ou de diminution. Si nous nous demandons maintenant quels sont les biens pour lesquels lutte un corps, nous voyons que ce sont des avantages moraux: le bon renom du corps, l'influence, la considération, le crédit. Ces avantages moraux ne sont sans doute que des moyens en vue d'assurer la prospérité matérielle du corps et de ses membres.' Ibid., p. 137.

104. Michel Onfray, *Georges Palante: essai sur un nietzschéen de gauche* (Bédée: Folle Avoine, 1989).

105. 'C'est dans cette grande loi générale d'*insincérité sociale* qu'il faut faire rentrer la tactique spéciale au moyen de laquelle un corps dissimule ses défauts.' Palante, 'L'esprit de corps', p. 138.

106. 'La concurrence est la grande loi qui domine l'évolution des sociétés; elle domine aussi la vie des corps constitués.' Ibid., p. 138.

107. 'comme une basse-cour se rue sur le poulet malade pour l'achever'; ibid., p. 138.

108. 'L'esprit de corps tend à étendre autant que possible sa sphère d'influence. Il est essentiellement envahisseur.' Ibid., p. 139.

109. 'Ces quelques remarques sur les faits et gestes de l'esprit de corps nous permettent de voir en lui une manifestation particulièrement énergique de ce que Schopenhauer appelle le vouloir-vivre. Un corps est, comme toute société organisée d'ailleurs, du *vouloir-vivre humain condensé*, et porté à un degré d'intensité que n'atteint jamais l'égoïsme individuel.' Ibid., p. 139.

110. 'Ce qu'il [le corps] exige de ses membres, c'est [. . .] une certaine tenue, une certaine persévérance dans la docilité au code moral du corps. C'est cette persévérance dans la docilité que, par je ne sais quel malentendu de langage, on décore parfois du titre de caractère. Par ce dernier mot un corps n'entendra nullement l'initiative dans la décision ni la hardiesse dans l'exécution, ni aucune des qualités de spontanéité et d'énergie qui font la belle et puissante individualité.' Ibid., p. 140.

6

The Mystique of Esprit de Corps in France in the Twentieth Century

The Moral Empire: The Persisting Ambiguity of Esprit de Corps in French

In the first decades of the twentieth century, two centuries after the birth of the signifier 'esprit de corps', many French uses of the phrase were still definitional, as if one of its attractions was its challenge to interpretation, or the possibility it offered for presenting an agonistic view on the relationship between groups and individuals. The war of connotations, webs of belief and nuances continued, for example in 1902 in a memoir about Napoleon:

> An esprit de corps contained within wise limits is appropriate; it can, as in the case of uniforms, have excellent effects, be a barrier against moral failings, develop in the officer the feeling of solidarity, raise him towards ever greater perfection, give him a clearer feeling for his duty. The spirit of caste [*l'esprit de caste*] has contrary effects: a spirit of selfishness and isolation, it manifests itself as a disdain for the rest of humanity, towards whom he then believes he can act as he pleases [. . .] The esprit de corps confers only duties; but the esprit de caste, privileges.[1]

A century after Louis de Bonald and his distinction between esprit de corps and *esprit de parti*, an author insisted again that 'esprit de corps' should have a good denotation only, proposing a new term for the negative connotation. Those were distinctions about distinctions – *corps* versus *caste*, after *corps* versus *parti* – a rhetorical way of separating the wheat from the chaff. This particular intertwining of military and political discourse comes as no surprise in a book about Napoleon.

Yet contrary to the UK and the USA, where esprit de corps became in the twentieth century a corporate cure, esprit de corps in France was still sometimes identified as a poison, or both a cure and a poison, a kind of *pharmakon*.[2] For instance, a discussion about solidarity among police forces held at the Sénat in 1902 hesitated between 'the disadvantages of esprit de corps' and its 'advantages'.[3] It was not rare to see esprit de corps still associated with 'intolerance, exclusivism'.[4] Most debaters felt the ambivalence of 'the esprit de corps, some-times strengthening, and sometimes thwarting the feeling of our general duties'.[5] Of course, the seeds of this dual view of esprit de corps were already present in the influential *Encyclopédie*'s definition of 1752: 'It is a kind of good or bad graft upon a great trunk.'[6] But the idea of esprit de corps as a good graft was quickly abandoned by the philosophers of the Enlightenment.

In 1902, distinctions were less sharp and assertive:

> The ground is slippery between the esprit de corps and the spirit of caste, and in the same manner one can easily fall from noble patriotism, formed by a feeling of love for compatriots, into the low patriotism of hate towards the foreigner.'[7]

It was now a Hegelian *lieu commun* of French undergraduate textbooks to profess that 'the Self emerges via oppositions' [*le moi se pose en s'opposant*],[8] but in the case of esprit de corps it felt as if the dialectics never found a solid ground upon which one could build unambiguously.

According to writer Émile Zola, who in the novel *Pot-Bouille* spoke of 'l'in-stinct de l'esprit de corps',[9] the slippery aspect of esprit de corps was due to the fact that it was both an instinct and a socially induced trait. He also suggested that esprit de corps was a cultural trait pertaining to class consciousness, for example among servants in a household animated by frustration and rancour.[10] Only by suppressing artificial divides and via the exercise of reason would one be able to minimise the pitfalls of esprit de corps: in his celebrated open letter on the Dreyfus affair, *J'accuse*, Zola explicitly compared the 'prejudices of esprit de corps' in the French army to a lack of intelligence. Esprit de corps was connected to our gregariousness; it was for Zola a reparable foolishness [*sottise*].[11]

Like Zola, a few *intellectuels* were busy with what the *Revue Internationale de Sociologie* called 'the controversy between partisans and opponents of esprit de corps'.[12] At the forefront of the critique of esprit de corps, we found a now even more radicalised Georges Palante, who in 1904 published a book-length manifesto that he defiantly called *Combat pour l'individu*.[13] In his crusade against most forms of collective human assemblage, Palante spotted the spectre of esprit de corps everywhere: 'the esprit de corps of married people', 'the esprit de corps of women', 'the esprit de corps of small towns', 'the esprit de corps of public employees'.[14] He concluded: 'Esprit de corps arrogates to itself a moral empire over individual consciences'.[15] If Palante was among the first authors to explicitly grant women the capacity to display esprit de corps, this was not a compliment, but rather part of a discourse of reductive biological metaphors and fuzzy psycho-economics: 'Women's esprit de corps has an interest in not leaving too many girls outside of the marriage market because this would depreciate the gender.'[16]

A more sober metaphor regarding the political dangers of esprit de corps was developed by the Hellenist Armand Delatte in his description of the ancient Pythagorean cult:

It is a kind of state within the state. This power is felt as a threat, an embarrass-ment or a tyranny by all those who do not have with it any relation of friend-ship and who cannot count upon its protection. The community of life of the Pythagoreans, their secret meetings, their practices, sometimes shocking, often bizarre, offer the appearance of a continual conspiracy, they arouse distrust, provoke fears, excite envy. Finally, their disdain and pride succeed in attracting the hatred of their fellow-citizens. The esprit de corps, which animates all the acts of their life, makes the [Pythagorean] Society look like a centre of all perfection, so that they think they are called to carry out a higher mission. To inspire and even lead the government is, for them, more than a right.[17]

A state within the state, or, remembering once more d'Alembert, a nation within the nation: this historical analysis echoed the old critique of the Jesuits. It was written with an impartial understanding of the rationale of both the insiders and the outsiders. Even the wisest of philosophical communities could develop forms of arrogance that transformed it into a political war machine. The integrity and discipline of esprit de corps, driven inwards, could be perceived by outsiders as a form of fundamentalism. Persistent cohesion and organised discipline created power; power created hegemonic tendencies, real or fantasised. 'The only really dangerous esprit de corps is that of men who participate in power',[18] wrote the inventor of the notion of *social synergy* in 1909.[19] But if esprit de corps is a synonym of collective power, such a claim is a tautology. Can there be esprit de corps without participation in power?

The Superior Self: Esprit de Corps as Honour in Terraillon and Bergson

The semantic field of esprit de corps was until the early twentieth century highly correlated to the notion of honour. According to Eugène Terraillon, a philos-ophy teacher who published in 1912 a book on the concept of honour, fidelity to a society and group solidarity were motivated first and foremost by a concern for good reputation, *le qu'en-dira-t-on* ('what will people say?'). Ironically, such a concern could be found even in criminal societies:

> The honour of the thief will proceed from respecting his commitments and maintaining the bonds of solidarity that unite him to his comrades. The worst bandit will obey the code of honour by following this kind of programme which is, in some way, printed in his mind, a programme whose emblems are sometimes even indelibly etched on his skin by a deep tattoo. Usually the man who follows the law of honour has a very clear vision of what the social group whose esteem he seeks would think and say of him.[20]

Esprit de corps was a form of allegiance based on a supposedly universal aversion to disrepute. Once again, group commitment was compared to an indelible mark: a literal character, a tattoo. The notion of solidarity as a sort of coded programme is even more striking: for Terraillon, the behaviour inspired by esprit de corps was *automatique*, as a *mécanisme*.[21] Esprit de corps was a social machine.

But Terraillon also compared esprit de corps to a feeling, a *passion*, a *cristallisation*, a *monoideism*, 'a very strong sentiment of solidarity' and attachment to 'a world'.[22] The combination of automatism and emotion is suggestive of the production of a second nature. The concept of monoideism was taken from the Scottish doctor James Braid, who coined the term in the first half of the eighteenth century in relation to hypnosis.[23] Esprit de corps was, according to Terraillon, a kind of mesmerism that turned humans into emotional automata. This phenomenon was ubiquitous, strong among thieves but also effective in upper-class 'elite'[24] groups such as the *grands corps d'État*: 'The esprit de corps is present in these great national organs with remarkable energy since without it, they would not exist.'[25] To some of his readers, the idea of public servants as workers under hypnosis probably did not feel very *honourable*.

Like Tarde, Terraillon thought that esprit de corps was a universal social glue on an expanding scale:

> Esprit de corps regularly passes through three successive phases: it is constituted first insofar as the group of which it expresses the aspirations gains a clearer sense of its existence and its importance; it is then vigorous, exclusive and jealous. Soon, its growth encounters obstacles and limits; internal contradictions or conflicts with rival organisations, older or newer, or with the largest society in which the group develops [. . .] Finally, it is reconstituted on a broader basis, better adapted to the social state of the community or civilisation, and thus the cycle of the evolution of esprit de corps begins again.[26]

This teleological view of progressive expansion and inclusion was consistent with the optimistic and religiously tinted view of esprit de corps synthesised twenty years later by the then world-famous philosopher Henri Bergson, who believed in the cosmopolitan ideal of 'the esprit de corps of the human kind'.[27] But Terraillon was more political and influenced by socialism: he insisted on 'the actual solidarity of all the workers of a country, and perhaps even of all the workers of the civilised world'.[28] Localised and concentrated esprit de corps was not civilised enough and had to be shown the path to transnational progress.

The idea of an extension of the borders of esprit de corps towards a universal solidarity, in which it might perhaps logically self-destruct in the end, was inspired both by Christianism and Marxism. Even twentieth-century French Jesuits now proclaimed carefully: 'Beware of esprit de corps; do not consider the interests of your group.'[29] One needed to accept only inclusive and tolerant forms of esprit de corps: it should be less about 'restrained solidarity' [*solidarité restreinte*] and more about 'enlarged solidarity' [*solidarité élargie*].[30] The universalisation or at least the expansion of the circles of esprit de corps could even become a utopian European project: 'Does the future hold wider social solidarity, such as could be achieved for example by a United States of Europe?'[31] But could there be a European esprit de corps? The question is still debated nowadays, for example by

French and German defence ministers: 'The EU should foster a European esprit de corps by creating a new military academy or by having European courses at national military schools.'[32]

Henri Bergson was known for his concepts of *creation* and *life*, but esprit de corps became a fundamental notion in his last major book, *Les deux sources de la morale et de la religion*, in which esprit de corps was closely related to the idea that one's social self was like a 'superior self' [*moi supérieur*]:[33]

> If we accept the idea of [...] a 'primitive mentality', within it self-respect will coincide with the feeling of such solidarity between the individual and the group that the group remains constantly present to the isolated individual, monitors him, encourages or threatens him, eventually demands to be consulted and obeyed [...] The pressure of the social self is exerted via an accumulation of these individual energies. Moreover, the individual obeys not only by habit of discipline or from fear of punishment: the group to which he belongs necessarily puts itself above the others [...] and the consciousness of this superiority of force assures [...] all the pleasures of pride [...] It suffices to observe what happens before our eyes in small societies that are constituted within the greater society, when men are brought closer to each other by some distinctive mark which underlines a real or apparent superiority, and which sets them apart [...] All the members of the group are 'bound' together; we observe the birth of a 'feeling of honour' that is identical to esprit de corps.[34]

Bergson presented here his synthesis of the ideas of authors such as Durkheim, Tarde, Palante and Terraillon. Esprit de corps was a tribal process of collective self-glorification. But Bergson's use of inverted commas reflected the fact that for him, this 'feeling of honour' was a fiction, a 'fabulation'.[35]

Fabulation is a cognitive capacity to manipulate symbols and fictional narratives in order to generate common beliefs. It functions for Bergson like a form of 'virtual instinct':

> It can be called a virtual instinct, because at the extremity of another line of evolution, in insect societies, we see instinct provoking a mechanical conduct comparable in its usefulness to the one that is induced, in the intelligent and free mind of man, by quasi-hallucinatory images.[36]

In Latin, *fabulari* means to speak and invent a story.[37] Bergson suggested that language and storytelling helped humans to create a mindset, a second nature that replaced and simulated animal instinct to a certain extent. Esprit de corps is here seen as a form of collective hallucination, a contagious social fiction, a more or less permanent altered state of consciousness. This would justify the use of the term *esprit* as a form of spiritual possession. The apparent paradox here was that freedom and intelligence were interlaced with illusion and insect-like instinct. How could one be free and at the same time hallucinating? How could one be intelligent while modelling one's conduct on a fable?

The answer, according to Bergson, relies upon our plastic capacity to recreate new ideologies, to modify our narratives, to regularly redesign our evolving virtual instinct, to which we then give our near-blind consent for a period of time, for the sake of social utility and mutual effect. Not unlike others before him, Bergson distinguished two interdependent and dialectical modes of human solidarity, one more conservative, the other more creative. Social pressure is comparable to the instinct of eusocial animals such as ants and bees, although it operates via 'habitude', language, and social fictions.[38]

Bergson agreed that the cohesion of a group was maintained through its opposition to an outside sphere, an out-group. Esprit de corps was a robust circular force, mainly hostile to the new and the different:

> Between the society we live in and humanity in general there is [. . .] the same contrast as between the closed and the open [. . .] Who does not see that social cohesion is due in large part to a society's necessity to defend itself against others, and that it is first in contradistinction to all other men that one loves the men with whom he lives?[39]

In other words, *esprit de caste* and antagonism between groups was inevitable. Bergson thought that the mortar that joined the bricks of a closed society was 'discipline', which prepared for an 'attitude' of 'war' before an 'enemy', a defensive mindset that subsisted even when covered by the 'varnish' of 'moral duty'.[40] There was a collective pressure on the members to remain united in a hermetic *corps* and surrender part of their individuality to the obligations and discipline of the in-group, for the sake of battles won.

But because life was dual, both structured and structuring, both spiritual and natural, because it was a process of 'creative evolution',[41] human societies, according to Bergson, also manifested a transnational flow of sentimental universalism, a slow and widening feeling of unity and solidarity that kept creating renewed and larger, more encompassing global fabulations. A more creative form of esprit de corps existed, if ephemerally, one that was about love and openness to humankind rather than antagonism. This second tendency, representative of our cosmic freedom, was often manifested in spiritual leaders who were at the forefront of the *élan vital*.[42] It is perhaps that cosmic *élan* that is present as a secret dynamic drive in the conquering aspect of all scales of esprit de corps. In that case, esprit de corps would contain its own contradiction or limit, as life contains death.

For Bergson, life evolves towards the 'ideal limit' of a 'mystical society that would encompass the whole of humanity':[43]

> Privileged souls arose who felt akin to all souls and who, instead of remaining within the limits of the group and holding on to the solidarity established by nature, moved towards humanity in general in a spirit of love. The appearance of each of them was like the creation of a new species composed of a single individual, the vital thrust arriving once in a while, in a determined man,

at a result which could not have been attained immediately by the whole of humanity.[44]

The mystical hero, a mutant of sorts, was the key to the evolution of humanity. Sociality tends to become antagonistic and closed, while life is also constant re-openness to a spiritual dimension, deeper and freer than natural or virtual instinct. Universalism and particularism, love and war, were for Bergson a creative process of dialectical humanism, a *crealectical* process that slowly aspired towards a cosmopolitan form of creation-friendly solidarity, even if it was constantly limited by local norms. The pressure of basic instinct was slowly overflowed by the aspiration of life towards creativity. Human virtual instinct was more plastic, not completely solid or automatic, but rather carrying the energy of life as cosmic creative flow. This energy was incarnated by rare role-model figures who kept reinventing humanity, such as, suggests Bergson, Teresa of Ávila.

Bergson agreed with Durkheim and Palante that esprit de corps was not only a societal notion but also a biological one: 'Any morality, of pressure or aspiration, is of biological essence.'[45] But Bergson's biology was holistic. For him the flow of life was a spiritual, creative flow, a dilation, an expansive aspiration towards the creation of new forms of society and intelligence, a movement that was regularly obstructed but never stopped by matter or reality contracted into the solidity and solidarity of collective niches. Societies were never totally rigidified because of the underground, crealectical momentum of life. Our existence is driven by this double dynamic movement of, on the one hand, 'dilation' and springing (inspiration, *esprit*), and on the other hand 'contraction', solidification by ordering (incorporation, *corps*).[46] Esprit de corps reflects the original, cosmic, dynamic duality between the multiple and the One, creation and unification.

Such is, for Bergson, the creative logos, the crealectic at work in human social processes: one movement is of creation and aspiration towards freedom, the other regulates the preservation of individuals into safer cohesive groups. To achieve the latter, a simulated or virtual instinct was often more efficient or less costly than intelligence: 'Intelligence would be an obstacle to serenity.'[47] The reduction of the unpredictable was the practical aim of esprit de corps as second nature: it had to somewhat contradict or restrict the impetus and agonism of creative evolution.[48]

More practically, esprit de corps was often quasi-military: 'Continually repeated exercises are necessary, such as those practised by the soldier, the automatism of which eventually fixes in his body the moral assurance which he will need on the day of danger.'[49] Groups and nations were war machines of collective fitness, group preservation and spiritual somnambulism. The feeling of solidarity that it slowly instilled within the group was a fabulation of commonness that lasted until a wider ideology was adopted.

Ultimately, esprit de corps, although morbid when too strong, was justified by the fact that humanity was industrious.[50] The creative dialectics of robustness and plasticity, automation and innovation are particularly visible in our relationship with the purview of work.

Professional Habitus: Esprit de Corps in Work, Management and French Education

In the recent literature of managerial studies, the French entrepreneur Henri Fayol is regularly mentioned as one of the most important figures of the twentieth century.[51] Among his often quoted fourteen principles of management are 'esprit de corps', and 'subordination of individual interests to the common good'.[52] But if we take a closer look at Fayol's original writings, we realise that the now globally influential characterisation of his principle of esprit de corps is in fact a biased translation of 'l'union du personnel',[53] which translates more literally as *union of the staff* or *employees*. This intriguing covering of the French original with a Gallicism contains in fact, metaphorically, an explanation for the success of esprit de corps in Anglo-Saxon corporate discourse.

Fayol never mentioned *esprit de corps* in his magnum opus *Administration industrielle et générale*, in which his principles are set out, probably because in French, esprit de corps was too ambivalent and still potentially negative:

14) The union of the staff
Unity is strength [. . .] *Harmony*, union in the personnel of a company is a great strength in the corporation [. . .] The principle to observe is *the unity of command* [. . .] There is no merit in sowing division among one's subalterns; any newcomer can do that. On the contrary, real talent is needed to coordinate efforts, stimulate zeal, draw on the faculties of all, and to reward the merit of each without arousing jealous susceptibilities and disturbing the harmony of relations.[54]

Fayol advocated 'harmony' under the authority of an integrating leader, as in an orchestra. Even if his metaphor of harmony was somewhat musical, the word *commandement* was more military. Such a praise of enlightened chief-commanders is indeed compatible with twentieth-century Anglo-Saxon views on management. However, a probable reason for the translations' avoidance of the phrase *union du personnel* and the choice of esprit de corps instead is the question of syndicalism.

Contrary to managerial eulogies of esprit de corps in English, which implicitly see employees as soldiers and esprit de corps as a convenient, non-legal form of solidarity, Fayol was explicitly in favour of strong trade unions and consensus between business leaders and workers, a model that has become rare in global capitalism:

It is not only by the effects of the harmony that prevails among agents of the same corporation that the power of union manifests itself: commercial agreements, trade unions [*syndicats*], associations of all kinds play a considerable role in the government of business [. . .] I saw in 1860 workers in large industries without cohesion, without connection, a complete atomisation of individuals; a union [*syndicat*] transforms them into collectives that discuss with the boss on an equal footing [. . .] Business leaders must take this development into account.[55]

One could not be clearer about the legal meaning of union and the critique of capitalist individualism. The kind of esprit de corps that Fayol advocates is a durable and social democratic one, protected by contracts, rules and a horizon of relative social equality. This was not about fostering in corporations an adventurous and ephemeral 'all for one, one for all' martial drive, typical of the American way described in detail in the next chapter.

Yet Fayol is not without contradictions: one could ask how a boss could be both a strong commander and on equal terms with the unions. Perhaps this ambivalence contributes to the partiality of the widespread English translations of Fayol's principles: 'Principle 14. Esprit de corps. The maintenance of high morale and unity among employees is imperative.'[56] No mention of unions, syndicates or labour associations in this occurrence: this indeed gives a clue as to why the exotic term 'esprit de corps' matters in English management discourse.[57] If the leader of a corporation can create unity and cohesion among employees without having to consult with unions and create legal protections for the workers, this constitutes a good deal from a capitalist perspective: the sense of belonging and esprit de corps is expected to replace to a certain extent the need for higher salaries and legislated working conditions. Enthusiasm is oblivious.

A similar comparative analysis of Fayol's principle 6 in English and French can be useful. First, the English translation offered by a management journal:

> Principle 6. Subordination of individual interests to the common good. The goals of the organization must take precedence over the interests of individuals or groups of individuals in the organization. Fundamentally, this principle proposes that employees must sacrifice their interests for the good of the organization. Thus, an organization should employ only individuals who are fully committed to its objectives and are willing to readily comply with its mandates.[58]

In this translation, 'common good' is not a political concept but rather a private one, related to a particular interest, 'the good of the organization'. The need for employees to become sacrificial beasts and the idea that corporations should recruit docile workers only seems extreme and in fact probably counterproductive today because it is unadapted to postmodern aspirations.

In any case, Fayol's original text showed more concern for society as a whole, for the state, and the *républicaine* idea of general interest. Here is a more honest translation:

> 6) Subordination of the particular interest to the general interest [*intérêt général*].
> This principle recalls that in a corporation, the interest of an agent, or of a group of agents, must not prevail against the interest of the enterprise [. . .] that

the interest of the State must take precedence over that of a citizen or a group of citizens [. . .] Ignorance, ambition, selfishness, laziness, weaknesses and all human passions tend to lose sight of general interest and favour particular interest. This principle is a continual battle to fight.[59]

Fayol added that the main instrument to maintain esprit de corps and virtuous subordination was not only the steadfastness of chief officers but also their fairness in negotiation with the French *syndicats*, thanks to 'des conventions équitables'.[60] *Convention* is an unambiguous unionist term in France, where different *conventions collectives de travail*, co-written by the unions and the corporate administration, regulate the working conditions of specific professional branches.[61]

In fact, in the first decades of the century, esprit de corps could be seen in France as an obsolete form of management when compared to socialist unions. In 1909, the Union des Charpentiers de la Seine, a *syndicat*, published a brochure against trade guilds:

> The esprit de corps rules among the members of the companion guilds. They despise [. . .] men who follow the rites of another 'Duty'. Among fellows, there used to be murderous quarrels. They called each other wolves or dogs, and it seemed as if, by continual battles, they were trying to justify their war names. To avenge the corporate honour, they killed each other.[62]

This is certainly not a very moderate kind of prose, even if metaphorical. According to the author, esprit de corps was an element of internal weaponisation of labour relationships that only united workers superficially and very locally. *Compagnonnage*, a surviving yet declining form of *Ancien Régime corporation* that is today nearly extinct, transformed guilds into war machines competing against similar guilds, opposing *ouvriers* to other *ouvriers*, creating dissension within a class which, in the view of several *syndicats* influenced by socialism or communism, should be united and organised against abuses by the leadership.

However, not everybody thought esprit de corps and socialist unionism were incompatible. An opponent of 'libre-échangisme'[63] and economic laissez-faire, the economist Jules Domergue, connected with a movement called Syndicalisme Agricole Catholique, published an article on the ways of 'developing esprit de corps among factory staff',[64] in which esprit de corps was related both to socialist unionism and Catholic fraternity. Other texts explained that a lack of esprit de corps among workers increased the risk of their exploitation by the bosses. Once more, women were believed to be less inclined to corporatism: 'Bosses readily accept women workers because they are more flexible instruments, more docile than men. Unlike men, female workers do not have esprit de corps.'[65] In 1906, France was still an androcentric democracy in which less than 10 per cent of working women belonged to a trade union, and indeed they participated less in strikes.[66]

In the field of professional education, France maintained its cautious attitude regarding manifestations of esprit de corps throughout the twentieth century:

'l'esprit de corps [. . .] un danger pour l'éducation'.[67] The connection between esprit de corps and educational elitism is often salient:

> Esprit de corps is undeniably one of the most remarkable effects of a close and exclusive solidarity: the young people who are preparing for the exam to enter one of the selective administration schools of the State are already in solidarity with one another, excluding other students because they despise them. They do not admit that 'one of them' should not be worthy of exceptional consideration, because they think they are all worthy of respect, since they are about to enter a highly honourable body, so much superior to other collectives.[68]

This association between esprit de corps, arrogant attitudes and self-entitled groups could also simply be discipline-related, as elegantly summarised by the Nobel Prize-winning poet and novelist Anatole France: 'According to the widespread esprit de corps, which is the intelligence of those who have none, the pupils in Literature and the pupils in Science despised each other.'[69]

Other voices maintained that educational esprit de corps was a constructive and necessary element of socialisation, for example among school teachers:

> For several years the candidate teacher is subjected to a form of animal training [dressage] that makes him eminently capable of accomplishing the obscure tasks that await him. An esprit de corps, so to speak, is imposed on him, willy-nilly, by the very nature of his studies [. . .] It is our belief that a certain esprit de corps expresses the dignity of the profession.[70]

This formulation was ironical: the paradox between the idea of forced *dressage* and the notion of *dignity* manifested the ambiguity between discipline as constraint and discipline as vocation or craft.

The ambivalence of esprit de corps was sometimes seen as a necessary evil in public administration. An editorial of *La Revue administrative* published in 1950 coined the term *esprit de bande, gang spirit*, and explained:

> The public servant [*fonctionnaire*], regardless of rank or position – even a 'director' – is still just a cog in a complex ensemble [. . .] From the moment he leaves the Grandes Écoles and passes the last impersonal and objective barrier of competitive entrance exams into the Administration, which will almost always be for him the last strictly impartial measure of his intellectual abilities, this eminently social being that the official then becomes will depend more than anyone else upon his fellow-men [. . .] All the special links that can bind individuals united in a common career engender this kind of solidarity. What is true of all ethnic or other minorities is also true in professional matters, and this is commonly called esprit de corps [. . .] The cement of such coalitions is constituted by an identical institutional formation which confers on all its former students [. . .] a discipline of mutuality in which camaraderie relies on a common feeling, justified or not, of superior vocation.[71]

French public administration was a mimetic social machine, fuelled by a stand-ardised and state-controlled education as well as complex instincts. This was a process of depersonification in which public officials were compared to ethnic minority groups, suggesting that they became not only cogs in a vast machine, but also primitive emotional beings.

Although this editorial indicated that esprit de corps was not a sublime virtue, but rather a gang spirit, its conclusion was that refusing to comply to the unwrit-ten rules of social esprit de corps was even more foolish, like an 'intellectual impairment'.[72] Such conformist compromise in spite of critical lucidity unveils the self-perpetuating aspect of esprit de corps: most of those who are aware of its limitations will end up conforming in order to avoid being segregated. The intellect becomes a serf to groupthink out of self-interest. Superiority complex and inferiority complex become intertwined.

The superiority complex associated with official esprit de corps was identified throughout the century:

> This esprit de corps still exists [in 1976] and it is useless to ignore the fact that, today, many engineers, officials or officers trained in the *Grandes Écoles* do not conceal a certain condescension towards colleagues who lack this background.[73]

Esprit de corps is about duty, drive, discipline and, last but not least, distinction. It plays with the emotions of pride and contempt.

An influential analysis of esprit de corps in elitist schools and state administra-tions was proposed in 1989 by the sociologist Pierre Bourdieu, who attempted a creative synthesis between Durkheim and Marx. Esprit de corps was, for Bourdieu, a form of (de)possession, a 'symbolic violence'[74] in which each group member is both a victim and a tormentor:

> This true magical action of influence, or, if the word is not too strong, of possession, succeeds only insofar as the one who suffers from it also contributes to its efficiency; it constrains him only to the extent that he is predisposed through prior learning to *recognise* it. This is only the case when the categories of perception and action which a member implements in the individual acts through which the 'will' and the power of the institution are achieved [. . .] are in agreement with the objective structures of the organisation, because they are the product of the incorporation of these structures. Throughout this book, we will meet many of these possessed souls who bow to the wishes of the insti-tution, because they are the institution made men. Dominated or dominant, they fully sustain or manifest its necessity because they have incorporated it, because they are one with it, and they give it a body.[75]

More than two hundred years of international discussion about esprit de corps did not bring about much scientific progress: esprit de corps is still seen by Bourdieu as a form of mysterious voodooism. More than a simple metaphor to designate the attachment of a subject to a group, the text points to a magical or diabolic possession, a form of institutional sorcery, a spirit made flesh and vice versa.

But how can an institution or a group-culture be individually incorporated? 'In the form of schemes of perception and action, principles of vision and division, mental structures',[76] answered Bourdieu, who did not expand on the mysterious circularity of esprit de corps: what came first, the collective body or the individual one? In fact, up to now, there is no consensual theory on how joint intentionality is generated and maintained: such uncertainties explain the persistent success of the pre-scientific, almost alchemical signifier 'esprit de corps'. The most inquisitive minds have failed to decode its complex rationale.

Bourdieu seemed eager to explain esprit de corps as a cognitive phenomenon, but he multiplied fuzzy metaphors:

> This affective enchantment, which arises from being able to love and admire oneself in one's peers, is one of the foundations, along with the *logical conformism* associated with the homogeneity of mental structures, of what is called *esprit de corps*: this sense of solidarity with the group is based on the community of schemes of perception, of appreciation, thought and action that support the instinctual connivance of the well-orchestrated unconscious minds.[77]

Poetic images suggest that cognitive, emotional and physical aspects cannot be easily dissociated in the comprehension of esprit de corps, turning any objective analysis into a challenge. In fact, 'Bourdieu thinks that it is this capacity to "think with the body" and to "know without concepts" that accounts for [. . .] the sense of "belief" and legitimacy of socially-produced structural orders.'[78] We find it hard to objectively analyse esprit de corps because it is mind and body interlaced, a human experience that does not pertain to analytical intelligence.

Esprit de Corps as a War Machine: From de Gaulle to Deleuze

Because one of the first historical meanings of esprit de corps signified loyalty and pride among soldiers of a specific regiment, the French army did not differ much from the US or British military in its valorisation of esprit de corps: 'The solidarity that results from this esprit de corps maintains the traditions of valour, probity, moral energy',[79] wrote Charles Ferrand, a *polytéchnicien* who became a military engineer, in 1911. Probity implied an allegiance to moral principles: it need not be a specifically martial virtue, neither did it suppose, in theory, a form of blind obedience to orders. The ideas of valour and moral energy supposed a personal engagement within a normative collective context.

Was esprit de corps mostly about common discipline? This is what the novelist André Maurois deduced from his military experience: 'It was hard, but what an esprit de corps, what a discipline these rough manners gave us!'[80] During the First World War, Maurois had served as an interpreter and a liaison officer between the French and the British armies; he had a first-hand experience of war. Through one of his characters, he suggested paradoxically that military esprit de corps was even more distinguishable in periods of peace:

Today's officer has seen real action, it's true, but at war, it's enough to be healthy and to have no more imagination than a fish. It is in peacetime that a soldier must be judged [. . .] How much I would like this war to be over to return to genuine peace-time military manoeuvres![81]

In other words, twentieth-century war was too chaotic and did not allow for much elegance or creativity. There was not only a tight link between discipline and esprit de corps, but also an aesthetic aspect to such discipline, visible when observed in simulated tactics, ordered manoeuvres and choreographed parades, outside the disorder of an actual battlefield. Esprit de corps was a stern and elegant way of doing things as a group. Interestingly, especially for our next chapter, Maurois also wrote: 'Business is a mixture of war and sport.'[82]

In combat, esprit de corps was interpreted in 1907 by the social philosopher Guillaume Duprat as a combination of cowardice and courage:

The consequence of esprit de corps is that individual cowardice, energetically stigmatised, either disappears or is transformed into a feeling that supposes that one takes shelter behind the group, that one marches with the others towards dangers that not only would one not dare to confront individually, but that are also confronted with the secret hope of being exposed to them as little as possible. The idea of collective danger is much less terrifying than that of individual danger [. . .] Men excite each other. Pushed by those behind them, those in the front rank would be ashamed to falter, and even if they are simply opting for what has been called 'the flight forward' [fuite en avant] rather than a dangerous retreat [. . .] it does not matter whether they obey more elevated motives or follow fierce survival instincts, provided that they display a brave posture.[83]

Esprit de corps compensated for strength in the form of alleviation of fear. It was a conditioned imitation, and it worked even when the individual parts were weak, because of group entrainment.

This mimetic aspect meant that esprit de corps could be, at least to some extent, socially engineered. The future president Charles de Gaulle, a commander during the war, taught at the national École militaire that the highest esprit de corps could and should be fostered via certain training protocols:

Instead of continual changes in the ranks and the men, and the kaleidoscope of commanders and comrades, we will build real regiments. Constant in their composition, in their rites and symbols [. . .] they will lead this interior life and take this marked form whence collective feeling is derived. The esprit de corps once established, must exert itself. This will be assured by emulation.[84]

This connection to character and its etymology as 'mark' revived the golden thread of the French original understanding of esprit de corps as esprit *du* corps, the specific style of each group, as we have seen in Montesquieu, d'Alembert, Tocqueville or early military descriptions of the *mousquetaires*. But this was also part of a conscious strategy of the state inherited from the Bonapartists. What was here described by de Gaulle, in terms that sounded more anthropological than martial (*rites et symboles, sympathie collective*), was a process of collective individ-uation, both internal (*vie intérieure*) and external (*figure*), engineered through protocols, rehearsals and habits. *Émulation* in French is suggestive of an admirable elevation, in which competition and respect are equally important.

The Politics of Grandeur, Philip G. Cerny's essay on the political philosophy of Gaullism, explains de Gaulle's philosophical view of esprit de corps:

> The nation-state, as a political system, results from the need for political effectiveness. For the state to be effective, it requires a social base, an ability to reflect psychological identity as well as goals [. . .] The result is not oppression or conflict, but the gradual realisation of a common consciousness, a common relationship to the nature of things. This is the sense of the whole, the holistic pattern – the *ensemble* – which reflects the essence of unity-in-diversity [. . .] 'Human passions, insofar as they remain diffused, realise nothing ordered, nor in consequence effective. It is necessary that they be crystallised in well-defined circumscriptions. That is why patriotism has always been something local, each religion builds temples and the cult of arms postulates an *esprit de corps*.'[85]

Esprit de corps is a channelling of identity feelings that could extend to the scale of the nation in a well-ordered state, but apparently no further – and even in the nation it needed sub-levels of cohesion, intermediary republican congre-gations. This sounded indeed like a reactivation of Bonapartism. De Gaulle, like Napoleon before him, proposed to blend military techniques, politics and the new spirit of management: 'We are at the age of effectiveness, efficiency. We are at the time of ensembles.'[86] The practico-absolutist nation-state was to prevent anti-national esprit de corps by organising a game of 'feudalities' between intermediate bodies and corporations.[87]

De Gaulle's grand meta-military politics ruled France until the spirit of May 1968 disrupted its order. Soon after, a quite anti-Gaullist influential reinterpreta-tion of 'war machines' was proposed. Despite the relatively bad reputation of the notion of esprit de corps within the French intelligentsia in the second half of the twentieth century, the philosophers Gilles Deleuze and Félix Guattari proposed a counter-intuitive laudatory reading of the 'revolutionary' aspect of esprit de corps.[88] Curiously, despite this being done in one of the most globally cited chap-ters of contemporary French philosophy, most commentators have missed the authors' insistence on esprit de corps: the phrase *esprit de corps* appears ten times in this chapter, revealing that Deleuze and Guattari were aware of subverting the long French tradition of intellectual critique of esprit de corps.

The strategy in this text is to criticise nationalist hegemonies and state ideologies of *grands ensembles* by favouring a return to the esprit de corps of small-scale
autonomous communities:

> Should we evoke a military origin of the corps and of esprit de corps? It is not
> 'military' that counts, but rather a distant nomadic origin. Ibn Khaldun defined
> the nomad war machine as: families or lineages, *plus* esprit de corps.[89]

To claim that the military origin of esprit de corps does not count is not only controversial, it might even seem contradictory in a celebration of 'war machines'.
But as we will see, the authors distinguish the military from the martial. Quoting
Ibn Khaldun only added to the provocation; we have seen that Khaldun's version
of esprit de corps implied, at least in the first French translations, racial notions of
pure blood:[90] Deleuze and Guattari also proposed here a disruptive redefinition of
race, of which more below. Since Deleuze was a visceral opponent of the British
school of analytic philosophy, it is possible that the italicised insistence on '*plus*
esprit de corps' was an implicit response to Ryle's notorious *The Concept of Mind*,
a book that insisted that esprit de corps was not something real: 'Exhibiting team-
spirit is not [. . .] a third thing such that we can say that the bowler first bowls *and*
then exhibits team-spirit or that a fielder is at a given moment *either* catching *or*
displaying *esprit de corps*.'[91]

The authors proposed a return to a communal and political autonomist spirit
against an over-controlling nation-state system. Any national body has its fringes
and minorities, which can function as guerrilla machines if they are able to
nurture their own esprit de corps.[92] Deleuze and Guattari insist on the spiritual
quality of esprit de corps, which cannot be state-controlled: 'It was always part
of the main business of the state [. . .] to defeat *band wander*, and *group nomadism*
[*nomadisme de corps*].'[93] Ibn Khaldun's medieval notion of *asabiyah* is conveyed
to defend the notion of a sacred revolutionary group dissolving the codes of
autocracy.

It is probable, however, that Deleuze and Guattari did not understand *asabiyah* properly and underestimated Ibn Khaldun's insistence on male individual
leadership:

> To impose himself upon others, an authoritative person can rely on what Ibn
> Khaldun calls *asabiyya* [. . .] We prefer translations such as 'esprit de corps'
> (de Slane), 'group feeling' (Rosenthal) or 'group spirit' [. . .] In Ibn Khaldun's
> work, power is always embodied by a man. For him, power cannot be divided:
> 'Politics requires the power of one. If power were to be shared among many,
> it would be a disaster.' A good leader, according to Ibn Khaldun, seems to be
> the one who guarantees the cohesion of the group, the one who plays the role
> of 'moderator' capable of intervening, if necessary, to separate men who are
> prone to natural aggressive tendencies, keeping for himself as much as possible
> a sovereign neutrality.[94]

Esprit de corps according to Ibn Khaldun was a form of group cohesion that needed to be orchestrated and controlled by a charismatic, if enlightened, leader. The latter might favour the common interest of the tribe above his personal interest and help maintain the unity of the group before potential enemies, but the cohesion of the tribe could not exist without his hegemonic authority.

A nineteenth-century English dictionary defined *corps* as 'a body of forces':[95] *body of forces*, in which forces can be concrete combat units or invisible energies, was the understanding that Deleuze and Guattari wanted to give to their renewed invocation of esprit de corps as a social machine of liberation: 'It is as if vague essences give things a determination which is more than the thingness, which is that of *corporeality*, and which perhaps implies an esprit de corps.'[96] Things are never isolated, they are part of embodied ensembles, even if the nature of these ensembles is more asymptotic than complete. I have argued elsewhere that this assembling is not, for Deleuze and Guattari, incompatible with the form of a quasi-leader or unifying principle, if the latter is an 'anomal', a strange attractor, a 'so(u)rcerer'.[97]

Mille plateaux opposes an autonomist and creative esprit de corps (nomadic) to a universalist and conformative esprit de corps (state-controlled). In what can indeed be read as an implicit response to Bonapartism and Gaullism, the authors present the state as a gigantic oppressor of the forces of creation and deeper knowledge:

> The State does not confer power on intellectuals or creators, quite the contrary, it transforms them into a closely dependent organ, which is autonomous only in dreams, a condition which nevertheless is good enough to withdraw all power from them, so they merely reproduce or execute.[98]

In fact, for Deleuze and Guattari, esprit de corps is more or less equivalent to their famous concept of BwO, or the 'body without organs':[99] this means, as we will see below, that they wish to strip the notion of esprit de corps of its connotation of automatism in favour of an equivalence between spirit and alchemical freedom.

A few zones of spiritual nomadism tend to emerge at the margins of regulated social automata when 'division of labour' – organic solidarity – is too constraining.[100] In order to prevent such scissions, the nation-state invented the fiction of *national esprit de corps*, which, as we have seen with Trump, Le Pen and Brexit, is a reappearing ghost today, inherited from the contradictions of the Enlightenment:

> The modern state defines itself as 'the rational and reasonable organisation of a community': community's particularity here becomes merely internal or moral (*people's spirit* [*esprit d'un peuple*]), at the same time as its organisation contributes to the harmony of a universal (*absolute spirit*) [. . .] Obey always, for the more you obey, the more you will be master, since you will be obeying pure reason, that is to say, yourself.[101]

We might want today to substitute *reason* with *jouissance*, as argued by the psychoanalyst Jacques Lacan.[102] For Deleuze and Guattari, the references to an official absolute spirit and an embodied pure reason confirmed that this chapter of *Mille plateaux* was not only a historically informed comment on French history, but also a philosophical response to Kantianism and Hegelianism, and in particular to the notion of the universal man, worth remembering:

> The ethical frame of mind [. . .] is rectitude and *esprit de corps*, i.e. the disposition to make oneself a member of one of the moments of civil society by one's own act, through one's energy, industry, and skill, to maintain oneself in this position, and to fend for oneself only through this process of mediating oneself with the universal, while in this way gaining recognition both in one's own eyes and in the eyes of others.[103]

Deleuze and Guattari, via their anti-Kant and anti-Hegel rhetoric, offered a post-1968 critique of Gaullism and French universalist centralisation, and a notorious defence of *singularities* and *multiplicities*, their version of particularism, influential in gender and minority studies. State universalism and its standardisation of psyches was the most visible enemy of rebellious assemblages of liberation: nomadic thought 'does not claim to be a universal thinking subject'.[104]

Against conformative and universalist esprit de corps, the authors advocated an outsiders' thought, a *pensée du dehors*.[105] What they called a *thought* was a collective embodiment: 'Any thought is already a tribe', 'a singular race.'[106] Race here had to be understood, the authors insisted, as a minority fabulation, nothing genetic, although they also mentioned that there was a risk that an imagined tribe or party slowly became a racist hegemonic state, a regime of 'dominant and encompassing fascism'.[107]

An important differentiation which meant to distinguish sedentary organisations from nomadic war machines was between discipline as code and drill, and discipline as know-how and careful practice of an art, craft, way, knowledge or skill – a discipline:

> For example, martial arts do not claim to be a *code*, as in a state affair, but a matter of *ways*, which are so many paths of affect; on these ways, one learns to 'unuse' weapons no less than to use them, as if the power and culture of affect was the true goal.[108]

On the one hand, quite Foucauldian, discipline could be a forced obedience to general codes and normalised protocols in pursuit of precise external goals (conformative and universalist esprit de corps); but on the other hand, discipline was an immersive feeling of attachment to a craft in itself, the goal then being a spiral of care (creative and autonomist esprit de corps). For Deleuze and Guattari, it was very important to insist on the difference between a creative *way*, 'the "not-doing" of the warrior',[109] and a series of externally imposed rules: a martial arts fighter was more than a soldier, a craftsman more than a worker, an artist not a simple producer, and a liberated person could not be the mere subject of the state, but should be animated by a spirit of philosophical health.

Autonomist and creative esprit de corps were moments of an 'affective semi-otic',[110] a passionate process of active arrangements or assemblages [*agencements*], as opposed to a technique of administrative ordering: 'Assemblages are passionate, they are compositions of desire.'[111] A good esprit de corps is a common feeling of belonging to a collective and open practice of autonomisation, one that pertains to a quasi-ensemble, neither a complete totality, neither a sum of particulars, but rather what we could call an *ensemblance*, a 'miraculate, enchanted surface'[112] of cohesion. Rather than imposing a shape or spirit on a body, esprit de corps is about slowly following, as a skilful craftsman, what the creative flow of matter has to reveal, in conjunction with a cosmic art of listening and in resonance with the nomadic *savoir-faire* of ancestral guilds:

> It's about following the wood, and in following the wood, connecting opera-tions and materiality, instead of imposing a form upon a material [. . .] We will therefore define the craftsman as one who is determined to follow a flow of matter, a *machinic phylum*. It is the *itinerant*, the *ambulating one*. To follow the flow of matter is to roam, it is to amble. It is intuition in action.[113]

This psycho-material flux is a creative and caring flow that a community follows in producing, revealing and actualising their sacred territory. It is a sort of imma-nent holy grail, a *Creal*, a creation of reality and a reality of creation.[114]

Most living entities, including humans, are partly composed of mineral salts and metal elements (sodium, potassium, calcium, magnesium, manganese, iron, cobalt, copper, zinc, etc.), as they are of electric fluxes. For Deleuze and Guattari, esprit de corps is an alchemical craft of transformation of mineral matter into a collective embodiment:

> The relationship of metallurgy with alchemy does not rest, as Jung believed, on the symbolic value of metal and its correspondence with an organic soul, but on the immanent power of corporeality in all matter, and on the esprit de corps that accompanies it [. . .] The metallurgist is the first specialised craftsman, and forms in this respect a *body* [*corps*] (secret societies, guilds, companionships). The artisan-metallurgist is itinerant because he follows the material flow of the subsoil.[115]

In this somewhat nostalgic view of traditional crafts and of a golden age of work, transformations from the invisible to the visible in communities of practice are a communal process of assemblages of matter and creative dialogue with our constitutive elements. Matter in us wants to engender bodies and ensembles, because the Multiple is infinitesimally attracted by the One and vice versa. Our common tools, machines and protocols are social secretions of desires, ideals and avoidances.

Esprit de corps was, according to Deleuze and Guattari, a passionate discipline that could sometimes appear bellicose before illegitimate obstacles – yet war was not its goal:

An artistic, scientific, 'ideological' movement can be a virtual war machine, precisely insofar as it traces a plan of consistency, a creative line of flight [. . .] It is not the nomad who defines this set of characters, it is this set that defines the nomad. [He] *can make war only if he creates something else at the same time*, even if only new non-organic social relations [. . .] in the face of the great conjunction of devices of capture or domination.[116]

This poetic notion of esprit de corps proposed a chivalrous fidelity to the spirit of creation, in which collateral damage could arm, *en passant*, structures of domination. In this view, the esprit de corps of a minority is a cosmopolitical force.

Ultimately, Deleuze and Guattari's philosophical interpretation proposed to reconnect esprit de corps to the alchemical medieval uses of the term 'esprit de', and once again to the fact that discipline is not only about coercion in a Foucauldian sense, but also about craft and what could be called *hieropoiesis*, a practice of co-creation producing a common space of focus and sacredness.

Vitalist philosophers such as Bergson or Deleuze are not the only ones who have attempted a renewal of the mystique of esprit de corps in the twentieth century – so did, for instance, the US army, as we will see in the next chapter.

The Future of a Gallicism: Canada as a Semantic Border Between French and English

A major difference between the French written meanings of esprit de corps and the English and American uses was that the latter were steadily depoliticised, while in French esprit de corps remains a polemical political term. This duality is particularly striking on a hybrid soil such as Canada, where French and English languages cohabit. We could still read recently in the *Dictionnaire canadien des relations du travail* the following definition:

> Esprit de corps. A distortion that consists of one person or group considering only the narrow interests of one professional category to the detriment of those of others or of society as a whole. One says: 'corporatist spirit', 'corporatist interests'.[117]

This critical definition suggests that the healthy attitude is conversely to consider the common good, which is still faithful to the spirit of the *Encyclopédie*, revived by Bourdieu in his analysis of professional groupthink.

On the other hand, an Ottawa-based governmental agency wrote in 1998 that for the sake of productivity, and in order to 'improve personal performance', a corporation could seek for 'ways to reinforce esprit de corps and engagement among employees'.[118] As trade unionism became less powerful by the end of the twentieth century, the influence of American managerial discourse about esprit de corps had some feedback effect: it is today more frequent to see 'esprit de corps' used eulogistically in French-language publications, especially those related to business and management.

In Québec, a management consultancy agency called 'Groupe Esprit de Corps' provides sport challenges to foster 'wellness in the workplace' and 'teambuilding'.[119] Its founder and director, Gilles Barbot, told me in a interview, when I mentioned the historical ambiguity and multiple views on esprit de corps, that for him there was 'only one definition of esprit de corps', one that was 'very positive', a synonym of 'team spirit'.[120] As we will see in the next chapter, the idea of esprit de corps as mere team spirit is an American capitalist tale.

Notes

1. 'L'esprit de corps, contenu dans de sages limites, est légitime; il peut, comme l'uniforme, avoir d'excellents effets, être une barrière contre telles défaillances morales, développer chez l'officier le sentiment de la solidarité, le hausser vers une perfection toujours plus grande, lui donner le sentiment plus net de son devoir. L'esprit de caste a des effets contraires: esprit d'égoïsme et d'isolement, il se manifeste par le dédain du reste de l'humanité, vis-à-vis de laquelle l'homme qui en est atteint se croit tout permis [. . .] L'esprit de corps ne confère que des devoirs; par l'esprit de caste, on se confère des privilèges.' Gustave Canton, *Napoléon antimilitariste* (Paris: Alcan, 1902), p. 270.
2. Jacques Derrida, 'La pharmacie de Platon', in *La Dissémination* (Paris: Seuil, 1972), pp. 77–214.
3. *Sénat: Compte-rendu in extenso* (Paris: Assemblée Nationale, 1902), p. 216.
4. Alexandre Lacassagne (ed.), *Archives d'anthropologie criminelle, de médecine légale et de psychologie normale et pathologique* (Lyons, 1900), p. 23.
5. 'L'esprit de corps, qui tantôt renforce, et tantôt contrarie le sentiment de nos devoirs généraux.' Eugène Terraillon, *L'honneur, sentiment et principe moral* (Paris: Alcan, 1912), p. 129.
6. 'C'est une espèce de greffe bonne ou mauvaise, entée sur un grand tronc.' D'Alembert, 'Caractère des sociétés ou corps particuliers', p. 666.
7. 'De l'esprit de corps à l'esprit de caste, on peut glisser vite, comme du patriotisme noble, fait d'un sentiment d'amour pour les compatriotes, on peut tomber au patriotisme bas, fait d'un sentiment haineux contre l'étranger.' Canton, *Napoléon antimilitariste*, p. 270.
8. Claude-Joseph Tissot, *Cours élémentaire de philosophie, rédigé d'après le programme de l'examen pour le baccalauréat ès-lettres* (Dijon: Popelain, 1837), p. 55.
9. Émile Zola, *Pot-Bouille* (Paris: Charpentier, 1883), p. 136.
10. 'la rancune de la domesticité'; ibid., p. 136.
11. Émile Zola, 'J'accuse, Lettre au Président de la République', *L'Aurore*, 13 January 1898, p. 1.
12. 'la controverse entre partisans et adversaires de l'esprit de corps'; V. Giard and E. Brière (eds), *Revue Internationale de Sociologie* (Paris: Institut International de Sociologie, 1908), p. 531.
13. Georges Palante, *Combat pour l'individu* (Paris, Alcan, 1904).
14. 'l'esprit de corps des gens mariés [. . .] l'esprit de corps des femmes', 'l'esprit de corps agissant dans les petites villes', 'l'esprit de corps fonctionnariste'; ibid., pp. 54, 4, 90.
15. 'L'esprit de corps s'arroge un véritable empire moral sur les consciences individuelles.' Ibid., p. 4.
16. 'L'esprit de corps des femmes a intérêt à ce qu'il n'y ait pas trop de filles restées pour compte sur le marché du mariage car cela déprécierait le sexe.' Ibid., p. 53.

17. 'C'est une sorte d'État dans l'État. Cette puissance est ressentie comme une menace, une gêne ou une tyrannie par tous ceux qui n'ont pas avec elle quelque rapport d'amitié et qui ne peuvent compter sur sa protection. La communauté de vie des Pythagoriciens, leurs réunions secrètes, leurs pratiques quelquefois choquantes, souvent bizarres, offrent les apparences d'une conspiration continuelle, éveillent la défiance, provoquent les craintes, excitent l'envie. Enfin leur dédain et leur orgueil achèvent de leur attirer la haine de leurs concitoyens. L'esprit de corps, qui anime tous les actes de leur vie, fait regarder la Société [pythagoricienne] comme un centre de toute perfection: aussi se croient-ils appelés à réaliser une haute mission. Inspirer et diriger le gouvernement est, pour eux, plus qu'un droit.' Armand Delatte, *Essai sur la politique pythagoricienne* (Liège et Paris: Bibliothèque de l'Université de Liège, 1922), p. 249.

18. 'Le seul esprit de corps vraiment dangereux, c'est celui des hommes qui détiennent une partie du pouvoir.' Henri Mazel, *Pour causer de tout: Petit dictionnaire des idées et des opinions* (Paris: Grasset, 1909), p. 195.

19. Henri Mazel, *La Synergie sociale* (Paris: Colin, 1896).

20. 'L'honneur du voleur tiendra dans le respect de ses engagements, dans le maintien des liens de solidarité qui l'unissent à ses camarades. Le pire bandit obéira à l'honneur s'il remplit cette sorte de programme dont la lettre est, en quelque façon, imprimée dans son esprit, et dont les emblèmes sont parfois même ineffaçablement gravés sur sa peau par un tatouage profond. D'ordinaire l'homme qui suit la loi de l'honneur se donne la vision très nette de ce que penserait et dirait de lui tel groupe social dont il recherche l'estime.' Terraillon, *L'honneur*, p. 11.

21. Ibid., p. 14.

22. Ibid., pp. 15, 210, 44.

23. James Braid, 'M. Braid on Hypnotism', *The Lancet* 45.1135 (1845), pp. 627–8.

24. Terraillon, *L'honneur*, p. 239.

25. 'L'esprit de corps se montre dans ces grands organes de la nation avec une puissance remarquable parce que, sans lui, ils n'existeraient pas.' Ibid., p. 209.

26. 'L'esprit de corps passe régulièrement par trois phases successives: il se constitue, d'abord, dans la mesure où le groupement dont il exprime les aspirations prend le sentiment plus net de son existence et de son importance; il est alors vigoureux, exclusif et jaloux. Bientôt, sa croissance rencontre des obstacles et des limites; des contradictions intérieures ou des conflits, soit avec des organismes rivaux, antérieurs ou plus récents, soit avec la plus grande société au sein de laquelle il se développe [. . .] Enfin il se reconstitue sur des bases élargies, mieux adapté à l'état social de la collectivité ou de la civilisation et il recommence ainsi le cycle de son évolution.' Ibid., p. 272.

27. 'l'esprit de corps du genre humain'; Odon Vallet, *L'Évangile des païens* (Paris: Albin Michel, 2003), p. 276.

28. 'la solidarité actuelle de tous les ouvriers d'un pays, et peut-être même, celle de tous les travailleurs de l'univers civilisé'; Terraillon, *L'honneur*, p. 272.

29. 'Gardez-vous de l'esprit de corps; ne considérez pas l'intérêt de votre groupe.' Henri Pinard de la Boullaye, *Exercices spirituels selon la méthode de Saint-Ignace*, 3 vols (Paris: Beauchesne, 1951), vol. II, p. 281.

30. Guillaume Léonce Duprat, *La Solidarité sociale, ses causes, son évolution, ses conséquences* (Paris: Doin, 1907), p. 87.

31. 'L'avenir nous réserve-t-il une solidarité sociale plus large encore, celle que pourraient, par exemple, réaliser des Etats-Unis d'Europe?' Ibid., p. 87.

32. Andrew Rettman, 'France and Germany Propose EU "Defence Union"', *Euobserver*, 12 September 2016, <https://euobserver.com/foreign/135022> (accessed 19 September 2019).

33. Henri Bergson, *Les deux sources de la morale et de la religion* (Paris: Presses Universitaires de France, 1990 [1932]), p. 65.

34. 'Si l'on admet [. . .] une "mentalité primitive", on y verra le respect de soi coïncider avec le sentiment d'une telle solidarité entre l'individu et le groupe que le groupe reste présent à l'individu isolé, le surveille, l'encourage ou le menace, exige enfin d'être consulté et obéi [. . .] La pression du moi social s'exerce avec toutes ces énergies accumulées. L'individu n'obéit d'ailleurs pas seulement par habitude de la discipline ou par crainte du châtiment: le groupe auquel il appartient se met nécessairement au-dessus des autres [. . .] et la conscience de cette supériorité de force lui assure [. . .] toutes les jouissances de l'orgueil [. . .] Il suffit d'observer ce qui se passe sous nos yeux dans les petites sociétés qui se constituent au sein de la grande, quand des hommes se trouvent rapprochés les uns des autres par quelque marque distinctive qui souligne une supériorité réelle ou apparente, et qui les met à part [. . .] Tous les membres du groupe 'se tiennent'; on voit naître un 'sentiment de l'honneur' qui ne fait qu'un avec l'esprit de corps.' Ibid., pp. 66–7.

35. Ibid., p. 111.

36. 'C'est de l'*instinct virtuel*, entendant par là qu'à l'extrémité d'une autre ligne d'évolution, dans les sociétés d'insectes, nous voyons l'instinct provoquer mécaniquement une conduite comparable, pour son utilité, à celle que suggèrent à l'homme, intelligent et libre, des images quasi hallucinatoires.' Ibid., p. 114.

37. 'Fabuler', *Centre National de Ressources Textuelles et Lexicales*, <https://www.cnrtl.fr/definition/fabuler> (accessed 19 September 2019).

38. Bergson, *Les deux sources*, p. 23.

39. 'Entre la société où nous vivons et l'humanité en général il y a [. . .] le même contraste qu'entre le clos et l'ouvert [. . .] Qui ne voit que la cohésion sociale est due, en grande partie, à la nécessité pour une société de se défendre contre d'autres, et que c'est d'abord contre tous les autres hommes qu'on aime les hommes avec lesquels on vit ?' Ibid., p. 27.

40. Ibid., p. 27.

41. Henri Bergson, *L'évolution créatrice* (Paris: Alcan, 1907).

42. Bergson, *Les deux sources*, p. 56.

43. 'société mystique qui engloberait l'humanité entière'; ibid., p. 85.

44. 'Des âmes privilégiées ont surgi qui se sentaient apparentées à toutes les âmes et qui, au lieu de rester dans les limites du groupe et de s'en tenir à la solidarité établie par la nature, se portaient vers l'humanité en général dans un élan d'amour. L'apparition de chacune d'elles était comme la création d'une espèce nouvelle composée d'un individu unique, la poussée vitale aboutissant de loin en loin, dans un homme déterminé, à un résultat qui n'eût pu être obtenu tout d'un coup pour l'ensemble de l'humanité.' Ibid., p. 97.

45. 'Toute morale, pression ou aspiration, est d'essence biologique.' Ibid., p. 103.

46. Bergson, *L'évolution créatrice*, pp. 46–149.

47. 'L'intelligence serait un obstacle à la sérénité.' Bergson, *Les deux sources*, p. 219.

48. Ibid., p. 147.

49. 'Des exercices continuellement répétés sont nécessaires, comme ceux dont l'automatisme finit par fixer dans le corps du soldat l'assurance morale dont il aura besoin au jour du danger.' Ibid., p. 212.

50. Bergson, *L'évolution créatrice*, p. i.

51. Ian Smith and Trevor Boyns, 'British Management Theory and Practice: The Impact of Fayol', *Management Decision* 43 (2005), pp. 1317–34.

52. Carl A. Rodrigues, 'Fayol's 14 Principles of Management Then and Now: A Framework for Managing Today's Organizations Effectively', *Management Decision* 39 (2005), pp. 880–9.

53. Henri Fayol, *Administration industrielle et générale* (Paris: Dunot and Pinat, 1917), p. 26.

54. '14° L'union du personnel *L'union fait la force* [. . .] *L'harmonie*, l'union dans le personnel d'une entreprise est une grande force dans cette entreprise [. . .] Le principe à observer c'est l'*unité de commandement* [. . .] Il n'est besoin d'aucun mérite pour semer la division parmi ses subordonnés; c'est à la portée du premier venu. Il faut au contraire un réel talent pour coordonner les efforts, stimuler le zèle, utiliser les facultés de tous et récompenser le mérite de chacun sans éveiller les susceptibilités jalouses et sans troubler l'harmonie des relations.' Ibid., p. 54.

55. 'Ce n'est pas seulement par les effets de l'harmonie qui règne entre les agents d'une même entreprise que se manifeste la puissance de l'*union*: les ententes commerciales, les syndicats, les associations de toutes sortes jouent un rôle considérable dans le gouvernement des affaires [. . .] J'ai vu, en 1860, les ouvriers de la grande industrie, sans cohésion, sans lien, véritable poussière d'individus; le syndicat en fait des collectivités qui traitent d'égal à égal avec le patron [. . .] Les chefs d'entreprise doivent tenir compte de cette évolution.' Ibid., p. 55.

56. Rodrigues, 'Fayol's 14 principles', p. 881.

57. To explore the differences between French *syndicalisme* and, for example, American trade unionism, see James B. Carey, *Trade Unions and Democracy: A Comparative Study of US, French, Italian, and West German Unions* (Washington, DC: National Planning Association, 1957).

58. Rodrigues, 'Fayol's 14 principles', p. 882.

59. '6° Subordination de l'intérêt particulier à l'intérêt général. Ce principe rappelle que, dans une entreprise, l'intérêt d'un agent, ou d'un groupe d'agents, ne doit pas prévaloir contre l'intérêt de l'entreprise; [. . .] que l'intérêt de l'État doit primer celui d'un citoyen ou d'un groupe de citoyens [. . .] L'ignorance, l'ambition, l'égoïsme, la paresse, les faiblesses et toutes les passions humaines tendent à faire perdre de vue l'intérêt général au profit de l'intérêt particulier. C'est une lutte continuelle à soutenir.' Fayol, *Administration industrielle*, p. 34.

60. Ibid., p. 34.

61. R. Pons, 'Le Code du Travail', *Civilisations* 3.3 (1953), p. 378.

62. 'L'esprit de corps règne parmi les membres des sociétés compagnonniques. Ils méprisent [. . .] les hommes qui suivent les rites d'un autre "Devoir". Entre compagnons, c'étaient autrefois de meurtrières querelles. Ils s'étaient appelés les uns: *loups*, les autres *chiens*, et il semblait que, par des batailles continuelles, ils voulussent justifier leurs noms de guerre. Pour venger l'honneur corporatif, ils s'entretuaient.' Jean Connay, *Le Compagnonnage* (Paris: Rivière, 1909), pp. 6–9.

63. Jules Domergue, *La comédie libre-échangiste* (Paris: Calmann Lévy, 1891).

64. 'développer l'esprit de corps parmi le personnel des usines'; Jules Domergue, 'L'esprit de corps dans les usines', in *La Réforme Economique* (Paris, 1908), p. 845.

65. 'Les patrons acceptent volontiers les ouvrières parce qu'elles sont des instruments plus souples, plus dociles que les hommes. Les ouvrières n'ont pas, comme les

ouvriers, d'esprit de corps.' Claude Weyl, *La réglementation du travail des femmes dans l'industrie* (Paris: Larose, 1898), p. 13.

66. Laura L. Frader, 'Femmes, genre et mouvement ouvrier en France aux XIXe et XXe siècles: bilan et perspectives de recherche', *Clio. Histoire, femmes et société en ligne* 3.1 (1996), <https://www.cairn.info/revue-clio-1996-1-page-14.htm> (accessed 19 September 2019).

67. Agathon, *L'Esprit de la nouvelle Sorbonne* (Paris: Mercure de France, 1911), pp. 360–1.

68. 'L'esprit de corps est sans contredit l'un des plus remarquables effets d'une solidarité étroite, exclusive: les jeunes gens qui se préparent au concours d'administration à l'une des grandes écoles de l'État sont déjà solidaires les uns des autres et à l'exclusion de leurs camarades du même établissement, parce qu'ils les méprisent. Ils n'admettent pas "qu'un des leurs" ne soit pas digne d'égards exceptionnels, parce qu'ils s'en jugent tous dignes comme devant entrer dans une collectivité au plus haut point honorable, tellement supérieure aux autres.' Duprat, *La Solidarité sociale*, p. 94.

69. 'Comme le voulait l'esprit de corps si répandu, et qui est l'esprit de ceux qui n'en ont pas, les élèves de lettres et les élèves de sciences se méprisaient réciproquement.' Anatole France, *La vie en fleur* (Paris: Calmann-Lévy, 1922), p. 87.

70. 'Pendant plusieurs années le candidat instituteur est soumis à un dressage qui le rend éminemment apte aux tâches obscures qui l'attendent. Un esprit de corps, si l'on peut dire, lui est imposé bon gré mal gré par la nature même de ses études [. . .] Nous pensons, quant à nous, qu'un certain esprit de corps exprime la dignité du métier.' Jean Lameere and Sylvain de Coster, *Esprit d'une politique générale de l'éducation* (Brussels: Lebègue, 1946), pp. 121–2.

71. 'Le fonctionnaire, quel que soit son rang ou son poste – même de "direction" – n'est toujours qu'un rouage dans un ensemble complexe [. . .] À partir du moment où il a quitté les Écoles et franchi le dernier cap impersonnel et objectif des examens et concours d'entrée dans l'Administration, qui constitueront presque toujours pour lui l'ultime mesure strictement impartiale de ses aptitudes intellectuelles, cet être éminemment social que devient dès lors le fonctionnaire relèvera plus que quiconque de ses congénères [. . .] Tous les liens particuliers qui peuvent unir des individus destinés à une carrière commune sont générateurs de cette sorte de solidarité. Ce qui est vrai de toutes les minorités ethniques ou autres l'est aussi en matière professionnelle, et cela s'appelle communément l'esprit de corps [. . .] Le ciment de telles coalitions est constitué par une formation d'Ecole identique qui confère à tous ses anciens élèves [. . .] une discipline de mutualité où la simple camaraderie s'appuie sur un complexe commun, justifié ou non, de vocation supérieure.' R. Catherine, 'L'esprit de bande', *La Revue administrative* 13 (1950), pp. 3–5 (p. 4).

72. 'défaillance intellectuelle'; ibid., p. 5.

73. 'Cet esprit de corps existe toujours et il est inutile de se voiler les yeux devant le fait que, de nos jours, bien des ingénieurs, fonctionnaires ou officiers formés dans les grandes écoles, dissimulent mal une certaine condescendance à l'égard des membres de leur profession qui n'en sont pas issus.' Jacques Aman, *Les officiers bleus dans la marine française au XVIIIe siècle* (Geneva: Droz, 1976), p. 21.

74. Bourdieu, *La Noblesse d'État*, p. 10.

75. 'Cette véritable action magique d'influence, ou, le mot n'est pas trop fort, de *possession*, ne réussit que pour autant que celui qui la subit contribue à son efficacité; qu'elle ne le contraint que dans la mesure où il est prédisposé par un apprentissage préalable à la *reconnaître*. Il n'en va vraiment ainsi que lorsque les catégories de perception et d'action qu'il met en œuvre dans les actes individuels à travers lesquels

s'accomplit la "volonté" et le pouvoir de l'institution [. . .] sont en accord immédiat avec les structures objectives de l'organisation parce qu'elles sont le produit de l'incorporation de ces structures. On rencontrera tout au long de ce livre de ces possédés qui font les quatre volontés de l'institution, parce qu'ils sont l'institution faite homme, et qui, dominés ou dominants, ne peuvent en subir ou en exercer pleinement la nécessité que parce qu'ils l'ont incorporée, qu'ils font corps avec elle, qu'ils lui donnent corps.' Ibid., p. 10.

76. 'Sous forme de schèmes de perception et d'action, de principes de vision et de division, de structures mentales.' Ibid., p. 14.

77. 'Cet enchantement affectif, qui naît de pouvoir s'aimer et s'admirer soi-même dans ses pareils, est un des fondements, avec le *conformisme logique* associé à l'homogénéité des structures mentales, de ce qu'on appelle *esprit de corps*: ce sentiment de solidarité avec le groupe repose en effet sur la communauté des schèmes de perception, d'appréciation, de pensée et d'action qui fonde la connivence réflexe des inconscients bien orchestrés.' Ibid., pp. 111–12.

78. Omar Lizardo, 'The Cognitive Origins of Bourdieu's *Habitus*', *Journal for the Theory of Social Behaviour* 34.4 (2004), pp. 376–401 (p. 390).

79. 'La solidarité qui résulte de cet esprit de corps maintient les traditions de vaillance, de probité, d'énergie morale.' Charles Ferrand, 'Comment Réformer la Marine?', *La Grande Revue* 68 (1911), p. 113.

80. 'C'était dur, mais quel esprit de corps, quelle discipline ces mœurs rudes nous donnaient!' André Maurois, *Les silences du Colonel Bramble* (Paris: Grasset, 1918), p. 137.

81. 'L'officier d'aujourd'hui a vu du service actif, c'est vrai, mais en somme il suffit, à la guerre, d'être bien portant et de n'avoir pas plus d'imagination qu'un poisson. C'est en temps de paix qu'il faut juger un soldat [. . .] Ah que je voudrais que cette guerre fût finie pour refaire de véritables manœuvres.' Ibid., p. 137.

82. 'Les affaires sont un mélange de guerre et de sport.' Alain Montoux, *Dictionnaire des organisations* (Paris: Publibook, 2012), p. 25.

83. 'L'esprit de corps fait que la lâcheté individuelle, énergiquement stigmatisée, ou disparaît ou se transforme en un sentiment qui veut que l'on s'abrite derrière la collectivité, qu'on "marche avec les autres" à des dangers que non seulement on n'affronterait pas individuellement, mais encore qu'on n'affronte qu'avec le secret espoir d'y être exposé le moins possible. La représentation du péril collectif est beaucoup moins terrifiante que celle du péril individuel [. . .] Les hommes s'excitent les uns les autres; poussés par ceux qui sont derrière eux, ceux qui se trouvent au premier rang auraient honte de faiblir, et même s'ils préfèrent ce qu'on a appelé "la fuite en avant" à la retraite dangereuse [. . .] ils en viennent à obéir à des mobiles plus relevés et parfois à des survivances d'instinct féroce, qui leur donnent au moins l'allure courageuse.' Duprat, *La Solidarité sociale*, pp. 93–4.

84. 'Au lieu des rangs sans cesse rompus, de la noria des effectifs, du kaléidoscope des chefs et des camarades, on fera de vrais régiments. Constants dans leur composition, dans leurs rites et symboles [. . .] ils mèneront cette vie intérieure et prendront cette figure marquée d'où procède la sympathie collective. L'esprit de corps une fois créé, il faut qu'il s'exerce. L'émulation y pourvoira.' Charles de Gaulle, *Vers l'armée de métier* (Paris: Berger-Levrault, 1934), p. 136.

85. Philip G. Cerny, *The Politics of Grandeur: Ideological Aspects of de Gaulle's Foreign Policy* (Cambridge: Cambridge University Press, 1980), p. 45.

86. 'Nous sommes à l'époque de l'efficacité, de l'efficience. Nous sommes à l'époque

des ensembles.' Charles de Gaulle, 'Discours à Dakar', 26 August 1958, <https://fresques.ina.fr/de-gaulle/fiche-media/Gaulle00329/discours-a-dakar.html> (accessed 19 September 2019).

87. Cerny, *The Politics of Grandeur*, p. 53.

88. Gilles Deleuze and Félix Guattari, 'Traité de nomadologie: la machine de guerre', in *Mille plateaux* (Paris: Minuit, 1980), pp. 434–527.

89. 'Faut-il évoquer une origine militaire du corps et de l'esprit de corps? Ce n'est pas "militaire" qui compte, mais plutôt une origine nomade lointaine. Ibn Khaldoun définissait la machine de guerre nomade par: les familles ou lignages, *plus* l'esprit de corps.' Ibid., p. 453.

90. Khaldoun, *Les Prolégomènes d'Ibn Khaldoun*, p. 341.

91. Gilbert Ryle, *The Concept of Mind* (Chicago: University of Chicago Press, 1949), p. 7.

92. Deleuze and Guattari, *Mille plateaux*, p. 455.

93. 'Ce fut toujours une des affaires principales de l'État [. . .] de vaincre *un vagabondage de bande*, et *un nomadisme de corps*.' Ibid., p. 456.

94. 'Pour s'imposer, un individu doué d'autorité peut s'appuyer sur ce qu'Ibn Khaldun appelle l'*asabiyya* [. . .] Nous préférons les traductions telles qu'"esprit de corps" (de Slane), "group feeling" (Rosenthal) ou "esprit de groupe" [. . .] Dans l'œuvre d'Ibn Khaldun, le pouvoir est toujours incarné par un homme. Le pouvoir, pour lui, ne se partage pas: "La politique exige le pouvoir d'un seul. S'il devait se partager entre plusieurs, ce serait la catastrophe." Un bon chef, selon Ibn Khaldun, semble être celui qui se fait le garant de la cohésion du groupe, celui qui joue le rôle de "modérateur", et qui, capable d'intervenir s'il le faut pour séparer des hommes en proie à leur agressivité naturelle, garde autant qu'il le peut une souveraine réserve.' Lilia Ben Salem, 'La notion de pouvoir dans l'oeuvre d'Ibn Khaldun', *Cahiers Internationaux de Sociologie* 55 (1973), pp. 293–314 (pp. 300–2).

95. *Johnson and Walker's Dictionary of the English Language* (London: Pickering, 1828), vol. I, p. 160.

96. 'On dirait que les essences vagues dégagent des choses une détermination qui est plus que la choséité, qui est celle de la *corporéité*, et qui implique peut-être même un esprit de corps.' Deleuze and Guattari, *Mille plateaux*, p. 455.

97. Luis de Miranda, 'Is a New Life Possible? Deleuze and the Lines', *Deleuze Studies* 7.1 (2013), pp. 106–52 (p. 134).

98. 'L'État ne confère pas un pouvoir aux intellectuels ou concepteurs, il en fait au contraire un organe étroitement dépendant, qui n'a d'autonomie qu'en rêve, mais qui suffit pourtant à retirer toute puissance à ceux qui ne font plus que reproduire ou exécuter.' Deleuze and Guattari, *Mille plateaux*, p. 456.

99. de Miranda, 'Is a New Life Possible?', p. 133.

100. Ibid.

101. 'L'État moderne va se définir comme "l'organisation rationnelle et raisonnable d'une communauté": la communauté n'a plus de particularité qu'intérieure ou morale (*esprit d'un peuple*), en même temps que son organisation la fait concourir à l'harmonie d'un universel (*esprit absolu*) [. . .] Obéissez toujours, car, plus vous obéirez, plus vous serez maître, puisque vous n'obéirez qu'à la raison pure, c'est-à-dire à vous-même.' Deleuze and Guattari, *Mille plateaux*, pp. 465–6.

102. Luis de Miranda, *Peut-on jouir du capitalisme? Lacan avec Heidegger et Marx* (Paris: Max Milo, 2009).

103. Hegel, *Philosophy of Right*, § 207, p. 133.

104. 'ne se réclame pas d'un sujet pensant universel'; Deleuze and Guattari, *Mille plateaux*, p. 469.

105. Ibid., p. 467.

106. 'Toute pensée est déjà une tribu', 'une race singulière'; ibid., pp. 467, 469.

107. 'fascisme dominant et englobant'; ibid., p. 469.

108. 'Aussi les arts martiaux ne se réclament-ils pas d'un *code*, comme une affaire d'État, mais de *voies*, qui sont autant de chemins de l'affect; sur ces voies, on apprend à se "desservir" des armes non moins qu'à s'en servir, comme si la puissance et la culture de l'affect était le vrai but.' Ibid., p. 498.

109. 'le "ne-pas-faire" du guerrier'; ibid., p. 498.

110. 'sémiotique affective'; ibid., p. 500.

111. 'Les agencements sont passionnels, ce sont des compositions de désir.' Ibid., pp. 495–7.

112. Gilles Deleuze and Félix Guattari, *Anti-Oedipus: Capitalism and Schizophrenia*, trans. Robert Hurley, Mark Seem and Helen R. Lane (London: Continuum, 2004), p. 14.

113. 'Il s'agit de suivre le bois, et de suivre sur le bois, en connectant des opérations et une matérialité, au lieu d'imposer une forme à une matière [. . .] On définira donc l'artisan comme celui qui est déterminé à suivre un flux de matière, un *phylum machinique*. C'est *l'itinérant, l'ambulant*. Suivre le flux de matière, c'est itinérer, c'est ambuler. C'est l'intuition en acte.' Ibid., pp. 508–9.

114. de Miranda, 'Is a New Life Possible?'.

115. 'Le rapport de la métallurgie avec l'alchimie ne repose pas, comme le croyait Jung, sur la valeur symbolique du métal et sa correspondance avec une âme organique, mais sur la puissance immanente de corporéité dans toute la matière, et sur l'esprit de corps qui l'accompagne [. . .] Le métallurgiste est le premier artisan spécialisé, et forme à cet égard un *corps* (sociétés secrètes, guildes, compagnonnages). L'artisan-métallurgiste est l'itinérant, parce qu'il suit la matière-flux du sous-sol.' Deleuze and Guattari, *Mille plateaux*, pp. 512–13.

116. 'Un mouvement artistique, scientifique, "idéologique", peut être une machine de guerre potentielle, précisément dans la mesure où il trace un plan de consistance, une ligne de fuite créatrice [. . .] Ce n'est pas le nomade qui définit cet ensemble de caractères, c'est cet ensemble qui définit le nomade. [Il] *ne peut faire la guerre qu'à condition de créer autre chose en même temps*, ne serait-ce que de nouveaux rapports sociaux non organiques [. . .] face à la grande conjonction des appareils de capture ou de domination.' Ibid., p. 527.

117. 'Esprit de corps. Déformation qui consiste pour une personne ou pour un groupement à ne considérer que les intérêts étroits d'une catégorie professionnelle au détriment de ceux des autres ou de l'ensemble de la société. On dit "esprit corporatiste", "intérêts corporatistes".' Gérard Dion, *Dictionnaire canadien des relations du travail* (Québec: Presses de l'Université Laval, 1986), p. 136.

118. 'moyens de renforcer l'esprit de corps et l'engagement chez les employés'; Charles Lusthaus, Marie-Hélène Adrien, Gary Anderson and Fred Carden, *Améliorer la performance individuelle: manuel d'auto-évaluation* (Ottawa: CRDI, 1998), p. 80.

119. Groupe Esprit de Corps online site, <www.espritdecorps.biz>.

120. Luis de Miranda, skype interview with Gilles Barbot, 24 February 2016.

7

The Way of Hilton: Esprit de Corps in the UK and the USA in the Twentieth Century

'A happy phrase': The Specificity of English Uses of Esprit de Corps

Anglophone references to esprit de corps in the twentieth century were not only frequent and popular, but also predominantly laudatory. Most English users of the phrase forgot about the pejorative political meaning invented by the *Philosophes* in the eighteenth century. If the phrase 'esprit de corps' continued to thrive in several discourses – military, political, intellectual and theoretical, corporate, and in sport – it was with a meaning that was increasingly generic and standard, often close to the general idea of *team spirit*, often with a bellicose twist. To be fair, this reduction of sense was never unanimously satisfying, and esprit de corps continued to be ungraspable for those who wanted to theorise it scrupulously: 'The expression esprit de corps covers so much ground that its meaning can no more be catalogued in a compact little definition.'[1]

Broadly speaking, the dominant English appropriation of the term was now much more about commanded collaboration than bias or partisanship. John Rowe, the president of a large American insurance company, explained that '"esprit de corps" [. . .] visualizes, as no idiom of our own does, the essence of co-operation'.[2] We must read in full his eloquent 'practical philosophy' article on esprit de corps, published in 1929 in a local newspaper of the western state of Washington:

A happy phrase is sometimes coined, so humanly expressive that barriers of language are swept aside and like music it becomes a universal sentiment. To the French we are indebted for such an expression, 'esprit de corps', which our English tongue has adopted and naturalized because it visualizes, as no idiom of our own does, the essence of co-operation. 'Esprit de corps' is the common spirit pervading men associated in business or social activity, implying sympathy, enthusiasm, devotion and jealous regard for the honor of the body as a whole. In concrete form it symbolizes the story of co-ordinated effort that has gradually raised humanity from the brutish isolation of history's dawn to the intensive inter-relations of today's high civilization. In proportion as 'esprit de corps' becomes a motivating force in men's lives do they transcend the narrow bounds of selfishness and become social beings, for it brings into action forces potent to lift men's thoughts from their own petty affairs to the contemplation of wider horizons. On this great co-ordinating emotion each of the component factors – sympathy, enthusiasm, devotion and jealous regard for honor – taken separately would be sufficient to elevate standards of conduct; taken together, they are the stuff that wins forlorn hopes, founds empires and conquers the world. A great business is very much like the human body, many different parts working together in close harmony. The human factors in business, each allotted to different tasks, are as dependent one on the other as are the organs and tissues of the body – one cannot do the job to the utmost if others fail to work to the same end. In a large organization 'esprit de corps' must be the soul that animates the body if the business is to function with the vigor of healthy growth, inspiring every one associated in the enterprise to pride in the purpose and value of his work, and to resolute determination to add his full quota to the total of achievement. A task of real importance devolves upon each one of us – so to imbue our associates by precept and example with 'esprit de corps' and all that it implies that we may work together as a great harmonious whole for the common welfare which, in the end, must be for the greatest good of each.[3]

On the surface, such a definition looks grandiose. It also epitomises the dominant American approach to esprit de corps, influenced by corporate imperialism and organicism. Rowe was a specialist in health and life insurance, which might partly explain his organicist metaphor. His insistence on the fact that esprit de corps was an emotion, a sentiment, a sympathy, masked his *parti pris* against state-controlled aspects of it: in a pamphlet against any official supervision of health insurance schemes, he explained that he was opposed to welfare-state forms of social security.[4] Rowe believed that corporate esprit de corps and economic laissez-faire walked hand in hand.

Behind the grandiloquence of universalising praise, one often finds a form of particular ideology, mystification or even self-deception. Here a bit of research shows that Rowe's case is embarrassing. In the journal of the Canadian Mathematical Society we find the following confidence written by Rowe's nephew decades later:

As I did every spring, I spent my Easter vacation visiting my Uncle John [. . .] Since he was in the insurance business, I expected he would be delighted when I told him I was going to be an actuary. He said, 'Hmmmmmmm.' Next day he invited me to the office [. . .] Finally he opened a door to an occupied room. There were 30 or 40 men there, sitting on high stools before slightly inclined desks. Each man wore a green eyeshade, had his coat off and satin sleeves over his shirt cuffs, and pounded almost continuously on a Comptometer. The racket was deafening. As Uncle John closed the door, he said, 'ACK-chu-air-ees.' All my life, I have been thankful for that wonderful lesson.[5]

So much for the harmonious esprit de corps in which every employee is a proud and admirable member of the corporate body: John Rowe intentionally discouraged his nephew from becoming a dehumanised employee. His public praise of esprit de corps was partly smoke and mirrors, an idealising generalisation, the self-deceitful speech of the president of a company who had a personal interest in keeping his workers disciplined and obedient, united by a vague feeling rather than by trade unions. Esprit de corps was good for the masses, but the enlightened sons of the dominant class should rather thrive to become independent-minded scientists or individualistic bosses.

The English-language attraction to esprit de corps was so enduring during the twentieth century that one is sometimes under the impression that the Gallicism served – and still serves – as a magic formula or an incantation to express the inexpressible or reconcile the irreconcilable, such as individualism and group spirit: 'The intellectual leaders of the country are striving frantically to find an American *esprit de corps* which is significant of American life.'[6] Sometimes written in italics, esprit de corps became a global idiom disseminated across the world via its English uses. One could, for example, find it in an English-language textbook for high schools and colleges published in Shanghai in 1926: 'Esprit de corps (Fr.) = spirit of collective body.'[7] Under the influence of the French sociologists, American academics also became sympathetic to the term, for example when Lewis Yablonsky noted that 'loyalty and esprit de corps are strong mobilizing forces',[8] or in studies which relied on the equivalence between esprit de corps and 'common cause'.[9] As we will see, scholarly attempts were even made to quantify esprit de corps statistically.

In corporate USA, and consequently in corporate global discourse, esprit de corps was perceived as a managerial asset, one that would favour employee retention and also help to construct an epic narrative comparing salaried work to a crusade on the battlefield of necessary capitalist battles. The American understanding of esprit de corps was often correlated to the idea of team-leading as a kind of paramilitary or meta-military strategy, within a paradigm of global competition and universal antagonism: 'Leaders may have a vested interest in conflict as a unity-producing mechanism so that they may accelerate already existing conflict [. . .] if internal dissension and dissatisfaction threaten their leadership',[10] and groups or corporations may 'actually search for an enemy whenever the esprit de corps threatens to become slack'.[11] Esprit de corps as a meta-military value was meant to serve hegemonic purposes. In the first decades of the twentieth century, the phrase was still used in imperialist and racialist discourses, for instance by British army officers: 'What race pride is to the Empire, so should esprit de corps be to the regiment.'[12] We have grasped already with the Bonapartists how imperialism favours the diffusion of military values into society.

Yet the martial denotation of esprit de corps was not always expressed unfiltered: euphemistic discourses exhibited what Bevir called, in his *Logic of the History of Ideas*, a 'distortion'.[13] A typical example of this is the frequent musical analogy of the chief as an orchestra conductor, which facilitates a discourse of oneness and harmony:

As musicians, our vernacular centers around words and phrases like: *ensemble, blend, focus, unity, working together, responsibility, commitment, expression creating a unified mood, bringing a sense of 'oneness' to the group, esprit de corps*, and so on. All these thoughts are generated from the fundamental philosophy that there is more benefit for the individual via emphasis on *we* and *us* rather than *I* and *me* [. . .] Ultimately, everyone grows because of the adjustment necessary in this group-goal endeavour.[14]

Does everyone grow thanks to esprit de corps? That is the question. Throughout the century, discourses of oneness were often correlated with a certain mystique, where esprit de corps was presented as both 'sacred' and 'secular'.[15] Even the more scientific attempts to redefine and measure esprit de corps would remain fascinated by the mysterious alchemy of the phenomenon, enhanced in English by the exoticism of the phrase.

Brothers in Arms: Esprit de Corps in Military Discourse

At the end of the nineteenth century, esprit de corps was considered a golden virtue by American military officials. Benjamin Harrison, the 23rd president of the USA, wrote solemnly when he retired in 1901: 'The soldier [. . .] is our countryman; he carries and keeps the flag. We must be tender, and careful that we do not spoil his *esprit de corps* by ingratitude.'[16] In 1904, the *Journal of the Military Service Institution of the United States* published a 'Gold Medal Essay' with the following title: 'Esprit de corps – How It May Be Strengthened and Preserved in Our Army.' In it, Peter Traub, a captain of the cavalry, wrote:

The military profession [. . .] has not a monopoly of esprit de corps [. . .] In every dignified profession in all countries there is a vital force, resulting from organization and association, that gives a stamp to the individuals composing it, that impels them to act for the good of the profession, and that may even urge them to the extreme of self-sacrifice, depending upon the ideal or standard they set up for themselves and *live up to*. Every trade, every society, every combination of individuals, has, to a greater or less degree, this moral, vitalizing force, which, through lack of a definite descriptive word in English, we designate by the French term, esprit de corps.[17]

The author justified military esprit de corps by suggesting that it was a universal quality, essentialised as a vital organic energy. Quite contradictory to this vitalism, the image of a 'stamp' was reminiscent of the French idea of esprit de corps as an *estampille*.[18] The reference to a 'moral force' was suggestive of a collective ethos, a perspective we have encountered in Durkheim and Bergson. Traub proposed a definition of esprit de corps in which a collective life force energised the individual member, a spirit so strong that it could defeat selfishness or even personal survival instinct. Finding a good recipe to produce self-sacrifice was vital for the army.

But vitality was not enough: ideas, values or beliefs needed to be rhetorically articulated to channel human resources in the expected direction. The force of esprit de corps was believed to be proportional to the elevation of 'the ideal or standard' it was connected to.[19] A belief in God, explained Traub, gave the most powerful esprit de corps, as shown by the 'marvellous' example of 'the Jesuits in North America in the middle of the seventeenth century'.[20] Just below the priest in the hierarchy of masters of esprit de corps came the doctor, who worked for the 'love of mankind'.[21] And just below medicine came military morale, rooted in patriotism, the love for 'the native land'.[22] This pyramidal perspective advocated large-scale esprit de corps and criticised small-scale manifestations based on internal competition among different platoons, 'frequently considered by the uninitiated as the essential characteristics of esprit de corps in an army'.[23] There was, for Traub, a grander and supposedly more authentic esprit de corps, of divine nature, compatible with patriotism and what the historian of ideas Betty Jean Graige called a form of 'political holism', in which 'the health of a group, like that of an organism, is defined by the productive interaction of all its members'.[24]

Once more, the expansion of the scope of esprit de corps produces speech acts soaked in religiosity, awe and wonder:

> What then is real esprit de corps? Esprit de corps is so like a real spirit, giving life to an army and to the various organizations composing it, that we experience difficulty at once when we try to seize upon it, define it and analyse it. It is such an intangible quality, it has its sources in so many secret springs [. . .] that, could we isolate it, we should scarcely be able to recognize it.[25]

Considering the Gold Medal Prize and the wide distribution of Traub's text within the US military administration, his mystique of esprit de corps was not just the expression of an isolated enthusiastic belief. It was also compatible with a national strategic programme. The discursive tactic here was to absolutise esprit de corps, making it natural to accept and espouse it at a national level.

Vitalist denotations of esprit de corps were not uncommon in the US military. Alfred Thayer Mahan, a navy admiral and historian, explained that 'the subtle influence for which we owe to the French the name of *esprit de corps* [. . .] is the breath of the body, the breath of life'.[26] This was both a metaphorical and somewhat literal reading of the signifier, reminiscent of the Latin etymology of spirit, which evoked breath. Life and the risk of death were one: if the state wanted soldiers to die for the fatherland, it seemed opportune to tell them that the spirited life that the state might be taking from them was never fully theirs, but was first conferred by the closer-to-God national body.

Adjacent to this rhetoric was the consideration of the army 'as a whole' instead of a sum of platoons.[27] A grand unit could be said to have a genuine spirit, and each national army displayed a specific character (a virtue once attributed to regiments and their esprit *du* corps). American esprit de corps, for example, was about being efficient:

The keystone of the esprit de corps of the British Army is tradition [. . .] The keystone of the esprit de corps of the American Army is efficiency – efficiency in the individual and in the various combinations of individuals from the lowest, or squad, to the highest, or army.[28]

This idea of a principle of efficiency at the source of military esprit de corps, a virtue that did not completely erase individual personalities but organised them organically for the sake of victory and glory, partly explains the success of the concept of esprit de corps in American managerial and corporate discourse, of which more below. One can run a conquering corporation according to the value of efficiency, which is innovation-friendly, perhaps less so according to the principle of tradition. The author did not speak of the keystone of French military esprit de corps, although the notion of élan would probably qualify.

The American military discourse that connected God, Life and Efficiency suggested that conquest was the meaning of life. In practice, military efficiency was first achieved by examining the moral character of applicants and by rejecting candidates with immoral antecedents, the list of which was often vague or subjective. Efficiency then consisted in following strict performative exercises and habits: hymns, uniforms, honours, colours, equal treatment, training, etc. Three 'cardinal principles' had to prevail: 'self-control, self-culture, and self-sacrifice'.[29] This suggested that the self was not totally erased – how could it be in an individualist culture? – but it was constrained through constant self- and mutual censorship, via limitation and monitoring of the self by the self under the surveillance of the group, thanks to an internalisation of the group's ethos. The three cardinal principles read like a chronological description of a soldier's existence: self-control meant *be mobilised*, self-culture meant *be trained*, self-sacrifice meant *be killed*. In this, group will and individual will were meant to be fused.

The value of equal treatment, not always practised on the field, meant that military esprit de corps relied ideally on practices of impartiality:

Nothing so soon undermines the very foundations of efficiency, nothing so soon stifles military ardor, loyalty, pride, and enthusiasm in the profession of arms, nothing so soon blights the esprit de corps, as to have the impression abroad amongst officers and men that political, personal, or social influence gives any claim to military preferment or to military reward.[30]

Efficiency was a managerial mode that ought to give at least 'the impression' that soldiers were treated equally. If the army was to be considered as a kind of corporation and its final product was self-sacrifice for the sake of national hegemony, then structural unfairness was a manufacturing flaw.

A pragmatic explanation for the defence of national esprit de corps was the relative nuisance of internally competing clusters within the US army, each defending their specificity and esprit. Immediately below the esprit de corps of the national army as a whole, which was more an ideal than a reality, esprit de corps in large branches such as the navy was preferred by the general administration

over esprit de corps in particular battalions, squadrons or batteries. Yet the less-
ening of the latter was not an easy task: according to the military historian
Mark Dunkelman, combat units that tend to display stronger esprit de corps are
the smaller companies in which soldiers come from the same villages, towns or
regions, with 'extensive family relationships'.[31] Because it was difficult to produce
an army in which every soldier would think of himself as part of a unique grand
body, speech acts in this direction were rewarded with gold medals. In reality,
internal semi-autonomist esprit de corps seems to be a feature of most armies,
since 'the military institutionalizes competition at all levels of organization'.[32]

The British army faced similar issues before the First World War, according to
the British *Journal of the Royal United Service Institution*:

> We Britons possess the best material; but we have our weak points and an
> inclination to selfishness and exclusiveness is one among them. *Esprit de corps*
> is all very well, and within bounds, commendable, but *esprit d'arme* is a vile,
> snobbish, and dangerous thing, where one branch of the service sets itself
> against another.[33]

Once again, we stumble upon vocabulary nuances, intended to avoid throwing
the baby of esprit de corps out with the bathwater of internal quarrels. What was
esprit d'arme? A definition could be found in a French encyclopaedia of military
history published in 1835: *L'esprit d'arme* was a *préjugé*, a prejudice according to
which each combat company wants to believe that they are the only real fighters
['lui seul fait la guerre'].[34] The contrast with esprit de corps was a difference of
scale. Controlling an army as a whole was the administrative goal. The more unified and homogenised a large military group was, the easier, perhaps, to win wars
and to channel soldiers into the idea of national service. But a perfect cohesion
would not be without national risks for those in power, and the practical military
tolerance towards esprit de corps in army branches in many nation-states could
be explained by the old political ruse of *divide et impera*. A very unified army,
or a very homogeneous and close-knit nation of citizens, could turn out to be a
double-edged menace of *coup d'état* or revolution.

Between 1915 and 1960, English occurrences of the signifier 'esprit de corps'
reached a peak in printed books and official documents. The 'cult of esprit de
corps'[35] was particularly high in the war decades of the twentieth century, when
nationalist fabulations had huge effects. Soon after the First World War, in the
British *Naval Review*, Lieutenant Colonel W. B. Barber hoped that officers would
in the future continue to 'instill *esprit de corps* into the minds of their men'.[36] He
proposed the following uncompromising 'definition':

> The best definition of this word seems to be one given by the French inter-
> preter at the original 3rd Army Infantry School in France. It is in simple words,
> admitting of no possible misunderstanding. '*Esprit de corps* is the feeling that
> prompts every man never to think of himself as an individual, but of the unit
> to which he belongs.'[37]

By 'unit', in this context, Barber meant 'regiment or corps'[38] rather than the whole of the army. It was perhaps a rhetorical artifice to cite the authority of a supposed French interpreter, and the vehement tone ('no possible misunderstanding') implies that the opinion was consciously polemical. Why was esprit de corps so important for regiments in times of war?

Drawing from the experience of 1914–18, Barber discovered that a small-scale esprit de corps could function as a proper adjuvant against boredom:

> None of the works on *esprit de corps* and morale, written before the war, make any mention of this factor. During the late war in France the insidious effect, one might almost call it a disease, of boredom on the minds of men holding a line of trenches for long periods, especially in the winter months, became a very real and threatening danger to the fighting spirit of the troops.[39]

The semantic proximity between esprit de corps and fighting spirit, as well as the bodily physiology of boredom in times of war, suggested that if the problem was physical, the solution could be also physical. Indeed, the main remedy that the British army proposed against boredom was sport: 'the Englishman's love of games and sport [. . .] a decisive factor in winning the war'.[40] Not far from the battlefield, football championships were supported by government funding. Performances, dinners and cheerful receptions were also instruments in the management of ennui.

During the Second World War, British parliamentary debates referred to the need to 'preserve tradition and esprit de corps' in the army.[41] The Royal Air Force was considered to be a paragon of esprit de corps, a quality 'of vital importance'.[42] Even when observed in adversary corps, such as the German army, the military efficiency of esprit de corps was recognised: 'Many a young "Black Knight" was sent into the cauldron of battle with little more than ideological conviction or *esprit de corps* to sustain him.'[43] This suggested, once again, a dangerous liaison between ideology and esprit de corps.

In the USA, official propaganda did appeal to 'the good of the State'[44] as the ultimate military goal, but it did not abandon the rhetoric of individual realisation. It was important to convince increasingly self-aware democratic soldiers that the army would magnify their persona. All soldiers had equal opportunity to prove that only the best among them would survive and triumph: efficiency was about the 'survival of the fittest'.[45] According to the *Proceedings of the United States Naval Institute* of 1903, 'esprit de corps is the moral foundation of the edifice of naval efficiency as well as the inspiration of individual success'.[46] In 1943, a magazine headline claimed that 'Uncle Sam Picks an All-Star Team', and the article explained: 'In the army they call it esprit de corps – the stuff that builds champion teams and victorious armies in which each man is doing the job he does best.'[47] To boost enlistment rates, it seemed best to ignore the self-sacrificial aspect of esprit de corps to focus on the more attractive, individualist metaphor of championship and professional excellence. The line between management and war was blurred.

Twentieth-century American readers were not likely to be exposed to a more critical meaning of esprit de corps, unless sporadically, for example via the occasional famous French author. In 1961, to explain why the Algerian War was turning some French military officers against President de Gaulle, the writer and diplomat Romain Gary published an article in *Life* magazine on the 'anger that turned generals into desperados':[48]

> A mystique of self-adoration, an *esprit de corps* was part of the army's greatness, but it was also responsible for a state of mind in which the army was becoming a thing in itself, a purpose in itself, a stronghold within a nation.[49]

This was reminiscent of the traditional French critique of esprit de corps, related since D'Alembert to a suspicion of anti-national forms of autonomy. Esprit de corps, equated to *esprit d'arme* or *de parti* even if it implied the entire army, was opposed to the common will. Gary's characterisation of the notion as a group mystique of self-adoration was an explicit religious metaphor, an echo of the anti-Jesuitism of the *Encyclopédie*. The formula 'thing in itself' referred to a vocabulary of metaphysics; if not explicitly to Kant's noumenon, certainly to ideas of reification and fetishism.

If one perceives a group as a thing in itself, one might tend to engage in 'group fetishism' by 'presuppos[ing] that the group may have moral characteristics that are neither identical with nor derived from the moral characteristics of its members'.[50] But a mystique is not only the constitution of an object of veneration; it also suggests a dismissal of the prosaic everyday routine, in favour of a more spiritual relation to existence, what Etienne Souriau, a contemporary of Gary, called *surexistence*, an ecstatic communion with 'the mysterious outline of a unique being'.[51] If in the twentieth century religious communities were no longer a practical heaven offering the experience of the bliss of esprit de corps, perhaps the military profession could provide an alternative.

Esprit de corps remains today an important notion in English military discourse, for reasons anticipated by the military historian Mike Chappel in 1987:

> With the 21st century almost upon us and the advent of 'Star Wars' now more than just a science-fiction writer's dream, the battlefield of the future seems destined to be dominated by the side with the superior technology. It is therefore remarkable that there is still a body of opinion which considers martial music, meticulously-performed drill, glittering uniforms, and even horses the outward signs of élite formations. The proponents of military pomp argue that it continues to foster esprit de corps in the same way it has done for centuries, and that a unit capable of performing faultless ceremonial will fight well in battle.[52]

As long as soldiers remain human beings rather than cyborgs or androids, esprit de corps might be a fundamental bodily technique. The phrase 'body of opinion' was suggestive, but esprit de corps was not only about shared opinions, it was also about drill and the slow co-creation of a momentum.

Are parades, manoeuvres, rituals or ceremonies key practices to foster esprit de corps even outside the army? Such was the thesis of the anthropologist David Kertzer – himself relying on Herbert Blumer's writings on the sociology of collective behaviour:

> If they are to be successful, social movements must create their own esprit de corps, which Blumer defines as the 'organizing of feelings on behalf of the movement' [. . .] But how is esprit de corps created? The answer, according to Blumer, is, in good part, through 'participation in formal ceremonial behaviour' [. . .] The psychology that is involved here is the psychology of being on parade.[53]

The management of feelings via ceremonial, uniforms and memory is a constant activity of nation-states. Unofficial social movements, protest assemblies or strikes tend to neglect this ritual aspect of solidarity.

The success in 2018 of the *Gilets jaunes* political movement is partly due to this simple fact: yellow vests are a uniform and contribute as such to the esprit de corps of the protesters. This is a paradox that political theorists tend to forget: in order to build autonomy, one needs to build homogeneity. Judith Butler is right to say that 'political claims are made by bodies as they appear and act',[54] but the theory of esprit de corps indicates that, to be effectual in the long term, performativity needs much more than temporary bodily assemblies: only discipline can undo discipline. Individualistic subjects of *jouissance* who gather occasionally find it hard to change the capitalist system because the latter is meta-military. The genealogy of esprit de corps tends to indicate that Deleuze and Guattari were right to suggest that to change the course of political history, a group needs to become a martial machine and manifest the ritual familiarity of a tribe.

The Purpose of Unity: Political and Institutional Aspects of Esprit de Corps

Does esprit de corps favour or prevent corruption? In 1904, the British House of Commons debated the decision to close the Royal Indian Engineering College, which had been training engineers for several decades to work in India. Opponents of the closure urged 'on the Secretary of State the importance of recruiting for the public service men who are gentlemen by character and training, and insist[ed] on the value of a College training with its accompanying esprit de corps'.[55] The elitist esprit de corps of the school was believed to function as a shield against corruption:

> The maintenance of a high standard of personal honour among engineers engaged in public works is of the utmost importance. The temptations to corruption (especially in India) to which engineers engaged in carrying out

public works are exposed are many and great. One of the best guarantees that these temptations will be resisted comes from a sense of esprit de corps in the Service, and it is therefore of great importance to do nothing which will weaken the sense of esprit de corps among Indian engineers.[56]

Underneath this capitalisation of *Service* lay a reversal of the Enlightenment view of esprit de corps, no longer equated with dishonesty but rather supposed to be a remedy against misconduct. This was the consciousness of participating in a dignified and well-functioning national system of responsibility and recognition. A state-administered esprit de corps, thanks to its distributed and internal surveillance, was supposed to generate loyalty in serving the empire.

Engineers were becoming a globally dominant profession and they helped build facilities used every day by thousands; it was important to ascertain that they were predictable and disciplined. In the USA, after the severe floods on the Passaic river in the state of New Jersey 1902–3, the duties of water resource engineers were emphasised in the following terms:

> In our work we must have not merely good engineers, but men who can and will study the reasons and underlying principles of national law [. . .] Everything depends on unity and continuity of purpose and of action and the creation of an esprit de corps, or what may be expressed as the holding of a unity of ideals by the entire body of men engaged in the work.[57]

Esprit de corps was an ideological asset in national narratives, telling a story of value-driven exemplarity, a professionally rooted unity of dedication to the greater good. The corps here was envisaged in a typically Bonapartist manner, as an emanation from the nation, allowing for a public or universalistic form of esprit de corps.

In 1904, British Members of Parliament did remember to distinguish the latter form from a more autonomist type:

> There are two kinds of esprit de corps – one is the esprit de corps which induces a man to do all he can to keep up the honour and efficiency of the public service to which he belongs, and the other is one which merely connects him socially with the body to which he belongs.[58]

National esprit de corps was better, but particularistic esprit de corps was not contradictory. Should the two be combined? Apparently yes, like Russian puppets scaling down homothetically from the level of the empire to the level of the individual, and vice versa.

A history book published in 1938 by Charles Jeffries with Cambridge University Press stated that the Colonial Office sought 'to create an *esprit de corps* for the Unified Service as a whole, complementary to and not in any way conflicting with that *esprit de corps* which is the natural and proud possession of the public service of each Colony'.[59] Here the suggested distinction was between a concrete and field-based esprit de corps, coinciding with local connections, and another, more symbolic, abstract or holistic, proceeding from the spirit of the British Empire. Larger units of people who did not know each other were expected to be cohered via an 'imagined' solidarity that should be 'consciously aspired to', and not only the result of habit and familiarity.[60]

With this idea of ensemblistic or organic imperialism, the critique of esprit de corps continued to wane in English, especially in the USA. Any derogatory political use of the Gallicism was becoming marginal. In 1927, in his book *The New Democracy*, the political thinker Walter Weyl wrote of 'professional politicians':

> By force and fraud at primary and convention, by party rules strengthening strategic and pivotal points, already pre-empted, by securing for themselves immunity from criminal prosecutions, by developing a special code of honor and *esprit de corps*, they obtained, subject to the right of the people to rebel, a strong firm grasp on party and government.[61]

The efficacy of esprit de corps was not in doubt, but it was equated in this swansong of the Enlightenment critique in the USA with a form of organised crime against the nation. Since d'Alembert and Diderot, both in English and French, almost no contemner of esprit de corps has denied its effectual power. Esprit de corps might be considered nefarious, but never ineffective or insignificant by those who use the phrase as a combat concept. Even if it were an illusion, it was – for a minority of historically minded intellectuals – a dangerous one in practice.

The dominant discourse, in the meantime, praised esprit de corps as a panacea. With the advent of Russian communism and the First World War, the political idea of esprit de corps continued to serve as a way of consolidating capitalist regimes. As we have seen in our examination of translations of Fayol's principles, esprit de corps was conveniently presented as the capitalist analogue of trade unionism, a substitute for the spectre of communist camaraderie: '*Esprit de corps* is a very good antidote to Bolshevism.'[62]

In 1942, the newly created United States Office of Civilian Defense aimed at organising civilian populations as a 'corps', officially to prepare them for a possible attack from a real or imaginary enemy. A proto-cybernetic booklet was issued, *The Control System of the Citizens' Defense Corps*, which stated that:

> *Esprit de corps* is an important factor in the success of any organization. In the work of the control system it is absolutely essential, inasmuch as even a slight failure to coordinate and cooperate by the workers may result in serious failures. No mechanical rules can be followed to develop this intangible but all-important element. It depends on the inner desire of each worker to give the very best possible service irrespective of how difficult and trying conditions may be. It will include a pride in the organization, rather than in personal accomplishment. In a larger sense it must be a reflection of the national consciousness that every individual must do his or her part, and do it well, for the protection and safety of all. Under emergency conditions absolute discipline

must be maintained. This requires instantaneous and unquestioned obedience on the part of each individual to the commands of his or her superior.[63]

There was a strange contradiction in this attempt to write a technically minded and bureaucratic manual to systematically control an intangible that it was also said to be impossible to create by following a mechanical protocol. But the authors did not seem – or want – to see the discrepancy between, for example, 'inner desire' and 'unquestioned obedience', or between individualism and 'absolute discipline', perhaps because they believed that 'personal accomplishment', 'organization pride' and 'national consciousness' were organically connected, thanks to a kind of homogeneous dilation from smaller to larger senses of esprit de corps.

This form of universalistic political cohesion could be called *homothetic belongingness*; its danger lies in the assumption that individual desire is bound to the state. Its manifestations are worryingly delirious: is 'absolute discipline' even possible? The very title of the booklet would seem to be extracted from a conspiracy theory pamphlet, were it not for the date, 1942, which allowed for a discourse of a state of emergency. Giorgio Agamben's *State of Exception* investigates how the modification of laws within a state of emergency or crisis can become a prolonged state of national being that institutionalises violence and neutralises the possibility of political change in the name of a war against 'anomie'.[64]

In our century and in times of peace, nation-states have tended until now to mask publicly their will-to-control with a more nuanced vocabulary than 'control of the citizen corps'. Yet there is still today in the USA a Citizen Corps Program coordinated by the Federal Emergency Management Agency, which was affiliated in 2003 with the Department of Homeland Security. These 'Freedom Corps' were given the following mission by President Bush:

> Since the terrorist attacks of September 11, 2001, Americans have acted with courage, compassion, and unity. To capture this spirit and to foster an American culture of service, citizenship, and responsibility, President George W. Bush has called upon all Americans to dedicate at least two years of their lives—the equivalent of 4,000 hours—in service to others. He launched the USA Freedom Corps initiative to inspire and enable all Americans to find ways to serve their community, their country, or the world. Citizen Corps is the component of USA Freedom Corps that creates opportunities for individuals to volunteer to help their communities prepare for and respond to emergencies [. . .] The goal is to have all citizens participate in making their communities safer, stronger, and better prepared for preventing and handling threats of terrorism, crime, and disasters of all kinds.[65]

Preparedness and readiness are emphasised, suggestive of a constant state of war against a diffuse and vague enemy that combines natural catastrophes, enemies of the nation, delinquents, etc. This device of esprit de corps relies on a mobilisation that does not offer a financial benefit, since it is supposed to be a training in civics.

Is this still about *control*? One could argue that we are in a cybernetic society in which random individuals contribute to general control often without a principled national consciousness, via their behavioural contribution to big data. In 1942, the protocol was clearly suggestive of what Foucault called a *mécanisme de contrôle*,[66] in which individual bodies are supervised and disciplined by a larger social body:[67] the Civilian Defense Corps booklet, blurring the line between peace and war, explicitly insisted on control and command. As in Bentham's infamous Panopticon, this meta-military system was expected to function by avoiding the need for face-to-face orders. Yet a corps leader had to 'know all that is happening in the area under his jurisdiction'.[68] Still today in the Citizen Corps, a combination of centralised and distributed power obscures the identification of a unique source of domination or homothetic centre. Under such forms of esprit de corps the risk is that individuals slowly forfeit their autonomy, their capacity for self-determination or existential integrity, and surrender to highly formalised, instrumental systems of action.

The tension between loss of freedom and bureaucracy is a well-known socio-political topic:

> Ever-fewer spheres of life are able to escape the straightjacket of formal reason [. . .] Instead, nearly all aspects of social life are regulated and predetermined – down to the innermost 'corpuscular' level, as Michel Foucault observes with reference to the growth of modern 'biopower'.[69]

The US 'weaponization'[70] of the ideas of 'corps' and 'esprit de corps', applied to civilians under a vague threat of war – or, as we will see, under the assumption that business administration is akin to a form of strategic war – is not always distinguishable from a paramilitary mode of social organisation.

Measure by Measure: Intellectual and Theoretical Uses of Esprit de Corps

In the twentieth century, the English-language attraction to esprit de corps continued to pervade scholarly translations. In the first British translation of Nietzsche's *Genealogy of Morals*, esprit de corps is connected to imperialist perceptions of race, within an anti-democratic frame:

> The pathos of nobility and distance [. . .] the chronic and despotic *esprit de corps* and fundamental instinct of a higher dominant race coming into association with [. . .] an 'under race', this is the origin of the antithesis of good and bad.[71]

However, Nietzsche's original text did not mention esprit de corps but *Gesammtgefühl*,[72] which implied a feeling of wholeness, an entireness, a totality.[73] Neither did he use a German domesticated version of esprit de corps, for instance *Korpsgeist* (literally *corps spirit*), which was used in German at least from 1855.[74] *Gemeingeist* (*common spirit*) was also an option: it was given as a synonym of 'esprit de corps' in a textbook on the proper usage of German published in 1795.[75]

Why did Horace Samuel, the English translator, choose 'esprit de corps'? Probably because in British English, esprit de corps was often associated in the nineteenth century with a notion of elitism, but perhaps also because of his familiarity with the French language: Samuel was also the translator of Stendhal's *Le Rouge et le Noir*.[76] Nevertheless, the then available French translation of Nietzsche's text (1900) did not use esprit de corps, but *sentiment général*.[77] The British translation's association between esprit de corps and the terms 'despotic', dominant 'instinct' and 'nobility' suggests that esprit de corps was understood as an exhilarating superiority complex against an out-group defined as inferior. In Nietzsche's then influential perspective, a dominant class ideologically defined its hegemony as beneficial, and its supremacy relied on a compact body of self-glorification and exclusion. Praising this state of affairs was quite remote from Enlightenment critiques of despotism.[78] Remember Rousseau's lucidity:

> I thought a hundred times with dread that if I had the misfortune to fill today such or such a position in certain countries, tomorrow I would be almost inevitably a tyrant, a torturer, destroyer of the people, harmful to the prince, enemy by estate of all humanity, of all fairness, of every kind of virtue.[79]

For Nietzsche, virtue could be cruel if it served the eschatological advent of the reign of the *Übermensch* – the uses and abuses of his philosophy by fascist regimes is well known.[80]

The phrase 'esprit de corps' was sometimes used in English translations to account for other enigmatic foreign notions, for example the Japanese notion of *seishin*, defined as 'the complex of loyalty, discipline, esprit de corps, and indomitable perseverance that is central to so many of the historical accomplishments of Japanese civilization'.[81] While in French the formula *esprit de* could evoke irrational notions of repetition, habit, *idée fixe*, stubbornness – as in *esprit de système*,[82] which meant the compulsion to elaborate a unifying system of interpretation at all cost – in twentieth-century English esprit de corps completely lost the idea of behavioural compulsion to refer to an experience of group unity.

In the first half of the century, this unity was often thought to be transcendent. A particularly exalted example of the spiritualisation of esprit de corps was a speech delivered before the medical department of the University of Michigan in 1912:

> It is an important and unquestioned truth that the greatest thing which a student takes from a classroom is not the facts which he may have learned here, but the spirit which he may have imbibed here [. . .] I shall take it for granted that the high qualities of that spirit are accepted as the characteristics of the ideal physician [. . .] It is chiefly as such a spirit is incarnated in a living man that it is impressed and perpetuated [. . .] The high *esprit de corps* of any body of men, family spirit, national spirit, patriotism in all its manifestations, is but

an expression of this same influence. The ideal is embodied in a man, and lo, a hero, a prophet, a saint is created and a world spirit is engendered or changed because a man has lived![83]

This grandiloquent speech seemed reminiscent of Hegel's description of Napoleon as 'the World-Spirit on horseback',[84] or of Bergson's idea about the men of action whose mystical *fabulations* have the power to renew the human species.[85] Yet for Bergson, heroic achievements could be led by a woman, such as Teresa of Ávila, Catherine of Siena or Joan of Arc,[86] while American lyrical speeches on esprit de corps tended to emphasise patriarchal and androcentric leadership. A mysterious universal soul was channelled by exceptional males who attracted disciples. Education was not presented as a democratic process of autonomisation and self-enlightenment, but as an imitation and influence process for the happy few.

To avoid mysticism or speculation, a few researchers in sociology or psychology felt that more empirical evidence was needed if one was to explain what esprit de corps was. This led in the second half of the twentieth century to expressions of extreme quantification, while the notion was momentarily losing its mystical connotation. In the 1950s, meticulous attempts were made to measure esprit de corps down to the decimal point. In a study about fraternities at Syracuse University, 'social-relations' indices were considered to be predictors of esprit de corps and group-effectiveness:

One measure of esprit de corps morale involved each fraternity member's listing all the unpleasant, and later all the pleasant, things he associated with his fraternity life [. . .] A second measure of esprit de corps morale was based on analysis of essays written by each member in defense of fraternities faced by a hypothetical but plausible threat to their continued existence at Syracuse University [. . .] A fourth measure of esprit de corps morale was obtained by having the subjects estimate how favorably they thought their fraternity brothers regarded them.[87]

The list went on, and the outcomes of this quantitative approach led to formulations such as 'This measure of esprit de corps morale ranged from .54 to .88 with a mid-correlation of .75.'[88] Repeated use of the sophisticated phrase 'esprit de corps morale', in which esprit de corps became adjectival, was meant to isolate a specific scientific object. Models to measure the phenomenon of esprit de corps could still be proposed at the end of the century. In 1997, a marketing study, of which more below, contained several exhibits of 'levels of esprit de corps', on a scale from 0 to 60.[89] In 1993, the academic *Journal of Institutional and Theoretical Economics* published a paper in which esprit de corps, abbreviated as 'e', was a mathematical variable within a complex equation measuring 'organizational effectiveness', explained in quantitative jargon: 'An exogenous increase in esprit de corps e will affect effort (x) indirectly.'[90]

After the Second World War, the new academic field of social psychology endeavoured to analyse the esprit de corps of the army[91] in relation to an emerging Theory of Small Groups, which remains today – more as a disparate bundle of more or less interesting claims or findings than a unified theory – an area of research in communication, psychology, management and political science. Throughout the twentieth century, sociology in general continued to be an important discipline for the intellectual propagation of the notion of esprit de corps. In the 1970s, it appeared on six different pages of a textbook, *Education Sociology*, still distributed to students in China at Shanghai College:[92]

> Persons in a group have their behaviour at least partially determined by the group processes and structure. This is the essence of social control [. . .] *Esprit de corps* is group loyalty, unity, or solidarity [. . .] *Esprit de corps* is sentimentalized identity; it represents assimilation of the values and attitudes, meanings and feelings that dominate the group.[93]

It was now well recognised that esprit de corps, defined as group identity, was not only about values and habits, but also about emotion. Social control was achieved not only through procedural protocols and speech acts, but also via sentiment and shared experiences. This definition is not far from Bourdieu's approach, and the correlation between identity and sociality remains today a key topic in sociology.[94]

In this context, esprit de corps was related to another French-imported signifier, *rapport*, used more or less as a synonym of *humane relation*. It was proposed that in human groups and in times of 'collective crises', 'rapport develops into esprit de corps [. . .] they are all in the same boat – the solution for one is the solution for all'.[95] An analogous boat metaphor was articulated in 1989 by the sociologist of religion Robert Wuthnow, who explained in neo-Darwinian fashion that some conditions favoured esprit de corps, chief among them scarcity of resources and a sense of shared adversity:

> The kind of environment in which collectivism is likely to be selected for can be illustrated by imagining a lifeboat adrift at sea with a handful of survivors aboard. Under these conditions 'each man for himself' is not likely to be an ideal ideology. A strong sense of *esprit de corps* is needed for the group to survive [. . .] A sense of *esprit de corps* in this instance protects scarce resources.[96]

The image of the lifeboat, a metaphor for a resource-poor environment, suggested that humans only cooperated efficiently and systematically in situations of collective emergency. One could argue the opposite: that in times of abundance, sharing and including the other is easier, whereas in a resource-limited environment, competition would increase. Most situations in life are not lifeboat situations because danger is often not as evident, as for example with the issue of global climate change. Despite the tempting and simplistic metaphor of the lifeboat, it is not an established scientific fact that esprit de corps is favoured only by limit-situations where the survival of the group is at stake.

Abundance or scarcity themselves do not have an objective and universal definition and are partly psychological, cultural and political constructs. For nomads, for example, a scarcity of material possessions can be a form of spiritual abundance. In the 1930s, in a volume of his major *Study of History*, Arnold J. Toynbee came back to Ibn Khaldun and his tribal version of esprit de corps:

> Ibn Khaldun [. . .] believed that an *esprit de corps* (*asabiyah*) which was manifestly the psychological cement of all political communities was a monopoly of Nomad peoples in their pristine habitat [. . .] The rises and falls of empires were simply functions of the strength and weakness of the *esprit de corps* of Nomad empire-builders.[97]

References to the old mystique of *asabiyah* continued to interpret esprit de corps as a collective *je-ne-sais-quoi* in which small-scale tribalism was related to large-scale nationalism and even imperialism. According to such views, esprit de corps was the very engine of history, the way through which history was made at least until the twentieth century in androcentric societies. A small motivated group could change the face of world history.

How could esprit de corps be an important ingredient towards civilisational politics? Olaf Stapledon's popular *Last and First Men*, a British science-fiction novel first published in 1931, mused on the idea of a consciousness composed of many telepathically linked individuals, called the 'group-mind':

> The designers of our species set out to produce a being that might be capable of an order of mentality higher than their own. The only possibility of doing so lay in planning a great increase of brain organization. But they knew that the brain of an individual being could not safely be allowed to exceed a certain weight. They therefore sought to produce the new order of mentality in a system of distinct and specialized brains held in 'telepathic' unity by means of ethereal radiation [. . .] There is always in the mind of each member a very special loyalty toward the whole group, a peculiar sexually toned esprit de corps unparalleled in other species.[98]

The fact that sexuality replaced the idea of sentiment gave a peculiar tonality to the idea of the hive mind. This eroticisation of esprit de corps was quite new in the genealogy of the Gallicism, and was a result of the recent invention of psychoanalysis. Stapledon was an avid reader of Freud.[99] The author of *Totem and Taboo* was known for suggesting that elements of homosexuality or sexual jealousy could be collectively instrumental in male-driven coteries.

Eroticism apart, could esprit de corps be a form of collective telepathy? Or was the idea of a hive mind an intellectualist myth with implicit origins in the eighteenth-century notion of esprit *du* corps? Could groups really have a character? In 1949, the British analytic philosopher Gilbert Ryle advised abandoning any conception of mind as a spirit independent of embodied practices. Any attempt to speak of *esprit* as located in a form of soul that could cause the body to move was, according to Ryle, a logical fallacy, a category mistake, a manifestation of the Cartesian dogma of the 'ghost in the machine':

> A foreigner watching his first game of cricket learns what are the functions of the bowlers, the batsmen, the fielders, the umpires and the scorers. He then says 'But there is no one left on the field to contribute the famous element of team-spirit. I see who does the bowling, the batting and the wicket-keeping; but I do not see whose role it is to exercise *esprit de corps*' [. . .] Certainly exhibiting team-spirit is not the same thing as bowling or catching, but nor is it a third thing such that we can say that the bowler first bowls *and* then exhibits team-spirit or that a fielder is at a given moment *either* catching *or* displaying *esprit de corps*.[100]

In his parable Ryle did not mention the captain, although it could be argued that the latter's main function was indeed to foster esprit de corps. Ryle did not deny that esprit de corps could be exhibited by bodies in action, but he insisted that it was just a way of doing things with a certain care, enthusiasm or goodwill, manifested by each individual in their acts: the feeling of ensemblance created by esprit de corps was 'roughly the keenness with which each of the special tasks is performed'.[101] Yet the political dimension was left unnoticed in Ryle's influential text: the assimilation of esprit de corps with the reductive idea of *team spirit* was unaware of the historical depoliticisation of the phrase. This is an example of the limits of analytic philosophy when it neglects to historicise its concepts. Looking at team spirit in order to understand esprit de corps is like looking at a lamp to understand light.

Sociologists were less keen to forget about politics. In the years after the Second World War, the journal *Social Forces*, published by Oxford University Press, presented a theory of political processes in which esprit de corps was a key factor:

> The effort to develop *esprit de corps* is especially important. Leaders who desire to intensify rapport as a means of transforming a mass of individuals into a psychological and/or acting crowd will employ *esprit de corps* as a means of social control. That is, they will foster it as a way of organizing and integrating loyalty to the movement – as a way of making people feel that they belong together and are identified with and engaged in a common undertaking. It is at once evident that *esprit de corps* is very necessary as a means of developing unity and solidarity in a movement [. . .] *Esprit de corps* must be buttressed by devices designed to develop group morale and ideology if disintegration is to be avoided.[102]

This speech act on social control is an interesting case in which discourse and historical impact are intertwined: the American author, Rex D. Hopper, was not only the 'head of the sociology programme at Brooklyn College', he was also 'specialized in Latin American area studies, travelling to that region on numerous occasions to lecture and conduct research. Hopper had a deep interest in revolution and its scientific management.'[103] In 1956, the US Pentagon chose him to be one of the directors of SORO (the Special Operations Research Office). There he would be the director of 'Project Camelot', intended to 'devise procedures for assessing the potential for internal war within national societies', and 'identify with increased degrees of confidence those actions which a government might take to relieve conditions which are accessed as giving rise to a potential for internal war'.[104] The USA, inspired by this Pentagon-driven research, intervened with counter-insurgency command operations in the affairs of nations such as Cuba, Guatemala, Chile, the Dominican Republic and Brazil.[105] Hopper and the Pentagon thought ideology and national politics could be manipulated with the help of esprit de corps, understood as an embodied web of belief: 'The ideology of a movement consists in a body of doctrines, beliefs, and myths which provide direction and the ability to withstand the opposition of out-groups.'[106] Indisputably, the antagonistic idea of being *in or out* is a recurrent theme in the history of esprit de corps – it was and still is a seductive trope for the 'paranoid style in American politics'.[107]

This idea of an inner group versus outer groups can also be related to the ethics of solidarity. It is not uncommon in the last one hundred years to observe an 'emphasis laid by *Ethics* upon solidarity, *esprit de corps*, communal and social necessities'.[108] The discipline of applied ethics discussed the relationship between collective responsibility and esprit de corps, wondering if a lack of the latter was a 'moral fault' of the whole group: 'We may ascribe responsibility to the collective for its lack of esprit de corps while remaining unwilling to ascribe individual responsibility for this to any member or group of members.'[109] Collective responsibility is an interesting and controversial notion, especially in its legal implications: can groups be considered to possess moral agency in the same way that an individual does? This problem influences the way one considers, for example, corporate responsibility over societal issues.[110]

The relationship between ethics and esprit de corps in corporations can be considered from an existential perspective, as in a recent paper describing an institutionalised group of anti-money-laundering analysts:

> Organizational ethics appears in a *living corps* continuously generated/ regenerated through shared active life, or *esprit de corps*. This means that individuals are united in their subjective uniqueness as are the different organs of the body each holding their own full responsibility. In other words, a renewed sense of self appears, that of being 'one among others' because remarkably, solidarity in praxis prevents the 'I can' from falling into feelings of despair, paralysis and inaction ('I can no more'). In that sense, active and affective life is thus reconnected with its ontological source: 'Community is an underground layer and everyone drinks the same water at that source.'[111]

The authors of this article are French scholars attached to business schools, one being an alumnus of the École normale supérieure and another a former

French Air Force officer, two institutions known for their strong esprit de corps. The praise of esprit de corps is here lyrically blended with a philosophical and even metaphysical discourse on community. The final sentence in the previous quotation is taken from the French phenomenologist Michel Henry, who serves as an intellectual authority to defend an ambitious version of corporate spirit as spiritual community, all-the-more defensible because the corporation described in the text is pursuing a noble task, the fight against money laundering. At this point in our study we can predict that in the future many French authors will espouse the Anglo-Saxon optimism about esprit de corps. The Enlightenment critique of esprit de corps was slowly lost in translation, and, as a result of a feedback loop, it could also be slowly lost in the donor language if we do not remain sympathetically vigilant regarding our fabulations of belongingness, as we can be about preposterous celebrations of individualism.

The Management of Men: Corporate and Managerial Discourse

The enthusiastic articulation of the phrase 'esprit de corps' in business and managerial discourse had a major influence on global corporate culture. As early as 1906, an American marketing magazine claimed:

> The very life of a corporation depends upon the esprit de corps which its chief officers impart to the rank and file of the organization. [The chief officer] should understand how to impart enthusiasm to his salesmen and to keep alive the esprit de corps.[112]

Androcentric military denotations were manifest in the praise of chiefs and 'officers'. As in the US army, the main concern was efficiency:

> *Esprit de corps is engendered* by two motives [. . .] the desire to perform efficient service to one's group, and the desire to receive appreciation. If, as it has always been recognized, *esprit de corps* is an enormous power binding associated individuals closely to each other and to the organization, and if the desire to do and the 'honor-motive' are the two great motor-activities leading to *esprit de corps*, then those two motives should be planted and stimulated in the microcosm of every organization as valuable aides to their effective administration.[113]

The idea of efficient service *to one's group* rather than to the outside user or client suggested that inner discipline and internal commitment was as important as customer satisfaction. It is a neglected aspect of capitalism that its major challenge is not only selling products but also – and perhaps even more – employee retention, especially in the last decades.

In 1921, *The Management of Men: A Handbook on the Systematic Development of Morale and the Control of Human Behavior* was widely distributed via a mainstream New York publisher. In it, 'esprit de corps' appeared no less than 43 times. It was defined as 'a mental state which represents the resultant of all forces making for cohesion of an organization. It is as necessary to commercial success as it is to military efficiency.'[114] The idea of a mental state confirmed that esprit de corps was perceived as a cognitive device, a way of generating obedience or internalised discipline that ought to be more efficient than orders, the latter being less and less accepted by the democratic individual. Contrary to slavery, the device of esprit de corps recognised that each member had a personal mind.

Still, the goal was to generate consent rather than critical thinking. The author of the book, Edward Lyman Munson, a Doctor in Medicine from Yale University, had also served as lieutenant in the Medical Army Corps, in which he was assigned to organise the Morale Section, 'a branch unprecedented in the United States Army'.[115] For Munson, esprit de corps, the core of 'morale', was related to our natural gregarious instinct, a flock-like manifestation of sociality that was to be methodically and ideologically enhanced – inspirationally rather than violently – for the sake of efficiency, order and obedience:

> Man is essentially a gregarious animal, although his gregariousness does not necessarily imply sociability, as the isolation of a stranger in a large community testifies [. . .] With many people, the mere presence of others adds to the enjoyment of any recreation. An inference is to use this instinct in promoting interest in mass games and contests, as well as for the exaltation of the group in promoting esprit de corps [. . .] Inspirational methods are those which tend to dramatize and idealize for the man the things he is doing or will be expected to do. They make him feel not an isolated unit but part of a great organization and plan. Thus parades, ceremonies, group singing and similar functions arouse the herd instinct and esprit de corps and glorify the humble part of the individual in that of an impressive whole. So, too, addresses and other methods for the creation of ideals serve the purpose.[116]

As a control technique, the fostering of corporate esprit de corps was meant to be a manipulation of natural existing tendencies. Collective inspiration was not fully spontaneous and had to be partly engineered in order to create an effective semblance of totality. The mental state was also an emotional state of conditioning: 'When esprit de corps is good, it furnishes one of the strongest appeals toward desired behaviour.'[117]

It was not enough to sublimate the instinct of gregariousness to produce esprit de corps. 'Enthusiasm' was to be nurtured as a synonym of 'God striving within us'.[118] This was not only an appeal to the Greek etymology of enthusiasm (being possessed by a god), it was also an epic discourse: enthusiasm had, since the historical French musketeers, been associated with esprit de corps as a joyful élan and drive serving a supposed higher cause. Reference to the now mythical musketeers was made obvious in The Management of Men:

> Where a high degree of esprit de corps exists in an organization, an appreciation of its high quality remains long after the efforts and difficulties that have been through are forgotten [. . .] The highest type of morale is found

where each man is so imbued with the spirit of his organization that he comes to believe that his own interest and those of his company are identical. An essential to esprit is living up to the motto 'All for one and one for all.'[119]

The pragmatic goal behind the storytelling was to limit employee turnover, people spending only one or two years in the corporation and then moving on. To prevent this, the focus was not factual, that is, actually creating attractive working conditions, such as high salaries and responsibility, but rather creating a belief, a corporate myth.

Munson revived more or less consciously the French alchemical origin of the expression *esprit de* in suggesting that esprit de corps was a 'sublimation'.[120] Sublimation was connected to esprit de corps as 'the sense of strength and pride which comes from feeling oneself a part of a distinguished and efficient organ-ization of splendid traditions, engaged in a noble work'.[121] Gregariousness and sublimation needed to be managed and articulated in hierarchical fashion: 'Esprit de corps is a quality developed by the commander and transmitted through subordinates until it pervades the mass.'[122] The leader ought to stimulate a form of admiring emulation, as if by contamination: 'Practical psychologists recognize the influence of contagion as of first importance in creating "a common mind to a common end".'[123] To propagate the fire of esprit de corps, direct violence was discouraged: the manager had to possess a mysterious capacity to be loved and followed, called the 'human touch'.[124]

Echoing American military discourse, theorists of management compared cor-porate esprit de corps to a form of vitalism: 'The agency by which the administra-tive system is vitalized [. . .] is *esprit de corps*.'[125] Organismic views of organisations and teamwork were common in English management discourses.[126] Most authors distinguished corporate esprit de corps from trade unionism or socialism. The former, it was advised, should not be 'transmuted' into 'trade-union' spirit.[127] It had to be controlled by leaders and chiefs. Corporate and business discourse was constructed as a continuation of politics and war by other means.

The convenient aspect of esprit de corps in terms of rhetorical appeal consists in the fact that its military roots are softened but not erased by its emotional appeal to solidarity. Emotional consent was achieved in bodies and not only in brains:

> The control of society over individuals is not only by consciousness or ideology, but also by the body and with the body. For capitalist society, it was biopolitics that mattered most, the biological, the somatic, the corporeal.[128]

Incorporated bodies seemed to perform better when meta-military. This approach we call *the way of Hilton*.

Thirty-eight years before the cover of *Time* magazine bestowed upon him the title of 'Innkeeper to the World',[129] Conrad Nicholson Hilton invested over a million dollars to build the first hotel that bore his name in Dallas. This grand investment was made possible thanks to the very profitable exploitation, since

1919, of the Mobley Hotel, Hilton's first hosting business, a two-floor brick build-ing of forty small rooms located near the train station in Cisco, at the epicentre of the Texas oil boom. In *Be My Guest*, his autobiography, Hilton remembered that around 1920, in the first stages of his career, he told his partner Drown, a former banker, about two original ideas that would become his lifelong business principles. Hilton's first principle was to make every inch of space as profitable as possible, for example by locating shops or newsstands in the lobbies. The second principle was 'esprit de corps':

> 'I know something that would make us a better hotel – and eventually more money,' I told Drown. '*Esprit de corps*.'
> 'I'm all for it,' said Drown. 'How do you get it?'
> 'Same way we got it in the Army,' I said. 'Pride plus incentive. Wages won't do all the job. We had to sell the idea that our men belonged to the best durn outfit in the A.E.F and they were the ones who made it that way.'
> I grant that our twenty-odd employees were stunned when I assembled them for our first pep talk. They liked the attention, however, and they were very pleased to hear that Mr. Drown and myself, while able to front for them at the bank and in the lobby, were completely at their mercy once a guest got beyond the front desk. 'You're the only ones who can give smiling service,' I said. 'Clean rooms, spotless halls, plenty of fresh soap and linen. Ninety per cent of the Mobley's reputation is in your hands. You get steady jobs, good money, pay raises, *if* Cisco means the Mobley to travellers. It's up to you.'
> Self-interest plus pride added up to increased efficiency and we simply blos-somed with *esprit de corps*.[130]

The AEF were the American Expeditionary Forces mobilised at the end of the First World War to fight alongside French and British troops against the German Empire, in which Second Lieutenant Conrad Hilton served two years in the 304th Labor Battalion. Esprit de corps, according to Hilton, was a military-inspired recipe that made each employee responsible for the commercial war against com-petitors. It could involve financial bonuses based on results, but more importantly it suggested that each worker, regardless of the complexity of their task, was made to feel like a warrior in battles won or lost. Regular pep talks, preferably uttered by a general officer, were intended to build sacrificial enthusiasm and generate full commitment and fervent loyalty. The conquering destiny of the firm became a grand imperialist narrative. Employees needed to feel constantly *mobilised*. The capitalist imperative of 'total mobilisation', reactivated today via digital addic-tions, in which having a smartphone in your hand means 'being in the hands of the world',[131] was identified in 1930 by the German essayist Ernst Jünger as the new mode of 'organizational thinking' in 'the age of masses and machines', in which 'each individual life' is forced into progress as a 'war of workers'.[132]

'Esprit de corps', a buzzword of business discourse, is today not only a catchphrase – it has become a global incantation in which capitalism is seen as total war. Michael Feuer, a celebrated American entrepreneur, founder of the large retail chain OfficeMax and author of *The Benevolent Dictator: Empower Your Employees, Build Your Business, and Outwit the Competition*,[133] recently published an article on 'How to create esprit de corps in your organization':

> The French term 'esprit de corps' is used to express a sense of unity, common interest and purpose, as developed among associates in a task, cause or enterprise. Sports teams and the military adopt the sometimes-overused cliché, 'One for all and all for one.' 'Semper Fi' is the Marine Corps' motto for 'always faithful.' We commonly hear, 'We're only as strong as our weakest link.' However, the real test of team-building and motivational sayings is that they are good only when they move from an HR/PR [Human Resources/ Public Relations] catchphrase to a way of doing business – every day [. . .] In my enterprises, I constantly tell my colleagues that the title following each person's name boils down to these three critical words: 'Whatever it takes.'[134]

This rash sense of urgency and state of war created by a boss who sees himself as a dictator is intended to place workers in a psychological state of shock, in order get them to place their work at the centre of their material and emotional existence. The somewhat psychopathic and paranoid formula 'Whatever it takes' suggests that the end – financial supremacy – justifies the means – ruthless corporate war – thus depriving esprit de corps of any ethical content. Esprit de corps is meant to serve a form of *regimental capitalism*.

In contemporary regimental capitalism, all employees should be equal in dedication, stress and mobilisation. To make sure this spirit of regimentation is quotidian, the leader becomes a 'benevolent dictator', a capitalist version of the enlightened despot of the eighteenth century, like Frederick the Great, who considered his Prussian army to be a giant clock. In 2011, the Institute of Economic Affairs, a free-market think tank, observed that 'mercantilism is back with a vengeance'.[135] A recent *New York Times* article claimed that 'Mr. Trump is bringing mercantilism back.'[136] Playing with Clausewitz's famed formula about war, the French sociologist Raymond Aron famously described *Ancien Régime* commercial practice and mercantilism as the continuation of war by other means.[137] From a global perspective, the capitalism of esprit de corps seems compatible with a return to a mercantilist worldview consisting of protectionism and the exacerbation of the combat paradigm.

The young Hilton saw himself as a benevolent general and gave grandiloquent inspirational speeches in front of his 'stunned' employees.[138] Success is about selling the company to its employees, since many of them accept lower pay in order to do a job that they feel is uplifting: 'People decide to take a job with less pay because they trust the leadership in place [. . .] Feeling personally fulfilled is far more powerful than we think.'[139] In democratic regimes, individuals are more efficient when they believe that they are performing meaningful tasks of their own volition. Already in 1919, in what was called the most important book for the 'intelligent employer' since Taylor's *Scientific Management*,[140] goodwill was presented as yet another essence of esprit de corps:

Goodwill is reciprocity [. . .] It is a beneficial reciprocity of wills [. . .] It is that unknown factor pervading the business as a whole, which cannot be broken up and measured off in motions and parts of motions, for it is not science but personality. It is the unity of a living being which dies when dissected. And it is not even the personality of a single individual, it is that still more pervasive personality to which the responsive French give the name, *l'esprit de corps*, the spirit of brotherhood, the solidarity of free personalities.[141]

Once more, it seemed important to insist on free participation and free will, even if it implied a conceptual ambiguity: was freedom only accessed within the collective mind? Was access to a 'free personality' a reward for those who abandoned part of their individual personality to embrace their collective psyche? Esprit de corps was presented both as a personal 'will to believe' and the 'soul of a corporation'.[142] Less poetically, goodwill has since become a common procedural accounting category in commercial corporations, one that is defined as a mix of reputation, potential to succeed, value of the team; this goodwill is evaluated financially, albeit not without issues and problems because of its intangible quality.[143]

Some attempts were made to avoid the dramatisation of business as a continuation of war by other means. The emotional appeal of corporate esprit de corps can also be related to the idea of play and joy. Already in 1907, US activist Jane Addams considered that children were a model for peaceful work relations in factories:

Play is the great social stimulus, and it is the prime motive which unites children and draws them into comradeship [. . .] We have not as yet utilized this joy of association in relation to the system of factory production which is so preeminently one of large bodies of men working together for hours at a time. But there is no doubt that it would bring a new power into modern industry if the factory could avail itself of that *esprit de corps*, that triumphant buoyancy which the child experiences when he feels his complete identification with a social group.[144]

It is very rare to see esprit de corps equated with play and buoyancy, and perhaps it took a woman's perspective on androcentric behaviour to decipher its infantilism. However, as often in twentieth-century management discourse, it is difficult to say if the term 'men' designated all adult humans, or if playful esprit de corps was advocated here for men rather than women, despite the fact that in the first decade of the century it was estimated that the percentage of female workers in 'Manufacturing and Mechanical Pursuits' was close to 25 per cent (while over 10 per cent were working in 'Trade and Transportation').[145] The definition of esprit de corps as childlike buoyancy experienced in a near state of group fusion suggested that the workplace was like a kindergarten and its workers immature boys who could not – should not? – access critical thinking. A journalist from the *New York Times* described his visit to the Google offices, known for their playful atmosphere:

Mr. Newman, 27, who joined Google straight from Yale, and Brian Welle, a 'people analytics' manager who has a Ph.D. in industrial and organizational psychology from New York University, led me on a brisk and, at times, dizzying excursion through a labyrinth of play areas.[146]

The paradigm of war and the paradigm of play have in common the idea of competition and agonism. Regimental capitalism is more direct in its message: kill or be killed. 'Ludic capitalism'[147] is more labyrinthine and therefore more in tune with the neo-romantic ideology of self-development, a regime in which the more you search for yourself the more you lose yourself, eventually surrendering to the company that seems to sponsor your narcissism.

Playful team-spirit perceptions of esprit de corps are very distant from the French intellectual tradition that associated the phrase with subjugation and cognitive prisons. But if there is a genealogical link between joyful corporate esprit de corps and the 'expeditious gaiety'[148] that Louis XIII admired in the esprit de corps of the musketeers, then *joy at work* is not incompatible with regimental capitalism. In Nietzschean fashion, one could be joyful and dauntless, for example according to a hagiographic *History of the Metropolitan Museum of Art* published in 1913:

> We are deeply impressed by the conviction that we, as an institution, possessed something in the initial enthusiasm and joyous service of the founders, those dauntless men who worked for the Museum as if it were the personal possession of each man and its success depended upon him, that the esprit de corps of no staff of men trained in museum work, however faithful and capable, can ever equal.[149]

Idealised models of the past were nostalgically presented as superior to contemporary workers. In general, esprit de corps evolved from being considered *too present* in France in the eighteenth century to something that is *not present enough* today in the USA and the corporate global world.

The field of business studies shows in the last decades a certain fascination for esprit de corps. A handbook on organisation theory argued in 1980 that the term 'esprit de corps' was richer and more promising than 'morale'.[150] A manual on managerial supervision ascertained that 'a term that symbolizes good feelings toward an organization is esprit de corps'.[151] Consensus is growing among American specialists: 'Agencies that have a strong sense of their own identities and of their mission – often referred to as organizational zeal or esprit de corps – have an edge over those that do not.'[152] Esprit de corps is defined both as identity and as project, bridging the past and the future: it is the force that is expected to maintain a coherent, collective integrity over time, even if the members of the corporation change, an idea that is reminiscent of the function of esprit de corps in the *Ancien Régime* guilds and royal military corps.

In 1991, research on state capitalism analysed the French national aircraft industry:

Aircraft manufacturers made use of an additional method for promoting loyalty [. . .] the cultivation of an esprit de corps based on participating in the excitement of aviation [. . .] Employers wanted their workers to perform as a labor aristocracy. As one former *chef d'atelier* recalled, managers encouraged workers to acquire an *esprit d'équipe* (team spirit) and an *esprit de maison* (company pride) and in so doing to view themselves as a laboring elite immune to the hostility that workers commonly felt toward their bosses.[153]

The American researcher noticed the connection between esprit de corps and elitism. It was expected that prestige could be instrumentalised in a manner that was meant to prevent workers from being too critical towards the hierarchy. But in the last decades of twentieth-century France and within its social democratic state, esprit de corps was an 'additional method' among others: it went along with social care, job security and acceptable wages frequently negotiated with the trade unions.

In France, the USA or anywhere else, only in rare cases was esprit de corps encouraged in corporations as a system in which the business enterprise modelled itself on the structure of cooperative associations. In this rare *creative esprit de corps* mind-frame, each worker could be a shareholder with the right to vote on the company's decisions:

As a social group, the cooperative was characterized by a collective mind manifesting itself as an 'esprit de corps', 'atmosphere', or 'climate' [. . .] It was this spirit alone that would form a coherent social group. Each true cooperative, therefore, would have to appeal not just to rational thinking but also to feelings.[154]

This still rather utopian managerial mode was intended to foster a climate of both emotional and rational solidarity, beyond team spirit: 'The term esprit de corps means "solidarity", not "team spirit" as some believe.'[155]

Overall, the idea of solidarity at work was much less popular in twentieth-century American management than regimental team spirit. The dominant capitalist interest in esprit de corps, even today, is best captured in the following sentence, already quoted in our introduction: 'Esprit de corps is a concept powerful enough to make soldiers go into battle knowing their odds of survival are slim: think how powerful it can be if harnessed in your marketing organization!'[156] More often than not, a strong leadership correlated with stressful/playful submissiveness is the spectre haunting the phenomenon of corporate esprit de corps. It is not surprising that in late twentieth-century marketing studies, a 'clear chain of command' was given a 'most positive' high coefficient in attempts to measure esprit de corps, immediately followed by 'well-defined procedures'. In this study called *Fostering Esprit de Corps in Marketing*, the most negative factor – given the lowest coefficient of relationship to esprit de corps – was 'no close personal friendships' at work.[157] Now that *camaraderie* is no longer a communist leitmotif, we can expect to see it flourish in managerial discourse. 'We All Need Friends

at Work' is the title of an article in the *Harvard Business Review*, concerned with
the fact that, according to a Gallup study, '70% of workers' are 'not engaged at
work'.[158] The article represents the current state of the art of regimental capitalist
discourse:

> Close work friendships boost employee satisfaction by 50% and people with a
> best friend at work are seven times more likely to engage fully in their work.
> Camaraderie is more than just having fun, though. It is also about creating a
> common sense of purpose and the mentality that we are in-it together. Studies
> have shown that soldiers form strong bonds during missions in part because
> they believe in the purpose of the mission, rely on each other, and share the
> good and the bad as a team. In short, camaraderie promotes a group loyalty that
> results in a shared commitment to and discipline toward the work. Camaraderie
> at work can create 'esprit de corps', which includes mutual respect, sense of
> identity, and admiration to push for hard work and outcomes.[159]

Esprit de corps is expected to transform friendship into hard work, via the military model of camaraderie as ideal-type. The article concludes by recommending
sport and common physical competitions.

And indeed, esprit de corps was in the twentieth century a recurrent phrase
in sports commentaries, partly explaining why it is now often used in English
as a synonym of *team spirit*. There is no real difference between corporate esprit
de corps and esprit de corps in sport: both are influenced by military discourse.
In 1937, a 500-page handbook on basketball compared players to 'warriors',
and praised 'true athletic esprit de corps' in order to 'add dynamic punch to the
athletic days ahead and to match the courage of today with that of yesterday'.[160]
Comparisons between players or athletes and warriors or gladiators is a mediatic
lieu commun, whether or not different nations are competing against each other.

We are now at this stage of the evolution of esprit de corps: for most English-
speakers it means team camaraderie and effective *élan* within a group with a
relatively short-term goal. It also carries fantasies of belonging in a world of
ambivalent individualism and tribalism. Moreover, in an era of artificial intelligence, robots and virtual relationships, esprit de corps feels like a reassuring
remnant of the past, a comforting and anachronistic *human touch*, suggestive of
the fascination a spectator might feel for a synchronised Bollywood dance or a
choral flash mob. The idea that we can still do miraculous things together, in
assembly, seems to promise – who knows? – a re-enchantment of the world.

Notes

1. Edward Lyman Munson, Jr, *Leadership for American Army Leaders* (Washington, DC:
   The Infantry Journal, 1941), p. 69.
2. John Scofield Rowe, 'Practical Philosophies: Esprit de Corps', *The Monroe Monitor*,
   9 August 1929, p. 2.
3. Rowe, 'Practical Philosophies: Esprit de Corps', p. 2.

4. Roy Lubove, *The Struggle for Social Security, 1900–1935* (Pittsburgh: University of Pittsburgh Press, 1986), p. 213.

5. R. Robinson Rowe, 'Cashing in on Mathematics', *Crux Mathematicorum* 4.7 (1978), pp. 189–90.

6. Marian Welles Hornberger, 'A Tour of Discovery', *The Michigan Alumnus* 35.1 (1928), p. 21.

7. Lee Teng-Hwee, *Lee's Rhetoric and Composition* (Shanghai: Commercial Press, 1926), p. 47.

8. Lewis Yablonsky, *Gangsters: Fifty Years of Madness, Drugs, and Death on the Streets of America* (New York: New York University Press, 1997), p. 37.

9. Nesta H. Webster, *Secret Societies and Subversive Movements* (Escondido, CA: The Book Tree, 2000 [1924]), p. 294.

10. Lewis A. Coser, *The Functions of Social Conflict* (New York: Free Press, 1956), p. 179.

11. Grace Coyle, *Social Process in Organized Groups* (New York: Smith, 1930), p. 161.

12. John Frederick Charles Fuller, *Training Soldiers for War* (London: Rees, 1914), p. 66.

13. Bevir, *The Logic of the History of Ideas*, p. 265.

14. Tim Lautzenheiser, *The Art of Successful Teaching: A Blend of Content and Context* (Chicago: GIA Publications, 1992), p. 72.

15. Harry Elmer Barnes and Howard Paul Becker, *Social Lore from Thought to Science*, 2 vols (Washington, DC: Harren Press, 1952), vol. I, p. 274.

16. Benjamin Harrison, *Views of An Ex-President*, compiled by Mary Lord Harrison (Indianapolis: Bowen-Merril, 1901), p. 229.

17. Peter E. Traub, 'Esprit de corps – How It May Be Strengthened and Preserved in Our Army Under the Present Organization and Method of Promotion', *Journal of the Military Service Institution of the United States* 34 (1904), pp. 181–217 (p. 181).

18. Palante, 'L'esprit de corps', p. 136.

19. Traub, 'Esprit de corps', p. 182.

20. Ibid., p. 182.

21. Ibid., p. 182.

22. Ibid., p. 182.

23. Ibid., p. 183.

24. Betty Jean Craige, *American Patriotism in a Global Society* (Albany, NY: State University of New York Press, 1996), p. 15.

25. Traub, 'Esprit de corps', p. 184.

26. Alfred Thayer Mahan, *From Sail to Steam, Recollections of Naval Life* (New York: Harper and Brothers, 1907), p. 52.

27. Traub, 'Esprit de corps', p. 185.

28. Ibid., p. 197.

29. Ibid., p. 198.

30. Ibid., p. 213.

31. Mark H. Dunkelman, *Brothers One and All: Esprit de Corps in a Civil War Regiment* (Baton Rouge: Lousiana State University Press, 2006), p. 22.

32. Edwin Hutchins, *Cognition in the Wild* (Cambridge, MA: MIT Press, 1995), p. 10.

33. Brigadier-General M. F. Rimington and Major-General R. S. S. Baden-Powell, 'The Spirit of Cavalry Under Napoleon', *Journal of the Royal United Service Institution* 50.344 (1906), p. 1236.

34. Anonymous, *Le Spectateur militaire, recueil de science, d'art et d'histoire militaire* (Paris: Noirot, 1835), vol. 19, p. 187.

35. W. B. Barber, 'Esprit de corps and morale', *The Naval Review* 8.2 (1920), pp. 129–40 (p. 129).
36. Ibid., p. 130.
37. Ibid., p. 129.
38. Ibid., p. 130.
39. Ibid., p. 133.
40. Ibid., p. 133.
41. *Parliamentary Debates, Official Report* (London: HMSO, 1943), vol. 391, p. 421.
42. Corporal K. E., 'An A.C. Squadron in Libya', *The Royal Air Force Quarterly* 14–15 (1942), p. 200.
43. George H. Stein, *The Waffen SS: Hitler's Elite Guard at War, 1939–1945* (Ithaca: NY: Cornell University Press, 1984 [1966]), p. 92.
44. Ibid., p. 227.
45. Fletcher Durell, *Fundamental Sources of Efficiency* (Philadelphia: Lippincott, 1914), preface.
46. Lieutenant C. L. Hussey, 'Systematic Training of the Enlisted Personnel of the Navy', *Proceedings of the United States Naval Institute* 29.1/105 (1903), <https://www.usni.org/magazines/proceedings/1903/january/systematic-training-enlisted-personnel-navy> (accessed 19 September 2019).
47. Wayne Whittaker, 'Uncle Sam Picks an All-Star Team', *Popular Mechanics Magazine* 80.1 (1943), p. 51.
48. Romain Gary, 'The Anger That Turned Generals into Desperados', *Life*, 5 May 1961, pp. 26–7.
49. Ibid., p. 27.
50. Amir Horowitz, 'Ronald Dworkin's Group Fetishism', *Journal of Markets and Morality* 5.2 (2002), pp. 415–23 (p. 415).
51. 'le contour mystérieux d'un être unique'; Étienne Souriau, *Les différents modes d'existence* (Paris: Presses Universitaires de France, 2009 [1943]), p. 179.
52. Mike Chappel, *The British Army in the 1980s* (Oxford: Osprey, 1987), p. 3.
53. David Kertzer, *Ritual, Politics, and Power* (New Haven, CT: Yale University Press, 1988), p. 72.
54. Judith Butler, *Notes Towards a Performative Theory of Assembly* (Cambridge, MA: Harvard University Press, 2015), p. 83.
55. An Engineer, 'Letter to the Editor of the Spectator', *The Spectator*, 30 July 1904, p. 16.
56. The Editor, 'Answer to the Letter to the Editor of the Spectator', *The Spectator*, 30 July 1904, p. 16.
57. Frederick Haynes Newell, 'Address by the Chief Engineer', in *Proceedings of the First Conference of Engineers of the Reclamation Service* (Washington, DC: Government Printing Office, 1904), p. 23.
58. 'Mr. F. R. Upcott', in *Sessional Papers of the House of Commons, Inventory control record 1* (1904), vol. 64, p. 36.
59. Charles Jeffries, *The Colonial Empire and its Civil Service* (Cambridge: Cambridge University Press, 1938), p. 104.
60. Anderson, *Imagined Communities*, p. 67.
61. Walter E. Weyl, *The New Democracy* (New York: MacMillan, 1927 [1912]), p. 61.
62. Barber, 'Esprit de corps and morale', p. 135.
63. US Office of Civilian Defense, *The Control System of the Citizens' Defense Corps* (Washington, DC: OCD, 1942), p. 27.

64. Giorgio Agamben, *State of Exception*, trans. Kevin Attell (Chicago: University of Chicago Press, 2005), p. 60.

65. FEMA, Federal Emergency Management Agency, <https://www.fema.gov/media-library-data/20130726-1859-25045-9954/citizen_corps_guide_for_local_officials.pdf>, p. 6 (accessed 19 September 2019).

66. Michel Foucault, *'Il faut défendre la société': Cours au Collège de France, 1976* (Paris: Gallimard/Seuil, 1997), p. 28.

67. Ibid., p. 27.

68. Office of Civilian Defense, *The Control System*, p. 1.

69. Richard Wolin, 'Habermas and Hermeneutics: From *Verstehen* to *Lebenswelt*', in Thomas Szanto and Dermot Moran (eds), *Phenomenology of Sociality: Discovering the 'We'* (London: Routledge, 2016), pp. 56–69 (p. 63).

70. UNIDIR, *The Weaponization of Increasingly Autonomous Technologies: Considering How Meaningful Human Control Might Move the Discusssion Forward* (Geneva: United Nations Institute for Disarmament Research, 2014).

71. Friedrich Nietzsche, *On the Genealogy of Morals*, trans. Horace Barnett Samuel (New York: Boni and Liveright, 1913), p. 4.

72. '*Das Pathos der Vornehmheit und Distanz, wie gesagt, das dauernde und dominirende Gesammt- und Grundgefühl einer höheren herrschenden Art im Verhältniss zu einer niederen Art, zu einem "Unten" – das ist der Ursprung des Gegensatzes "gut" und "schlecht".*' Nietzsche, *Zur Genealogie der Moral* (Leipzig: Naumann, 1887), in Nietzsche Source, Digital Critical Edition, <http://www.nietzschesource.org/#eK GWB/GM> (accessed 19 September 2019).

73. *Oxford German-English Dictionary Online*, <http://www.oxforddictionaries.com>.

74. *Allgemeine Schweizerische Militärzeitung* (Basel: S.V., 1855), p. 135.

75. Johann Friedrich August Kinderling, *Über die Reinigkeit der Deutschen Sprache* (Berlin: Maurer, 1795), p. 129.

76. Stendhal, *The Red and the Black: A Chronicle of 1830*, trans. Horace Barnett Samuel (London: Kegan Paul, Trench, Trübner, 1916).

77. 'La conscience de la supériorité et de la distance, je le répète, le sentiment général, fondamental, durable et dominant d'une race supérieure et régnante . . .' Friedrich Nietzsche, *La Généalogie de la Morale*, trans. Henri Albert, in *Oeuvres complètes de Frédéric Nietzsche* (Paris: Mercure de France, 1900), vol. XI, p. 31.

78. Richard Whatmore, 'Enlightenment Political Philosophy', in George Klosko (ed.), *The Oxford Handbook of the History of Political Philosophy* (Oxford: Oxford University Press, 2011), pp. 296–318 (p. 301).

79. 'J'ai pensé cent fois avec effroi que si j'avais le malheur de remplir aujourd'hui tel emploi que je pense en certains pays, demain je serais presque inévitablement tyran, concussionnaire, destructeur du peuple, nuisible au prince, ennemi par état de toute humanité, de toute équité, de toute espèce de vertu.' Rousseau, *Émile ou de l'Éducation*, p. 173.

80. Max Whyte, 'The Uses and Abuses of Nietzsche in the Third Reich: Alfred Baeumler's "Heroic Realism"', *Journal of Contemporary History* 43.2 (2008), pp. 171–94.

81. Anna Wierzbicka, *Understanding Cultures through their Key Words* (Oxford: Oxford University Press, 1997), p. 272.

82. To understand how in French *esprit* could have little to do with *a spiritual realm*, see, for instance, Tore Frängsmyr, J. L. Heilbron and Robin E. Rider (eds), *The Quantifying Spirit in the Eighteenth Century* (Berkeley: University of California Press, 1990).

83. Lewis S. Pilcher, 'An Antitoxin for Medical Commercialism', *The Michigan Alumnus* 18 (1912), p. 321.

84. Eric R. Lybeck, 'Geist (Spirit): History of the Concept', in *International Encyclopedia of the Social and Behavioral Sciences* (Amsterdam: Elsevier, 2015), vol. IX, pp. 666–70 (p. 667).

85. Bergson, *Les deux sources*, p. 266.

86. Ibid., p. 241.

87. Eric F. Gardner and George G. Thompson, *Social Relations and Morale in Small Groups* (New York: Appleton-Century-Crofts, 1956), pp. 297–8.

88. Ibid., p. 298.

89. Thomas E. Boyt, Robert F. Lusch and Drue K. Schuler, 'Fostering Esprit de Corps in Marketing', *Marketing Management* 6.1 (1997), pp. 20–8.

90. Christopher Clague, 'Rule Obedience, Organizational Loyalty, and Economic Development', *Journal of Institutional and Theoretical Economics* 149.82 (1993), pp. 393–414.

91. Samuel Stouffer et al., *Studies in Social Psychology in World War II* (Princeton: Princeton University Press, 1950), vol. IV, p. 54.

92. Siu-Lun Wong, *Sociology and Socialism in Contemporary China* (London: Routledge, 1979), p. 28.

93. Daniel Harrison Kulp II, *Education Sociology* (New York: Longmans, Green, 1932), p. 300.

94. Neil J. MacKinnon and David R. Heise, *Self, Identity, and Social Institutions* (New York: Palgrave Macmillan, 2010).

95. Kulp, *Education Sociology*, p. 306.

96. Robert Wuthnow, *Meaning and Moral Order: Explorations in Cultural Analysis* (Berkeley: University of California Press, 1987), p. 167.

97. Arnold Joseph Toynbee, *A Study of History* (Oxford: Oxford University Press, 1935), vol. X, pp. 85–6.

98. Olaf Stapledon, *Last and First Men & Star Maker* (New York: Dover, 1968 [1931]), pp. 221, 222.

99. Robert Crossley, *Olaf Stapledon: Speaking for the Future* (Syracuse, NY: Syracuse University Press, 1994), p. 156.

100. Ryle, *The Concept of Mind*, pp. 5, 7

101. Ibid., p. 7.

102. Rex D. Hopper, 'The Revolutionary Process: A Frame of Reference for the Study of Revolutionary Movements', *Social Forces* 28.3 (1950), pp. 270–9 (pp. 274–5).

103. Mark Solovey, 'Project Camelot and the 1960s Epistemological Revolution: Rethinking the Politics-Patronage-Social Science Nexus', in Howard Lunde, Enrique S. Pumar and Ross Koppel (eds), *Perspectives in Social Research Methods and Analysis* (Thousand Oaks: Sage, 2010), pp. 166–94 (p. 177).

104. Irving Louis Horowitz, *The Rise and Fall of Project Camelot: Studies in the Relationship Between Social Science and Practical Politics* (Cambridge, MA: MIT Press, 1967), pp. 47–9.

105. William Blum, *Killing Hope: US Military and CIA Interventionism Since World War II* (Monroe, ME: Common Courage Press, 1995).

106. Hopper, 'The Revolutionary Process', p. 276.

107. Richard Hofstadter, *The Paranoid Style in American Politics and Other Essays* (Cambridge, MA: Harvard University Press, 1967).

108. Edward Bullough, *Aesthetics: Lectures and Essays* (Stanford: Stanford University Press, 1957), p. 81.

109. R. S. Downie, 'Collective Responsibility', in Larry May and Stacey Hoffman (eds), *Collective Responsibility: Five Decades of Debate in Theoretical and Applied Ethics* (Lanham, MD: Rowman and Littlefield, 1991), p. 48.

110. Bertram Gross, *Friendly Fascism: The New Face of Power in America* (Cambridge: South End Press, 1980), p. 206.

111. Mar Pérezts, Eric Faÿ and Sébastien Picard, 'Ethics, Embodied Life and *Esprit de Corps*: An Ethnographic Study with Anti-Money Laundering Analysts', *Organization* 22.2 (2015), pp. 217–34 (p. 231).

112. Forrest Crissey, 'Esprit de Corps', *Ad Sense* 20 (1906), p. 30.

113. William Hemphill Bell, 'Administration: Its Principles and Their Application', *Efficiency Society Journal* 2 (1917), pp. 75–6.

114. Edward Lyman Munson, *The Management of Men: A Handbook on the Systematic Development of Morale and the Control of Human Behavior* (New York: Holt, 1921), p. 435.

115. S. P. Lucia, 'Edward Lyman Munson', 1947, University of California: In Memoriam, Calisphere California Digital Library, <http://texts.cdlib.org/view?docId=hb1m3n-b0fr&doc.view=frames&chunk.id=div00007&toc.depth=1&toc.id=> (accessed 19 September 2019).

116. Munson, *The Management of Men*, pp. 61, 159.

117. Ibid., p. 161.

118. Ibid., p. 424.

119. Ibid., p. 437.

120. Ibid., p. 436.

121. Ibid., p. 435.

122. Ibid., p. 435.

123. Ibid., p. 436.

124. Barber, 'Esprit de corps and morale', p. 134.

125. Bell, 'Administration: Its Principles and Their Application', p. 75.

126. Tom Burns and G. M. Stalker, *The Management of Innovation* (London: Tavistock, 1961).

127. Ibid., p. 76.

128. 'Le contrôle de la société sur les individus ne s'effectue pas seulement par la conscience ou par l'idéologie, mais aussi dans le corps et avec le corps. Pour la société capitaliste, c'est le biopolitique qui importait avant tout, le biologique, le somatique, le corporel.' Michel Foucault, 'La naissance de la médecine sociale', in *Dits et Ecrits II, 1976–1988* (Paris: Gallimard, 2001), pp. 209–10.

129. Annabella Fick, 'Conrad Hilton, *Be My Guest* and American Popular Culture', *The European Journal of Life Writing* 2 (2013), pp. 18–34 (p. 20).

130. Conrad Nicholson Hilton, *Be My Guest* (New York: Simon and Schuster, 1957), pp. 114–15.

131. Maurizio Ferraris, 'Total Mobilization: Recording, Documentality, Normativity', *The Monist* 97.2 (2014), special issue 'Documentality', ed. M. Ferraris and L. Caffo, pp. 201–22 (p. 201).

132. Ernst Jünger, 'Total Mobilization', trans. Joel Golb and Richard Wolin, in Richard Wolin (ed.), *The Heidegger Controversy: A Critical Reader* (Cambridge, MA: MIT Press, 1993), pp. 128, 134.

133. Michael Feuer with Dustin S. Klein, *The Benevolent Dictator: Empower Your*

Employees, Build Your Business, and Outwit the Competition (Hoboken, NJ: Wiley, 2011).

134. Michael Feuer, 'How to Create Esprit de Corps in Your Organisation', *Smart Business Online*, 8 March 2013, <http://www.sbnonline.com/article/michael-feuer-how-to-create-esprit-de-corps-in-your-organization-2/> (accessed 19 September 2019).

135. Terry Arthur, 'Mercantilism is Back with a Vengeance', *Institute of Economic Affairs Blog*, 31 August 2011, <https://iea.org.uk/blog/mercantilism-is-back-with-a-vengeance> (accessed 19 September 2019).

136. Binyamin Applebaum, 'On Trade, Donald Trump Breaks With 200 Years of Economic Orthodoxy', *The New York Times*, 10 March 2016, <https://www.nytimes.com/2016/03/11/us/politics/-trade-donald-trump-breaks-200-years-economic-orthodoxy-mercantilism.html> (accessed 19 September 2019).

137. Raymond Aron, *Peace and War: A Theory of International Relations*, trans. Richard Howard and Annette Baker Fox (New Brunswick, NJ: Transaction, 2003), p. 253.

138. Hilton, *Be My Guest*, p. 114.

139. Martha C. White, '5 Reasons to Consider Actually Sticking with a Low-Paying Job', *Time*, 6 January 2014, <http://140.234.252.185/c/articles/93576129/5-reasons-consider-actually-sticking-low-paying-job> (accessed 19 September 2019).

140. Bruce E. Kaufman, *The Global Evolution of Industrial Relations* (New Delhi: Academic Foundation, 2006), p. 143.

141. John Rogers Commons, *Industrial Goodwill* (New York: McGraw-Hill, 1919), p. 20.

142. Ibid., p. 96.

143. Hugh P. Hugues, *Goodwill in Accounting: A History of the Issues and Problems* (Atlanta, GA: Georgia State University Press, 1982).

144. Jane Addams, *Newer Ideals of Peace* (New York: MacMillan, 1907), pp. 171–2.

145. Charles E. Persons, 'Women's Work and Wages in the United States', *The Quarterly Journal of Economics* 29.2 (1915), pp. 201–34 (p. 202).

146. James B. Stewart, 'Looking for a Lesson in Google's Perks', *The New York Times*, 15 March 2013, <http://www.nytimes.com/2013/03/16/business/at-google-a-place-to-work-and-play.html?_r=0&pagewanted=all> (accessed 19 September 2019).

147. Alexander R. Galloway, *The Interface Effect* (Cambridge: Polity, 2012), p. 26.

148. Saint-Foix, 'Les deux companies des Mousquetaires', pp. 304–32.

149. Winifred E. Howe, *A History of the Metropolitan Museum of Art* (New York: Metropolitan Museum of Art, 1913), pp. 183–4.

150. Richard Osborn, James G. Hunt and Lawrence R. Jauch, *Organization Theory: An Integrated Approach* (Hoboken, NJ: Wiley, 1980), p. 80.

151. Stan Kossen, *Supervision: A Practical Guide to First-Line Management* (New York: Harper and Row, 1981), p. 301.

152. Jeanne Nienaber-Clarke and Daniel McCool, *Staking Out the Terrain: Power Differentials Among Natural Resource Management Agencies* (Albany, NY: State University of New York Press, 1985), p. 8.

153. Herrick Chapman, *State Capitalism and Working-Class Radicalism in the French Aircraft Industry* (Berkeley: University of California Press, 1991), p. 54.

154. Holger Bonus, 'The Cooperative Association as a Business Enterprise. A Study in the Economics of Transactions', in G. Furubotn and Rudolf Richter (eds), *The New Institutional Economics* (Tübingen: Mohr, 1991), pp. 171–2.

155. Boyt, Lusch and Schuler, 'Fostering Esprit de Corps in Marketing', p. 21.

156. Ibid., p. 21.

157. Ibid., p. 23.

158. Gallup, *State of the American Workplace, 2010–2012*, <https://news.gallup.com/reports/178514/state-american-workplace.aspx> (accessed 19 September 2019).

159. Christine M. Riordan, 'We All Need Friends at Work', *Harvard Business Review*, 3 July 2013, <https://hbr.org/2013/07/we-all-need-friends-at-work> (accessed 19 September 2019).

160. Forrest Claire Allen, *Better Basketball: Technique, Tactics and Tales* (New York: MacGraw-Hill, 1937), p. 90.

Conclusion: Ensemblance

'Large issues within a small compass': Histosophy

I have demonstrated that esprit de corps is a very important historical, social and political notion, and I have offered arguments that allow us to understand why. To construct the present diachronic narrative, I have analysed transnational and translingual interdiscursive 'relics from the past that are available to us in the present',[1] systematically privileging primary sources that made explicit use of the Gallicism. Despite my philosophical sensibility, I was not trying to attain objective knowledge about an exemplary, essential and universal definition of esprit de corps. Conversely, neither was I assembling historical data for the sake of erudition, disconnected from their relevance to understanding our modernity and present epoch. In this sense, I echoed Foucault's intention to write a 'history of the present'.[2] I believe I have practised a specific combination of history and philosophy, a kind of intellectual history that could also be called *histosophy*, an interdiscursive approach that is correlated to what Foucault called genealogy or 'archaeology of knowledge'[3] and to the method of *Les mots et les choses*.[4] It is particularly adapted to a lateral approach to 'ideology' and an 'analysis of representations'.[5]

The possibility of a 'histosophy' defined as 'the art of surveying large issues within a small compass'[6] was alluded to three decades ago by the historian David Walker in the journal *Labour History*. Walker did not proceed to explore the promise of his throwaway remark, but he did mention that a histosophical approach could be 'a provocative introduction to a range of issues which others are [. . .] examining in more historically specific contexts'.[7] The phrase 'esprit de corps' was, in 2014, when I started to take notes towards the present book, a scholarly neglected 'small compass', a notion that was not considered to be a significant keyword of modernity. Here is what Walker answered from his office at Deakin University in Australia after I reminded him of his 'histosophy' coinage:

Having now returned from Peking University I have my books around me and perhaps that copy of *Labour History*. Your approach sounds an interesting one to me though I am not able to do what you have done. I did meet colleagues in China who were doing interesting work comparing editorial practices/vocabularies in key publications to discern cultural differences and commonalities. They did a great deal of word crunching. As someone who thinks of himself as a cultural historian the use of words and phrases over time strikes me as a very fruitful line of inquiry.[8]

Indeed, computer crunching and data mining were essential tools in my research, as I have explained in the article 'Big Data, Small Concepts: Histosophy as an Approach to *longue-durée* history', published in *Global Intellectual History*.[9]

On the one hand, too many philosophers, especially analytic philosophers, neglect to look at the social and cultural history of the notions they discuss, thus cultivating the illusion that concepts are a universal totality and that they can be conceived as depoliticised abstractions in a disembodied realm of pure intellect. I believe I have avoided as far as possible this kind of 'foundationalist' discourse of truth.[10] My chapters have contributed to strengthening the web of belief according to which 'ideas are social forces',[11] and to the understanding that 'the history of ideas is central to all the human sciences'.[12] More generally, ideas and notions are embodied in action and speech: 'human practices are always significant and cannot be understood independently of their "meaning"'.[13]

On the other hand, many historians and intellectual historians, chief among them Quentin Skinner, have tended until now to be more or less distrustful of a kind of transdiscursive history covering several centuries and regions of the world. True enough, specialists in the specific periods I have surveyed might demand more granularity in the description of synchronic contexts, which in the case of the genealogy of esprit de corps would demand a dozen volumes at least. Still, I hope I have proven that there can be an inspiring and careful way to follow the evolution of a notion – I am still reluctant to call esprit de corps a concept because of its fuzziness – over long periods and vast geographic zones, in a manner that is not a simple collection of random occurrences. Further research could include more nations across the globe and also domesticated synonyms in other languages than French or English. This again would imply several volumes, authors and years: I do encourage others to take on the challenge.

In developing 'a narrative that moves from object to object though time', I made progress 'through a process of criticising and comparing rival sets of theories', to achieve a 'holistic understanding', relating 'the various historical objects [. . .] to one another'.[14] I started my research without a theoretical or perspectival *a priori* in order to avoid any form of eisegesis and, if possible, allow the empirical collection of data to facilitate an objective interpretation. 'Objective interpretation' might sound like an oxymoron. We should still speak of interpretation because a complete avoidance of authorial subjectivity is probably a fiction, and a damaging one at that, in a century where even the so-called human sciences are being challenged by automation. The author of *Explaining Explanation*, the philosopher of science Lee McIntyre, wrote recently that:

Today, too much social research remains embarrassingly unrigorous. Not only are the methods sometimes poor, much more damning is the non-empirical attitude that lies behind them [. . .] The truth is that such questions are open to empirical study and it is possible for social science to study them scientifically. There are right and wrong answers to our questions about human behavior.[15]

The final sentence is, of course, a worrying self-contradictory claim, itself unevidenced. While I agree that we need to avoid any self-indulgent lack of rigour or complacent logorrhoea in academic presentations and writing, I don't believe we will succeed in universalising the quantitative scientific model and applying it conveniently to all human realities. The humanities and the social sciences need to continue to invent hybrid methods and philosophically-healthy research strategies, partly empirical but avoiding reductionism.

I would like to think that my work is not too distant from Bevir's optimistic ideal, expressed in *The Logic of the History of Ideas*: 'Although historians of ideas [. . .] construct narratives by postulating conditional and volitional connections between objects, their doing so does not constitute an imposition of subjective structures on to the past.'[16] I have tried to demonstrate that a systematic use of primary sources and a confrontation of differential discourses and transnational logics allow for the asymptotical possibility of approaching a form of veracity. The element of subjectivity present in any narrative, even if unconscious, can be partly neutralised via 'consistency', interdiscursivity, 'comparing rival webs of theories'[17] and, more precisely, in the case of esprit de corps, plural signifieds connected by the use of an invariable signifier.

Interdiscursivity, the interplay of discourses, is not only a formal exchange of worldviews between intellectuals and authors. It is also a social dynamic in which different embodied codes and subjects interact agonistically. Discourses and webs of belief are political. In the case of esprit de corps, it would be impoverishing the richness of the term to suppress its sociopolitical denotations in an attempt to think about collective intelligence in a *pure* analytical and abstract manner, as is often done today. Philosophy and history are intertwined in a crealectical process in which ideas and events mutually engender one another, without ever reaching the status of closed totality. The cosmos, according to process philosophers, is likely to be a creative flow in which wholeness is never fully achieved and completeness is a human convention. In fact, even science finds it hard to constitute a complete description of ensembles, and Gödel's theorem of incompleteness continues to be much discussed today. Because 'creal' multiplicity implies unity as its ontological opposite,[18] we may hypothesise that there is everywhere a unifying principle at work in conjunction with what Deleuze called the disparating principle.[19] However, the belief that wholes and ensembles are real and totally unified pertains to what the philosopher Alfred North Whitehead called 'the fallacy of misplaced concreteness'.[20] Coherent and unified human ensembles are a fabulation, a dynamic and performative ensemblance.

Is a General Theory of Esprit de Corps Possible?

This book has demonstrated via a careful and processual study of the phrase 'esprit de corps' that normative vocabularies are ideological, and the history of ideas is 'a style of political theorizing'.[21] While some might use the notion of esprit de corps today as an exotic cliché to express a form of team spirit, the notion remains polemical and politically relevant; the fact that nationalists have made attempts recently to revive it must be vigilantly monitored in the years to come. Now, some readers may still ask: could this book have been different, less historical and more theoretical?

In 2005, Jean Vauvilliers, a former professor at HEC – France's highest institution for business studies and economics, an elitist school of which I am an alumnus, often presented, along with the Polytéchnique, as a temple of esprit de corps – called for a general theory of esprit de corps in a nicely synthetic article worth translating here at length:

> We are not always aware of the need for esprit de corps, we do not understand its principles, its foundations, it is difficult to define the word [. . .] A *general theory* of esprit de corps relates to the theory of the social body, the theory of bureaucracy (and political power), the theory of *state duties*, the theory of order and disorder in any body, to the theory of action (what makes one act?), to the theory of conformity [*médiocrité*].[22]

The author then sketched seven principles that he believed could help to elaborate a formalised political theory of esprit de corps:

> *First principle*: legitimacy: we are within a system that is legitimate, which is about order [. . .] *Second principle*: duration: the esprit de corps is anchored in tradition, it is a form of control of time, we had predecessors, we will have *successors* [. . .] we must be worthy of our *predecessors*, and transmit the *inheritance* in good condition to the successors. *Third principle*: the community of views within a body [. . .] There is a way to view things, there are forms of thought, methods to conduct one's ideas, to regulate one's conduct, which are essentially 'common' and from which one should not deviate to avoid being faulty [. . .] *Fourth principle*: the distinction of what is *appropriate* and what is not [. . .] What is suitable is what is first of all consistent with the interest of the body [*corps*] [. . .] *Fifth principle* [. . .] each body has its own state duties, related to the *officium*, and the esprit de corps forces its members – in the general interest – to observe regularly, wisely, their state duties, and to respect the servitude they impose [. . .] *Sixth principle*: the regularity – or rather the *optimisation* – of career management; a certain security is conferred upon internal careers [. . .] which makes it possible to avoid disorderly ambitions, a source of conflicts and divisions, and *to control* the rebellious spirits or those who observe their duties badly [. . .] *Seventh principle*: solidarity. Inside the body, in principle, one must be tolerant, courteous, not to attack one's peers, not to engage in intrigue or

cabals [. . .] Vis-à-vis the outside world, the corps must be united, protect the members of the body who are in difficulty or who have committed mistakes (the corps is a system of assurance).[23]

These principles, which we have encountered separately in our previous chapters, are of course more empirical than scientific. The priority given to legitimacy seems pertinent, if subjective. Whether esprit de corps is described as a good or bad quality depends on one's perception of the legitimacy of the corps unit. In a capitalist society, the commercial corporation is a legitimate unit, for example. Where a perceived ensemble has not itself gained full legitimacy, or when its legitimacy is contested, its esprit might be subordinated to a wider one, for example the nation-state. Vauvilliers perpetuates the French tradition in connecting esprit de corps with a belief in a supervising nation-state, representing the general will. Social bodies can be allowed to develop a relative form of autonomy, but only in relation to a republican ideal of service: 'We serve the Republic, not the government.'[24]

Vauvilliers also notes that esprit de corps can be a politically risky 'police des esprits',[25] echoing d'Alembert's critique of esprit de système:

> Esprit de corps is frowned upon, often it has been strongly denounced [. . .] even the members of the bodies, when they speak freely, detail the misdeeds of esprit de corps, which ends up corrupting the judgment and encouraging the esprit de système (we see the world through a deforming prism) [. . .] First risk: the esprit de corps is based on fictions, creates an imaginary system: one believes one has an autonomous power, a particular mandate given by the social body, one tends to redefine the general interest from the corps' perspective [. . .] Second risk: the esprit de corps limits autonomy, the sense of responsibility, it is confining, it pushes towards conformism, it imposes blinkers, it maintains narrow-mindedness: the members of the body are no longer capable of initiative, they become specialised insects [. . .] a brilliant personality becomes dull, fearful, he becomes oblivious of how to think for himself [. . .] Third risk: esprit de corps defines codes of conduct and codes of thought [. . .] that become sooner or later obsolete [. . .] and we end up with a sort of calcification [. . .] The average [mediocre] member easily adopts the style, the outward appearances, the modes of reasoning, the language of the corps.[26]

These risks, which again we have encountered across our study, lead Vauvilliers to an intellectual aporia: 'Must we maintain – and develop – esprit de corps? It is an irresolvable question, everything varies depending on the times [. . .] A general theory is inevitably incomplete, unfinished.'[27] Hence the need for a genealogical and diachronic strategy, to let the various principles of esprit de corps emerge within a process of temporal, societal and transnational manifestations.

A perspective on esprit de corps needs to encompass a creative dialectic between social autonomy and social automatism, although, etymologically speaking, heteromatism would perhaps be a more convenient term to designate subordination and subservience, as noted by Bruno Latour: 'There is nothing more "heteromaton" than an automaton.'[28] We have seen that if esprit de corps is often about normalisation, uniformity and describes a *heteromatisation* of humans, it can also and conversely be about collective co-creation and a sociopolitical aspiration to autonomy. When modern forms of universalism and globalisation generate standardised identities without nurturing the capacity for regeneration, reinvention, autonomy and pluralism, they produce indeed a calcified world of social heteromata who might still *fabulate* or believe that they are free.

If a form of standardised, conformative and meta-military competition becomes ubiquitous as it sometimes seems to be in capitalist societies, on the other hand a sense of co-creative discipline as singular craft and care – which I agree with Deleuze and Guattari is another meaning of esprit de corps – might be a rampart of solidarity against deskilling or dispirited economic imperatives.[29] Corporate and business discourse was often constructed in the twentieth century with a meta-military connotation of *continuation of war by other means*, or, as André Maurois put it: 'Business is a mixture of war and sport.'[30] In this context, the rhetorical appeal of the multifaceted phrase 'esprit de corps' consists in the fact that its military combative roots are softened but not erased by its camaraderie and solidarity connotations. One could also argue that the contemporary dominant global meaning (esprit de corps as a form of combative team spirit) is a return to the original French military meaning, implying an enthusiastic collective *élan*. The evolution of esprit de corps would then be a circular revolution: the now dominant use would have returned to its supposedly apolitical point of origin, after a political, intellectualist and polemical journey of three centuries. But history never returns to an exact point performed in the past: rather than circles, it performs spirals of combined novelty and regression. About esprit de corps, there is something obviously old-fashioned, but there is also something perpetually new: the asymptotic ideal of becoming one.

Drive, Discipline, Duty and Distinction: Four Scales of Esprit de Corps?

We now understand why caution about rigid theorisation is advisable in sociopolitical matters. Nevertheless, heuristic typologies are possible, if easily criticisable. A diachronic comparison of esprit de corps discourses has allowed us to distinguish at least four evaluative perspectives on the notion, identified in the previous chapters as *conformative*, *autonomist*, *universalist* and *creative*, corresponding to the four core values of duty, discipline, distinction and drive.

The first aspect of esprit de corps in organised groups I called *conformative*. Conformative collectives exhibit strong internal conformity and an enclosed form of solidarity. Entering or exiting the group is likely to be a difficult process, while most members tend to obey the strict ethos of this type of group, mainly according to the central value of *duty*. Historically, this is typical of religiously grounded communities or armies, but traditional families or rigid institutions could qualify, for example hospitals. In such groups, hierarchy is an important relational mode: decision making relies on hierarchical structures of power and on a sustained uniformity.[31] A recurrent mode of control in such a group is coercion.

The second aspect of esprit de corps groups I have called *autonomist*. Its core value is discipline as craft: skill, knowledge, art, know-how, empathetic expertise, careful practice. Its main mode of control or cohesion is what we could call *co-excellence*. Autonomist esprit de corps is typical of communities of practice, such as labour guilds, corporations based on craftsmanship, some research clusters or gender communities, or other groups that exhibit forms of peer-equality. One of the most beautiful and effectual examples of autonomist esprit de corps is the Nicolas Bourbaki Group, a twentieth-century secret society of mathematicians, the members of which successfully renounced their individual names for the sake of knowledge.[32]

The third aspect we have encountered, often applied to nation-state levels of esprit de corps, can be called *universalist*. It is a construct that leans towards legal standards, officialised forms of distinction, an organised division of labour and an organicist form of solidarity. Distinction and service are interconnected core values in universalistic ensembles. A fourth perspective on esprit de corps can be called *creative*. Its main agentic mode is drive, shared enthusiasm, zeal, *élan*, aspiration, and it is often – but not always – related to smaller or emerging groups.

This schematic division of social cohesive groups into four aspects should be read as dynamic or homothetic, with differently sized circles of identity that can partly intersect. Even if some groups in theory can be dominated by one of the values or dimensions, we are more likely to find, in practice, intertwined examples of creative, conformative, autonomist and universalist esprit de corps. Such a typology is to be read as an example of how perhaps a study of varieties of esprit de corps could help us to introduce more pluralism into our perception of human ensembles.[33] This is especially important if digital automation reaches a ubiquitous momentum, redefining our identities and modes of belonging in the context of techno-social systems. Inspired by the repetitive historical metaphors of human groups as social machines, I developed this perspective in a line of inquiry that I have taken to calling *anthrobotics*.[34] The genealogy of esprit de corps suggests that individual well-being is highly correlated to the question of belonging, but further research needs to be done in anthrobotic belonging and what one could call *well-belonging*.

The Contingency of Ensembles: Six Questions Raised and Answered

I will now briefly re-examine six important questions that have emerged in the course of this book and attempt for each of them a concise answer. Is esprit de corps an essentially contested concept? Is esprit de corps a leader-independent phenomenon? If the phrase 'esprit de corps' was so successful in English, was it because the phenomenon of esprit de corps did not exist in English-speaking cultures before the French signifier was adopted? Has there been an evolution from 'esprit *du* corps' designating the specific spirit of a group, to a notion of 'esprit *de* corps' as a standardised global quality of team spirit? Is esprit de corps an androcentric notion? What is the relevance of the notion of esprit de corps in contemporary debates on communitarianism, multiculturalism and universalism?

First question: is esprit de corps an 'essentially contested concept'?[35] This well-known definition of concepts as tools in argumentative combats was clearly pertinent and rightfully influential in late twentieth-century research. As I have pointed several times, I am reluctant to call a *concept* any idea that is multifarious, indistinct and unresolved. I believe the definitions of esprit de corps are contested because esprit de corps is not a concept but a notion, contrary to *bicycle* or *photosynthesis*. Human history is notional rather than conceptual. Gallie's use of the term 'essentially' means, for example, that polemics about the meaning of esprit de corps imply that each side will maintain that they know what the unique essence of the concept is: solidarity, discipline, fear, cowardice, love, loyalty, fidelity, subjugation, truth, etc. I would rather speak of *essentialising polemical notions*. Esprit de corps is indeed an essentialising polemical notion.

Second question: is esprit de corps a leader-independent phenomenon? We have learned from the intellectual history of the notion that it is more often than not associated with ideas of hierarchy and subordination. The phenomenon of esprit de corps seems to imply a form of leadership, even if the leader is not necessarily embodied by a single human: abstract values or internalised imperatives and norms can function as an idealised master. Human sublimation means to serve something grander than the individual ego. Experience shows that even in highly horizontal groups with minimal hierarchy and maximal distributed power, such as the aforementioned Bourbaki Group, a few individuals emerge who embody the truth of the group in a more evident manner. They gain their authority from the fact that they devote themselves to *subjectivating* the collective body, like Spartacus leading the slaves towards freedom.

Among the spheres of ideas that are more likely to function historically as *strange attractors* or 'truth-procedures' of group fidelity, the philosopher Alain Badiou distinguishes love, science, art and politics.[36] A close reader of Badiou, Quentin Meillassoux, explains that:

> These truths, moreover, cannot exist in a Heaven of Ideas: they are the result of an undecidable event and of a fidelity of subjects that attempt to investigate their world in light of it [. . .] This appearance of truth in a world, Badiou calls a *subject-body*: a mode of appearance in a world determined by a [usually collective] subject that has developed a fidelity to the trace of an event [. . .] The fact that the subjectivated body is organised also means that this body is essentially 'split', 'crossed out', i.e. that it is never totally adapted to the actual situation.[37]

If the ground of the Real is a Creal, that is, a virtual stream of infinite multiplicities, real unity is but a horizon and group oneness not an essence, but still something that matters and that can count as one for the purposes of a faithful realisation. Human ensembles are never entities that would be essentially one; they are always open, cracked, fissured along what Deleuze called a molecular line: 'The fissure of the molecular line seems to be the human compromise between the whirl of the undifferentiated and the social mechanisms.'[38] Ensembles of esprit de corps are a historical and crealectical experience of becoming one and multiple in various modes of appearance: an *ensemblance*.

Third question: if the phrase 'esprit de corps' was so successful and without a satisfactory synonym in English, was it because the phenomenon of esprit de corps did not exist in English-speaking cultures before the French signifier was adopted? This question presupposes that we use words to describe existing realities, a presupposition that was vaguely disputed by Benjamin Constant: 'The word illusion is not found in any ancient language, because a word is created only when the thing no longer exists.'[39] The idea that our abstract political or philosophical notions appear when a concrete reality is lost is intriguing. Perhaps the notion of esprit de corps appeared in the eighteenth century in French and English when the possibility of deep social-body cohesion, grounded in Catholicism and strong class divides, was vanishing, as suggested by Tocqueville. The pejorative view of esprit de corps invented by the *Philosophes* was clearly one in which the *corps* was seen as a quasi-dead *corpse*, as opposed to the vitality of nature, reason and a republic of free citizens.

It is worth noting here that the English language has developed its own suggestive words to describe the pejorative aspects of esprit de corps. Adam Smith spoke of 'corporation spirit' in terms that echoed the French eighteenth-century critique:

> The usual corporation spirit, whenever the law does not restrain it, prevails in all regulated companies. When they have been allowed to act according to their natural genius, they have always, in order to confine the competition to as small a number of persons as possible, endeavored to subject the trade to many burdensome regulations [. . .] Members [. . .] are likely to make a common cause, to be all very indulgent to one another, and every man to consent that his neighbor may neglect his duty, provided he himself is allowed to neglect his own.[40]

A more recent influential coinage in tune with the French critical views of esprit de corps is of course 'groupthink'. It was proposed by Irving Janis, a social psychologist at Yale University, who was inspired by 'the words in the newspeak vocabulary George Orwell used in his dismaying world of *1984*':[41]

> Groupthink involves non-deliberate suppression of critical thoughts as a result of internalization of the group's norms [. . .] The more amiability and esprit de corps there is among the members of a policy-making group, the greater the danger that independent critical thinking will be replaced by groupthink, which is likely to result in irrational and dehumanizing actions directed against outgroups.[42]

Interestingly, this article suggested that 'esprit de corps' and 'groupthink' were highly correlated but not equivalent, probably because esprit de corps was by 1971, in the USA, as we have seen, generally felt to be a positive and desirable quality. If the present genealogy of esprit de corps possesses any practical quality, let it be this: whenever capitalist or nationalist discourse today calls for more esprit de corps, the English reader may now remember that this might mean alienation, *groupthink* and *esprit de corpse*.

Fourth question: has there been, over the last three centuries, an evolution from 'esprit *du* corps' designating the specific spirit of a group – each society, class or caste nurturing a different character or style – to a notion of 'esprit *de* corps' as a standardised global quality of body cohesion or team spirit? This is indeed, as is now evident, the evolution of the phrase in the new lingua franca. As the references to esprit de corps were globalised in English, the phrase was progressively reduced to a laudatory, general, essentialising quality, often applied indifferently to any type of group, as if all forms of group cohesion were equivalent.

Fifth question: is esprit de corps an androcentric notion? This has been mostly true until recently. Over the last hundred years, even though women have been a growing part of the corporate workforce and more recently of the military, they have rarely been referred to in esprit de corps discourses, perhaps because of 'a pervasive tendency to see men as representative of categories that technically should include women as much as men'.[43] Today, however, mentions of a female esprit de corps have become a possibility, as seen for instance in the *Wall Street Journal* in 2015, apropos a popular Hollywood movie: 'Funny, likeable, and energetic, Pitch Perfect was a surprise hit, thanks to its catchy tunes and girl power esprit de corps.'[44]

Other signifiers might have been preferred in the past to designate female forms of solidarity. The French studies specialist Marilyn Schuster, in her account of 'lesbian resistance' in the USA, speaks of 'passionate communities'.[45] She also suggests that each historian, 'whether straight or queer', and despite the academic ethos of objectivity, might manifest in his or her writing a form of unconscious esprit de corps and 'group or community identity'.[46] Moreover, the androcentric habitus of esprit de corps discourses might be at work in the very digitisation of 'publicly available documents (magazines, newspapers, written documents)', the partiality of which might underestimate gynocentric 'social scripts'.[47] Who digitises what? Since researchers, including myself, often use Google's plethoric sources, it is worth noting that nearly 70 per cent of Google's employees were male when I started my research for this book.[48] Ironically, an opinion article published in *The Economist* about Silicon Valley's digital companies claims that 'the Valley's testosterone-infused culture needs to change so as to address' its 'sexism', 'without losing the esprit de corps that seems essential to its success'.[49] Contrary to what this article suggests, I don't think that gender is a core factor in the subjective possibility of actualising effectual ensemblances of bodies in alliance. To put it in Judith Butler's terms:

> It is possible to say, 'I am myself an alliance, or I ally with myself or my various cultural vicissitudes.' That means only that the 'I' in question refuses

to background one minority status or lived site of precarity in favour of any other; it is a way of saying, 'I am the complexity that I am, and this means that I am related to others in ways that are essential to any invocation of this 'I'. Such a view, which implicates social relationality in the first-person pronoun, challenges us to grasp the insufficiency of identitarian ontologies for thinking about the problem of alliance. For the point is not that I am a collection of identities, but that I am already an assembly, even a general assembly, or an assemblage, as Jasbir Puar has adapted the term from Gilles Deleuze.[50]

Assembly and assemblage are influential terms that are highly correlated with ensemblance. I prefer ensemblance because it avoids, in my view, the risk of creating a new, if more sophisticated, reification of the spirit of collectives, an ideology of hive minds and human swarms that won't be much better politically than the hazardous ideology of individualism.

Sixth and last question: what is the relevance of esprit de corps in contemporary debates on communitarianism, multiculturalism and universalism? The above reference to Butler's work already offers elements towards an answer. Yet, to be fair, I have not found that 'esprit de corps' is a signifier that appears frequently in the way minorities describe themselves today. In the USA or the UK, this might be because esprit de corps tends to be hijacked by managerial or nationalist discourse. In French, this is because the phrase *esprit de corps* has become rare yet still sporadically used by intellectuals in reference to corporatism, bias, sectism and groupthink. Globally, discourses that are identified as anti-communitarian seem to find the phrase 'esprit de corps' appealing within a nationalist connotation. Ideas of patriotism and xenophobia are still conflated with notions of duty, sacrifice, distinction and the metaphor of national embodiment.

The intentionally ambivalent idea of ensemblance points to the untruth – or asymptotic truth – of identity, the fact that a feeling of being one, or the appearance of closed unity, do not suppose a complete substance. In his *Negative Dialectics*, the German philosopher Theodor W. Adorno insisted that finite social wholes are often ideological, and that any historical totality was socially a 'necessary semblance':[51] 'The semblance cannot be decreed away, as by avowal of a being-in-itself outside the totality of cogitative definitions.'[52] Any societal totality is an appearance, even if such semblance is a useful collective fabulation, as we have recognised with Bergson and Deleuze.

We tend to form contingents – our contingents are positively contingent on their incompleteness. In times of globalised ideological divisions and essentialising claims about human groups, the question of the necessity of our belonging, collective identities and the *well-being* they might generate calls for more research in experiences and anticipations of *well-belonging*, and how they relate to physical, psychological, political and philosophical health.

Notes

1. Bevir, *The Logic of the History of Ideas*, p. 309.
2. Michael S. Roth, 'Foucault's History of the Present', *History and Theory* 20.1 (1981), pp. 32–46.
3. Michel Foucault, *L'archéologie du savoir* (Paris: Gallimard, 1969).
4. Michel Foucault, *Les mots et les choses: une archéologie des sciences humaines* (Paris: Gallimard, 1966).
5. Foucault, *L'archéologie du savoir*, p. 206.
6. Walker, '*Holy Virility*, by Emmanuel Reynaud', p. 121.
7. Ibid., p. 121.
8. David Walker to Luis de Miranda, email, 17 February 2017.
9. de Miranda and Chabal, 'Big Data, Small Concepts'.
10. Bevir, *The Logic of the History of Ideas*, p. 125.
11. Whatmore, *What is Intellectual History?*, p. 9.
12. Bevir, *The Logic of the History of Ideas*, p. 314.
13. Thomas Hippler, *Citizens, Soldiers, and National Armies: Military Service in France and Germany, 1789–1830* (London: Routledge, 2008), pp. 5–6.
14. Bevir, *The Logic of the History of Ideas*, pp. 311–12.
15. Lee McIntyre, 'To Fix the Social Sciences, Look to the "Dark Ages" of Medicine', *The MIT Press Reader* (2019), <https://thereader.mitpress.mit.edu/social-sciences-dark-ages/> (accessed 19 September 2019).
16. Ibid., p. 314.
17. Bevir, *The Logic of the History of Ideas*, p. 116.
18. de Miranda, 'On the Concept of Creal'.
19. de Miranda, 'Is a New Life Possible?', p. 120.
20. Alfred North Whitehead, *Science and the Modern World* (New York: Free Press, 1997), p. 51.
21. Kari Palonen, 'The History of Concepts as a Style of Political Theorizing', *European Journal of Political Theory* 1.1 (2002), pp. 91–106.
22. 'On n'est pas toujours conscient de la nécessité de l'esprit de corps, on ne saisit pas ses principes, ses fondements, on peine à définir le mot [. . .] Une *théorie générale* de l'esprit de corps touche à la théorie du corps social, à la théorie de la bureaucratie (et du pouvoir politique), à la théorie des *devoirs d'état*, à la théorie de l'ordre et du désordre dans un corps quelconque, à la théorie de l'action (qu'est-ce qui fait agir?), à la théorie de la médiocrité.' Vauvilliers, 'Pour une théorie générale de l'esprit de corps', pp. 489–90.
23. '*Premier fondement*: la légitimité: on est à l'intérieur d'un système qui est légitime, qui tient à l'ordre [. . .] *Deuxième fondement*: la durée: l'esprit de corps est ancré dans la tradition, c'est une forme de maîtrise du temps, on a eu des *prédécesseurs*, on aura des *successeurs* [. . .] on doit être à la hauteur de ses prédécesseurs, et transmettre *l'héritage* en bon état aux successeurs. *Troisième fondement*: la communauté de vues à l'intérieur d'un corps [. . .] On a une vision des choses, des formes de pensée, des méthodes pour conduire ses idées, régler sa conduite, qui sont communes "pour l'essentiel", et dont on ne peut s'écarter, sous peine d'être en faute [. . .] *Quatrième fondement*: la distinction de ce qui est *convenable* et ne l'est pas [. . .] Ce qui est convenable, c'est ce qui est d'abord conforme à l'intérêt du corps [. . .] *Cinquième fondement*: [. . .] chaque corps a ses devoirs d'état propres, liés à l'*officium*, et l'esprit de corps oblige – dans

l'intérêt général – à observer régulièrement, sagement, ses devoirs d'état, à respecter les servitudes qu'ils imposent [. . .] *Sixième fondement*: la régularité – ou plutôt *l'optimisation* – de la gestion des carrières; on donne une certaine sécurité de carrière [. . .] ce qui permet d'éviter les ambitions désordonnées, sources de conflits, de divisions, et de *contrôler* les esprits rebelles ou qui observent mal leurs devoirs [. . .] *Septième fondement*: la solidarité. A l'intérieur du corps, en principe, on doit être tolérant, courtois, ne pas attaquer ses pairs, intriguer, cabaler [. . .] Vis-à-vis de l'extérieur le corps doit se montrer uni, protéger les gens du corps qui sont en difficulté, ont commis des fautes (le corps est un système d'assurances).' Ibid., pp. 491–3.

24. 'On sert la République, non le gouvernement.' Ibid., p. 494.

25. Ibid., p. 493.

26. 'L'esprit de corps est mal vu, souvent on l'a dénoncé vivement [. . .] même les membres des corps, quand ils parlent librement, détaillent les méfaits de l'esprit de corps, qui finit par corrompre le jugement et encourager *l'esprit de système* (on voit le monde à travers un prisme déformant) [. . .] *Premier risque*: l'esprit de corps repose sur des *fictions*, crée un système imaginaire: on croit avoir un pouvoir *autonome*, un mandat particulier du corps social, on veut définir à sa manière l'intérêt général [. . .] *Deuxième risque*: l'esprit de corps limite l'autonomie, le sens des responsabilités, il est claustrant, il pousse au conformisme, il donne des œillères, il entretient l'étroitesse d'esprit: les membres du corps ne sont plus capables d'initiative, ils deviennent des *insectes spécialisés* [. . .] une personnalité brillante devient terne, craintive, elle ne sait plus *penser par elle-même* [. . .] *Troisième risque*: l'esprit de corps définit des *codes de conduite*, des *codes de pensée* [. . .] tôt ou tard obsolètes [. . .] et on finit par une sorte de *calcification* [. . .] Les médiocres adoptent facilement le style, les apparences extérieures, les modes de raisonnement, le langage du corps.' Ibid., pp. 497–8.

27. 'Faut-il maintenir – et developer – l'esprit de corps? C'est une question insoluble, tout varie suivant les temps [. . .] Une théorie générale est par force partielle, inacheveé.' Ibid., p. 596.

28. 'Rien de plus "hétéromate" qu'un automate.' Bruno Latour, *Enquête sur les modes d'existence: Une anthropologie des modernes* (Paris: La Découverte, 2013), p. 215.

29. Fabiane Santana Previtali and Cilson César Fagiani, 'Deskilling and Degradation of Labour in Contemporary Capitalism: The Continuing Relevance of Baverman', *Work Organisation, Labour and Globalisation* 9.1 (2015), pp. 76–91.

30. 'Les affaires sont un mélange de guerre et de sport.' Montoux, *Dictionnaire des organisations*, p. 25.

31. Michiel Schwarz and Michael Thompson, *Divided We Stand: Redefining Politics, Technology, and Social Choice* (Philadelphia: University of Pennsylvania Press, 1990), p. 75.

32. Maurice Mashaal, *Bourbaki, A Secret Society of Mathematicians* (Providence: American Mathematical Society, 2006).

33. This typology might be compatible with the Grid-Group Theory, which looks at how much of people's lives is controlled by the group they belong to. See Mary Douglas, 'A History of Grid-Group Cultural Theory', Semiotics Institute Online, University of Toronto, <http://projects.chass.utoronto.ca/semiotics/cyber/douglas1.pdf> (accessed 19 September 2019).

34. Luis de Miranda, Subramanian Ramamoorthy and Michael Rovatsos, 'We, Anthrobot: Learning from Human Forms of Interaction and Esprit de Corps to Develop More Plural Social Robotics', in Johanna Seibt et al. (eds), *What Social Robots Can and Should Do: Proceedings of Robophilosophy 2016* (Amsterdam: IOS Press, 2016).

35. Gallie, 'Essentially Contested Concepts', pp. 167–98.

36. Quentin Meillassoux, trans. Thomas Nail, 'History and Event in Alain Badiou', *Parrhesia* 12 (2011), pp. 1–11 (p. 1).

37. Ibid., pp. 1–6.

38. de Miranda, 'Is a New Life Possible?', p. 120.

39. 'Le mot illusion ne se trouve dans aucune langue ancienne, parce que le mot ne se crée que lorsque la chose n'existe plus.' Constant, *De l'esprit de conquête*, p. 114.

40. Adam Smith, *An Inquiry into the Nature and Causes of the Wealth of Nations* (New York: Random House Modern Library, 1937 [1776]), pp. 692–718.

41. Irving L. Janis, 'Groupthink', *Psychology Today Magazine* 5 (1971), pp. 43–6, 74–6 (p. 43).

42. Ibid., p. 44.

43. Bailey and LaFrance, 'Who Counts as Human?', p. 2.

44. WSJ staff, '"Mad Max: Fury Road", "Pitch Perfect 2": Review Revue', <https://blogs.wsj.com/speakeasy/2015/05/15/mad-max-fury-road-pitch-perfect-2-review-revue/> (accessed 25 February 2016).

45. Marilyn R. Schuster, *Passionate Communities: Reading Lesbian Resistance in Jane Rule's Fiction* (New York: New York University Press, 1999).

46. Ibid., p. 57.

47. Ibid., p. 58.

48. Jay McGregor, '2% of Google Employees Are Black and Just 30% Are Women', *Forbes*, 29 May 2014, <https://www.forbes.com/sites/jaymcgregor/2014/05/29/2-of-google-employees-are-black-and-just-30-are-women/#7ff55990490e> (accessed 19 September 2019).

49. Schumpeter, 'Valley of the Dudes', *The Economist*, 4 April 2015, <https://www.economist.com/business/2015/04/04/valley-of-the-dudes> (accessed 19 September 2019).

50. Butler, *Notes Towards a Performative Theory of Assembly*, p. 68.

51. Theodor W. Adorno, *Negative Dialectics*, trans. E. B. Ashton (London: Continuum, 1981), p. 312.

52. Ibid., p. 5.

Bibliography

Adams, Julia, 'The Rule of the Father: Patriarchy and Patrimonialism in Early Modern Europe', in Charles Camic, Philip S. Gorski and David M. Trubek (eds), *Max Weber's Economy and Society* (Stanford: Stanford University Press, 2005), pp. 237–66.

Addams, Jane, *Newer Ideals of Peace* (New York: MacMillan, 1907).

Addison, Joseph, *The Campaign: A Poem, To His Grace the Duke of Marlborough* (London: Tonson, 1705).

Adorno, Theodor W., *Negative Dialectics*, trans. E. B. Ashton (London: Continuum, 1981).

AFP, 'Devant ses jeunes, Marine Le Pen decline ses fondamentaux', *Le Point*, 9 September 2011, <https://www.lepoint.fr/societe/devant-ses-jeunes-marine-le-pen-decline-ses-fondamentaux-09-09-2011-1371678_23.php> (accessed 19 September 2019).

Agamben, Giorgio, *State of Exception*, trans. Kevin Attell (Chicago: University of Chicago Press, 2005).

Agathon, *L'Esprit de la nouvelle Sorbonne* (Paris: Mercure de France, 1911).

D'Alembert, Jean le Rond, 'Caractère des sociétés ou corps particuliers', in Denis Diderot and Jean le Rond d'Alembert (eds), *Encyclopédie ou dictionnaire raisonné des sciences, des arts et des métiers* (Paris: Briasson, David, Le Breton and Durand, 1751–65), vol. II (1752), p. 666.

D'Alembert, Jean le Rond, 'Character of Societies and Particular Groups', in *The Encyclopedia of Diderot & d'Alembert Collaborative Translation Project* (2003), trans. Nelly S. Hoyt and Thomas Cassirer, University of Michigan Library, <https://quod.lib.umich.edu/d/did/did2222.0000.352/--character-of-societies-and-particular-groups?rgn=main;view=fulltext;q1=character+of+societies> (accessed 19 September 2019).

D'Alembert, Jean le Rond, 'Discours préliminaire des éditeurs', in *Encyclopédie*, ARTFL Encyclopédie Project, University of Chicago (2013), <https://artflsrv03.uchicago.edu/philologic4/encyclopedie1117/navigate/1/3/> (accessed 19 September 2019).

D'Alembert, Jean le Rond, *Traité de Dynamique* (Paris: David, 1758).

'D'Alembert to Voltaire, 14 July 1767', Electronic Enlightenment Project,

Bodleian Libraries, Oxford, 2008–14, <http://www.e-enlightenment.com/item/voltfrVF1160202a1c/?letters=decade&s=1760&r=14802> (accessed 19 September 2019).

Allen, Forrest Claire, *Better Basketball: Technique, Tactics and Tales* (New York: McGraw-Hill, 1937).

Allgemeine Schweizerische Militärzeitung (Basel: S.V., 1855).

Alonso, Facundo, 'Shared Intention, Reliance, and Interpersonal Obligations', *Ethics* 119.3 (2009), pp. 444–75.

Aman, Jacques, *Les officiers bleus dans la marine française au XVIIIe siècle* (Geneva: Droz, 1976).

Anderson, Benedict, *Imagined Communities: Reflections on the Origin and Spread of Nationalism* (London: Verso, 1991).

Anonymous, 'Du serment civique', *Révolutions de Paris, dédiées à la nation*, 27 (1790).

Anonymous, *L'Esprit d'intérêt, ou la censure des deux libelles intitulés l'Esprit de paix, et l'Esprit de guerre* (Paris: Nicolas Guérard, 1652).

Anonymous, *Mémoire des fruitiers-orangers*, 1776, BNF, Coll. Joly 462, fol. 120–1.

Anonymous, 'Observations sur le rétablissement de la discipline militaire', in *Manuscrits du Service historique de la défense* (1766), <http://www.servicehistorique.sga.defense.gouv.fr/?q=content/nos-ressources> (accessed 19 September 2019).

Anonymous, 'Organisation de la liberté d'enseignement', *Le Correspondant* (Paris: Sagnier & Bray, 1847), vol. XVII.

Anonymous, *Le Spectateur militaire, recueil de science, d'art et d'histoire militaire* (Paris: Noirot, 1835), vol. 19.

Applebaum, Binyamin, 'On Trade, Donald Trump Breaks With 200 Years of Economic Orthodoxy', *The New York Times*, 10 March 2016, <https://www.nytimes.com/2016/03/11/us/politics/-trade-donald-trump-breaks-200-years-economic-orthodoxy-mercantilism.html> (accessed 19 September 2019).

Archer, Crina, Ephraim, Laura, and Maxwell, Lida, 'Politics in the Terrain of Second Nature', in Crina Archer, Laura Ephraim and Lida Maxwell (eds), *Second Nature: Rethinking the Natural through Politics* (New York: Fordham University Press, 2013).

Archives parlementaires de 1787 à 1860, ed. Jérôme Madival and Émile Laurent (Paris: Centre national de la Recherche Scientifique, 1961), vol. XLVIII.

Archivum Romanum Societatis Iesu, Archives of the Society of Jesus, <http://www.sjweb.info/arsi>.

Arendt, Hannah, *Eichmann in Jerusalem: A Report on the Banality of Evil* (New York: Viking, 1963).

Arendt, Hannah, *The Human Condition* (Chicago: University of Chicago Press, 1998 [1958]).

Arendt, Hannah, 'Karl Marx and the Tradition of Western Political Thought', *Social Research* 69.2 (2002), pp. 273–319.

Aristotle, *Politics*, in *Aristotle*, trans. Horace Rackham, 23 vols (Cambridge, MA: Harvard University Press, 1944), vol. XXI.

Armitage, David, *Civil Wars: A History in Ideas* (New York: Knopf, 2017).

Armitage, David, 'What's the Big Idea? Intellectual History and the *Longue Durée*', *History of European Ideas* 38.4 (2012), pp. 493–507.

Armitage, David, and Guldi, Jo, *The History Manifesto* (Cambridge: Cambridge University Press, 2014).

Aron, Raymond, *Peace and War: A Theory of International Relations*, trans. Richard Howard and Annette Baker Fox (New Brunswick, NJ: Transaction, 2003).

Arthur, Terry, 'Mercantilism is Back with a Vengeance', *Institute of Economic Affairs Blog*, 31 August 2011, <https://iea.org.uk/blog/mercantilism-is-back-with-a-vengeance>(accessed 19 September 2019).

Augustine, *Sermons*, in Emile Mersch, *The Whole Christ* (London: Dobson, 1962).

Austin, John Langshaw, *How to Do Things with Words* (Cambridge, MA: Harvard University Press, 1975).

'Austrian Netherlands', *Oracle*, 10 November 1789, in *The 17th and 18th Century Burney Collection*, <http://tinyurl.galegroup.com/tinyurl/PAZj0> (accessed 19 September 2019).

Baecque, Antoine de, *Le corps de l'histoire. Métaphores et politique 1770–1800* (Paris: Calmann-Lévy, 1993).

Bailey, April H., and LaFrance, Marianne, 'Who Counts as Human? Antecedents to Androcentric Behaviour', *Sex Roles* 76.11–12 (2017), pp. 682–93, <https://link.springer.com/article/10.1007/s11199-016-0648-4> (accessed 19 September 2019).

Balbany, André-Christophe, *Acceptation du défi hazardé par l'auteur d'un libelle intitulé Réplique aux apologies des Jésuites* (Avignon, 1762).

Baldet, Marcel, *La vie quotidienne dans les armées de Napoléon* (Paris: Hachette, 1964).

Baldwin, James Mark, *Social and Ethical Interpretations in Mental Development: A Study in Social Psychology* (New York: Macmillan, 1899).

Banning, T. C. W., *The French Revolutionary Wars, 1787–1802* (London: Hodder Education, 1996).

Barber, W. B., 'Esprit de corps and morale', *The Naval Review* 8.2 (1920), pp. 129–40.

Bareau, Jean-Michel (ed.), *Dictionnaire des inégalités scolaires* (Issy-les-Moulineaux: ESF, 2007).

Barnes, Harry Elmer, and Becker, Howard Paul, *Social Lore from Thought to Science*, 2 vols (Washington, DC: Harren Press, 1952).

Barret, Robert, *The Theoric and Practic of Modern Wars* (London: Ponsonby, 1598).

Bary, René, *L'Esprit de cour, ou les conversations galantes. Divisées en cent dialogues dédiés au Roi* (Paris: Charles de Sercy, 1662).

Baudelaire, Charles, 'Salon de 1846', in *Œuvres complètes de Charles Baudelaire*, 7 vols (Paris: Lévy, 1868), vol. II.

Belhoste, Bruno, and Chatzis, Konstantinos, 'From Technical Corps to

Technocratic Power: French State Engineers and Their Professional and Cultural Universe in the First Half of the 19th Century', *History and Technology* 23.3 (2007), pp. 209–25.

Bell, David A., *The Cult of the Nation in France, Inventing Nationalism, 1680–1800* (Cambridge, MA: Harvard University Press, 2003).

Bell, William Hemphill, 'Administration: Its Principles and Their Application', *Efficiency Society Journal* 2 (1917), pp. 75–6.

Benjamin, John, 'Are You Making Sure Your Team is Set for Success', *The Greeley Tribune*, 9 April 2016.

Bentham, Jeremy, *An Introduction to the Principles of Morals and Legislation* (London: Payne, 1789).

Béranger, Pierre-Jean de, 'L'Académie et le Caveau, Chanson de récéption au Caveau Moderne', in *Chansons complètes* (Paris, 1832).

Berg, Gunnar, 'School Culture and Teachers' Esprit de Corps', in Éva Balazs, Fons van Wieringen and Leonard Watson (eds), *Quality and Educational Management* (Budapest: Wolters Kluwer, 2000), <https://www.ofi.hu/qual ity-and-educational-090617/school-culture-and> (accessed 19 September 2019).

Bergier, Nicolas Sylvestre, 'Communautés ecclesiastiques', in *Encyclopédie méthodique*, 26 vols (Paris: Panckoucke, 1782–1832), vol. XV (1789), p. 384.

Bergson, Henri, *Les deux sources de la morale et de la religion* (Paris: Presses Universitaires de France, 1990 [1932]).

Bergson, Henri, *L'évolution créatrice* (Paris: Alcan, 1907).

Berk, Isaac, 'The Walking Dead as a Critique of American Democracy', *Cineaction* 95 (2015), pp. 48–55.

Berns, Thomas, and Frydman, Benoît, 'Généalogie de l'esprit de corps', in Gilles J. Guglielmi and Claudine Haroche (eds), *Esprit de corps, démocratie et espace public* (Paris: Presses Universitaires de France, 2005).

Bertaud, Jean-Paul, *La vie quotidienne des soldats de la Révolution, 1789–1799* (Paris: Hachette, 1985).

Bevir, Mark, *The Logic of the History of Ideas* (Cambridge: Cambridge University Press, 1999).

Biet, Christian, 'Mémoires, Saint-Simon', *Encyclopædia Universalis* (2014), <https://www.universalis.fr/encyclopedie/memoires-saint-simon/> (accessed 19 September 2019).

Biet, Christian, 'Pensées, livre de Blaise Pascal', *Encyclopædia Universalis* (2014), <https://www.universalis.fr/encyclopedie/pensees/> (accessed 19 September 2019).

Bignon, Louis, *Histoire de France* (Brussels: Meline, Cans, 1839).

Bihl-Wilette, Luc, *Des tavernes aux bistrots, une histoire des cafés, Lausanne* (Lausanne: L'Age d'Homme, 1997).

Blitman, Sophie, 'Fundraising: Polytéchnique a levé 31,6 M€ en misant sur son réseau d'anciens', *L'étudiant*, 23 May 2012 <https://www.letudiant.fr/educpros/ actualite/fundraising-polytechnique-a-leve-316-mEUR-et-ne-compte-pas-sar reter-la.html> (accessed 19 September 2019).

Blount, Thomas, *Glossographia or a Dictionary* (London: Newcomb, 1656).

Blum, William, *Killing Hope: US Military and CIA Interventionism Since World War II* (Monroe, ME: Common Courage Press, 1995).

Bodin, Jean, *Les six Livres de la République* (Paris: Jacques du Puys, 1576).

Bonafous, Louis Abel de, *Du rétablissement des Jésuites et de l'éducation publique* (Emmerick: Romen, 1800).

Bonald, Louis Gabriel Ambroise de, *Législation primitive, considérée dans les derniers temps par les seules lumières de la Raison*, 3 vols (Paris: Le Clère, 1802).

Bonald, Louis de, *De l'esprit de corps et de l'esprit de parti* (Paris: Le Clère, 1828).

'Bonald, Louis Gabriel Ambroise, viscount de', *Encyclopædia Britannica Online*, <https://www.britannica.com/biography/Louis-Gabriel-Ambroise-vicomte-de-Bonald> (accessed 19 September 2019).

Bonus, Holger, 'The Cooperative Association as a Business Enterprise. A Study in the Economics of Transactions', in G. Furubotn and Rudolf Richter (eds), *The New Institutional Economics* (Tübingen: Mohr, 1991).

Boucher, Jean, *Les œuvres spirituelles* (Paris: Moreau, 1621).

Boullaye, Henri Pinard de la, *Exercices spirituels selon la méthode de Saint-Ignace*, 3 vols (Paris: Beauchesne, 1951).

Bourdet, Eugène, *Principes d'éducation positive* (Paris: Germer-Baillière, 1877).

Bourdieu, Pierre, *La Noblesse d'État. Grandes écoles et esprit de corps* (Paris, Minuit, 1989).

Bourdieu, Pierre, 'Les trois états du capital culturel', *Actes de la recherche en sciences sociales* 30 (1979), pp. 3–6.

Boyt, Thomas E., Lusch, Robert F., and Schuler, Drue K., 'Fostering Esprit de Corps in Marketing', *Marketing Management* 6.1 (1997), pp. 20–8.

Bradshaw, John, *The Letters of Philip Dormer Stanhope, Earl of Chesterfield*, 3 vols (London: Allen and Unwin, 1913).

Braid, James, 'M. Braid on Hypnotism', *The Lancet* 45.1135 (1845), pp. 627–8.

Brandist, Craig, 'The Risks of Soviet-Style Managerialism in UK Universities', *Times Higher Education*, 5 May 2016, <https://www.timeshighereducation.com/comment/the-risks-of-soviet-style-managerialism-in-united-kingdom-universities> (accessed 19 September 2019).

Braudel, Fernand, 'Histoire et sciences sociales. La longue durée', *Annales* 13.4 (1958), pp. 725–53.

Braun, Theodore E. D., and Radner, John B., *The Lisbon Earthquake of 1755: Representations and Reactions* (Oxford: Voltaire Foundation, 2006).

Breen, Henry Hegart, *Modern English Literature, Its Blemishes and Defects* (London: Longman, 1857).

Briasson et Chaubert, *Mémoires pour l'Histoire des sciences et des beaux-arts*, ARTFL-Frantext, pp. 118–20, <https://artfl-project.uchicago.edu/content/journal-de-trévoux> (accessed 19 September 2019).

'M. Le Duc de Broglie', *Discussion de la loi sur l'instruction secondaire* (Paris: Moniteur Universel and Hachette, 1844), vol. I.

Bruin, Boudewijn de, 'We and the Plural Subject', *Philosophy of the Social Sciences* 39 (2009), pp. 235–59.

Brubaker, William Rogers, 'The French Revolution and the Invention of Citizenship', *French Politics and Society* 7.3 (1989), pp. 30–49.

Brunet, Jacques-Charles, *Manuel du libraire et de l'amateur de livres* (Paris: Sylvestre, 1843).

Brunton, Mary, *Discipline* (Edinburgh: Ramsay, 1814).

Bublitz, Jan Christoph, and Merkel, Reinhard, 'Crimes against Minds: On Mental Manipulations, Harms and a Human Right to Mental Self-Determination', *Criminal Law and Philosophy* 8.1 (2014), pp. 51–77.

Buchwalter, Andrew, *Dialectics, Politics, and the Contemporary Value of Hegel's Practical Philosophy* (New York: Routledge, 2012).

Bullough, Edward, *Aesthetics: Lectures and Essays* (Stanford: Stanford University Press, 1957).

Burns, Tom, and Stalker, G. M., *The Management of Innovation* (London: Tavistock, 1961).

Butler, Judith, 'Competing Universalities', in Judith Bulter, Ernesto Laclau, and Slavoj Žižek, *Contingency, Hegemony, Universality: Contemporary Dialogues on the Left* (London: Verso, 2000).

Butler, Judith, *Notes Towards a Performative Theory of Assembly* (Cambridge, MA: Harvard University Press, 2015).

Butler, Nicholas Michael, *Votaries of Apollo: The St. Cecilia Society and the Patronage of Concert Music in Charleston, South Carolina, 1766–1820* (Columbia: University of South Carolina Press, 2007).

Byron, George Gordon, Lord, 'Letter CCCCXXVIII to Mr. Moore, May 20th, 1821', in Thomas More, *Life and Journals of Lord Byron*, 2 vols (Hamburg: Lebel, Truttel & Wrutz, 1831), vol. II.

Calvocoressi, Peter, *World Politics Since 1945* (Harlow: Pearson, 2009 [1968]).

Canton, Gustave, *Napoléon antimilitariste* (Paris: Alcan, 1902).

Carey, James B., *Trade Unions and Democracy: A Comparative Study of US, French, Italian, and West German Unions* (Washington, DC: National Planning Association, 1957).

Castillon, André Le Blanc de, *Arrêt du parlement de Provence* (Aix en Provence, 1762).

Catalogus officinalis (Frankfurt: Kopf, 1610).

Catherine, R., 'L'esprit de bande', *La Revue administrative* 13 (1950), pp. 3–5.

Censer, Jack, *The French Press in the Age of Enlightenment* (Oxford: Routledge, 1994).

Cerny, Philip G., *The Politics of Grandeur: Ideological Aspects of de Gaulle's Foreign Policy* (Cambridge: Cambridge University Press, 1980).

Cerutti, Joseph-Antoine, *Œuvres diverses, ou Recueil de pièces composées avant et depuis la Révolution* (Paris: Desenne, 1792).

Chabal, Emile, *A Divided Republic: Nation, State, and Citizenship in Contemporary France* (Cambridge: Cambridge University Press, 2015).

Chapman, Herrick, *State Capitalism and Working-Class Radicalism in the French Aircraft Industry* (Berkeley: University of California Press, 1991).

Chappel, Mike, *The British Army in the 1980s* (Oxford: Osprey, 1987).

Chappey, Jean-Luc, 'La formation d'une technocratie. L'école polytéchnique et ses élèves de la Révolution au Second Empire', *Annales Historiques de la Révolution Française* 137 (2004), pp. 223–7.

Charbonnel, Nanine, *Comme un seul homme: corps politique et corps mystique* (Lons Le Saunier: Aréopage, 2010).

Chateaubriand, François-René de, *Génie du Christianisme ou beautés de la religion chrétienne*, 5 vols (Paris: Migneret, 1803).

Chenaye-Desbois, François-Alexandre de la, and Badier, Jacques, *Dictionaire de la Noblesse* (Paris: Schlesinger, 1865–67).

Chervel, André, *Histoire de l'enseignement du français du XVIIe au XXe siècle* (Paris: Retz, 2006).

Chervel, André, and Compère, Marie-Madeleine, 'Les candidats aux trois concours pour l'agrégation de l'Université de Paris (1766–1791)', *Ressources numériques en histoire de l'éducation* (2002), <http://rhe.ish-lyon.cnrs.fr/?q=agregar> (accessed 19 September 2019).

Chesterfield, Lord, 'To Dr. Rev. Chenevix, Lord Bishop of Waterford, Blackheath (June 26, 1755)', in *Miscellaneous Works of Lord Chesterfield*, 3 vols (Dublin: Maty, 1777), vol. III.

Chichester, Henry Manners, 'Jardine, Alexander', in *Dictionary of National Biography* (London: Smith, Elder, 1885–90), vol. XXIX (1892).

Cicero, *De Officiis*, trans. Walter Miller (Cambridge, MA: Harvard University Press, 1913).

Clague, Christopher, 'Rule Obedience, Organizational Loyalty, and Economic Development', *Journal of Institutional and Theoretical Economics* 149.82 (1993), pp. 393–414.

Clarke, Rachel, 'The Moral in "Morale" Is, Take it Seriously, Mr Hunt', *The Huffington Post*, 29 February 2016, <https://www.huffingtonpost.co.uk/rachel-clarke/the-moral-in-morale-is-ta_b_9341244.html> (accessed 19 September 2019).

Clifton, Gloria C., *Professionalism, Patronage, and Public Service in Victorian London* (London: Bloomsbury, 2015).

Code des délits et des peines, servant de supplément au procès verbal des séances du corps législatif (Paris: Hacquart, 1810).

Coeffeteau, Nicolas, *Réponse au livre intitulé: Le Mystère d'iniquité, du Sieur du Plessis* (Paris: Cramoisy, 1614).

Commons, John Rogers, *Industrial Goodwill* (New York: McGraw-Hill, 1919).

Compte rendu des débats du Grand Conseil du canton de Vaud sur le projet de loi ecclésiastique, ou recueil des discours qui ont été prononcés (Lausanne: Dépôt Bibliographique, 1839).

Condorcet, Nicolas de, *Eloge de Michel de l'Hôpital, chancelier de France, discours présenté à l'Académie française en 1777* (Paris: Demonville, 1777).

Condorcet, Nicolas de, *Essai sur l'application de l'analyse à la probabilité des décisions rendues à la pluralité des voix* (Paris: Imprimerie Royale, 1785).

Condorcet, Nicolas de, *Vie de Monsieur Turgot* (Paris or London, 1786).

Connay, Jean, *Le Compagnonnage* (Paris: Rivière, 1909).

Constant, Benjamin, *De l'esprit de conquête et de l'usurpation, dans leurs rapports avec la civilisation européenne* (London: John Murray, 1814).

Coontz, Stephanie, *The Social Origins of Private Life: A History of American Families, 1600–1900* (London: Verso, 1988).

Coser, Lewis A., *The Functions of Social Conflict* (New York: Free Press, 1956).

Cottrell, H., Pearse, T. D., et al., *Remarks on the petition of the British inhabitants of Bengal, Bihar, and Orissa, to Parliament. By the gentlemen of the Committee at Calcutta, appointed to transmit the petition to England, and transact the business appertaining thereto* (London, 1780).

Courcelle-Seneuil, Jean-Gustave, 'Corps', in *Dictionnaire politique* (Paris: Pagnerre, 1842), p. 290.

Courtenay, John, *Philosophical Reflections on the Late Revolution in France, and the Conduct of the Dissenters in England* (London: Becket, 1790).

Coyle, Grace, *Social Process in Organized Groups* (New York: Smith, 1930).

Craige, Betty Jean, *American Patriotism in a Global Society* (Albany: State University of New York Press, 1996).

Crespet, Pierre, *Le Jardin de plaisir et récréation spirituelle* (Paris: Nouë, 1587).

Crissey, Forrest, 'Esprit de Corps', *Ad Sense* 20 (1906), p. 30.

Crossley, Robert, *Olaf Stapledon: Speaking for the Future* (Syracuse: Syracuse University Press, 1994).

Cueva, Edmund P., Byrne, Shannon N., and Benda, Frederik (eds), *Jesuit Education and the Classics* (Newcastle: Cambridge Scholars Publishing, 2009).

Dainville, François de, *L'Éducation des Jésuites, XVIe–XVIIIe siècles* (Paris: Minuit, 1978).

Davenport, Ken, 'Obama May Offend on Brexit, but He's Right', *The Wall Street Journal*, 29 April 2016, <https://www.wsj.com/articles/obama-may-offend-on-brexit-but-hes-right-1461946482> (accessed 19 September 2019).

Davis, David, 'With the EU Referendum Looming, the Government Must Give Us Reliable Immigration Figures', *ConservativeHome*, 2 March 2016, <https://www.conservativehome.com/thetorydiary/2016/03/david-davis-with-the-eu-referendum-looming-the-government-must-give-us-reliable-immigration-fig ures.html> (accessed 19 September 2019).

Day, C. R., 'Making Men and Training Technicians: Boarding Schools of the Ecoles d'Arts et Métiers during the Nineteenth Century', *Historical Reflexions* 7.2/3 (1980), pp. 381–96.

Deckard, Michael Funk, and Losonczi, Péter (eds), *Philosophy Begins in Wonder: An Introduction to Early Modern Philosophy, Theology, and Science* (Cambridge: James Clarke, 2011).

'Décret portant suppression des maîtrises et jurandes, article 7, Séance à l'Assemblée du 2 mars 1791', in Jérôme Madival and Émile Laurent (eds), *Archives parlementaires de 1787 à 1860* (Paris: Centre national de la Recherche Scientifique, 1961), vol. XXIII.

de Gaulle, Charles, 'Discours à Dakar', 26 August 1958, <https://fresques.ina.fr/de-gaulle/fiche-media/Gaulle00329/discours-a-dakar.html> (accessed 19 September 2019).

de Gaulle, Charles, *Vers l'armée de métier* (Paris: Berger-Levrault, 1934).

Delatte, Armand, *Essai sur la politique pythagoricienne* (Liège and Paris: Bibliothèque de l'Université de Liège, 1922).

Deleuze, Gilles, 'Post-scriptum sur les sociétés de contrôle', in *Pourparlers* (Paris: Minuit, 1990).

Deleuze, Gilles, and Guattari, Félix, *Anti-Oedipus: Capitalism and Schizophrenia*, trans. Robert Hurley, Mark Seem and Helen R. Lane (London: Continuum, 2004).

Deleuze, Gilles, and Guattari, Félix, *Mille plateaux* (Paris: Minuit, 1980).

Déloye, Yves, 'Penser l'esprit de corps: L'actualité de l'anthropologie des corps et des esprits chez Alexis de Tocqueville', in Gilles J. Guglielmi and Claudine Haroche (eds), *L'esprit de corps, démocratie et espace public* (Paris: Presses Universitaires de France, 2005).

De Marco, Donald, 'Personalism vs Abstract Humanism', *The Linacre Quarterly* 45.3 (1978), pp. 258–63.

de Miranda, Luis, *Ego Trip: La société des artistes-sans-oeuvre* (Paris: Max Milo, 2003).

de Miranda, Luis, 'Is a New Life Possible? Deleuze and the Lines', *Deleuze Studies* 7.1 (2013), pp. 106–52.

de Miranda, Luis, 'On the Concept of Creal: The Politico-Ethical Horizon of a Creative Absolute', in Paulo de Assis and Paolo Giudici (eds), *The Dark Precursor: Deleuze and Artistic Research* (Louvain: Leuven University Press, 2017), pp. 510–16.

de Miranda, Luis, *Peut-on jouir du capitalisme? Lacan avec Heidegger et Marx* (Paris: Max Milo, 2009).

de Miranda, Luis, and Chabal, Emile, 'Big Data, Small Concepts: Histosophy as an Approach to *longue-durée* History', *Global Intellectual History* (2019), <https://www.tandfonline.com/doi/full/10.1080/23801883.2019.1592871> (accessed 19 September 2019).

de Miranda, Luis, Ramamoorthy, Subramanian, and Rovatsos, Michael, 'We, Anthrobot: Learning from Human Forms of Interaction and Esprit de Corps to Develop More Plural Social Robotics', in Johanna Seibt et al. (eds), *What Social Robots Can and Should Do: Proceedings of Robophilosophy 2016* (Amsterdam: IOS Press, 2016).

Derrida, Jacques, 'La pharmacie de Platon', in *La Dissémination* (Paris: Seuil, 1972).

Descartes, René, *Méditations métaphysiques* (Paris: Camusat & Petit, 1647).

Desmons, Eric, 'Réflexions sur la politique et la religion, de Rousseau à Robespierre', *Revue française d'histoire des idées politiques* 1.29 (2009), pp. 77–93.

Dewey, John, 'The Historic Background of Corporate Legal Personality', *Yale Law Journal* 35.6 (1926), pp. 655–73.

Dewey, John, and McLellan, James Alexander, *Applied Psychology. An Introduction to the Principles and Practice of Education* (Boston: Educational Publishing Company, 1889).

Dictionnaire de l'Académie française, 2 vols (Paris: Smits, 1789).

Dictionnaire de l'Académie française, 2 vols (Paris: Firmin-Didot, 1835).

Dictionnaire politique, Encyclopédie du langage et de la science politiques, rédigé par une réunion de députés, de publicistes et de journalistes (Paris: Pagnerre, 1842).

Dictionaire historique de la Suisse, <http://www.hls-dhs-dss.ch>.

Dictionnaire Universel de Commerce (Genève: Cramer and Philibert, 1742).

Diderot, Denis, 'Encyclopédie', in Denis Diderot and Jean le Rond d'Alembert (eds), *Encyclopédie, ou dictionnaire raisonné des sciences, des arts et des métiers* (Paris: Briasson, David, Le Breton and Durand, 1751–65), vol. V (1755), p. 649.

Diderot, Denis, *Mémoires, correspondance et ouvrages inédits de Diderot, publiés d'après les manuscrits confiés, en mourant, par l'auteur à Grimm* (Paris: Paulin, 1834).

DiMaggio, Paul J., and Powell, Walter W., 'The Iron Cage Revisited: Institutional Isomorphism and Collective Rationality in Organizational Fields', *American Sociological Review* 48 (1983), pp. 147–60.

Dion, Gérard, *Dictionnaire canadien des relations du travail* (Québec: Presses de l'Université Laval, 1986).

Domergue, Jules, *La comédie libre-échangiste* (Paris: Calmann Lévy, 1891).

Domergue, Jules, 'L'esprit de corps dans les usines', in *La Réforme Economique* (Paris, 1908).

'Domestic Intelligence', *The Philadelphia Magazine and Review; or, Monthly Repository of Information and Amusement*, January 1799, vol. 1, p. 53.

'Donald Trump Hosts a Made in America Event at The White House – July 23, 2018', Factbase Videos, YouTube, https://youtu.be/d0fp_X4MVP8 (accessed 19 September 2019).

Dorschel, Andreas, 'The Idea of Order: Enlightened Revisions', *Archiv für Rechts- und Sozialphilosophie* 98.2 (2012), pp. 185–96.

Douglas, Mary, 'A History of Grid-Group Cultural Theory', Semiotics Institute Online, University of Toronto, <http://projects.chass.utoronto.ca/semiotics/cyber/douglas1.pdf> (accessed 19 September 2019).

Douglas, Mary, *How Institutions Think* (London: Routledge and Kegan Paul, 1987).

Douglas, Stuart, *A military dissertation, containing a plan for recruiting the British army and improving its establishment* (London, 1781).

Downie, R. S., 'Collective Responsibility', in Larry May and Stacey Hoffman (eds), *Collective Responsibility: Five Decades of Debate in Theoretical and Applied Ethics* (Lanham, MD: Rowman and Littlefield, 1991).

Dufresny, Charles Rivière, *L'Esprit de contradiction, comédie* (Paris: Barbin, 1700).

Dumas, Alexandre, *Les Trois Mousquetaires* (Paris: Baudry, 1844).

Dunbar, Robin, 'Coevolution of Neocortical Size, Group Size and Language in Humans', *Behavioral and Brain Sciences* 16 (1993), pp. 681–735.

Dunkelman, Mark H., *Brothers One and All: Esprit de Corps in a Civil War Regiment* (Baton Rouge: Lousiana State University Press, 2006).

Duperron, Jacques Davy, *Traité du Saint Sacrement de l'Eucharistie* (Paris: Estiene, 1612).

Dupin, Frédéric, 'Réformer la médicine par la littérature: l'éducation des médecins dans la philosophie positive d'auguste Comte', *Cahiers de Narratologie* 18 (2010), <https://journals.openedition.org/narratologie/5981> (accessed 19 September 2019).

Dupont, André, *Rabaut de Saint-Etienne, 1743–1793* (Geneva: Labor and Fidès, 1989).

Duprat, Guillaume Léonce, *La Solidarité sociale, ses causes, son évolution, ses conséquences* (Paris: Doin, 1907).

Durkheim, Émile, *De la division du travail social* (Paris: Félix Alcan, 1893).

Durkheim, Émile, *Le Suicide* (Paris: Alcan, 1897).

Durkin, Philip, *Borrowed Words: A History of Loanwords in English* (Oxford: Oxford University Press, 2014).

Durell, Fletcher, *Fundamental Sources of Efficiency* (Philadelphia: Lippincott, 1914).

Eagles, Julian, 'Marxism, Anarchism, and the Situationist's Theory of Revolution', *Critical Sociology* 43.1 (2017), pp. 13–36.

The Editor, 'Answer to the Letter to the Editor of the Spectator', *The Spectator*, 30 July 1904, p. 16.

Edwards, Bryan, *The History, Civil and Commercial, of the British West Indies*, 5 vols (London: Miller, 1819).

Efrahem, Zael, *De l'association des ouvriers de tous les corps d'état* (Paris: Mie, 1833).

Egret, Jean, *La pré-Révolution française, 1787–1788* (Paris: Presses Universitaires de France, 1962).

Encyclopédie méthodique, 210 vols (Paris: Panckoucke, 1787).

An Engineer, 'Letter to the Editor of the Spectator', *The Spectator*, 30 July 1904, p. 16.

'Esprit', in *Dictionnaire de l'Académie française* (1694), ARTFL-Frantext, <http://portail.atilf.fr/cgi-bin/getobject_?p.4:66./var/artfla/dicos/ACAD_1694/IMAGE/> (accessed 19 September 2019).

'Esprit', in *Centre National de Ressources Textuelles et Lexicales*, <https://www.cnrtl.fr/definition/esprit> (accessed 19 September 2019).

The Esprit de Corps Pointer, <https://researchonespritdecorps.wordpress.com> (accessed 19 September 2019).

'Esprit de corps, n.', *OED Online*, Oxford University Press, <http://oxforddictionaries.com/definition/english/esprit-de-corps> (accessed 19 September 2019).

'Esprit de corps', *Merriam-Webster Dictionary*, <https://www.merriam-webster.com/dictionary/esprit%20de%20corps> (accessed 19 September 2019).

'Esprit de corps', *The British Architect: Journal of Architecture and the Accessory Arts* 27 (1887), p. 283.

'Fabuler', *Centre National de Ressources Textuelles et Lexicales*, <https://www.cnrtl.fr/definition/fabuler> (accessed 19 September 2019).

Fantin-Désodoards, Antoine Etienne Nicolas, *Histoire philosophique de la Révolution de France*, 10 vols (Angers: Belin and Calixte, 1801).

Farr, James, and Williams, David Lay (eds), *The General Will: The Evolution of a Concept* (Cambridge: Cambridge University Press, 2015).

Faveau de Frénilly, François-Auguste, *Considérations sur une année de l'histoire de France* (Paris: Chaumerot, 1815).

Fayol, Henri, *Administration industrielle et générale* (Paris: Dunot and Pinat, 1917).

Ferrand, Charles, 'Comment Réformer la Marine?', *La Grande Revue* 68 (1911), p. 113.

Ferraris, Maurizio, 'Total Mobilization: Recording, Documentality, Normativity', *The Monist* 97.2 (2014), special issue 'Documentality', ed. M. Ferraris and L. Caffo, pp. 201–22.

Feuer, Michael, 'How to Create Esprit de Corps in Your Organization', *Smart Business Online*, 8 March 2013, <http://www.sbnonline.com/article/michael-feuer-how-to-create-esprit-de-corps-in-your-organization-2/> (accessed 19 September 2019).

Feuer, Michael, with Dustin S. Klein, *The Benevolent Dictator: Empower Your Employees, Build Your Business, and Outwit the Competition* (Hoboken, NJ: Wiley, 2011).

Fick, Annabella, 'Conrad Hilton, *Be My Guest* and American Popular Culture', *The European Journal of Life Writing* 2 (2013), pp. 18–34.

Flotte, Paul de, *La Souveraineté du peuple: essais sur l'esprit de la Révolution* (Paris: Pagnerre, 1851).

Follesdal, Andreas, 'The Principle of Subsidiarity as a Constitutional Principle in International Law', *Global Constitutionalism* 2.1 (2013), pp. 37–62.

Fonvielle, Bernard François Anne, *Situation de la France et de l'Angleterre à la fin du 18e siècle*, 2 vols (Paris, 1800).

Forbonnais, François Véron Duverger de, 'Communauté (commerce)', in Denis Diderot and Jean le Rond d'Alembert (eds), *Encyclopédie, ou dictionnaire raisonné des sciences, des arts et des métiers* (Paris: Briasson, David, Le Breton and Durand, 1751–65), vol. III (1753).

Fortescue, Earl Hugh, *Public schools for the middle classes* (London: Ridgway, 1880).

Fosdick, Raymond B., *The Story of the Rockefeller Foundation* (New Brunswick, NJ: Transaction Publishers, 1989 [1952]).

Foucart, Émile Victor, *Éléments de droit public et administratif*, 3 vols (Paris: Videcoq, 1843).

Foucault, Michel, *L'archéologie du savoir* (Paris: Gallimard, 1969).

Foucault, Michel, *'Il faut défendre la société': Cours au Collège de France, 1976* (Paris: Gallimard/Seuil, 1997).

Foucault, Michel, *Les mots et les choses: une archéologie des sciences humaines* (Paris: Gallimard, 1966).

Foucault, Michel, 'La naissance de la médicine sociale', in *Dits et ecrits II, 1976–1988* (Paris, Gallimard, 2001), pp. 209–10.

Foucault, Michel, 'Nietzsche, la généalogie, l'histoire', in *Hommage à Jean Hyppolite* (Paris: Presses Universitaires de France, 1971).

Foucault, Michel, *L'ordre du discours* (Paris: Gallimard, 1971).

Foucault, Michel, *Surveiller et punir* (Paris: Gallimard, 1975).

Fouillée, Alfred, *La Démocratie politique et sociale en France* (Paris, 1900).

Fouillée, Alfred, *L'Évolutionisme des idées-forces* (Paris: Alcan, 1890).

Fourier, Charles, 'Le groupe hypermajeur', in *Manuscrits de Fourier* (Paris: Librairie Phalanstérienne, 1849).

Fourier, Charles, *Théorie des quatre mouvements et des destinées générales* (Leipzig, 1808).

Frader, Laura L., 'Femmes, genre et mouvement ouvrier en France aux XIXe et XXe siècles: bilan et perspectives de recherche', *Clio. Histoire, femmes et société en ligne* 3.1 (1996), <https://www.cairn.info/revue-clio-1996-1-page-14.htm> (accessed 19 September 2019).

France, Anatole, *La vie en fleur* (Paris: Calmann-Lévy, 1922).

Frängsmyr, Tore, Heilbron, J. L., and Rider, Robin E. (eds), *The Quantifying Spirit in the Eighteenth Century* (Berkeley: University of California Press, 1990).

Frank, Tibor, 'Hegel in England: Victorian Thought Reconsidered', *Hungarian Studies in English* 13 (1980), pp. 49–58.

Franklin, Alfred, *Dictionnaire historique des arts, métiers et professions exercés dans Paris depuis le treizième siècle* (Paris: H. Welter, 1906).

Frauenheim, Ed, and Peters, Kim, 'Here's the Secret to How the Best Employers Inspire Workers', *Fortune*, 22 August 2016, <https://www.greatplacetowork.com/resources/articles/here-s-the-secret-to-how-the-best-employers-inspire-workers> (accessed 19 September 2019).

Frost, David, 'Liam Fox May Be a Virtual Minister – but he's Vital to Britain's Future Success', *The Telegraph*, 27 July 2016, <https://www.telegraph.co.uk/news/2016/07/27/fox-may-be-a-virtual-minister--but-hes-vital-to-britains-future/> (accessed 19 September 2019).

Frost, Tom, 'The *Dispositif* between Foucault and Agamben', *Law, Culture and the Humanities* 15.1 (2019), pp. 151–71, <https://journals.sagepub.com/doi/abs/10.1177/1743872115571697> (accessed 19 September 2019).

Fuller, John Frederick Charles, *Training Soldiers for War* (London: Rees, 1914).

Furet, François, *Marx et la Révolution Française* (Paris: Flammarion, 1992).

Gallie, Walter Bryce, 'Essentially Contested Concepts', *Proceedings of the Aristotelian Society* 56 (1956), pp. 167–98.

Galloway, Alexander R., *The Interface Effect* (Cambridge: Polity, 2012).

Gallup, *State of the American Workplace, 2010–2012*, <https://news.gallup.com/reports/178514/state-american-workplace.aspx> (accessed 19 September 2019).

Gannett, Cinthia, and Brereton, John C. (eds), *Traditions of Eloquence, The Jesuits and Modern Rhetorical Studies* (New York: Fordham University Press, 2016).

Gardner, Eric F., and Thompson, George G., *Social Relations and Morale in Small Groups* (New York: Appleton-Century-Crofts, 1956).

Gary, Romain, 'The Anger that Turned Generals into Desperados', *Life*, 5 May 1961, pp. 26–7.

Gauchet, Marcel, *La Révolution des droits de l'homme* (Paris: Gallimard, 1989).

Gaxotte, Pierre, *L'Académie française* (Paris: Hachette, 1965).

Genlis, Félicité de, 'La Femme Auteur', in *Nouveaux Contes moraux et nouvelles historiques*, 3 vols (Paris: Maradan, 1802), vol. III.

Gervaisais, Nicolas Magon de la, *La péninsule en tutelle* (Paris: Pihan-Delaforest, 1828).

Giard, V., and Brière, E. (eds), *Revue Internationale de Sociologie* (Paris: Institut International de Sociologie, 1908).

Gin, Pierre-Louis-Claude, *Discours sur l'histoire universelle, depuis Charlemagne jusqu'à nos jours* (Paris: Bertrand-Pottier, 1802).

Goffart, A., 'Les esprits animaux', *Revue néo-scolastique* 26 (1900), pp. 153–72.

Gold, Natalie, and Sugden, Robert, 'Collective Intentions and Team Agency', *The Journal of Philosophy* 104.3 (2007), pp. 109–37.

Goodman, Dena, *The Republic of Letters: A Cultural History of the French Enlightenment* (Ithaca: Cornell University Press, 1994).

Gourden, Jean-Michel, *Gens de métiers et sans-culottes: Les artisans dans la Révolution* (Paris: Créaphis, 1988).

Gournay, Jacques Claude Vincent de, *Mémoire à la chambre de commerce de Lyon* (Lyons: Archives Municipales, 1752).

Granada, Louis of, *L'exercice spirituel pour tous les jours de la semaine*, trans. François Primault du Mans (Lyons: Pillehotte, 1590).

Grivel, Guillaume, *Mélanges de philosophie et d'économie politique* (Paris: Briand, 1789).

Grofman, Bernard, and Feld, Scott L., 'Rousseau's General Will: A Condorcetian Perspective', *The American Political Science Review* 82.2 (1988), pp. 567–76.

Gross, Bertram, *Friendly Fascism: The New Face of Power in America* (Cambridge: South End Press, 1980).

Groult, Benoîte, *Ainsi soit Olympe de Gouges: la déclamation des droits de la femme et autres textes politiques* (Paris: Grasset, 2013).

Gueudeville, Nicolas, *L'Esprit des cours de l'Europe* (The Hague: Étienne Foulque, 1701).

Guglielmi, Gilles J., and Haroche, Claudine (eds), *Esprit de corps, démocratie et espace public* (Paris: Presses Universitaires de France, 2005).

Guilhaumou, Jacques, 'Sieyès et le non-dit de la *sociologie*: du mot à la chose', *Revue d'histoire des sciences humaines* 15 (2006), pp. 117–34.

Guillermou, Alain, *Saint Ignace de Loyola et la Compagnie de Jésus* (Paris: Seuil, 1960).

Guillo, Dominique, 'La Place de la biologie dans les premiers textes de Durkheim: un paradigme oublié?', *Revue française de sociologie* 47.3 (2006), pp. 507–35.

Guinier, Arnaud, *L'honneur du soldat: Éthique martiale et discipline guerrière dans la France des Lumières* (Paris: Champ Vallon, 2014).

Gündogdu, Ayten, 'Potentialities of Second Nature: Agamben on Human Rights', in Crina Archer, Laura Ephraim and Lida Maxwell (eds), *Second Nature: Rethinking the Natural through Politics* (New York: Fordham University Press, 2013).

Hacking, Ian, 'Jacques Bernoulli's Art of Conjecturing', *British Journal for the Philosophy of Science* 22.3 (1971), pp. 209–29.

Hallé, C., 'Discours prononcé dans la séance publique de l'École de Médicine, par le C. Hallé, président de l'École', in *Mercure de France, littéraire et politique* 11 (1803), p. 421.

Hamon, Thierry, 'Corporations et compagnonnage en Bretagne d'Ancien Régime', *Mémoires de la Société d'Histoire et d'Archéologie de Bretagne* (Rennes: SHAB, 1999), vol. LXXVII, pp. 165–221.

Harrison, Benjamin, *Views of An Ex-President*, compiled by Mary Lord Harrison (Indianapolis: Bowen-Merril, 1901).

Hazlitt, William, *A Reply to The Essay on Population by The Rev. T. R. Malthus* (London: Longman, 1807).

Hegel, G. W. F., *Philosophy of Right*, trans. Thomas Malcolm Knox (Oxford: Oxford University Press, 1942 [1820]).

Heilbron, Johan, *French Sociology* (Ithaca: Cornell University Press, 2015).

Helvétius, Claude Adrien, *De l'Esprit* (Paris: Durand, 1758).

Helvétius, Claude Adrien, 'Lettre de Helvétius à Saurin', in *Œuvres complètes d'Helvétius*, 5 vols (Paris: Servière, 1795), vol. V.

Hilton, Conrad Nicholson, *Be My Guest* (New York: Simon and Schuster, 1957).

Hippler, Thomas, *Citizens, Soldiers, and National Armies: Military Service in France and Germany, 1789–1830* (London: Routledge, 2008).

'Histoire du livre des Lumières', *Statistiques de la Bibliothèque Nationale de France*, <http://classes.bnf.fr/livre/arret/histoire-du-livre/lumieres/index.htm> (accessed 19 September 2019).

Hobbes, Thomas, *Leviathan*, ed. A. P. Martinich and Brian Battiste (Peterborough, ON: Broadview, 2010).

Hobbes, Thomas, 'Of Systemes Subject, Political, and Private', in *Leviathan, Reprinted from the Edition of 1651* (Oxford: Clarendon Press, 1909).

Hofstadter, Richard, *The Paranoid Style in American Politics and Other Essays* (Cambridge, MA: Harvard University Press, 1967).

Holcroft, Thomas, 'A view of Amsterdam', *The Lady's Magazine, or Entertaining Companion for the Fair Sex; Appropriated Solely to their Use and Amusement* 35 (1804), p. 80.

Hopper, Rex D., 'The Revolutionary Process: A Frame of Reference for the Study of Revolutionary Movements', *Social Forces* 28.3 (1950), pp. 270–9.

Hornberger, Marian Welles, 'A Tour of Discovery', *The Michigan Alumnus* 35.1 (1928), p. 21.

Horowitz, Amir, 'Ronald Dworkin's Group Fetishism', *Journal of Markets and Morality* 5.2 (2002), pp. 415–23.

Horowitz, Irving Louis, *The Rise and Fall of Project Camelot: Studies in the Relationship Between Social Science and Practical Politics* (Cambridge, MA: MIT Press, 1967).

Howarth, David, and Howarth, Stephen, *Nelson: The Immortal Memory* (London: Conway Maritime Press, 2004).

Howe, Winifred E., *A History of the Metropolitan Museum of Art* (New York: Metropolitan Museum of Art, 1913).

Hugues, Hugh P., *Goodwill in Accounting: A History of the Issues and Problems* (Atlanta: Georgia State University Press, 1982).

Hunter, Ian, 'Secularization: The Birth of a Modern Combat Concept', *Modern Intellectual History* 12.1 (2015), pp. 1–32.

Hussey, Lieutenant C. L., 'Systematic Training of the Enlisted Personnel of the Navy', *Proceedings of the United States Naval Institute* 29.1/105 (1903), <https://www.usni.org/magazines/proceedings/1903/january/systematic-training-enlisted-personnel-navy> (accessed 19 September 2019).

Hutchins, Edwin, *Cognition in the Wild* (Cambridge, MA: MIT Press, 1995).

Icher, François, *Le compagnonnage* (Paris: Gallimard, 1994).

Jackson, Colonel J. R., *On National Education; With Remarks on Education in General* (London: Alexander and Co., 1840).

Jackson, Philip W., *Life in Classrooms* (New York: Holt, Rinehart and Wilson, 1968).

Jacob, Margaret C., 'Newtonianism and the Origins of the Enlightenment', *Eighteenth-Century Studies* 11.1 (1977), pp. 1–25.

Janet, Paul, *Traité élémentaire de philosophie à l'usage des classes* (Paris: Delagrave, 1899).

Janis, Irving L., 'Groupthink', *Psychology Today Magazine* 5 (1971), pp. 43–6, 74–6.

Jardine, Alexander, 'Letter III from Portugal to Friends in England', in *Letters from Barbary, France, Spain, Portugal, etc., by an English officer*, 2 vols (London: Cadell, 1788), vol. II.

Jefferson, Thomas, 'Thomas Jefferson to The Secretary of The Treasury (Albert Gallatin), 13 December 1803', in *The Works of Thomas Jefferson*, ed. Paul Leicester Ford, 12 vols (New York and London: Putnam, 1904–5), vol. X, p. 56.

Jeffries, Charles, *The Colonial Empire and its Civil Service* (Cambridge: Cambridge University Press, 1938).

Johnson, Samuel, *A Dictionary of the English Language*, 5 vols (London: Longman, 1818).

Johnson and Walker's Dictionary of the English Language (London: Pickering, 1828).

Journal des débats et décrets de l'Assemblée Nationale (Paris: Baudoin, 1790).

Journal de Médicine et de Chirurgie Pratique, à l'usage des médecins praticiens (Paris: Crapelet, 1844), vol. XV.

Julia, Dominique, 'Les professeurs, l'Eglise et l'État après l'expulsion des Jésuites', *Historical Reflections* 7.2–3 (1980), pp. 459–81.

Jünger, Ernst, 'Total Mobilization', trans. Joel Golb and Richard Wolin, in Richard Wolin (ed.), *The Heidegger Controversy: A Critical Reader* (Cambridge, MA: MIT Press, 1993).

Ka, Pauline, 'The Concept of National Character in Eighteenth-Century France', *Cromohs*, 7 (2002), pp. 1–6, <http://www.fupress.net/index.php/cromohs/article/view/15716/14605> (accessed 19 September 2019).

Kafker, Frank A., and Kafker, Serena L., *The Encyclopédistes as Individuals: A*

Biographical Dictionary of the Authors of the Encyclopédie (Oxford: Voltaire Foundation, 1988).

Kant, Immanuel, *Vorlesungen über Moralphilosophie* (Berlin: de Gruyter, 1975).

Kantorowicz, Ernst H., *The King's Two Bodies* (Princeton: Princeton University Press, 1958).

Kaplan, Steven L., *La fin des corporations*, trans. Béatrice Vierne (Paris: Fayard, 2001).

Kaplan, Steven, 'Réflexions sur la police du monde du travail, 1700–1815', *Revue Historique* 261 (1979), pp. 17–77.

Kaufman, Bruce E., *The Global Evolution of Industrial Relations* (New Delhi: Academic Foundation, 2006).

Kay, Oliver, 'Ronaldo Revels in his New Image as Ultimate Team Man', *The Times*, 12 July 2016, <https://www.thetimes.co.uk/article/ronaldo-takes-glory-in-his-finest-hour-as-first-among-equals-5fv3pgc8t> (accessed 19 September 2019).

Kawano, Kenji, 'The French Revolution and the Progress of Capitalism', *Kyoto University Economic Review* 30.2 (1960), pp. 31–42.

K. E., Corporal, 'An A.C. Squadron in Libya', *The Royal Air Force Quarterly* 14–15 (1942).

Kertzer, David, *Ritual, Politics, and Power* (New Haven, CT: Yale University Press, 1988).

Kessler, Marie-Christine, 'Les grands corps de l'État', *La Revue administrative* 231 (1996), pp. 221–8.

Khaldun, Ibn, *Les Prolégomènes d'Ibn Khaldoun*, trans. William de Slane (Paris: Imprimerie Impériale, 1863), pp. 341–97.

Kinderling, Johann Friedrich August, *Über die Reinigkeit der Deutschen Sprache* (Berlin: Maurer, 1795).

Kingston, Rebecca, *Montesquieu and the Parlement de Bordeaux* (Geneva: Droz, 1996).

Kossen, Stan, *Supervision: A Practical Guide to First-Line Management* (New York: Harper and Row, 1981).

Kulp II, Daniel Harrison, *Education Sociology* (New York: Longmans, Green, 1932).

Kwass, Michael, 'Consumption and the World of Ideas: Consumer Revolution and the Moral Economy of the Marquis de Mirabeau', *Eighteenth-Century Studies* 37.2 (2004), pp. 187–213.

La Mettrie, Julien Offray de, *L'Homme-machine*, in *Œuvres philosophiques*, ed. Francine Markovits, 2 vols (Paris: Fayard, 1987), vol. I.

La Valine, Joseph, 'Memoir of G. F. Poullain de Saint-Foix', *Gentleman's Magazine* 19 (1843), p. 37.

Lacassagne, Alexandre (ed.), *Archives d'anthropologie criminelle, de médecine légale et de psychologie normale et pathologique* (Lyons, 1900).

Lagardelle, Hubert, *L'Évolution des syndicats ouvriers en France. De l'interdiction à l'obligation* (Paris: L'Émancipatrice, 1901).

Lakoff, George, *Moral Politics: How Liberals and Conservatives Think* (Chicago: University of Chicago Press, 2002).

Lameere, Jean, and de Coster, Sylvain, *Esprit d'une politique générale de l'éducation* (Brussels: Lebègue, 1946)

Latour, Bruno, *Enquête sur les modes d'existence: Une anthropologie des modernes* (Paris: La Découverte, 2013).

Lauring, Jakob, and Selmer, Jan, 'Multicultural Organizations: Common Language and Group Cohesiveness', *International Journal of Cross Cultural Management* 10.3 (2010), pp. 267–84.

Lautzenheiser, Tim, *The Art of Successful Teaching: A Blend of Content and Context* (Chicago: GIA Publications, 1992).

Lavie, Jean-Charles de, *Des corps politiques et de leurs gouvernements*, 3 vols (Lyons: Duplain, 1764–66).

Le Chapelier, Isaac René Guy, 'Séance du mardi 14 juin 1791 à l'Assemblée nationale', *Archives parlementaires*, French Revolution Archive <https://frda. stanford.edu/en/catalog/ph525xc1642_00_0203> (accessed 19 September 2019).

Le Prévost d'Exmes, François, *La revue des feuilles de Mr. Fréron, Lettres à Madame de **** (London, 1756).

Lefranc, Georges, *Histoire du travail et des travailleurs* (Paris: Flammarion, 1957).

Legret, G. P., *Sur les corporations* (Paris: Scherff, 1818).

Lemmings, David, *Professors of the Law: Barristers and English Legal Culture in the Eighteenth Century* (Oxford: Oxford University Press, 2000).

'Lennox, Charles, Third Duke of Richmond', *Encyclopaedia Britannica Online* (2008), <https://www.britannica.com/biography/Charles-Lennox-3rd-duke-of-Richmond> (accessed 19 September 2019).

Leroux, Pierre, 'Religion. Aux philosophes', in *Revue Encylopédique, ou analyse raisonnée des productions les plus remarquables dans la littérature, les sciences et les arts* (Paris: Sédillot, 1831), vol. LI.

Leroy, Michel, *Le Mythe jésuite: de Béranger à Michelet* (Paris: Presses Universitaires de France, 1992).

Leroy-Beaulieu, Paul, 'Un nouveau pas dans la voie du socialisme. Le syndicat obligatoire', *L'Économiste Français*, 29 September 1900, p. 423.

Lespinasse, René de, *Les métiers et corporations de la ville de Paris du XIVe au XVIIIe siècle* (Paris: Imprimerie Nationale, 1886).

Levacher-Duplessis, Antoine, *Réponse des délégués des marchands en détail et des maîtres artisans de la ville de Paris aux Rapports et délibérations des conseils généraux du commerce et des manufactures établis auprès de Son Excellence le ministre de l'Intérieur* (Paris: Dondey-Dupré, 1821).

Lev-Ari, Shiri, San Giacomo, Marcela, and Peperkamp, Sharon, 'The Effect of Domain Prestige and Interlocutors' Bilinguism on Loanword Adaptations', *Journal of Sociolinguistics* 18.5 (2014), pp. 658–84.

Levinger, Matthew, 'La rhétorique protestataire du Parlement de Rouen (1753–1763)', *Annales: Économies, Sociétés, Civilisations* 3 (1990), pp. 589–613.

Litton, Edward Arthur, *University Reform, A Letter to the Right Hon. Lord John Russel* (London: Hatchard, 1850).

Littré, Emile, *Dictionnaire de la langue française* (Paris: Hachette, 1872).

Lizardo, Omar, 'The Cognitive Origins of Bourdieu's *Habitus*', *Journal for the Theory of Social Behaviour* 34.4 (2004), pp. 376–401.

Lojkine, Stéphane, 'Le décentrement matérialiste du champ des connaissances dans l'Encyclopédie', *Recherches sur Diderot et sur l'Encyclopédie* 26 (1999), <http://rde.revues.org/1041> (accessed 19 September 2019).

Louis XVI, *Édit du Roi: portant suppression des communautés d'art & métiers ci-devant établies dans les villes du ressort du parlement de Paris* (Versailles: Imprimerie Royale, 1777).

Lovejoy, Arthur O., *The Great Chain of Being. A Study in the History of an Idea* (Cambridge, MA: Harvard University Press, 1936).

Loyd Jones, I. D., 'Charles Fourier: Faithful Pupil of the Enlightenment', in Peter Gilmour (ed.), *Philosophers of the Enlightenment* (Edinburgh: Edinburgh University Press, 1990).

Lubove, Roy, *The Struggle for Social Security, 1900–1935* (Pittsburgh: University of Pittsburgh Press, 1986).

Lucia, S. P., 'Edward Lyman Munson', 1947, University of California: In Memoriam, Calisphere California Digital Library, <http://texts.cdlib.org/view?docId=hb1m3nb0fr&doc.view=frames&chunk.id=div00007&toc.depth=1&toc.id=> (accessed 19 September 2019).

Lukács, Georg, *History and Class Consciousness* (London: Merlin Press, 1971).

Lusthaus, Charles, Adrien, Marie-Hélène, Anderson, Gary, and Carden, Fred, *Améliorer la performance individuelle: manuel d'auto-évaluation* (Ottawa: CRDI, 1998).

Lybeck, Eric R., 'Geist (Spirit): History of the Concept', in *International Encyclopedia of the Social and Behavioral Sciences* (Amsterdam: Elsevier, 2015), vol. IX, pp. 666–70.

Lyons, John O., *The Invention of the Self, The Hinge of Consciousness in the Eighteenth Century* (Carbondale, IL: Southern Illinois University Press, 1978).

Macdonnel, David Evans, *A Dictionary of Quotations in Most Frequent Use, Taken chiefly from the Latin and French, but comprising many from the Greek, Spanish, and Italian Languages* (London: Wilkie and Robinson, 1809).

Mackenzie, Alex Muir, *General Observations upon the probable effects of any measures which have for their object the increase of the regular army* (Edinburgh: Manners and Miller, 1807).

Maclear, James F. (ed.), *Church and State in the Modern Age: A Documentary History* (Oxford: Oxford University Press, 1995).

MacKinnon, Neil J., and Heise, David R., *Self, Identity, and Social Institutions* (New York: Palgrave Macmillan, 2010).

Madeline, Félix, *Jean-Noël Hallé (1754–1822): Médecin ordinaire de Napoléon* (Paris: Office Parisien, 2011).

Mahan, Alfred Thayer, *From Sail to Steam, Recollections of Naval Life* (New York: Harper and Brothers, 1907).

Maison-Neuve, Jean de la, *Colloque social de paix, justice, miséricorde, et vérité pour l'heureux accord des très augustes rois de France et d'Espagne* (Paris: Martin L'Homme, 1559).

Maistre, Joseph de, *Étude sur la souveraineté*, in *Œuvres complètes* (Lyons: Vitte, 1884 [1794]).

Malthus, Thomas Robert, *An Essay on The Principle of Population: Or a View of Its Past and Present Effects on Human Happiness* (London: Bensley, 1803).

Mandeville, Bernard, *The Fable of the Bees, or, private vices, publick benefits* (London: Roberts, 1714).

Marana, Jean-Paul, *L'espion du Grand-Seigneur et ses relations secrètes envoyées à Constantinople* (Paris: Barbin, 1686).

Marshall, Max S., 'The Concept of Immunity', *The Centennial Review of Arts and Science* 3.1 (1959), pp. 95–113.

Maruyama, Magoroh, 'Cultural Engineering Toward Mental Health: Individual, Intracultural and Transcultural Solutions', *Zeitschrift für Ethnologie* 90.2 (1965), pp. 282–92.

Marx, Karl, and Engels, Friedrich, *The German Ideology*, trans. Richard Dixon and Clemens Dutt (Amherst, MA: Prometheus Books, 1976).

Marx, Karl, and Engels, Friedrich, *Manifest der Kommunistischen Partei* (London: Burghard, 1848).

Mashaal, Maurice, *Bourbaki, A Secret Society of Mathematicians* (Providence: American Mathematical Society, 2006).

Maurois, André, *Les silences du Colonel Bramble* (Paris: Grasset, 1918).

May, Louis-Philippe, 'Note sur les origines maçonniques de l'Encyclopédie suivie de la liste des encyclopédistes', *Revue de synthèse* 58 (1939), pp. 5–110.

Mazel, Henri, *Pour causer de tout: Petit dictionaire des idées et des opinions* (Paris: Grasset, 1909).

Mazel, Henri, *La Synergie sociale* (Paris: Colin, 1896).

McFadden, Robert D., 'Robert H. B. Baldwin, Transformer of Morgan Stanley, Dies at 95', *The New York Times*, 6 January 2016, <https://www.nytimes.com/2016/01/07/business/dealbook/robert-hb-baldwin-transformer-of-morgan-stanley-dies-at-95.html> (accessed 19 September 2019).

McGregor, Jay, '2% of Google Employees Are Black and Just 30% Are Women', *Forbes*, 29 May 2014, <https://www.forbes.com/sites/jaymcgregor/2014/05/29/2-of-google-employees-are-black-and-just-30-are-women/#7ff55990490e> (accessed 19 September 2019).

McKerrow, Mary, *Mary Brunton: The Forgotten Scottish Novelist* (Kirkwall: The Orcadian, 2001).

McIntyre, Lee, 'To Fix the Social Sciences, Look to the "Dark Ages" of Medicine', *The MIT Press Reader* (2019), <https://thereader.mitpress.mit.edu/social-sciences-dark-ages/> (accessed 19 September 2019).

Meggle, George (ed.), *Social Facts and Intentionality* (Frankfurt: Hänsel-Hohenhausen, 2002).

Mehlman, Jeffrey, 'The "Floating Signifier": From Lévi-Strauss to Lacan', *Yale French Studies* 48 (1972), pp. 10–37.

Meillassoux, Quentin, 'History and Event in Alain Badiou', trans. Thomas Nail, *Parrhesia* 12 (2011), pp. 1–11.

Meiskins Wood, Ellen, *Liberty & Property: A Social History of Western Political Thought from Renaissance to Enlightenment* (New York: Verso, 2012).

Mercier, Hugo, and Sperber, Dan, *The Enigma of Reason: A New Theory of Human Understanding* (London: Penguin Random House, 2018).

Mercier, Hugo, and Sperber, Dan, 'Why Do Humans Reason? Arguments for an Argumentative Theory', *Behavioral and Brain Sciences* 34 (2011), pp. 57–111.

Mercier, Louis Sébastien, *Tableau de Paris* (Amsterdam, 1782).

Mercklé, Pierre, 'La "science sociale" de Charles Fourier', *Revue d'Histoire des Sciences Humaines* 2 (2006), pp. 69–88.

Merey, Pierre Soufflot de, *Considérations sur le rétablissement des jurandes et maîtrises* (Paris: Marchant, 1805).

Mérilhou, Joseph, *Œuvres de Mirabeau, Discours et opinions*, vol. II (Paris: Dupont and Brissot-Thivars, 1825).

Michaud, Louis-Gabriel (ed.), *Biographie universelle ancienne et moderne*, 52 vols (Paris: Michaud, 1811–28), vol. XXXIX (1825).

Michel, Jean-Baptiste, et al., 'Quantitative Analysis of Culture Using Millions of Digitized Books', *Science* 311 (2011), pp. 176–82.

Mintzker, Yair, '"A Word Newly Introduced into Language"': The Appearance and Spread of "Social" in French Enlightened Thought, 1745–1765', *History of European Ideas* 34.4 (2008), pp. 500–13.

Mirabeau, *Courrier de Provence* (Paris: François, 1789).

Mirabeau, *De la monarchie prussienne sous Frédéric Le Grand*, 8 vols (London: Brunel, 1788).

Mirabeau, *Enquiries concerning Lettres de Cachet, the Consequences of Arbitrary Imprisonment and a History of the Inconveniences, Distresses, and Sufferings of State Prisoners*, 2 vols (London: Robinson, 1787).

Moleville, Antoine François Bertrand de, *Annals of the French Revolution*, 4 vols (London: Cadell and Davies, 1800).

Moleville, Antoine François Bertrand de, *Histoire de la Révolution de France pendant les dernières années du règne de Louis XVI*, 10 vols (Paris: Giguet and Michaud, 1800).

Montandré, Claude Du Bosc de, *L'esprit de la vérité, Représentant nuëment la Puissance et l'Authorité du Roy* (Paris, 1652).

Montesquieu, Charles-Louis de Secondat, Baron de, *De l'Esprit des Loix, ou du rapport que les Loix doivent avoir avec la Constitution de chaque Gouvernement, les Mœurs, le Climat, la Religion, le Commerce, &c.*, 2 vols (Geneva: Barillot, 1748).

Montesquieu, Charles-Louis de Secondat, Baron de, *De l'esprit des lois* (London: Nourse, 1772).

Montesquieu, Charles-Louis de Secondat, Baron de, *Lettres persanes*, 2 vols (Amsterdam: Brunel, 1721).

Montoux, Alain, *Dictionnaire des organisations* (Paris: Publibook, 2012).

More, Hannah, *Strictures on the Modern System of Female Education, with a view of the principles and conducts prevalent among women of rank and fortune*, 2 vols (London: Cadell and Davies, 1799).

Mouffe, Chantal, *Agonistics: Thinking the World Politically* (London: Verso, 2013).

Mouffe, Chantal, 'Hearts, Minds and Radical Democracy', interview, *Red Pepper*, <https://www.redpepper.org.uk/hearts-minds-and-radical-democracy/> (accessed 19 September 2019).

Mouffe, Chantal, *On the Political* (London: Routledge, 2005).

'Mr. F. R. Upcott', in *Sessional Papers of the House of Commons, Inventory control record 1* (1904), vol. 64.

'Mr. Grey's motion for a Reform in Parliament, Debate', *The Parliamentary History of England* (London: Hansard, 1817), vol. XXX.

Muir, Rory, *Tactics and the Experience of Battle in the Age of Napoleon* (New Haven, CT: Yale University Press, 1998)

Munson, Edward Lyman, Jr, *Leadership for American Army Leaders* (Washington, DC: The Infantry Journal, 1941).

Munson, Edward Lyman, Jr, *The Management of Men, A Handbook on the Systematic Development of Morale and the Control of Human Behavior* (New York: Holt, 1921).

Nafziger, George F., *Historical Dictionary of the Napoleonic Era* (Lanham, MD: Scarecrow Press, 2002).

Namier, Lewis, and Brooke, John, *The History of Parliament: The House of Commons, 1754–1790* (London: Secker and Warburg, 1964).

Napoléon, 'Note sur les Lycées du 16 février 1805', *Correspondance de Napoléon Ier*, 32 vols (Paris: Plon and Dumaine, 1858–70), vol. X.

Ndrianaivo, 'Esprit de groupe', *La Vérité*, 31 May 2016, <https://researchone spritdecorps.wordpress.com/2016/06/01/solidarity-madagascar/> (accessed 19 September 2019).

Newell, Frederick Haynes, 'Address by the Chief Engineer', *Proceedings of the First Conference of Engineers of the Reclamation Service* (Washington, DC: Government Printing Office, 1904).

Nienaber-Clarke, Jeanine, and McCool, Daniel, *Staking Out the Terrain: Power Differentials Among Natural Resource Management Agencies* (Albany: State University of New York Press, 1985).

Nietzsche, Friedrich, *La Généalogie de la Morale*, trans. Henri Albert, in *Oeuvres complètes de Frédéric Nietzsche* (Paris: Mercure de France, 1900), vol. XI.

Nietzsche, Friedrich, *On the Genealogy of Morals*, trans. Horace Barnett Samuel (New York: Boni and Liveright, 1913).

Nietzsche, Friedrich, *Zur Genealogie der Moral* (Leipzig: Naumann, 1887), in Nietzsche Source, Digital Critical Edition, <http://www.nietzschesource.org/#eKGWB/GM> (accessed 19 September 2019).

Nussbaum, Martha C., 'Patriotism and Cosmopolitanism', *Boston Review*, 1 October 1994, <http://bostonreview.net/martha-nussbaum-patriotism-and-cosmopolitanism> (accessed 19 September 2019).

Oakeshott, Michael J., *The Social and Political Doctrines of Contemporary Europe* (Cambridge: Cambridge University Press, 1939).

Olivier-Martin, François, *L'organisation corporative de la France d'ancien régime* (Paris: Sirey, 1938).

Olson, Richard, *Science Deified and Science Defied: The Historical Significance of Science in Western Culture*, 2 vols (Berkeley: University of California Press, 1990).

Onfray, Michel, *Georges Palante: essai sur un Nietzschéen de gauche* (Bédée: Folle Avoine, 1989).

Orwell, George, *Burmese Days* (London: Penguin, 1975).

Osborn, Richard, Hunt, James G., and Jauch, Lawrence R., *Organization Theory: An Integrated Approach* (Hoboken, NJ: Wiley, 1980).

Osrecki, Fran, 'Constructing Epochs: The Argumentative Structures of Sociological Epochalisms', *Cultural Sociology* 9.2 (2015), pp. 131–46.

Palante, Georges, *Combat pour l'individu* (Paris: Alcan, 1904).

Palante, Georges, 'L'Esprit de corps', *Revue philosophique de la France et de l'étranger* 48 (1899), pp. 135–45.

Palonen, Kari, 'The History of Concepts as a Style of Political Theorizing', *European Journal of Political Theory* 1.1 (2002), pp. 91–106.

Parker, Walter C., *Teaching Democracy: Unity and Diversity in Public Life* (New York: Teachers College Press, 2003).

Parliamentary Debates, Official Report (London: HMSO, 1943), vol. 391.

The Parliamentary History of England From the Earliest Period to the Year 1803 (London: Hansard, 1814), vol. XX.

Pastoors, Martin, 'Exponential Growth in the Number of Words Used for the European Common Fisheries Policy (CFP): Does Better Management Require More Text?', *Marine Policy* 46 (2014), pp. 101–4.

Pearson, Hesketh, *Sir Walter Scott: His Life and Personality* (New York: Harper, 1964).

Pellarin, Charles, *Théorie sociétaire* (Paris: Librairie Phalanstérienne, 1850).

Pérezts, Mar, Faÿ, Eric, and Picard, Sébastien, 'Ethics, Embodied Life and *Esprit de Corps*: An Ethnographic Study with Anti-Money-Laundering Analysts', *Organization* 22.2 (2015), pp. 217–34

Perry, John, *Winston Churchill* (New York: Thomas Nelson, 2010).

Persons, Charles E., 'Women's Work and Wages in the United States', *The Quarterly Journal of Economics* 29.2 (1915), pp. 201–34.

Peyronnet, Pierre, 'François Le Prévost d'Exmes', in *Dictionnaire des journalistes 1600–1789*, <http://dictionnaire-journalistes.gazettes18e.fr/journaliste/499-francois-le-prevost-dexmes> (accessed 19 September 2019).

Pickering, Mary, *Auguste Comte: An Intellectual Biography*, 2 vols (Cambridge: Cambridge University Press, 1993).

Piercey, Robert, *The Uses of the Past from Heidegger to Rorty: Doing Philosophy Historically* (Cambridge: Cambridge University Press, 2009).

Piguet, Marie-France, 'Individualisme: Origine et reception initiale du mot', *Œuvres et critiques* 33.1 (2008), pp. 39–60.

Pilcher, Lewis S., 'An Antitoxin for Medical Commercialism', *The Michigan Alumnus* 18 (1912), p. 321.

'Pinckney, Charles Cotesworth', *Encyclopaedia Britannica Online* (2009), <https://www.britannica.com/biography/Charles-Cotesworth-Pinckney> (accessed 19 September 2019).

Plato, *Republic*, trans. Allan Bloom (New York: Basic Books, 1991).

Playfair, Lyon, *On Teaching Universities and Examining Boards* (Dublin: Hodges, Foster, 1873).

Pocock, John Greville Agard, 'The History of Political Thought: A Methodological Enquiry', in P. Laslett and W. Runciman (eds), *Philosophy, Politics and Society* (Oxford: Basil Blackwell, 1962), pp. 183–202.

Pocock, John Greville Agard, *Political Thought and History: Essays on Theory and Method* (Cambridge: Cambridge University Press, 2009).

Pons, R., 'Le Code du Travail', *Civilisations* 3.3 (1953), p. 378.

Porritt, Edward, *The Unreformed House of Commons* (Cambridge: Cambridge University Press, 1909).

Previtali, Fabiane Santana, and Fagiani, Cilson César, 'Deskilling and Degradation of Labour in Contemporary Capitalism: The Continuing Relevance of Baverman', *Work Organisation, Labour and Globalisation* 9.1 (2015), pp. 76–91.

Proust, Jacques, 'L'idée de nature en France dans la première moité du XVIIIe siècle', *Annales Historiques de la Révolution Française* 178 (1964), pp. 478–88.

Pugliese, David, 'Canadian Army Generals to Get Maple Leaf Insignias Back', *National Post*, 1 April 2016, <https://nationalpost.com/news/canada/canadian-army-generals-to-get-maple-leaf-insignias-back> (accessed 19 September 2019).

Rabaut Saint-Étienne, Jean-Paul, *Considérations trés-importantes sur les intérêts du Tiers-État, adressées au peuple des Provinces, par l'Auteur de l'Avis Important sur le Ministère et sur l'Assemblée prochaine des États-Généraux* (1788).

Rabaut de Saint-Etienne, Jean-Paul, *The History of the Revolution of France* (London: Debrett, 1792).

Rabaut Saint-Étienne, Jean-Paul, *Précis historique de la Révolution Française* (Paris: Onfroy, 1792).

Randolph, Edmund, *Germanicus* (Philadelphia, 1794).

Raynal, Guillaume 'Abbé', *Histoire philosophique et politique des établissements et du commerce des Européens dans les deux Indes* (La Haye, 1776).

Reddy, William M., *The Rise of Market Culture: The Textile Trade and French Society, 1750–1914* (Cambridge: Cambridge University Press, 1984).

Rehberg, August Wilhelm, *Recherches sur la Révolution Française*, trans. Lukas K. Sosoe (Paris: Vrin, 1998).

Remontrances de la Cour Souveraine de Lorraine et Barrois au Roi (Nancy: Charlot, 1755).

'Remontrances du parlement de Metz au sujet de ce qui s'est passé en Bretagne, 15 Mai 1765', in *La clef du cabinet des Princes de l'Europe* (Luxembourg: Chevalier, 1765), vol. CXXIII.

Rettman, Andrew, 'France and Germany Propose EU "Defence Union"', *Euobserver*, 12 September 2016, <https://euobserver.com/foreign/135022> (accessed 19 September 2019).

'Richmond, The Duke of', *The Parliamentary register; or, History of the proceedings and debates of the House of Commons*, 17 vols (London: Wilson, 1802), vol. X.

Rimington, Brigadier-General M. F., and Baden-Powell, Major-General R. S. S., 'The Spirit of Cavalry Under Napoleon', *Journal of the Royal United Service Institution* 50.344 (1906), p. 1236.

Riordan, Christine M., 'We All Need Friends at Work', *Harvard Business Review*, 3 July 2013, <https://hbr.org/2013/07/we-all-need-friends-at-work> (accessed 19 September 2019).

Ritter, Joachim, *Hegel and the French Revolution* (Cambridge, MA: MIT Press, 1982).

Roberge, Marie-Hélène, Xu, Qiumei Jane, and Rousseau, Denise M., 'Collective Personality Effects on Group Citizenship Behavior?', *Small Group Research* 43.4 (2012), pp. 410–42.

Rodrigues, Carl A., 'Fayol's 14 Principles of Management Then and Now: A Framework for Managing Today's Organizations Effectively', *Management Decision* 39 (2005), pp. 880–9.

Roosbroeck, Gustave Leopold van, *Persian Letters before Montesquieu* (New York: Institute of French Studies, 1932).

Rosanvallon, Pierre, *Le Modèle politique français: la société civile contre le jacobinisme de 1789 à nos jours* (Paris: Seuil, 2004).

Roth, Michael S., 'Foucault's History of the Present', *History and Theory* 20.1 (1981), pp. 32–46.

Rousseau, Jean-Jacques, 'De la patrie', in *Œuvres complètes*, 5 vols (Paris: Bibliothèque de la Pléiade, 1969), vol. III.

Rousseau, Jean-Jacques, *Discours sur l'origine et les fondements de l'inégalité parmi les hommes* (Geneva: Rey, 1755).

Rousseau, Jean-Jacques, *Du contrat social ou principes du droit politique* (Amsterdam: Rey, 1762).

Rousseau, Jean-Jacques, *Émile ou de l'Éducation*, in *Collection complète des oeuvres*, 4 vols (Geneva: Société Typographique, 1782 [1762]), vol. IV.

Rousseau, Jean-Jacques, *Lettres écrites de la montagne* (Amsterdam: Rey, 1764).

Rousset, Camille, *Les Volontaires: 1791–1794* (Paris: Didier, 1870).

Roux, Vital, *De l'influence du gouvernement sur la prospérité du commerce* (Paris: Fayolle, 1800).

Rowe, John Scofield, 'Practical Philosophies: Esprit de Corps', *The Monroe Monitor*, 9 August 1929.

Rowe, R. Robinson, 'Cashing in on Mathematics', *Crux Mathematicorum* 4.7 (1978), pp. 189–90.

Ryle, Gilbert, *The Concept of Mind* (Chicago: University of Chicago Press, 1949).

Saint-Foix, Germain Poullain de, *Essais historiques sur Paris*, 5 vols (London: Duchesne, 1766).

Saint-Foix, Germain Poullain de, *Lettres de Nedim Coggia, Secrétaire de l'Ambassade de Mehemet Effendi à la Cour de France* (Amsterdam: Pierre Mortier, 1732).

Saint-Foix, Germain Poullain de, *Œuvres complètes de M. de Saint-Foix*, 5 vols (Paris: Duchesne, 1778).

Saint Lambert, Jean-François de, *Œuvres philosophiques*, 5 vols (Paris: Agasse, 1800).

Saint-Pierre, Jacques-Bernardin-Henri de, *Etudes de la nature*, 4 vols (Paris: Didot and Mequignon, 1788).

Saint-Simon, *Mémoires complets et authentiques du duc de Saint-Simon*, 21 vols (Paris: Sautelet, 1830).

Salem, Lilia Ben, 'La notion de pouvoir dans l'oeuvre d'Ibn Khaldun', *Cahiers Internationaux de Sociologie* 55 (1973), pp. 293–314.

Salmon, Jacob, *The Origins of Totalitarian Democracy* (London: Mercury Books, 1919).

Sand, George, *Histoire de ma vie*, 10 vols (Paris: Lévy, 1893 [1856]).

Sandras, Gatien de Courtilz de, *Mémoires de Mr. d'Artagnan, Capitaine Lieutenant de la première Compagnie des Mousquetaires du Roi* (Cologne: Marteau, 1700).

Saussure, Ferdinand de, *Cours de linguistique générale* (Paris: Payot, 1995 [1916]).

Say, Léon, *Turgot* (Paris: Institut Coppet, 2014 [1887]).

Schmitt, Carl, *The Concept of the Political*, trans. George Schwab (Chicago: University of Chicago Press, 1996).

Schofield, Philip, 'Jeremy Bentham's "Nonsense upon Stilts"', *Utilitas* 15.1 (2003), pp. 1–26.

Schor, Naomi, 'The Crisis of French Universalism', *Yale French Studies* 100 (2001), p. 43.

Schroeder, Prosper, *La loi de la gravitation universelle, Newton, Euler et Laplace* (Paris: Springer, 2007).

Schumpeter, Joseph, *Capitalism, Socialism, and Democracy* (New York: Harper and Brothers, 1942).

Schumpeter, 'Valley of the Dudes', *The Economist*, 4 April 2015, <https://www.economist.com/business/2015/04/04/valley-of-the-dudes> (accessed 19 September 2019).

Schuster, Marilyn R., *Passionate Communities: Reading Lesbian Resistance in Jane Rule's Fiction* (New York: New York University Press, 1999).

Schwarz, Michiel, and Thompson, Michael, *Divided We Stand: Redefining Politics, Technology, and Social Choice* (Philadelphia: University of Pennsylvania Press, 1990).

Schwob, Marcel, and Guieysse, Georges, *Études sur l'argot français* (Paris: Bouillon, 1889).

Scott, Hamish, 'The Seven Years War and Europe's *Ancien Régime*', *War in History* 18.4 (2011), pp. 419–55.

Scott, Walter, 'On the present state of periodical criticism', *The Edinburgh Annual Register For 1809* (Edinburgh: Ballantyne, 1811), vol. II.

Scott, William, 'Commerce, Capitalism, and the Political Culture of the French Revolution', *History of European Ideas* 11 (1989), pp. 89–105.

Searle, John, 'Collective Intentions and Actions', in Philip R. Cohen, Jerry Morgan and Martha E. Pollack (eds), *Intentions in Communication* (Cambridge: Bradford Books, 1990).

Segev, Elad, *Google and the Digital Divide: The Bias of Online Knowledge* (Oxford: Chandos, 2010).

Sénat: Compte-rendu in extenso (Paris: Assemblée Nationale, 1902).

Servan, Joseph-Michel-Antoine, *Doutes d'un provincial* (Lyons: Prault, 1784).

Sewell, William H., Jr, 'Connecting Capitalism to the French Revolution: The Parisian Promenade and the Origins of Civic Equality in Eighteenth-Century France', *Critical Historical Studies* 1.1 (2014), pp. 5–46.

Sewell, William H., Jr, 'La confraternité des prolétaires: conscience de classe sous la Monarchie de Juillet', *Annales. Histoire, Sciences Sociales* 4 (1981), pp. 650–71.

Sewell, William H., Jr, *Work and Revolution in France: The Language of Labor from the Old Regime to 1848* (Cambridge: Cambridge University Press, 1980).

Shenhav, Yehouda, *Manufacturing Rationality: The Engineering Foundations of the Managerial Revolution* (Oxford: Oxford University Press, 2002).

Shorter, Edward, and Tilly, Charles, 'Le déclin de la grève violente en France de 1890 à 1835', *Le Mouvement social* 76 (1971), pp. 95–118.

Sibalis, Michael David, 'Corporatism after the Corporations: The Debate on Restoring the Guilds under Napoleon I and the Restoration', *French Historical Studies* 15.4 (1988), pp. 718–30.

Sieyès, Emmanuel Joseph, *Qu'est-ce que le Tiers état?* (Paris: Boucher, 2002 [1822]).

Simonde de Sismondi, and Jean-Charles-Léonard, *Histoire des Français* (Paris: Treuttel and Würtz, 1842).

Sinha, Mrinalini, 'Britishness, Clubbability, and the Colonial Public Sphere: The Genealogy of an Imperial Institution in Colonial India', *Journal of British Studies* 40.4 (2001), pp. 489–521.

Skinner, Quentin, 'Rhetoric and Conceptual Change', in Margrit Pernau and Dominic Sachsenmaier (eds), *Global Conceptual History, A Reader* (London: Bloomsbury, 2016), pp. 136–7. Originally published in *Finnish Yearbook of Political Thought* (Helsinki: SoPhi, 1999).

Skinner, Quentin, *Visions of Politics. Vol. I: Regarding Method* (Cambridge: Cambridge University Press, 2002).

Slater, Ian, *Orwell: The Road to Airstrip One* (Montreal and Kingston: McGill-Queen's University Press, 2003).

Smaldino, Paul, Pickett, Cynthia, Sherman, Jeffrey, and Schank, Jeffrey, 'An Agent-Based Model of Social Identity Dynamics', *Journal of Artificial Societies and Social Simulation* 15.4 (2012), http://jasss.soc.surrey.ac.uk/15/4/7.html (accessed 19 September 2019).

Smith, Adam, *An Inquiry into the Nature and Causes of the Wealth of Nations* (New York: Random House Modern Library, 1937 [1776]).

Smith, Ian, and Boyns, Trevor, 'British Management Theory and Practice: The Impact of Fayol', *Management Decision* 43 (2005), pp. 1317–34.

Smith, Jay M., *The Culture of Merit: Nobility, Royal Service, and the Making of Absolute Monarchy in France, 1600–1789* (Ann Arbor: University of Michigan Press, 1996).

Smith, Olivia, *The Politics of Language 1791–1819* (Oxford: Oxford University Press, 1986).

Society of the Friends of the People, *The State of the Representation of England and Wales, delivered to the Society of the Friends of the People, associated for the Purpose of obtaining a Parliamentary Reform* (London: Society of the Friends of the People, 1793).

Solovey, Mark, 'Project Camelot and the 1960s Epistemological Revolution: Rethinking the Politics-Patronage-Social Science Nexus', in Howard Lunde, Enrique S. Pumar and Ross Koppel (eds), *Perspectives in Social Research Methods and Analysis* (Thousand Oaks: Sage, 2010), pp. 166–94.

Soret, Jean, *Essai sur les mœurs* (Brussels, 1756).

Souriau, Étienne, *Les différents modes d'existence* (Paris: Presses Universitaires de France, 2009 [1943]).

Spitz, Jean-Fabien, 'Quentin Skinner', *Revue française d'histoire des idées politiques* 40 (2014), pp. 347–77.

Staël-Holstein, Anne-Louise-Germaine de, *De la littérature, considérée dans ses rapports avec les institutions sociales*, 2 vols (Paris: Maradan, 1800).

'Stanhope, Philip Dormer, 4th earl of Chesterfield', *Encyclopædia Britannica Online* (2007), <https://www.britannica.com/biography/Philip-Dormer-Stanhope-4th-Earl-of-Chesterfield> (accessed 19 September 2019).

Stanhope, Philip, aka Lord Mahon (ed.), *The Letters of Philip Dormer Stanhope, Earl of Chesterfield*, 4 vols (London: Bentley, 1845).

'Stanhope, Philip Dormer', *A Cambridge Alumni Database*, University of Cambridge <http://venn.lib.cam.ac.uk/cgi-bin/search-2018.pl?sur=Stanhope&suro=w&fir=&firo=c&cit=&cito=c&c=all&z=all&tex=&sye=&eye=&col=all&maxcount=50> (accessed 19 September 2019).

Stapledon, Olaf, *Last and First Men & Star Maker* (New York: Dover, 1968 [1931]).

Stein, George H., *The Waffen SS: Hitler's Elite Guard at War, 1939–1945* (Ithaca: Cornell University Press, 1984 [1966]).

Stendhal, *The Red and the Black: A Chronicle of 1830*, trans. Horace Barnett Samuel (London: Kegan Paul, Trench, Trübner, 1916).

Stewart, James B., 'Looking for a Lesson in Google's Perks', *The New York Times*, 15 March 2013, <http://www.nytimes.com/2013/03/16/business/at-google-a-place-to-work-and-play.html?_r=0&pagewanted=all> (accessed 19 September 2019).

Stouffer, Samuel, et al., *Studies in Social Psychology in World War II* (Princeton: Princeton University Press, 1950).

Stunt, Timothy C. F., 'Litton, Edward Arthur (1813–1897)', *Oxford Dictionary of National Biography*, <https://www.oxforddnb.com/view/10.1093/ref:odnb/9780198614128.001.0001/odnb-9780198614128-e-47639> (accessed 19 September 2019).

Suleiman, Ezra N., *Elites in French Society: The Politics of Survival* (Princeton: Princeton University Press, 1978).

Susane, Louis, *La Maison du Roi, Histoire de la cavalerie Française* (Paris: Hetzel, 1874).

Talleyrand, Charles Maurice de, 'Rapport au Conseil d'État du 20 avril 1800', in Louis Bastide, *Vie religieuse et politique de Talleyrand-Périgord, Prince de Bénévent* (Paris: Faure, 1838).

Taminiaux, Jacques, and Crease, Robert, 'Merleau-Ponty: From Dialectic to Hyperdialectic', *Research in Phenomenology* 10 (1980), pp. 58–76.

Tarde, Gabriel, *L'esprit de groupe, Conférence faite au Collège Libre des Sciences Sociales le 6 Novembre 1899* (Lyons: Storck, 1900).

Tarde, Gabriel, *On Communication and Social Influence: Selected Papers*, ed. Terry N. Clark (Chicago: University of Chicago Press, 1969).

Taubman, Antony, 'Is There a Right to Collective Personality', *European Intellectual Property Review* 28.9 (2006), pp. 485–92.

Teng-Hwee, Lee, *Lee's Rhetoric and Composition* (Shanghai: Commercial Press, 1926).

Terraillon, Eugène, *L'honneur, sentiment et principe moral* (Paris: Alcan, 1912).

Teysseire, Daniel, 'Un modèle autoritaire: le discours de "la flagellation"', *Mots* 43.1 (1995), pp. 118–27.

Thibaut, Pierre, *Cours de Chimie* (Paris: Iolly, 1667).

Thion, Stéphane, *Les armées françaises de la guerre de Trente Ans* (Auzielle: LRT, 2008).

Thuillier, Guy, and Tulard, Jean, *Histoire de l'administration française* (Paris: Presses Universitaires de France, 1994).

'Thursday, June 21, 1787', *The Records of the Federal Convention of 1787, American Memory from the Library of Congress*, <https://oll.libertyfund.org/titles/1057#lf0544-01_head_189> (accessed 19 September 2019).

Tissot, Claude-Joseph, *Cours élémentaire de philosophie, rédigé d'après le programme de l'examen pour le baccalauréat ès-lettres* (Dijon: Popelain, 1837).

Tocqueville, Alexis de, *De la démocratie en Amérique* (Paris: Gosselin, 1835–40).

Tocqueville, Alexis de, *Democracy in America*, trans. Henri Reeve (Cambridge: Sever and Francis, 1863).

Tocqueville, Alexis de, *Democracy in America*, trans. Arthur Goldhammer (New York: Library of America, 2004).

Tocqueville, Alexis de, 'Lettre du 25 juin 1838 à Francisque de Corcelle', in *Œuvres complètes*, 16 vols (Paris: Gallimard, 1983), vol. XV.

Tocqueville, Alexis de, *Mélanges, fragments historiques et notes sur l'ancien régime, la Révolution et l'empire* (Paris: Lévy, 1865).

Tombs, Robert, *France: 1814–1914* (London: Routledge, 2014).

Toynbee, Arnold Joseph, *A Study of History* (Oxford: Oxford University Press, 1935).

Traub, Peter E., 'Esprit de corps – How It May Be Strengthened and Preserved in Our Army Under the Present Organization and Method of Promotion', *Journal of the Military Service Institution of the United States* 34 (1904), pp. 181–217.

'Travail', *Dictionnaire de l'Académie française* (1694), ARTFL-Frantext, <https://

artflsrv03.uchicago.edu/philologic4/publicdicos/navigate/4/8207/> (accessed 19 September 2019).

Twain, Mark, 'General Grant's Grammar', in *Mark Twain's Civil War*, ed. David Rachels (Lexington: University Press of Kentucky, 2007).

Udias, Agustin, 'Jesuits', in David Gubbins and Emilio Herrero-Bervera (eds), *Encyclopedia of Geomagnetism and Paleomagnetism* (Dordrecht: Springer, 2007), p. 460.

UNIDIR, *The Weaponization of Increasingly Autonomous Technologies: Considering How Meaningful Human Control Might Move the Discusssion Forward* (Geneva: United Nations Institute for Disarmament Research, 2014).

'Unité, indivisibilité de la République, liberté, égalité, fraternité ou la mort', estampe (Paris: Basset, 1792).

US Office of Civilian Defense, *The Control System of the Citizens' Defense Corps* (Washington, DC: OCD, 1942).

Valade, Bernard, 'Droit de grève (France)', *Encyclopaedia Universalis*, <https://www.universalis.fr/encyclopedie/droit-de-greve/> (accessed 19 September 2019).

Vallet, Odon, *L'Évangile des païens* (Paris: Albin Michel, 2003).

Vardi, Liana, *The Physiocrats and the World of the Enlightenment* (New York: Cambridge University Press, 2012).

Vauvilliers, Jean, 'Pour une théorie générale de l'esprit de corps', *Revue administrative* 347–8 (2005), pp. 489–98, 589–96.

Vauxcelles, Simon Bourlet de, *L'esprit de l'Encyclopédie* (Paris: Fauvelle et Sagnier, 1798).

Venuti, Lawrence, *The Translator's Invisibility* (London: Routledge, 1995).

Vernon, Keith, *Universities and the State in England, 1850–1939* (London: Routledge, 2004).

Villepin, Dominique de, *De l'esprit de cour: la malédiction française* (Paris: Perrin, 2010).

Vincent, Andrew, 'Can Groups be Persons?', *Review of Metaphysics* 42 (1989), pp. 687–715.

Vogel, Christine, 'The Suppression of the Society of Jesus, 1758–1773', *European History Online* (2010), http://www.ieg-ego.eu/vogelc-2010-en (accessed 19 September 2019).

Voltaire, 'Les Cabales', 1772, in *Oeuvres complètes de Voltaire* (Paris: Renouard, 1819), vol. XII.

Voltaire, 'Esprit (Philos. & Belles-Lettr.)', in Denis Diderot and Jean le Rond d'Alembert (eds), *Encyclopédie, ou dictionnaire raisonné des sciences, des arts et des métiers* (Paris: Briasson, David, Le Breton and Durand, 1751–65), vol. V (1755), p. 975.

Voltaire, *An Essay on Universal History, the Manners, and Spirit of Nations, from the Reign of Charlemeign to the Age of Lewis XIV*, trans. Thomas Nugent, 4 vols (London: Nourse, 1759).

Voltaire, 'Lettre CCCIII à Milord Chesterfield (24 Sept. 1771)', in *Œuvres complètes de Voltaire* (Paris: Société Littéraire-Typographique, 1784), vol. LXVIII.

Voltaire, *Œuvres complètes* (Paris: Garnier, 1877–95).

Voltaire, *Le Siècle de Louis XIV* (Berlin: Henning, 1751).

Wahnich, Sophie, *La Révolution Française* (Paris: Hachette, 2012).

Waldeck-Rousseau, Pierre René, 'Le droit de grève et le gouvernement (18 janvier 1900, Chambre des députés)', in Georges Pellissier (ed.), *Anthologie des prosateurs français contemporains*, 3 vols (Paris: Delagrave, 1910), vol. II.

Walker, David, '*Holy Virility: The Social Construction of Masculinity*, by Emmanuel Reynaud', book review, *Labour History* 48 (1985), p. 121.

Wang, Fade, 'An Approach to Domestication and Foreignization from the Angle of Cultural Factors Translation', *Theory and Practice in Language Studies* 4.11 (2014), pp. 2423–7.

Webster, Nesta H., *Secret Societies and Subversive Movements* (Escondido: The Book Tree, 2000 [1924]).

Weyl, Claude, *La réglementation du travail des femmes dans l'industrie* (Paris: Larose, 1898).

Weyl, Walter E., *The New Democracy* (New York: MacMillan, 1927 [1912]).

Whatmore, Richard, 'Enlightenment Political Philosophy', in George Klosko (ed.), *The Oxford Handbook of the History of Political Philosophy* (Oxford: Oxford University Press, 2011), pp. 296–318.

Whatmore, Richard, *What is Intellectual History?* (Cambridge: Polity, 2016).

White, Martha C., '5 Reasons to Consider Actually Sticking with a Low-Paying Job', *Time*, 6 January 2014, <http://140.234.252.185/c/articles/93576129/5-reasons-consider-actually-sticking-low-paying-job> (accessed 19 September 2019).

Whitehead, Alfred North, *Science and the Modern World* (New York: Free Press, 1997).

Whittaker, Wayne, 'Uncle Sam Picks an All-Star Team', *Popular Mechanics Magazine* 80.1 (1943), p. 51.

Whyte, Max, 'The Uses and Abuses of Nietzsche in the Third Reich: Alfred Baeumler's "Heroic Realism"', *Journal of Contemporary History* 43.2 (2008), pp. 171–94.

Wierzbicka, Anna, *Understanding Cultures through their Key Words* (Oxford: Oxford University Press, 1997).

Winegarten, Renee, *Germaine de Staël and Benjamin Constant: A Dual Biography* (New Haven, CT: Yale University Press, 2008).

Wolin, Richard, 'Habermas and Hermeneutics: From *Verstehen* to *Lebenswelt*', in Thomas Szanto and Dermot Moran (eds), *Phenomenology of Sociality: Discovering the 'We'* (London: Routledge, 2016), pp. 56–69.

Wong, Siu-Lun, *Sociology and Socialism in Contemporary China* (London: Routledge, 1979).

Woodcock, George, *The Crystal Spirit: A Study of George Orwell* (Montreal: Black Rose, 2005).

Woodward, Calvin M., 'Domestic and Intercollegiate Athletics', *The Popular Science Monthly*, October 1902.

Wuthnow, Robert, *Meaning and Moral Order: Explorations in Cultural Analysis* (Berkeley: University of California Press, 1987).

Wyckoff, Jason, 'Rousseau's General Will and the Condorcet Jury Theorem', *History of Political Thought* 32.1 (2011), pp. 49–62.

Yablonsky, Lewis, *Gangsters: Fifty Years of Madness, Drugs, and Death on the Streets of America* (New York: New York University Press, 1997).

Yvon, Claude, 'Aristotélisme', in Denis Diderot and Jean le Rond d'Alembert (eds), *Encyclopédie, ou dictionnaire raisonné des sciences, des arts et des métiers* (Paris: Briasson, David, Le Breton and Durand, 1751–65), vol. I (1751), p. 654.

Zenner, Eline, Speelman, Dirk, and Geeraerts, Dirk, 'Cognitive Sociolinguistics Meets Loanword Research: Measuring Variation in the Success of Anglicisms in Dutch', *Cognitive Linguistics* 23 (2012), pp. 749–92.

Zola, Émile, *Pot-Bouille* (Paris: Charpentier, 1883).

Index